The Law of Theft

Learning Centre

Park Road, Uxbridge Middlesex UB8 1NQ
Telephone : 01895 853326

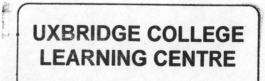

The Law of Theft

EIGHTH EDITION

Sir John Smith CBE, QC, LLD, FBA
Honorary Bencher of Lincoln's Inn
Honorary Fellow of Downing College, Cambridge
Emeritus Professor of Law, University of Nottingham

Butterworths
London, Edinburgh, Dublin
1997

United Kingdom	Butterworths a Division of Reed Elsevier (UK) Ltd, Halsbury House, 35 Chancery Lane, LONDON WC2A 1EL and 4 Hill Street, EDINBURGH EH2 3JZ
Australia	Butterworths, SYDNEY, MELBOURNE, BRISBANE, ADELAIDE, PERTH, CANBERRA and HOBART
Canada	Butterworths Canada Ltd, TORONTO and VANCOUVER
Ireland	Butterworth (Ireland) Ltd, DUBLIN
Malaysia	Malayan Law Journal Sdn Bhd, KUALA LUMPUR
New Zealand	Butterworths of New Zealand Ltd, WELLINGTON and AUCKLAND
Singapore	Reed Elsevier (Singapore) Pte Ltd, SINGAPORE
South Africa	Butterworths Publishers (Pty) Ltd, DURBAN
USA	Michie, CHARLOTTESVILLE, Virginia

A CIP Catalogue record for this book is available from the British Library.

ISBN 0 406 89545 7

Printed by Redwood Books, Trowbridge, Wiltshire

Preface

The principal reason for this new edition is the decision of the House of Lords in *R v Preddy* [1996] 3 All ER 481 and the Theft (Amendment) Act 1996 which rapidly followed to fill the serious lacunae in the law created by *Preddy*, and, incidentally, to effect some other reforms. My discussion of the law relating to theft and obtaining by deception of cheques and of things in action has been revised in the light of that decision and the new offences created by the 1996 Act have been incorporated into the text.

The dust has not yet completely settled on *Gomez*, as the differing attitudes of the judges in the two decisions in *Mazo* [1996] Crim LR 435 and *Hopkins and Kendrick* [1997] Crim LR 359 show. I have substantially re-organised Chapter 2, on theft, contrary to s. 1 of the 1968 Act, in order to bring together all the possible limitations which may exist on that far-reaching case. There have been interesting decisions on most of the offences under the Theft Acts and I have tried to incorporate the effect of all of these.

Since the last edition of this book, Professor A.T.H. Smith has published his monumental *Property Offences*, Anthony Arlidge and Jacques Parry have produced a second and much enlarged version of their very perceptive work on *Fraud*, and the late Edward Griew has left us the 7th edition – the last, alas, from his own pen, and I think, the best – of *The Theft Acts 1968 and 1978*. I have tried to take account, as far as possible, of the opinions expressed by these authors, especially where they differ from those I have expressed, either by revising, or justifying, my opinion, as seemed right.

Once again, I am greatly indebted to Professor Michael Gunn of De Montfort University whose reading of the whole of the proofs has enabled me to remove many blemishes. I alone am responsible for any remaining errors.

I have tried to take account of all the relevant changes in the law up to 1 May 1997.

John Smith

Contents

Contents

Table of Statutes

References in the Table to *Statutes* are to Halsbury's Statutes of England (Fourth Edition) showing the volume and page at which the annotated text of an Act may be found.
References in the right-hand column are to paragraph numbers (set in roman type) and page numbers (set in *italic*).
References in **bold** roman and ***bold italic*** type indicate where the section of an Act is set out in part or in full.

Table of Cases

NOTE. Cases are listed under the name of the accused whenever the usual method of citation would cause them to be preceded by the abbreviation "R v" signifying that the prosecution was undertaken by the Crown.

PARA

A

Q

R

Abbreviations

The following are the abbreviations used for the principal textbooks and other materials cited in this book. References are to the latest editions, as shown below, unless it is specifically stated otherwise. The particulars of other works referred to in the text are set out in the relevant footnotes.

Archbold	*Criminal Pleading, Evidence and Practice*, by John Frederick Archbold. 1997 edition by P.J. Richardson and others
Arlidge & Parry	*Arlidge & Parry on Fraud,* 2nd ed. (1996)
A.T.H. Smith	*Property Offences*, by A.T.H. Smith (1994)
Blackstone, *Commentaries*, I	*Commentaries on the laws of England*, by Sir William Blackstone, Vol 1 (4 Vols) 17th ed. (1830) by E. Christian
Blackstone CP	*Blackstone's Criminal Practice* (1997)
Eighth Report, Cmnd 2977	Criminal Law Revision Committee, Eighth Report "Theft and Related Offences" (1966) Cmnd 2977
Griew	*The Theft Acts 1968 and 1978*, 7th ed. (1995) by Edward Griew
Hale, 1 PC	*The History of the Pleas of the Crown*, by Sir Matthew Hale, Vol 1 [2 Vols] (1736)
Hawkins, 1 PC	*Pleas of the Crown*, by W. Hawkins, Vol 1 [2 Vols] (1916)
JCrL	Journal of Criminal Law (English)
Kenny	*Outlines of Criminal Law*, by C.S. Kenny, 19th ed. (1965) by J.W.C. Turner
LQR	Law Quarterly Review
MLR	Modern Law Review
NLJ	New Law Journal
Russell	*Crime*, by Sir W.O. Russell, 12th ed. (1964) by J.W.C. Turner [2 Vols]
Smith and Hogan	*Criminal Law*, by J.C. Smith and Brian Hogan, 8th ed. (1996)
Thirteenth Report, Cmnd 6733	Criminal Law Revision Committee, Thirteenth Report, "Section 16 of the Theft Act 1968" (1977) Cmnd 6733
Williams, CLGP	*Criminal Law: The General Part*, by Glanville L. Williams, 2nd ed. (1961)
Williams, TBCL	*Textbook of Criminal Law*, by Glanville L. Williams, 2nd ed. (1983)

CHAPTER 1

Introduction

1–01 Until 1968 the English law of stealing developed in a haphazard fashion over several centuries. The common law began with a crude notion of stealing which covered only the most obvious and direct taking by one person of property which was in the possession of another. As the inadequacies of the law were exposed by the ingenuity of rogues, so the courts and, later, Parliament, extended the law to punish more sophisticated forms of dishonesty. The courts generally achieved their purpose by extending the ambit of the original crime of larceny by means of fictions and strained interpretations of the concepts which constitute the definition of that crime – particularly the concept of possession. Parliament's method was to create a new crime to supplement the old.

1–02 In one way or another most varieties of dishonest appropriation of the property of another were brought within the ambit of the criminal law and, with one or two exceptions, the gaps through which the dishonest might slip were narrow and did not present a serious problem. But this was at the price of tolerating an immensely and unnecessarily complicated structure, full of difficult distinctions of a purely technical character and bristling with traps for the judges, magistrates, prosecutors and police who had to administer the law.

1–03 The Theft Act 1968, which was based largely on the Eighth Report of the Criminal Law Revision Committee[1] (hereafter "CLRC"), swept all this away and gave us a completely fresh start. The definition of theft embraces all – or virtually all – of the kinds of dishonest conduct which came within the definitions of the old crimes of larceny (in all its various forms), obtaining by false pretences, embezzlement and fraudulent conversion. This was, in itself, an immense simplification, for the boundaries between these offences were difficult to draw precisely and, right up to the time of their repeal, were the subject of controversy. It has, however, been decided that the simplification effected by the Act was greater than the CLRC intended. They did not think it practicable for the definition of theft to include the offence of obtaining by false pretences. The effect of the decision of the House of Lords in *Gomez*[2] is that it includes that offence (now obtaining by deception, contrary to s. 15) with the unimportant exception of obtaining land.

---

[1] Cmnd 2977, "Theft and Related Offences".
[2] [1993] 1 All ER 1, below, paras **2–04** to **2–09**.

1–04 Notwithstanding this simplification, many difficulties remain and some, at least, are unavoidable. Stealing consists in interference with other persons' rights in property, their rights of ownership, whether legal or equitable, their possession and control over chattels and things in action – intangible property. These rights are regulated by the civil law and, in an advanced society, their structure is inevitably complicated. This is something of which the reformer of the criminal law must take account in the legislation which he proposes, but which he cannot alter. The concepts of the civil law must be utilised in the definition of the crime. Moreover, while many borderlines are eliminated by the use of a broadly-based definition of theft, there must always remain the borderline between interferences with another's property which are criminal and those which are not. One section of the 1968 Act, s. 16, a provision introduced while the Bill was passing through Parliament without scrutiny by the CLRC, proved to be so obscure and unsatisfactory that as early as 1972 it was referred to the CLRC for re-consideration. On the recommendation of the Committee, part of the section (s. 16 (1) (a)) was repealed and replaced by new offences in the Theft Act 1978. New methods of transferring funds created other difficulties, not foreseen by the CLRC, which have been met by the Theft (Amendment) Act 1996.

Unfortunately the interpretation of the Theft Acts has produced a mass of complex case-law. Whether this is due to inherent defects in the Acts or failures on the part of the courts to construe and apply them properly is debatable. The law of theft is once again being considered by the Law Commission[1] who cite the opinion of Beldam LJ, a former chairman of the Commission, that it is "in urgent need of simplification and and modernisation, so that a jury of 12 ordinary citizens do not have to grapple with the antiquated 'franglais' of choses in action and scarce public resources are not devoted to hours of semantic argument divorced from the true merits of the case".[2] In fact the Acts do not use the expression "chose in action" or any other franglais. If juries are being confused by the use of such terms, that is the fault of the judges. The law must utilise the concept of a thing in action because that is a variety of intangible property which is frequently the object of offences under the Acts. It is the duty of the judge to explain this and other legal concepts to the jury in terms which are intelligible to them.

---

[1]   Law Com No 228 (1994). For some proposals, see JCS, (1996) 28 Bracton LJ 27.
[2]   *Hallam* 1994, CA, No 92/4388. (The report in [1995] Crim LR 323 does not include this dictum). Contrast the opinion of Lord Diplock, below, para **1–07**. Lord Diplock was speaking before, and Beldam LJ after, the courts got seriously to work on the 1968 Act.

1–05   Like many nineteenth-century statutes, the Larceny Acts of 1861 and 1916 created a multitude of separate crimes to provide an aggravated punishment where a single circumstance of aggravation was present. Simple larceny was punishable with five years' imprisonment, but there were many types of stealing with greater or less penalties according to the nature of the property stolen, the place where it was stolen and the relationship between the thief and the owner. The fact that the subject of the larceny was a will, title deeds or a mail-bag was a sufficient circumstance of aggravation to raise the maximum to life. Other single circumstances which allowed for an enhanced punishment were that the larceny was of cattle or goods in the process of manufacture, from the person, from a ship, by a clerk or servant, or by a tenant or lodger. On the other hand, lesser punishments were provided, for example, if the larceny was of ore from a mine or of a dog. Any court in sentencing a thief today will take account, in determining the sentence, of very many factors in addition to such single elements of aggravation or mitigation – indeed it is very unlikely that the factors enumerated will be the most important in the court's decision. Society's view as to what aggravates an offence changes from time to time.

1–06   In place of all these aggravated forms of larceny the 1968 Act provided a single offence of theft with a single penalty.[1] As the definition comprehends within it offences which were formerly punishable with imprisonment for life and for fourteen years, it was thought right that the maximum penalty provided should be more than the five years available for simple larceny. Following the recommendation of the CLRC, s. 7 of the Act provided a maximum of ten years. From 1 October 1992, this was reduced to seven years.[2] This is a more realistic maximum in the light of the practice of the courts, but it creates an anomaly in that obtaining by deception, contrary to s. 15, an offence which heavily overlaps theft, still carries a maximum of ten. As with all the offences under the Act, these maxima should, in accordance with general principles,[3] be reserved for the worst type of the offence which comes before the court; and sentences in other cases should be proportionately lower.

---

[1] A step back was taken by the Criminal Justice Act 1991, providing a higher penalty for burglary when it is committed in a dwelling, below, para **11–02**.
[2] Criminal Justice Act 1991, s. 26 (1).
[3] *Ambler* [1976] Crim LR 266.

---

1 THE INTERPRETATION OF THE THEFT ACTS[1]

1–07 The Theft Acts represented an almost completely fresh start, and their words should be interpreted in their natural meaning to produce sensible results,[2] without harking back unnecessarily to the concepts of the common law and the Larceny Acts.

> "[The 1968 Act] is expressed in simple language as used and understood by ordinary literate men and women. It avoids so far as possible those terms of art which have acquired a special meaning understood only by lawyers in which many of the penal enactments which it supersedes were couched."[3]

Very little attention was paid to the actual words of the Larceny Act 1916. The courts constantly had recourse to the common law and assumed that the Act was intended to preserve it, even when the wording was somewhat difficult to reconcile with this view. The definition of larceny in the 1916 Act was a new statutory definition, but it did not purport to do more than codify the common law. There is therefore a fundamental difference between the Act of 1916 and the Theft Acts. The Theft Acts enact, for the most part, completely new law. Only in a limited number of cases is it necessary or desirable to resort to earlier case-law. When the 1968 bill was before the House of Lords, Lord Wilberforce introduced an amendment[4] to the effect that it should not be permissible "to refer to any decisions of any Courts prior to the passing of this Act, other than decisions in general terms dealing with the interpretation of Statutes".

It is submitted that this amendment was wisely withdrawn. Such a rule might be workable in some statutes but only if they were drafted with such a rule of interpretation in mind, which the Theft Acts were not. In this field, moreover, it would simply not be possible to dispense with the previous case-law altogether. The Theft Acts assume the existence of the whole law of property, much of which is to be found only in decided cases; and any such Act must surely make a similar assumption. The Acts include expressions like "thing in action", "tenancy", "proprietary right or interest", "trust", and many other terms describing concepts of the civil law which it would be quite impracticable to spell out in an Act concerned with theft. The court can be informed as to the circumstances in which a person is "under an obligation to make restoration" of property, its proceeds or its value,[5] only by reference to the law of contract and quasi-contract which is embodied in case-law.

---

[1] See R. Brazier "The Theft Act: Three Principles of Interpretation" [1974] Crim LR 701.
[2] *Baxter* [1971] 2 All ER 359 at 362, per Sachs LJ.

3   *Treacy v DPP* [1971] AC 537 at 565, [1971] 1 All ER 110 at 124, per Lord Diplock.
4   Parl. Debates, Official Report (HL) Vol 290, col 897.
5   Section 5 (4), below, para **2–81**.

1–08   No doubt Lord Wilberforce had in mind not the civil law, but the old cases on the criminal law of larceny and related offences with all their technicalities. Most of these cases are now irrelevant because the criminal concepts employed in the Act are new. Where the interpretation of the Act requires an answer to some question of civil law – for example, when the ownership in property passes – it is particularly undesirable that resort should be had[1] to those cases in which the concepts of the civil law were distorted in order to force a case within the confines of one of the old offences. Where, however, the Act incorporates the substance of the provisions of earlier statutes – as, for example, with the amended version of taking motor vehicles[2] – it is surely undesirable that the courts should have to go back to square one and reconsider points of construction previously settled, with perhaps different and not necessarily better results. Again, where terms with a well-settled meaning under the Larceny Acts have been used in a similar context in the Theft Act, it would seem desirable – and certainly in accord with the intention of the framers of the Act – that those concepts should be given their well-settled meaning. Examples are the use of the word "menaces" in blackmail[3] and "receives" in handling stolen goods.[4]

1   As occurred in *Gilks* [1972] 3 All ER 280, below, para **2–87**, where *Middleton* (1873) LR 2 CCR 38 was applied and extended. See [1972] Crim LR 586–590.
2   Section 12, below, para **8–01**.
3   Section 21, below, para **10–01**.
4   Section 22, below, para **13–01**.

1–09   The old law is also relevant as an aid to construction insofar as its inadequacies illuminate the mischief at which the Act is aimed and in that it may persuade the court that Parliament could not have intended to legalise conduct which it thinks ought to be criminal and which was criminal under the old law.[1] On the other hand, the courts should " . . . shun the temptation which sometimes presses on the mind of the judiciary, to suppose that because a particular course of conduct . . . was anti-social and undesirable, it can necessarily be fitted into some convenient criminal pigeon-hole". And where an act was an offence under a provision repealed by the Theft Act, "it does not follow that there is necessarily a convenient alternative criminal pigeon-hole provided which fits the facts under the provisions of the 1968 Act".[2]

1   *Treacy v DPP* [1971] AC at 557–558, [1971] 1 All ER at 118, per Lord Hodson.
2   *Charles* [1976] 1 All ER 659 at 666, per Bridge LJ.

1–10   Lord Wilberforce's amendment would also have provided that the 1968 Act should be interpreted "according to the plain and natural meaning of the words used, read in the context of the Act as a whole, and given a fair, large and liberal construction". It is submitted that the Acts should be interpreted according to the plain and natural meaning of the words used (if they have one) except where it appears that the word has a technical meaning which, in the context, it is intended to bear. Thus, if the word "menaces" were given its plain and natural meaning, it might be held to be confined to threats of violence and the like. This would result in a drastic narrowing of the offence of blackmail and would plainly defeat the intention of Parliament. The word should be given the extended meaning which, in this context, it has long borne in the law.

1–11   No one could object to the words of the Acts being given a "fair" construction but the other expressions used in the amendment, "large and liberal", are of much more doubtful import. They suggest that the Acts should be given an extensive meaning, so as to prohibit acts not clearly within their terms. It is submitted that the Act should not be so interpreted. There is much to be said for ignoring the rule (only applied spasmodically and inconsistently) that penal statutes should be strictly construed; but this is achieved by giving words their plain and natural meaning and adopting the "fair" interpretation – "fair", that is, to both sides. It is not desirable that the courts should go to the other extreme and extend the meaning of penal provisions by a "large and liberal" construction. The principle, *nulla poena sine lege*, is of as great importance today as ever it was. An important feature of the interpretation of the Act in practice has been the tendency of the courts to leave the meaning of words and phrases to be determined by the jury as "a question of fact". This has been criticised as an abdication of judicial responsibility leading to uncertainty and inconsistency in the application of the law.[1] Recently, however, the courts have resumed their proper role as the interpreters of statutes.[2]

---

[1]   See *Feely* [1973] QB 530, [1973] 1 All ER 341, below, para **2–121**; *Hale* (1978) 68 Cr App Rep 415, below, para **3–09**; *Dawson* [1976] Crim LR 692, below, para **3–04**; *Reader* (1977) 66 Cr App Rep 33, below, para **13–41**; Elliott "Law and Fact in Theft Act Cases" [1976] Crim LR 707. *Hayes* (1976) 64 Cr App Rep 82, an extreme case, seems, in effect, to have been overruled by *Mainwaring* (1981) 74 Cr App Rep 99, below, para **2–72**.

[2]   See Elliott, "*Brutus v Cozens*, Decline and Fall" [1989] Crim LR 323.

1–12   Where the words of the Act are ambiguous, reference may be made to the appropriate report of the CLRC in accordance with the general principles for the construction of statutes.[1] In numerous cases the courts have not hesitated to follow this course.[2] If only they had done so consistently, most of the difficulties which have arisen under the Acts would have been avoided. That they have not done so may be largely due to the fact that they were not invited by counsel to consider the report. In *Gomez*,[3] however, the majority of the House of Lords declined to look at the Eighth Report, saying that to do so "serves no useful purpose at the present time". Their reason was that there was, in Lord Keith's opinion, a clear decision of the House on the point which had stood for twelve years; but the House in the earlier case did not have the advantage of reference to the Report; and not everyone agrees that it was a clear decision. Lord Lowry, dissenting, demonstrated pretty clearly that the decision of the majority defeated the intention of the Committee which Parliament had espoused by enacting provisions virtually identical with the Committee's draft bill.

---

[1]   *Black-Clawson International Ltd v Papierwerke Waldhof-Aschaffenburg AG* [1974] QB 660, [1974] 2 All ER 610, CA, [1975] AC 591, [1975] 1 All ER 810, HL. In exceptional circumstances the courts may now refer even to Hansard: *Pepper (Inspector of Taxes) v Hart* [1991] 1 All ER 42.

[2]   See, for example, *Hall* [1968] 2 QB 788, [1968] 2 All ER 1009, CA; *Scott v Metropolitan Police Comr* [1975] AC 819, at 836–7, HL; *Ghosh* [1982] 2 All ER 689, CA; *Kassim* [1993] 3 All ER 713 at 718; *Kassim* [1992] 1 AC 9 at 16, HL; *Preddy* [1996] 3 All ER 481 at 486.

[3]   [1993] 1 All ER 1 at p 13. Cf Lord Lowry at p 18.

2   THE LAW OF STEALING UNDER THE LARCENY ACTS

1–13   A very brief *résumé* of the position before the 1968 Act will assist the understanding of some of its provisions.[1] There existed the following crimes:

A. SIMPLE LARCENY

Simple larceny was most commonly committed where D by a trespass took possession of goods which were in the possession or custody of P without P's consent. It was from this notion that the common law began. The concept of "taking" was expanded by the courts until, in the 1916 consolidation, it was defined to include:

"obtaining the possession –
(a) by any trick;
(b) by intimidation;
(c) under a mistake on the part of the owner with knowledge on the part of the taker that possession has been so obtained;
(d) by finding, where at the time of the finding the finder believes that the owner can be discovered by taking reasonable steps".[2]

It was essential in all these forms of larceny that, as well as a taking there should be a "carrying away" and the Act provided:

"the expression 'carries away' includes any removal of anything from the place which it occupies, but in the case of a thing attached, only if it has been completely detached".[3]

At common law a possessor could not steal but legislation from 1857 onwards made it larceny for a bailee to misappropriate the bailed goods and the 1916 Act provided:

" . . . a person may be guilty of stealing any such thing notwithstanding that he has lawful possession thereof, if, being a bailee or part owner thereof, he fraudulently converts the same to his own use or the use of any person other than the owner".[4]

Here a physical "taking and carrying away" was unnecessary. It was enough, for example, that D should have contracted to sell goods bailed to him, without laying hands on them at all. Though larceny was commonly (and, in general, accurately) described as an offence against possession, larceny by a bailee was plainly an offence by a possessor against ownership.

---

[1]   A full account is to be found in Smith & Hogan, *Criminal Law* (1st edn, 1965) and *Russell on Crime* (12th edn, 1964).
[2]   Larceny Act 1916, s. 1 (2) (i).
[3]   Ibid, s. 1 (2) (ii).
[4]   Ibid, s. 1 (1), proviso.

B. LARCENY BY A SERVANT

1–14   Where a master (or, as we would now say, employer) entrusted his servant (employee) with goods it was held at an early stage in the development of the common law that possession remained in the master and the servant merely had custody, so that a misappropriation of the goods by the servant amounted to a "taking" out of the master's possession and, therefore, larceny. This was an aggravated form of larceny under s. 17 (1) (a) of the 1916 Act.

C. EMBEZZLEMENT

1–15   The position was different where the servant received goods from a third party to transmit to the possession of the master. Here the servant was held to acquire possession and therefore to be incapable of larceny at common law. He was, no doubt, a bailee; but, in 1799, before legislation dealt with bailees generally, Parliament created the offence of embezzlement to deal with the particular case here discussed. The distinction between embezzlement and larceny by a servant was a subtle one. If D received money for his master and put it straight into his pocket this was embezzlement; but if he put the money into his master's till and then took it out again this was larceny, since putting the money into the till reduced it into the possession of the master. Like larceny by a servant, embezzlement was punishable with fourteen years' imprisonment.[1]

---

[1]   Larceny Act 1916, s. 17 (1) (b).

D. FRAUDULENT CONVERSION

1–16   By a series of statutes from 1812 onwards the offence known as fraudulent conversion was created and extended. By s. 20 of the 1916 Act it was provided that anyone who had been entrusted or become entrusted[1] with property for various purposes or had received property for or on account of another should, if he converted the property, be guilty of a misdemeanour, punishable with seven years' imprisonment. On the face of it, the definition of this offence comprehended within it larceny by a bailee, larceny by a clerk or servant and embezzlement. It also clearly applied to another category of persons – those who had been entrusted not merely with the possession but with the ownership of the property.

---

[1]   *Grubb* [1915] 2 KB 683.

E.   OBTAINING BY FALSE PRETENCES

1–17   Where D by a false statement induced P to transfer to him possession of the goods with intent to appropriate them, this was larceny by a trick at common law. Where D by a false pretence induced P to transfer to him *ownership* of the goods with intent to appropriate them, this was no offence at common law but was made a misdemeanour by statute in 1757; and, by s. 32 of the 1916 Act, it was an offence punishable with five years' imprisonment. The distinction between larceny by a trick and obtaining by false pretences was a fine one and a fruitful source of difficulties. As an example, if D by false pretences induced P to let him have goods on hire purchase intending to appropriate them, this was larceny by a trick since the property did not pass; but if he induced him to let him have the same goods on credit-sale terms, this was obtaining by false pretences, since the property did pass.

3   JURISDICTION UNDER THE THEFT ACTS

1–18   *The Criminal Justice Act 1993, ss. 1–6.* A matter which is conveniently dealt with at this point, because it must be mentioned in the discussion of particular offences, is that of territorial jurisdiction. Our courts will generally accept jurisdiction only over offences committed in England and Wales. A crime requiring proof of a result of some kind is usually regarded as committed here if conduct abroad causes that result in this country; but conduct in this country causing the prohibited result abroad is not. This rule caused serious difficulties which were the subject of a Law Commission Consultation Paper and Report[1] making recommendations which were enacted in the Criminal Justice Act 1993.[2]

This Act applies to what it calls "Group A" and "Group B" offences. Group

A offences include many of the crimes with which this book is concerned – that is the offences under the Theft Act 1968 of theft (s. 1), obtaining property by deception (s. 15), obtaining a money transfer by deception (s. 15A), obtaining a pecuniary advantage by deception (s. 16), false accounting (s. 17), false statements by company directors, etc., (s. 19), procuring the execution of a valuable security by deception (s. 20 (2)), blackmail (s. 21), handling stolen goods (s. 22) and retaining credits from dishonest sources (s. 24A[3]); and the offences under the Theft Act 1978 of obtaining services by deception (s. 1) and avoiding liability by deception (s. 2).[4]

Group B offences include conspiracy, attempt or incitement to commit a Group A offence, and offences of conspiracy and attempt triable by virtue of new sections inserted by the 1993 Act in the Criminal Law Act 1977 and the Criminal Attempts Act 1981 respectively.[5]

---

[1] Law Com No 180 (1989).
[2] The provisions of this Act are also discussed by Griew, 17-02 and by Arlidge and Parry, 12–019.
[3] The references to ss. 15A and 24A were introduced by the Theft (Amendment) Act 1996, s. 3.
[4] The other Group A offences are offences under ss. 1, 2, 3, 4, and 5 of the Forgery and Counterfeiting Act 1981 and the common law offence of cheating the public revenue.
[5] The only other Group B offence is conspiracy to defraud.

1–19   The 1993 Act, s. 2, provides that a person may be guilty of a Group A offence if any relevant event occurs in England and Wales, and "relevant event" means –

"any act or omission or other event (including any result of one or more acts or omissions) proof of which is required for conviction of the offence".

So it is sufficient if any one element of the offence is committed or occurs here. It is not sufficient that a merely preparatory act is done here; but if the act is more than merely preparatory to bringing about a result which is an element of a Group A offence, it will be an attempt triable here. It does not matter for the purposes of Group A or B offences (or conspiracy or attempt to commit them) whether a defendant was a British citizen at the time of the relevant event or whether he was in England and Wales at that time. Fritz, a German citizen, posting from Germany a deceitful letter which results in an obtaining of property in England (a relevant event) commits offences under s. 15 and s. 1 of the 1968 Act. It also appears to be immaterial whether a Group A offence is an offence under the law of the foreign jurisdiction in which it takes place. Even if Fritz commits no offence under German law by posting the letter, he is guilty of offences in England; but there may, of course, be difficulty in bringing him to trial.

1–20   *Conspiracy, attempt and incitement to commit Group A offences triable here*. The general principles of conspiracy, attempt and incitement are stated in Smith & Hogan, *Criminal Law* (8th edn) and are not discussed in this book. These "inchoate offences" are however, in general, confined to conspiracy, attempt or incitement to commit an offence triable in England and Wales so it is necessary to note the extension of jurisdiction made by the 1993 Act for Theft Acts offences. Where a contemplated Group A offence includes an event in England and Wales, an agreement to commit it is a conspiracy under s. 1 of the Criminal Law Act 1977, an attempt is an offence under s. 1 of the Criminal Attempts Act 1981 and incitement is an offence at common law. It is immaterial that D joined the conspiracy or made the attempt outside England and Wales and that nothing was done here (s. 3 (2) and (3) of the 1993 Act); but (it seems) the incitement must occur in England and Wales though the inciter need not be here.

1–21 *Conspiracy, attempt and incitement to commit Group A offences not triable here.* The 1993 Act goes further in respect of all three inchoate offences. Section 5 (1) and (2) creates new sections of the Criminal Law Act 1977 and the Criminal Attempts Act 1981 which extend the application of those Acts to agreements and attempts respectively to do what would, if done, amount to a Group A offence which is *not* triable in England and Wales; i.e. where no element of the contemplated Group A offence will be committed or occur in England and Wales. Section 5 (4) makes a similar provision for the common law offence of incitement.

An agreement to commit a non-triable Group A offence is indictable here if a party to the agreement, personally or through his agent, (a) did anything in England and Wales in relation to it before its formation or (b) joined it in England and Wales, or (c) did or omitted anything in pursuance of it in England and Wales. Consider an agreement by Germans to steal in Germany. If that is all, our courts have no jurisdiction over either the conspiracy or the theft if it is committed. But if D, a party to the agreement, has written from England (a) advising the formation of such an agreement, or (b) joining it after it has been made, or (c) done any act in England in pursuance of it, the conspiracy is indictable here, though the theft is not. Perhaps there are five other parties who never left or did anything outside Germany. They are all liable to conviction here. It may even be that D himself (and every other party to the agreement) was in Germany throughout. If he has a secretary, an innocent agent, in England, through whom he does any of (a), (b) or (c), above, all the parties are indictable in the English courts. There is a similar provision (s. 5 (3)) in relation to conspiracy to defraud.

1–22 *Attempt or incitement to commit non-triable Group A offences.* It is not easy to think of a Group A offence which, when an attempt or incitement has been made in England to commit it, will not be triable in England if it is committed. But, if there should be such an offence, the attempt is made triable here by the new s. 1A of the Criminal Attempts Act 1981 and the incitement by s. 5 (4) of the 1993 Act. These provisions contemplate, rather strangely, a situation in which D is triable for attempting or inciting to commit a crime but not triable for the full crime, even though he has in fact committed it or procured its commission. If D in England prepares false documents with a view to deceiving his German bank manager to allow him increased borrowing by way of overdraft (a "pecuniary advantage" under s. 16 of the Theft Act 1968), this is probably a merely preparatory act; but if he posts or attempts to post the documents to Germany, this is probably more than merely preparatory. Assuming that obtaining the pecuniary advantage would be an offence in Germany, it does not matter whether that offence would be triable here or not: D is guilty of an attempt under the new s. 1A. In fact it appears that the offence would be triable here as a Group A offence. By s. 4 of the 1993 Act –

"(a) there is an obtaining of property in England and Wales if the property is
     either despatched from or received at a place in England and Wales; and
(b) there is a communication in England and Wales of any information,
     instruction, request, demand or other matter if it is sent by any means –
     (i) from a place in England and Wales to a place elsewhere; or
     (ii) from a place elsewhere to a place in England and Wales."

It follows from (b) (ii) above that, if the attempt succeeds, D's deception is deemed to have been practised in England, a "relevant event" occurs here, and the obtaining of the pecuniary advantage is an offence triable in England. In that event it is immaterial whether it is an offence triable in Germany. The attempt is triable under s. 1 of the Criminal Attempts Act and the new s. 1A is inapplicable.

1-23 *Relevance of external law.* For the purposes of these extensions of the law of conspiracy and attempt the 1993 Act applies, in effect, a presumption that any conduct amounting to a Group A offence is punishable under any foreign criminal law. The prosecution do not, in the first instance, have to prove it. If the defendant wishes to challenge this presumption, he must give notice stating the grounds for his opinion and requiring the prosecution to prove to the satisfaction of the judge that the contemplated conduct is indeed punishable (however it is described) under the foreign law.

1-24 *Commencement and transitional provision.* Remarkably, these provisions of the 1993 Act have still not been brought into force at the time of writing (May 1997). If and when they are brought into force, they will then apply only to acts, omissions and events occurring on or after the date of commencement: s. 78 (5). Even where the prosecution is started after that date, the old law will apply to acts, omissions and events occurring before it.

CHAPTER 2
Stealing under the Theft Act

2–01 Section 1 (1) of the Theft Act 1968 provides:

"A person is guilty of theft if he dishonestly appropriates property belonging to another with the intention of permanently depriving the other of it; and 'thief' and 'steal' shall be construed accordingly."

1 THE ACTUS REUS OF THEFT

2–02 The *actus reus*, then, consists simply in the *appropriation of property belonging to another*. The two questions which require detailed consideration are, What is an appropriation? and, When does property belong to another?

A. APPROPRIATION

(a) Morris *and* Gomez

2–03 By s. 3 (1) of the Act,

"Any assumption by a person of the rights of an owner amounts to an appropriation, and this includes, where he has come by the property (innocently or not) without stealing it, any later assumption of a right to it by keeping or dealing with it as owner."

This provision, said the CLRC,[1] is a "partial definition . . . which is included partly to indicate that this is the familiar concept of conversion. . . ." "Conversion" is the name of a tort concerning which there exists a substantial body of civil law. It may be familiar to lawyers but it is certainly not familiar to laymen in its legal sense – essentially the usurpation of rights of property belonging to another. A similar concept already existed in the criminal law of larceny by a bailee and the offence of fraudulent conversion. The CLRC thought that "appropriation" and "conversion" had the same meaning but preferred "appropriation" because it more aptly describes the whole range of acts it is intended to cover.

---

[1] Cmnd 2977, para 34.

2–04 The above provisions now have to be read in the light of two decisions of the House of Lords. In *Morris*,[1] it was held that –

"the assumption by a person of *any* of the rights of an owner in property amounts to an appropriation of the property";

and in *Gomez*[2] it was held that –

"there may be an assumption of a right and, therefore, an appropriation of property belonging to another although the owner consents to or authorises the act in question".

It is questionable whether either of these propositions is a correct interpretation of the Act but they have to be accepted as clear decisions of the highest court. The effect is that the *actus reus* of theft is reduced to a minimum. Where P is the absolute owner of property the general principle is that only he has any right to do anything to or with it. Anyone else who does anything to or with it is therefore exercising a right of the owner. If P has consented to or authorised the exercise of that right we would not, it is submitted, ordinarily describe that exercise as an "assumption" or "appropriation"; but, since it has been decided that consent and authority are immaterial, it is both. And, since the assumption of any one of the owner's rights in the property is an appropriation of the property itself, this amounts to theft if done dishonestly and with intent permanently to deprive.

---

¹   [1984] AC 320, [1983] 3 All ER 288.
²   [1993] 1 All ER 1.

2–05   *Morris* also establishes that it is not necessary to prove an intention permanently to deprive *by the act of appropriation*; it is sufficient that the appropriator has a present intention to deprive, either by that act or by some future act. As interpreted by these cases, the definition of theft may now be more fully stated as follows:

> Anyone doing anything whatever to property belonging to another, with or without the authority or consent of the owner, appropriates it; and, if he does so dishonestly and with intent, by that act or any subsequent act, permanently to deprive, he commits theft.

2–06   Whether this statement requires qualification in any respect is considered below. The statement is illustrated by the decision in *Morris*: a person, D, who switches the labels on two articles lying on the shelves of a supermarket, with the intention of buying the more expensive article for the price of the less expensive one, steals the more expensive article.¹ Only the owner has the right to label the goods so D, by assuming that right of the owner, appropriates both articles. He has no intention to deprive the owner of the less expensive article, so he does not steal that. The act of re-labelling the more expensive article will not deprive the owner of it; but D intends to take it to the cash point, offer to buy it, and, when it has been sold to him, carry it off as his own. The theft, however, is complete as soon as the label switching is done. It is immaterial (so far as liability to conviction is concerned) that, for whatever reason, D thereupon desists. This does not look like theft because the article remains safely in the possession of its owner; but, in law, the theft is complete. The article in D's hands was stolen goods. It ceased to be "stolen" when it was replaced on the shelf ² but that could not undo the theft that had been committed.

---

¹   [1984] AC 320, [1983] 3 All ER 288, HL, holding that *Anderton v Wish* (1980) 72 Cr App Rep 23, DC, followed (reluctantly) in *Oxford v Peers* (1980) 72 Cr App Rep 19, DC, was rightly decided. Lord Roskill at [1983] 3 All ER 293 thought it material that D had removed the goods from the shelves but, it appears, only as evidence that he intended to steal and was not merely a misguided practical joker. *Gomez* at p 9 makes it completely clear that the mere switching of the labels without more is an appropriation.
²   Theft Act 1968, s. 24 (3), below, para **13–10**.

2–07   The dishonest label switcher of course acted without the consent of the owner; but, following *Gomez*, even the shop assistant, performing his duty to label the goods, is appropriating them. Of course he has the authority of the owner to do this, but, so far as appropriation is concerned, that is immaterial. A customer taking goods from the shelf in the supermarket also has the consent of the owner but he is appropriating the goods[1] and, if he does so dishonestly intending permanently to remove the goods from the shop without paying, he commits theft then and there. Motorists are invited to fill their tanks at self-service petrol stations but when they do so, they appropriate the petrol. If a motorist, D, fills his tank intending to drive off without paying, he is guilty of theft when the petrol goes into his tank.[2]

---

[1]   *McPherson* [1973] Crim LR 191, approved in *Gomez*, pp 11–12, as a case where goods where appropriated when taken from shelves and before being concealed in D's shopping bag. *Eddy v Niman* (1981) 73 Cr App Rep 237, DC, though not expressly overruled, must be regarded as wrongly decided.
[2]   *McHugh (David)* (1976) 64 Cr App Rep 92.

2–08   *Gomez* resolved a conflict between two earlier unanimous pronouncements of the House of Lords. In *Lawrence v Metropolitan Police Comr*,[1] it was held that s. 1 of the 1968 Act is not to be read as if it contained the words, "without the consent of the owner" (words included in the definition of larceny in the Larceny Act 1916 and omitted from the 1968 Act), and that it followed that D was guilty of theft although he took the property with the consent of the owner. Ten years later, in *Morris*,[2] the House was apparently unanimous in asserting that "the concept of appropriation . . . involves not an act expressly or impliedly authorised by the owner but an act by way of adverse interference with or usurpation of the owner's rights". Some judges attempted to reconcile these propositions (theft could be committed if D took with the owner's consent but not if he took with the owner's authority) but, generally, *Morris* rather than *Lawrence* was followed in the Court of Appeal, Criminal Division. In a case in the Civil Division, *Dobson v General Accident Fire and Life Assurance Corp plc*,[3] *Lawrence* was preferred. In *Gomez*, the whole House acknowledged that the propositions are irreconcilable and, Lord Lowry dissenting, held that *Lawrence* was right and *Morris* (in this respect) wrong. The majority gave scant consideration to the merits of the two views. The proposition in *Lawrence* was *ratio decidendi*, that in *Morris obiter dictum*, and that was good enough for the majority. They thought[4] it would serve "no useful purpose" to seek to construe the Act by reference to the CLRC Report. Lord Lowry, who did refer to the Report, demonstrated convincingly in his dissenting speech that it was the dictum in *Morris* which truly represented the intention of the CLRC and therefore that of Parliament which enacted the CLRC's proposals with no material change.

---

[1]   [1972] AC 626, [1971] 2 All ER 1253, HL.
[2]   [1984] AC 320, [1983] 3 All ER 288, HL.
[3]   [1990] 1 QB 274, [1989] 3 All ER 927, CA (Civ Div).
[4]   [1993] 1 All ER 1 at 13.

2–09   *The facts of Gomez*. Gomez, the assistant manager of a shop, persuaded the manager to agree to sell goods to the value of £17,000 to his accomplice and to accept payment by two cheques. The cheques (as X and Gomez knew) were stolen and worthless. This was a straightforward case of obtaining property by deception contrary to s. 15 of the Act; but for some reason the defendants were charged with theft. The Court of Appeal, following *Morris*, quashed their convictions: the contract of sale, being induced by fraud, was voidable but not void, ownership in the goods passed to X and so there was no appropriation; X was entitled to take possession and did so with the consent and express authority of the owner. The question certified for the House of Lords was:

"When theft is alleged and that which is alleged to be stolen passes to the defendant with the consent of the owner, but that has been obtained by a false representation has (a) an appropriation within the meaning of section 1 (1) of the Theft Act 1968 taken place, or (b) must such a passing of property necessarily involve an element of adverse interference with or usurpation of some right of the owner?"

The House answered (a) in the affirmative and (b) in the negative.

2–10 *May dishonest acquisition of ownership without deception be theft?* The questions for the House of Lords in *Gomez* were limited to cases involving deception and the House might have confined their ruling to such cases. They did not. No significance was attached to the fact that property was obtained by deception. The *ratio decidendi* is wider, namely that, whether there is a deception or not, it is no answer to a charge of theft that the act was done with the consent or authority of the owner. This is consistent with *Lawrence v Metropolitan Police Comr*[1] which was followed by the majority. P, an Italian with very little English, asked D, a taxi-driver, to take him to a certain address and tendered £1, which was more than sufficient for the fare. D said it was not enough. P's wallet was still open and D took from it a further £6. Although P agreed that he had "permitted" the taking of the money and although there was no finding that it was obtained by deception, D's conviction for stealing the excess was upheld. It was irrelevant that P consented to the taking. Such consent must have been to the passing of the entire interest in the money; but it was enough that "the money in the wallet which [D] appropriated belonged to [P]". There seems to have been ample evidence of obtaining by deception but there was no finding to that effect and it was not an element in the decision. It will be submitted below, however, that circumstances not envisaged by the House in *Gomez* may require some qualifications of the apparent *ratio decidendi*.[2]

---

[1] [1972] AC 626, [1971] 2 All ER 1253.
[2] Below, para **2–18**.

2–11 If, as *Gomez* decides, a person who acquires ownership with consent may commit theft, *a fortiori*, one who takes only possession or custody with consent commits theft if he does so with the dishonest intention permanently to deprive the owner. A customer in a supermarket who removes goods from the shelves, dishonestly intending to deprive the owner of them, commits theft although the owner consents to, and indeed invites, the removal of the goods.[1] The customer practises no deception. In *Gomez*, Lord Browne-Wilkinson said:[2]

"For myself . . . I regard the word 'appropriation' in isolation as being an objective description of the act done irrespective of the mental state of either the owner or the accused."

So it is irrelevant that D intended to deceive or that P was deceived. According to this opinion, both their mental states are irrelevant to the question whether there was an appropriation.

---

[1] Per Lord Keith at p 12.
[2] At p 39. But no meaning can sensibly be given to the word "in isolation". One has only to compare the phrase "appropriates goods to the contract" in the Sale of Goods Act 1979 to see that its meaning depends entirely on the context in which it is used. When the word is read in either of these contexts it is submitted that it clearly imports a mental element.

(b)   Cases overruled by Gomez

2–12   *Fritschy*[1] was one of only two cases expressly overruled by *Gomez*. Fritschy was instructed by the owner of some krugerrands to collect them from bullion dealers in England and take them to Switzerland. He collected the property and took it to Switzerland, exactly as instructed, and there, as he intended from the beginning, disposed of it for his own benefit. It was held, following *Morris*, that, as everything he did in England was authorised by the owner, he committed no theft within the jurisdiction of the court.[2] According to the law in *Gomez*, he was guilty of theft at the latest when he got his hands on the property with intent to steal it.[3]

---

[1]   [1985] Crim LR 745.

[2]   Even if the theft was not committed until D disposed of the property in Switzerland such a case will be triable here when Part I of the Criminal Justice Act 1993 is brought into force, the act of acquiring control of the property and taking it abroad being a "relevant event": para **1–18**, above. In the meantime, it may be triable here, following *Smith (W.D.)* [1996] 2 Cr App Rep 1.

[3]   In *Gallasso*, the court thought *Fritschy* distinguishable probably because Fritschy "took" the gold with a theftuous intent whereas Gallasso may have already taken the cheque when she formed her dishonest intention. It is submitted that this is an immaterial distinction.

2–13   The other case overruled was *Skipp*.[1] D, "posing as a genuine haulage contractor", obtained instructions to collect three loads from different places in London and deliver them to customers in Leicester. It was unsuccessfully argued that a single count for theft of the goods was bad for duplicity in that there were three separate appropriations. It was held that, though D may have had a dishonest intention permanently to deprive the owner at the time he received each load, he had done nothing inconsistent with the rights of the owner by loading the goods and probably not until he diverted the goods from their proper destination. It is now clear that he committed three thefts.[2]

---

[1]   [1975] Crim LR 114.

[2]   Whether the indictment should be regarded as duplicitous is perhaps less clear. Cf *DPP v McCabe* [1992] Crim LR 885, DC, where an information alleging theft of 76 library books from some or all of 32 different branch libraries over a period of two years was held not to be duplicitous. But in that case (i) the thefts were all from the same owner and (ii) it was impossible to particularise locations and dates.

2–14   Other cases are impliedly overruled. In *Hircock*,[1] D obtained possession of a car under a hire-purchase agreement by deception. Fourteen days later he dishonestly sold the car. It was held that he was guilty of an offence under s. 15 when he acquired the car and of theft contrary to s. 1 when he sold it. The court distinguished between obtaining and appropriation and held that he did not commit theft when he obtained possession of the car, considering it significant that he acknowledged at that time that he was not the owner. It is now clear that he stole the car when he obtained possession and there was no separate or continuing theft when he sold it.[2] In *Dip Kaur v Chief Constable for Hampshire*,[3] a shop displayed two racks of shoes, one rack bearing a price label of £6.99 and the other of £4.99. D found in the £6.99 rack a pair of shoes, one of which was labelled £6.99 and the other £4.99. She took the shoes to the cashier, hoping that she would see the lower and not the higher price. This indeed occurred. D's conviction for theft was quashed on the ground that the cashier had authority to accept D's offer to buy at the lower price and the ownership passed to D. It now seems clear that D was guilty of theft as soon as she did anything with the shoes with the dishonest intent – probably

when she picked them up, certainly not later than when she tendered them to
the cashier.

1   (1978) 67 Cr App Rep 278, [1979] Crim LR 184.
2   Cf *Atakpu* [1994] QB 69, [1993] 4 All ER 215.
3   [1981] 2 All ER 430.

2–15 *Gomez misunderstood: Gallasso.* It is submitted that the effect of
the decision in *Gomez* is accurately described above, para **2-05**, but, if so, it
was not immediately apparent to the Court of Appeal. On the very day that the
Lords gave judgment in *Gomez* the Court of Appeal heard the appeal in
Gallasso.[1] D, a nurse responsible for the care of[2] mentally handicapped patients,
quite properly received cheques on behalf of one of them, J, who was incapable
of managing his own affairs. Although there were already two trust accounts at
a building society in existence in which J was named as the beneficiary, D
opened a third trust account, a cashcard account at the same building society,
and paid in a cheque belonging to J. The prosecution alleged that her purpose
was to make it easier for her to make unauthorised withdrawals. The particular
question for the court was whether the paying-in of the cheque, if done
dishonestly and with intent permanently to deprive, amounted to theft of the
cheque. They held that it did not because there was no appropriation. The court
was convinced by counsel's argument that, while *Gomez* makes clear that a
taking without consent may be an appropriation, "there must still be a taking"
and here there was no taking. Lloyd LJ, clearly with the law of larceny[2] in
mind, said:

> "This is not to reintroduce the concept of carrying away into the definition of
> appropriation. It is to do no more than to give appropriation its ordinary meaning
> in section 1 and the same for the assumption of owner's rights in section 3 (1)."

Sadly, only Lord Lowry in *Gomez* was prepared to give these words their
ordinary meaning and the decision of the majority excludes it.

1   (1992) 98 Cr App Rep 284, [1993] Crim LR 459. See commentary and criticism at [1993]
     Crim LR 307. Griew, *Theft,* 2-91, thinks the case may "defy rationalisation", A.T.H. Smith,
     Property Offences, 5-56, fn 6, thinks it "simply wrong" and Archbold, 21-40 that it "overlooks
     the essence of the decision in *Gomez*". To the same effect, Arlidge & Parry, 3-091, Blackstone,
     CP, B4.26.
2   Above, para **1–13**.

2–16 *Taking not an essential element of theft.* Most thefts (shoplifting,
picking pockets, stealing of or from cars and in houses) involve a taking and,
not unnaturally, Lord Keith spoke of taking with and without consent in
discussing cases such as *Lawrence*; but it is impossible to believe that "taking"
is now an element in the definition of theft. It was because the common law of
larceny required a taking that Parliament had to create the offences of larceny
by a bailee, embezzlement, fraudulent conversion and obtaining by false
pretences. But all these (except obtaining by false pretences, i.e. deception)
have been abolished. The re-introduction of "taking" would set the law back
200 years. The word "appropriates" was used because it comprehended both
taking and other assumptions of ownership. Section 3 (1),[1] according to the
CLRC, is a "partial definition . . . which is included partly to indicate that this
is the familiar concept of conversion . . . ".[2] There is nothing in *Gomez* to
support the argument that "there must still be a taking". On the contrary, Lord
Keith's opinion that mere label swapping with intent is theft is inconsistent

with that view. As for authority, the cases in which convictions for theft have been upheld where there was a "conversion" but no taking are legion. *Gallasso* is inconsistent with these decisions and must surely be regarded as decided *per incuriam* and not a precedent binding on the Court of Appeal or lower courts.

---

[1]   Above, para **2–03**.
[2]   *Eighth Report*, Cmnd 2977, para 34.

2–17   *Analysis* of *Gallasso*. Assuming that she had the dishonest intention alleged by the prosecution, D, when she paid in J's cheque, was exercising a right of the owner and, as consent and authority are irrelevant, she assumed that right and appropriated the cheque. When the cheque was honoured, J's property, a thing in action consisting in his right to sue the drawer of the cheque, ceased to exist. It was converted into another thing in action, namely J's right to sue the building society for the same amount of money. It was alleged that D intended to deprive J permanently of that thing, or part of it, by drawing on the account for her own purposes. If so, it is submitted that the theft was committed not later than when she paid in the cheque. If she had formed the dishonest intent when she took it from the envelope (which would be a dishonest taking), the theft began then and presumably continued until the cheque was paid in. In taking possession of the cheque and in paying it in D was exercising rights of the owner and it is immaterial that she was doing so with authority or consent.

(c)   Possible qualifications of Gomez

2-18 Notwithstanding the apparently all-embracing nature of the decision in *Gomez*, there remains the possibility of a number of qualifications to it which later courts may find it desirable or even necessary to impose. These are considered below.

(i) Appropriation which is not "unlawful"

2–19   It has been forcefully argued that no act should amount to theft unless it is unlawful in the civil law.[1] Of course the vast majority of thefts do amount to civil wrongs but it does not necessarily follow that civil unlawfulness is a constituent of the offence. Section 1 (1) of the 1968 Act does not include the word "unlawfully" nor does it say "misappropriate".This opinion has not yet been accepted by any court[2] and, after *Gomez*, it looks untenable. The mere removal of goods by a customer from the shelves of a supermarket and the filling of his tank by a motorist at a self-service petrol station do not amount to civil wrongs merely because the act is done with a secret dishonest intent. *Fritschy*[3] committed no civil offence by carrying out his employer's instructions to take the property to Switzerland but *Gomez* tells us that he committed theft by doing so.

---

[1]   Williams, "Theft, Consent and Illegality" [1977] Crim LR 127, *TBCL* 770–773. ". . . if the civil law sees no reason to permit the owner to complain of an interference with his property why should the criminal law do so?" – A.T.H. Smith, *Property Offences*, 5–49.
[2]   It has been held that a person may be guilty of theft although his act does not amount to the tort of conversion and the court did not find it necessary to look for any other form of civil wrong: *Bonner* [1970] 2 All ER 97n, [1970] 1 WLR 838, CA, below, para **2–26**. D's act was, however, certainly unlawful in the sense that it was a breach of contract.
[3]   Above, para **2-12**.

(ii) Appropriation which is not "dishonest"

2–20   Another argument[1] is that the word "dishonestly" has an objective as well as a subjective meaning. This is true, at least to the extent required by the first part of the *Ghosh* test,[2] to be applied by a jury for the meaning of "dishonestly": Was what was done dishonest according to the ordinary standards of reasonable and honest people? If not, D is not guilty.

If a jury should think, as a senior clergyman of the Church of England apparently thinks, that shoplifting from supermarkets is not dishonest according to the ordinary standards of reasonable people like themselves, the particular shoplifting which has occurred is not a crime, whatever the state of mind of the shoplifter. A jury will, however, not usually be instructed to apply this test unless the defendant claims that he does not regard his conduct as dishonest. Moreover, "what was done" refers to D's act *and* the state of mind with which he did it. A typical case is where D takes money from his employer's till but claims that this is not dishonest because he intended one day to pay it back. The first limb of the *Ghosh* test is really only a necessary first step to assessing the mind of the particular defendant.

Whether dishonesty qualifies the concept of appropriation generally is another matter. There is a passage in the speech of Lord Browne-Wilkinson in *Gomez* which, at first sight, encourages the view that the appropriation must be objectively "dishonest". Lord Browne-Wilkinson said:[3]

> "Parliament has used a composite phrase, 'dishonest appropriation'. Thus it is not every appropriation which falls within the section but only an act which answers the composite description."

If that were right it would surely follow that only a *mis*appropriation would satisfy the Act. "Appropriation" is neutral – it might be rightful (e.g., by a bailiff) or wrongful. "Dishonest appropriation" is certainly not neutral – if it describes the act, it must be, in some sense, a wrongful act. But in fact, the Theft Act nowhere uses the "composite phrase, 'dishonest appropriation'". Lord Browne-Wilkinson seems to have been looking at an earlier analysis of the section by the Court of Appeal, not at the Act. The definition of theft in s. 1 says "dishonestly appropriates", which is not the same thing. "Dishonestly" does not appear to qualify the objective meaning of "appropriates" any more than "maliciously wounds" qualifies "wounds". It is true that s. 2 begins, "A person's appropriation of property belonging to another is not to be regarded as dishonest . . .", but the sidenote to the section is "Dishonestly", indicating that it is merely spelling out the meaning of the adverb, not qualifying the noun; and it then goes on to specify three beliefs, not objective facts, giving no support to the view that the word "dishonestly" is meant to include anything other than a state of mind. Lord Browne-Wilkinson, in any event, failed to follow through his reading (or misreading) of the Act because he went on to hold that appropriation is entirely unqualified, except by the intent with which the act is done. He criticised *Morris* because it treated the word "appropriation" as being tantamount to "misappropriation"; but what could be wrong about treating the imagined "composite phrase, 'dishonest appropriation'", as tantamount to misappropriation? As the law stands, it seems that appropriation need not be "dishonest" or *mis*appropriation.

---

[1]   Arlidge and Parry (1st edn), 1.10.

[2]   Below, para **2–122**.

[3]   [1993] 1 All ER 1 at 39. This is part of a longer passage cited by the court in *Hopkins and Kendrick,* below, para **2–21** And see above, para **2–11**.

(iii)   Where D acquires an absolute, indefeasible title

2–21   *Gift.* We turn then to a narrower, more specific, qualification. As we have noted, in *Gomez* the property was in fact obtained by deception. The title which D obtained to it was, therefore, voidable. In *Morris* the article when taken from the supermarket shelves continued to belong to, and, indeed, probably to remain in the possession of, the shopkeeper. There was no finding of any deception in *Lawrence* but the dishonest taxi-driver certainly had no right to retain the fare which he knew exceeded that permitted by law. In all these cases any title D had to the property was defeasible. They may, therefore, be distinguishable where D acquires an indefeasible right to the entire proprietary interest – i.e., where there is no deception, duress or other vitiating factor to render the transaction void or voidable, and its effect is to divest P wholly of his proprietary interest. Two recent cases required the courts to consider whether the recipients of gifts made by an elderly lady of failing powers were guilty of theft. In the first of these, *Mazo*,[1] a lady's maid was convicted of theft of large sums of money given to her by her by P. Quashing her conviction, the court, referring to *Gomez*, said that it was clear that an act could be theft notwithstanding the owner's consent *if* that consent was obtained by deception but no deception was proved in this case; and it was –

"common ground that the receiver of a valid gift *inter vivos* should not be the subject of a conviction for theft".

In *Hopkins and Kendrick* [2] some doubt was cast on that premise:

"It is not for these purposes necessary to consider whether or not that apparent gloss on *Gomez* is well-founded."

The court considered counsel's submission–

"if the donor's mind is such that the donor has the capacity to make a gift or to consent to the transfer of property, then there is no appropriation and no theft" – "bold and perhaps surprising".

---

[1]   [1996] Crim LR 435 and Smith & Hogan, 521.
[2]   [1997] Crim LR 359.

2–22   It is submitted that the proposition in *Mazo*, "gloss" or not, and counsel's submission are well-founded. Otherwise there would be an intolerable conflict with the civil law. If the gifts in these cases were valid in the civil law – neither void nor voidable for fraud, duress, undue influence or any other reason – the donees acquired an absolute, indefeasible title to the property. If it were seized from them by the police, they, not the donors or anyone else, would be entitled to recover it. They would have an action in conversion against the police – or the donor, if the police returned the property to her. It is submitted then that the question in both *Mazo* and *Hopkins*, in the absence of proof of deception, duress or undue influence, was whether P was competent to make the disposition she did. If she was, it should be immaterial that her actions might be regarded by others as eccentric, imprudent, or irrational; and that the actions of the donee in relation to the gift were grasping and despicable. If a sane and wealthy woman, persuaded by reading the Bible that she should give her property to the poor, goes down the street and gives her Rolex to the first seller of *The Big Issue* she meets, it is submitted that he cannot be guilty of theft, even if he tells his friends that she must be a "complete nutter".[1]

The two cases are reconcilable on the facts. In *Hopkins*, in the court's judgment, the evidence of the lady's mental capacity was very different from that in *Mazo*; and the summing up could not have resulted in the jury being confused "as to whether Mrs Clare was somebody who is just 'not quite up to it', with reduced mental capacity, which was said of Lady S [in *Mazo*] or lacking the capacity manage her own affairs". An instruction to convict only if Mrs Clare lacked the capacity to manage her own affairs was, indeed, unnecessary if *Mazo* was wrong. If she lacked that capacity, the dispositions were invalid and the property continued to belong to her; and, if the appellants were aware of her incapacity, they intended a dishonest appropriation of her property. There was ample evidence to support the jury's verdict that they were dishonest.

---

[1] Arguably, it might be attempted theft under the Criminal Attempts Act 1981, s. 1 (1) and (3).

2–23 *Sale.* The arguments in the last paragraph relating to gifts apply *a fortiori* to sale. Take a case like *Smith v Hughes*.[1] S contracted to sell some oats to H. Even on the assumption that S knew (i) that the oats were new oats and (ii) that H was buying the oats only because he believed they were old, new oats being useless to him, it was held that S was entitled to recover the price. Suppose H had paid the price before discovering that the oats were new. S made no false pretence so there was no question of obtaining the price by deception; but suppose he were now to be charged with theft. The question in the civil law was not "what a man of scrupulous morality or nice honour would do under such circumstances"; and, in a criminal case, a jury might well consider such an unscrupulous and dishonourable seller to be "dishonest" under the principle in *Ghosh*.[2] He obviously has an intention to deprive the buyer permanently of the money. But, if the law says he is entitled to recover the price, it cannot also say that he steals it. If this were theft the law would be assisting him to commit the crime. To hold the conduct to be theft would be, in effect, to alter the civil law.

---

[1] (1871) LR 6 QB 597.
[2] Below, para **2–114**.

2–24 Another example may be *Deller*.[1] D induced P to accept his car in part-exchange for a new one by representing that it was free from encumbrances. D had previously executed a document purporting to mortgage the car to a finance company. He probably believed that this was effective in which case the car was subject to an encumbrance. If so, he intended to tell a lie; but the document was probably void in law as an unregistered bill of sale. In that case the car was not subject to any encumbrance: " . . . quite accidentally and, strange as it may sound, dishonestly, the appellant had told the truth". Clearly D could not be guilty of obtaining the new car by deception but would his dishonest obtaining of it without deception now be theft? Probably not, because the contract of part-exchange was an enforceable contract. Whatever his intention, objectively he had done nothing wrong. Where, on the other hand, D has no enforceable right to the property, the mere fact that P has no civil remedy should not inhibit the court from finding that D has stolen P's property if the definition of theft is satisfied. For example, if D dishonestly and without authority offers to sell P's property to E,[2] D may not yet be guilty of any civil wrong against P but it would be strange to say that the civil law gave D a "right" to do such an act; and it seems that, if the words of s. 1 fit D's act, he may be convicted of theft. Even before *Gomez* such an unauthorised usurpation of the owner's rights in the thing was clearly "an appropriation".

[1]   (1952) 36 Cr App Rep 184, CCA. D could probably now be convicted of an attempt to obtain by deception (Smith & Hogan 35, 327 – but see also p 333, (c) (i)) and, since *Gomez*, of an attempt to steal.

[2]   Cf *Pitham and Hehl* (1976) 65 Cr App Rep 45, below, para **2–36**. The position was the same under the Larceny Acts: *Rogers v Arnott* [1960] 2 QB 244, [1960] 2 All ER 417. Where goods are obtained by deception under a voidable contract of sale a receiver who knows the goods have been so obtained is guilty of handling, below, para **13–06**; but, while the contract remains unrescinded, he is not guilty of conversion.

(iv)   Appropriation of the property of another authorised by the civil law

2–25   There are many cases where the civil law authorises or even requires D to appropriate P's property with the intention of permanently depriving P of it.[1] If, in such a case, D is aware of the law, it is submitted that he cannot be considered to be acting dishonestly and he commits no offence, however evil his motive might be. Suppose, however, that D is unaware of the civil law which authorises or requires him to act as he does and he proceeds in a furtive manner evincing a dishonest intention. He now falls literally within the terms of the Act unless "dishonestly" is interpreted to include the objective element at one time discerned by Arlidge and Parry.[2] The court would, it is submitted, have to find some means of avoiding the conviction of D for doing no more than the civil law expressly authorised or required him to do.

[1]   E.g. a sale of uncollected goods under Sch 1 of the Torts (Interference with Goods) Act 1977.
[2]   Above, para **2.20**.

2–26   An express authority or right in the strict sense must, however, be distinguished from a mere liberty or power. D has a liberty under the civil law to do an act if the performance of that act does not amount to a civil wrong. There is no reason why the criminal law should not curtail such liberties in appropriate cases,[1] and the Theft Act has done so in the case of a co-owner who dishonestly appropriates the joint property;[2] and where D has the power to pass a good title, he may nevertheless in some cases be properly convicted of theft when he does so. For instance, the mercantile agent who is in possession of goods with the consent of the owner passes a good title if he sells to a bona-fide purchaser, even though he does so dishonestly and in breach of the arrangement made with the owner.[3] This is clearly theft by the mercantile agent.

The distinction between power and right appears in s. 48 of the Sale of Goods Act 1979 and it is instructive to consider the effect of the Theft Act upon the situations there envisaged. By subsections (1) and (2):

"(1) Subject to the provisions of this section, a contract of sale is not rescinded by the mere exercise by an unpaid seller of his right of lien or retention or stoppage in transitu."

"(2) Where an unpaid seller who has exercised his right of lien or retention or stoppage in transitu re-sells the goods, the buyer acquires a good title thereto as against the original buyer."

The unpaid seller who re-sells after the property has passed has clearly appropriated the property of another (the first buyer) and commits the *actus reus* of theft although in doing so he passes a good title to the second buyer. It is unlikely that he could be convicted in most cases, for it would be difficult to prove dishonesty where no part of the price had been paid. But a seller is unpaid[4] until he receives the *whole* price, and a seller would certainly be dishonest if, having received 90 per cent of the price, he were to re-sell the goods, intending not to repay. This subsection gives the seller a mere power, not a right. The re-sale is a wrongful one and the first buyer, if he were to tender the price, could sue in conversion. There seems to be no reason why this should not be a crime. A quite different situation is created by subsection (3):

> "Where the goods are of a perishable nature, or where the unpaid seller gives notice to the buyer of his intention to re-sell, and the buyer does not within a reasonable time pay or tender the price, the unpaid seller may re-sell the goods and recover from the original buyer damages for any loss occasioned by his breach of contract."

Though it is now established that the re-sale rescinds the contract and terminates the first buyer's property in the goods, the goods belong to the first buyer up to the moment of sale. It would be intolerable that the law should say, at one and the same time, that "the unpaid seller may re-sell the goods" and that he is guilty of theft if he does this, not knowing that the law permits him to do so. He is not guilty.[5] The position is the same under subsection (4):

> "Where the seller expressly reserves the right of re-sale in case the buyer should make default, and on the buyer making default, re-sells the goods, the original contract of sale is thereby rescinded, but without prejudice to any claim the seller may have for damages."

---

[1]   This passage in the seventh edition of this book is closely analysed by Arlidge & Parry, 1–063 to 1–069. They have particular difficulty with the distinction between a liberty and a right "in the strict sense". But the distinction between right *stricto sensu* and liberty has been recognised by jurists from Bentham onwards, though, admittedly, not in this context. See, e.g., Dias, *Jurisprudence* (2nd edn) 226.

[2]   *Bonner*, above, para **2-19**. There was a breach of contract in that case, but co-owners are not necessarily in a contractual relationship – they may have inherited the property – and this should make no difference to the liability for theft of the one who appropriates the other's proprietary interest.

[3]   Factors Act 1889, s. 2 (1).

[4]   Sale of Goods Act 1979, s. 38.

[5]   *Ward Ltd v Bignall* [1967] 1 QB 534, [1967] 2 All ER 449, CA.

2–27   It has already been noticed that the most common method of appropriation is by taking property from the possession of another. It is now time to take a closer look at other types of appropriation.

(d)   Appropriation without taking

(i)   Appropriation by one already in possession

2–28   It is very common for one person, D, to be in possession of property which belongs to another, P. Clearly P retains some of the rights of an owner which may be dishonestly assumed by D. The commonest examples are bailments, where P, the bailor, has entrusted D, the bailee, with possession for some limited purpose – he has loaned D a book, hired a car to him, let him have a television on hire-purchase or pledged his watch to him as security for a loan. If, in any of these cases, D destroys the property or gives it away or sells it to another, he does something which only the owner, P, can lawfully do and he has assumed P's rights. Even if D has only gone so far as to offer to sell the thing, he has assumed the right to dispose of the owner's entire interest and it is clear that there is an appropriation.[1] Even an invitation to E to make an offer to buy P's property might be regarded as an assumption of P's right. But a mere decision by D to sell P's property, even if it could be proved (he has declared his intention in a letter or by musing aloud), would not be enough. A decision to assume rights is not an assumption of them. Appropriation requires conduct of some kind even if it is no more than "keeping" property already held.

---

[1] *Pitham and Hehl* (1976) 65 Cr App Rep 45, CA. Though there is a complete theft at the instant the offer is made, it does not necessarily follow that the theft does not continue for some time thereafter. *Gregory* (1982) 77 Cr App Rep 41, [1982] Crim LR 229, CA, and below, para **2–49**.

2–29 *Exercise of one's own proprietary right is not an appropriation.* Notwithstanding the decision in *Gomez* that appropriation may be committed by an authorised act, it is submitted that D, a bailee, does not commit an offence by any act which he has a right to do under the terms of the bailment. This is because the ownership in the thing is divided between bailor and bailee. The bailee has his own proprietary interest. In exercising the rights vested in him by the bailment, D is not assuming or appropriating any right belonging to another. For example, D hires a car from P for a month. During the month he decides to take the car to a neighbouring town and sell it to a secondhand car dealer. He does not commit theft by driving the car to the dealer. As a bailee he has proprietary rights in the car which include, say, the right to drive the car anywhere in Great Britain. He is exercising his own rights, not assuming any right belonging to another. P has no right that he shall not drive the car to any place that the terms of the bailment permit.[1] Of course, D steals the car as soon as he offers to sell it, for he is now exercising a right which still belongs to P.

---

[1] It was argued in *Rogers v Arnott* [1960] 2 QB 244, [1960] 2 All ER 417, DC. "Once the defendant decided to keep the appointment to sell the tape recorder, and certainly once he had put it into the car, he committed an act of conversion" (Basil Wigoder); but the decision was that the offence of larceny was complete when the bailee of the tape recorder offered to sell it.

2–30 *An agent, exercising his principal's rights, may steal.* It is now clear that D may commit theft if, as P's authorised agent, he takes P's property into his possession or custody with intent to steal. But suppose that he does so without any such intention – e.g. that in *Fritschy*[1] D had obtained P's krugerrands from the depositary, as instructed by P, without any intention to steal but had conceived the theftuous intent before he left (again, as instructed) for Switzerland. Is it arguable that D, in taking the gold abroad, like the hirer of the car above (para **2–29**), would have been exercising his own proprietary rights, not P's? It is submitted not. The agent (though he may be a bailee) is exercising the rights of the principal. His conduct is lawful in the civil law, not because he has a proprietary right but because he is authorised by the principal to do the act in question. When he exercises a right belonging to the principal, even with the principal's consent, he appropriates it and if he has a theftuous intent, he steals the property.

---

[1] Above, para **2–12**.

2–31 *Theft by possessors who are not bailees.* A person may come into possession of the property of another in ways other than bailment and may commit theft by the exercise of any proprietary right of the owner. Any possible doubts are dispelled by the provision of s. 3 (1) that appropriation includes –

" . . . where he has come by the property (innocently or not) without stealing it, any later assumption of a right to it by keeping or dealing with it as owner".[1]

To the reader unfamiliar with the law of larceny, this provision probably seems quite unnecessary – and indeed it is. It was a principle of larceny that, except in the case of a bailee, the intention to steal must exist at the moment of taking possession. The purpose of s. 3 (1) is to ensure that this principle was not applied to the new offence. It is now entirely clear that the following acts amount to theft.

(i) D receives property which he knows to be stolen. He intends to restore it to the true owner or the police so he is not dishonest and commits no offence. Later he changes his mind and conceals the thing, dishonestly intending to deprive the owner permanently of it.

(ii) D, a lorry-driver, receives a number of sacks of pig-meal into his employer's lorry for carriage from A to B. When he arrives, D discovers that ten sacks too many have been loaded. He keeps them for himself or sells them for his own benefit.

In these two examples, D did not assume *all* the rights of the owner when he first received the property; he intended to hold it for another. When he later assumed the entire rights of the owner he committed theft. The same principle applies, however, where D intends innocently to assume the entire ownership at the start. For example:

(iii) D finds a banknote in the highway. There appears to be no reasonable means of ascertaining the owner and D decides to keep it for himself. This is no offence – D has "come by the property . . . innocently". Two days later, being still in possession of it, he discovers that P is the owner and then uses the note for his own purposes.

(iv) In the dark P hands a banknote to D. Both believe it to be a £5 note. In fact it is a £20 note. Some time later, D discovers it is a £20 note and spends it. It is assumed that the property in the note does not pass in this situation. If this assumption is wrong, D will not escape liability, but it will then be necessary to rely on s. 5 (4).[2]

(v) D is handed his workmate's pay packet by mistake. When he has been in possession of it for some hours he discovers that it contains more than he is entitled to and appropriates the money.

In cases (iii), (iv) and (v), it has been suggested that, since D intended to assume *all* the rights of an owner when he first took the thing, there is no room for any "later assumption of a right to it", i.e. that one cannot assume what one has already assumed. It is submitted, however, that the words "later assumption" pre-suppose an earlier assumption; and that the later assumption envisaged may be an exercise of rights which have been assumed on "coming by" the thing in question.[3]

---

[1]   Section 3 (1).
[2]   Cf *Ashwell* (1885) 16 QBD 190; below, para **2–81**.
[3]   The contrary view would be disastrous for, it should be noted, s. 5 (4), below, para **2–81**, does no more than vest a fictitious property in the prosecutor and leaves open the necessity for an appropriation.

(ii)   Appropriation by acquiring ownership without possession

2–32   Ownership may pass under a contract of sale which is voidable because induced by deception, before possession is transferred. Under section 18, rule 1, of the Sale of Goods Act 1979, where there is an unconditional contract for the sale of specific goods in a deliverable state, the ownership, in the absence of a contrary intention, passes to the buyer when the contract is made and it is immaterial that the time of payment or delivery or both are postponed. In *Dobson v General Accident Fire and Life Insurance Corpn plc*,[1] a civil action, the plaintiff claimed from his insurers the value of a watch and ring which a rogue had induced him to sell for a worthless cheque. The plaintiff's insurance policy covered loss by theft. It was not enough for him to prove that his property had been obtained by deception, contrary to s. 15. The insurers argued that the ownership in the goods passed when a contract was made over the telephone, two days before delivery; so that, when the rogue collected the goods, he was taking delivery of his own property. The response of Parker LJ to this argument was:

> " . . . the result would merely be that the making of the contract constituted the appropriation. It was by that act that the rogue assumed the rights of an owner and at that time the property did belong to the plaintiff ".

The goods remain, for the time being, safely in the owner's possession; but they are already stolen.

---

[1] [1990] 1 QB 274, [1990] Crim LR 271, CA, Civ Div. Much of Parker LJ's judgment was cited with approval by Lord Keith in *Gomez*. This particular passage was not cited but is probably to be regarded as approved. Cf cases discussed below, para **4–40**.

(iii)   Appropriation by the mere assumption of the rights of an owner

2–33   When the common law of larceny required a taking and carrying away of the property alleged to have been stolen, the theft could occur only when and where that event took place. But "asportation", as it was known, is no longer necessary. It never was necessary in the statutory extension of larceny – "conversion" by a bailee. Consequently it was held in *Rogers v Arnott* that the bailee of a tape-recorder committed larceny when he offered to sell it. That case has been doubted[1] and it has been argued[2] that the owner "has no general right that [others] shall not contract to sell [his property], or to purport to pass ownership in it" and that there is therefore no assumption of the rights of the owner, no appropriation.   It is true that A, without the knowledge or consent of B, might lawfully *contract* to sell B's car to C next week, a contract which he might be able to perform by buying the car from B in the interval. But to purport to *sell*, or to purport to pass ownership, is a different matter. Even here the purported sale will usually be ineffective and not amount to a civil wrong;   but it gives C a bona fide, though invalid, claim to B's property, which it may not always be easy to rebut. The right to sell is surely a right of the owner and, in normal circumstances, of him alone.

Under the 1968 Act it must be proved that D "appropriated" the property and "Any assumption by a person of the rights of an owner amounts to an appropriation . . . ". The question arises, does D assume the rights of an owner, (i) as soon as he does acts in relation to the property which only the owner may lawfully do or, (ii) only when those acts take effect on the property? In *Tomsett*,[3] the Court of Appeal acted on the assumption that the latter view was correct. The P Bank transferred US $7m to a New York bank to earn overnight interest. The "money" should have been returned to England the next day. D, a telex operator employed by the P Bank, sent a telex from London diverting the $7m plus interest to another bank in New York for an account at its Geneva branch which his accomplice had opened a month earlier. D covered up his dishonest conduct by making it appear that a second telex had been sent giving the correct destination of the money but this was "killed" before it was transmitted. D's conviction for conspiracy to steal was quashed on the ground that the theft took place either in Geneva or New York outside the jurisdiction of the court: the alleged conspiracy was not, at that time,[4] an agreement to commit an offence "triable in England and Wales", as required by the Criminal Law Act 1977, s. 1 (1) and (4).

---

¹   A.T.H. Smith, *Property Offences,* 5–45, drawing attention to earlier conflicting cases which have been overlooked.
²   Ibid, 5–49.
³   [1985] Crim LR 369, CA.
⁴   Even if *Tomsett* was rightly decided at the time, it seems clear that D could be convicted under Part 1of the Criminal Justice Act 1993 when it comes into force. In order to establish the theft, proof would be required of D's act which was therefore a "relevant event" occurring in England. See para **1–19** above. He and his accomplices would be guilty of conspiracy to steal.

2–34   However, in *Re Osman*,¹ an extradition case, a Divisional Court comprised of Lloyd LJ and French J, who were both members of the court in *Tomsett*, refused to follow that case. Prosecuting counsel in *Tomsett* had declined the court's invitation to argue that the theft was committed in England and, said Lloyd LJ, "The law of England cannot be made or unmade by the willingness of counsel to argue a point . . . the present point was left undecided." *Re Osman* was concerned with acts done in Hong Kong (where the law of theft is the same as in England) in relation to property in other countries; but the effect of the application of the *ratio decidendi* to *Tomsett* is that Tomsett would be guilty of stealing in England the property situated in New York when he, in England, assumed the rights of the owner by directing a disposition of the property which could be lawfully done only by the owner.

---

¹   [1988] Crim LR 611. Archbold (44th edn), 21–29, doubted this proposition in *Osman*; (the doubt is not repeated in the current (1997 edition). In *Shuck* [1992] Crim LR 209 D was held liable for appropriations of property committed by his innocent agent in the Isle of Man – presumably because D directed them from England.

2–35   The property alleged to be stolen in both *Tomsett* and *Re Osman* was intangible property, a thing in action. In *Tomsett* it was the P Bank's credit balance with the New York bank, i.e. the debt owed by the New York bank to the P Bank. But the *ratio* of *Re Osman* is not confined to things in action. Suppose that P's Rolls-Royce is in Scotland. D has found the registration document and, purporting to be P, he in England produces the document and "sells" the car to a bona-fide purchaser, E. Whether or not ownership in the car passes to E, this is surely an assumption by D of the rights of the owner, P, and theft is committed in England.¹ Of course, theft also requires an intention permanently to deprive the owner of his property. Whether such an intention can be discerned in circumstances such as these is considered below.²

---

¹   See the discussion in the fifth and earlier editions of this book (5th edn, paras [25] and [26]), cf *Bloxham* (1943) 29 Cr App Rep 37, CCA.
²   Para **2–128**.

2–36   Even in the light of *Re Osman* and of *Gomez*, the earlier decision in *Pitham*¹ is difficult to justify. D offered to sell P's property to Pitham. It was held that the mere offer to sell amounted to a completed theft so that when the goods were delivered to Pitham he received them "otherwise than in the course of the stealing"² and was therefore guilty of handling the stolen goods. But in this case, unlike the example of the Rolls-Royce,³ Pitham, the buyer, knew very well that D had no authority to sell P's property; and D knew that the buyer knew that. D did not purport to be the owner or to be acting with his authority. It was not really an offer to sell at all but a proposal for a joint theft of the goods. To demonstrate the absurdity of *Pitham*, Williams⁴ puts the case of a butler who tells the maid that he has found the key to the Duke's safe and invites her to help herself to the silver. Williams says that it would be preposterous to hold that the butler has already stolen the silver. It would indeed. The butler never purports to be, or to exercise any of the rights of, the owner or his agent. The maid does not acquire a claim of right to the property. To invite another to steal is not to assume or exercise any right of the owner. If it were otherwise, all those conspiring to steal specific property would already be guilty of theft.

---

1   (1976) 65 Cr App Rep 45.
2   Below, para **13–33**.
3   Above, para **2–35**. It is also unlike *Bloxham*, above, para **2–35** fn 1, where D purported to sell his employer's refrigerator to a bona-fide purchaser and was held not guilty of an attempt to commit larceny because he had made no attempt (and presumably did not intend to make any attempt) to take the refrigerator and carry it away. Bloxham was not a bailee.
4   *TBCL* 764.

(e)   Other aspects of appropriation

(i)   No appropriation by the sole owner

2–37   Although P consents to, and does, transfer his entire proprietary interest to D, D is guilty of theft if he receives that entire interest dishonestly and with intent permanently to deprive, at least if the transaction is voidable for fraud.[1] That is the effect of *Gomez* and of *Lawrence v Metropolitan Police Comr*.[2] But if D receives the entire interest innocently he cannot thereafter be guilty of theft: there is no longer any property "belonging to another" for him to appropriate. It makes no difference that D is dishonest. For example, D, believing that P has left a fountain pen on D's desk by mistake, takes it, dishonestly intending to keep it for himself. In fact P put the pen there intending to make D a gift and by this delivery made D the owner of the pen. D is not guilty of theft – but he might now be convicted of an attempt to steal. Where D, a motorist, fills his tank at a self-service petrol station, intending to pay, and then dishonestly decides to drive off without paying, he commits no theft.[3] The owner has consented to D's acquiring, and he has acquired, the entire proprietary interest in the petrol. It no longer belongs to another. It is the same as where a customer in a restaurant honestly consumes a meal and then dishonestly leaves without paying. Clearly, he does not steal the food.[4] These acts are offences of making off without payment under 1978, s. 3.[5]

---

1   See *Mazo*, above, para **2–21**.
2   [1972] AC 626, above, para **2–08**.
3   *Greenberg* [1972] Crim LR 331 (Judge Friend); *Edwards v Ddin* [1976] 3 All ER 705, DC. It is assumed that P, having parted with possession, has no lien. For the case where D dishonestly fills his tank, see *McHugh*, para **2–07**.
4   *Corcoran v Whent* [1977] Crim LR 52, DC. D had arrived home before he formed the dishonest intention; but it makes no difference to the result. The food was incapable of being stolen as soon as it was consumed. Cf *Buckmaster* (1887) 20 QBD 182, CCR (the welshing bookmaker), criticised in Kenny 264–265, Russell 935–938, Smith & Hogan (1st edition) 352, n. 15, and in the fifth edition of this book, para [41].
5   Below, paras **5–01** to **5–09**.

2–38   Since generally[1] D cannot steal from P after he has acquired P's entire proprietary interest, it is sometimes necessary to have recourse to the law of contract to determine whether and, if so, when the ownership in property has passed from P to D. Ownership may pass under a contract for the sale of goods as soon as the contract is made and before the price has been paid.[2] Whether or not it does so pass in any particular case is, however, a question of intention; and it has been held that, in a sale in a supermarket, it is presumed that the ownership in the goods is not intended to pass until the goods are paid for.[3] In *Davies v Leighton*,[4] the presumption was held to be applicable, not only to the ordinary case where the customer collects the goods and tenders them to the cashier, but also to the case where the goods were weighed, bagged, priced and handed by an assistant to a customer, D, who, instead of tendering them to the cashier, dishonestly removed them from the store. It is possible that the contract of sale was made with the assistant but whether it was so or not was immaterial. The ownership had not passed and D was guilty of theft. In *Davies v Leighton* the court thought it might have been different if the assistant had been in a managerial capacity. But, even if it had been intended that the ownership in the goods should pass immediately to D, and therefore did pass to him, it is inconceivable that the manager would have intended to give up the seller's lien, i.e. his right to retain possession until the payment of the price. The customer would have only custody of the goods in his hands, until he paid the price, possession continuing in the seller,[5] to whom the property would still therefore "belong": s. 5 (1). Similarly, it may be necessary to decide whether a contract has been rescinded so as to revest property in the seller. In *Walker*,[6] D sold to P an unsatisfactory video recorder which was returned to him for repair. P then served on D a summons claiming the return of the price as the "return of money paid for defective goods". Two days later, D sold the recorder. He was convicted of theft of the recorder and obtaining the price by deception but his conviction was quashed. The service of the summons probably operated to rescind the contract. The effect would be to restore the parties to the position they were in before the contract was made. D would be the absolute owner, perfectly entitled to sell the recorder and to receive the price.[7]

---

[1]   For exceptions, see s. 5 (3) and (4) of the Act below, paras **2–71** to **2–87**.
[2]   Sale of Goods Act 1979, s. 18, r. 1.
[3]   *Martin v Puttick* [1968] 2 QB 82, [1967] 1 All ER 899, DC; *Lacis v Cashmarts* [1969] 2 QB 400, DC.
[4]   (1978) 68 Cr App Rep 4, [1978] Crim LR 575, DC, and commentary.
[5]   Cf *Chissers* (1678) T Raym 275, 3 Salk 194.
[6]   [1984] Crim LR 112, CA.
[7]   Cf Lord Roskill in *Morris*, "it is on any view wrong to introduce into this branch of the criminal law questions whether particular contracts are void or voidable on the ground of mistake or fraud or whether any mistake is sufficiently fundamental to vitiate a contract": [1983] 3 All ER 288 at 294, [1983] Crim LR 813 and commentary. But, as Bingham LJ said in *Dobson v General Accident Fire and Life Insurance Corpn plc* [1989] 3 All ER 927 at 937: "Whether, in the ordinary case . . . goods are to be regarded as belonging to another is a question to which the criminal law offers no answer and which can only be answered by reference to civil law principles."

(ii)   Agent exceeding authority

2–39   Before *Gomez* it was held that where D has a limited authority to deal with P's property, he may appropriate it by dealing with it in excess of that authority. *A fortiori*, this is so after *Gomez*. Dealing with P's property is an appropriation whether authorised or not and the excess of authority is now important only as evidence of a dishonest intention permanently to deprive. The director of a company who has a general authority to deal in its export quotas (which, if assignable, is "intangible property") commits theft if he dishonestly sells quotas at an undervalue.[1] In *Pilgram v Rice-Smith*,[2] goods were dishonestly underpriced by an assistant in a supermarket, acting in collusion with a customer, D, who then tendered the underpriced goods at the checkout. It is now clear that the underpricing of the goods by the assistant amounted to an appropriation. It was immaterial that the customer was going to behave as such, and not as owner, by offering to buy the goods at the checkout. In *Bhachu*,[3] a dishonest cashier in collusion with a customer undervalued the goods by ringing up a price below the authorised price. The court thought that the appropriation was committed by the customer when she put the goods in the wire basket provided and wheeled them out of the shop. It seems, however, that the cashier appropriated the goods when she sold them at an undervalue. If so, according to *Pitham*, the customer might have been convicted of handling as well as of theft.

---

[1]   *A-G of Hong Kong v Chan Nai-Keung* (1987) 86 Cr App Rep 174, [1988] Crim LR 125, PC.
[2]   [1977] 2 All ER 658, DC.
[3]   (1977) 65 Cr App Rep 261, CA.

(iii)   Buyer not intending to pay

2–40   It appears that a buyer who receives the goods not intending to pay may now be guilty of theft even though he practises no deception or does any other wrongful act. He appropriates the goods when he receives them and it is immaterial that the property passes to him with the owner's consent. He obviously intends permanently to deprive so the only question is whether he dishonestly appropriates. A jury which was satisfied that he never intended to pay would presumably answer the question in the affirmative. This is different from the *Smith v Hughes* example discussed in para **2–23**. Though there is a contract, the buyer has no indefeasible right to the goods: a court aware of his intention not to pay – a fundamental breach of contract – would not enforce any such right. A decision not to pay after acquiring the ownership and possession of the property, however, cannot be theft because there is no longer any property belonging to another to appropriate.

(iv)   Appropriation of property obtained by intimidation

2–41   Theft may be committed by intimidation falling short of force or threats of force and so not amounting to robbery. In *Bruce*,[1] D generated such an "atmosphere of menace" that P was frightened into parting with his money. A verdict of not guilty of robbery and guilty of theft was legitimate. Before *Gomez* it was thought that the outcome depended on whether the intimidation prevented the property passing from P to D. It seems that this is no longer material. There is no difference in this respect from the case in which property is obtained by deception. The only question is whether the intimidation was such as to preclude D from enforcing any right to the property. If it was, the *Smith v Hughes* principle (para **2–23**) would be excluded. It is then sufficient that the property belonged to P at the instant when D appropriated it and that he did so with a dishonest intention. If he knew that P parted with his property unwillingly and only because he was intimidated a jury would presumably find dishonesty proved.

---

[1]   (1975) 61 Cr App Rep 123, see the 6th edition of this work, para [45].

(v)   Appropriation by a handler of stolen goods[1]

2–42   The wide definition of theft means that almost every person who would have been a receiver of stolen goods under the Larceny Acts and almost everyone who is a "handler" under the 1968 Act will be guilty of theft. Dishonest handling of stolen goods will normally amount to an appropriation of property belonging to another and will generally be done with the intention of permanently depriving the other of his property.

---

[1] See A.T.H. Smith "Theft and or Handling" [1977] Crim LR 517. On the problem of proving theft or handling, see below, para **13–44**.

(vi) Appropriation by a purchaser in good faith of stolen goods

2–43   Section 3 (2) creates an exception to the general rule that appropriation of the property of another is theft. It provides:

> "Where property or a right or interest in property is or purports to be transferred for value to a person acting in good faith, no later assumption by him of rights which he believed himself to be acquiring shall, by reason of any defect in the transferor's title, amount to theft of the property."

The words, "which he believed himself to be acquiring", relate to the moment when D received the property.[1] This subsection is designed to except from the law of theft the case where D purchases goods in good faith and for value and then later discovers that the seller had no title and that the goods still belong to a third party, P. P may simply have lost the goods or they may have been stolen from him. Having paid for the goods, D may well, in many cases, be innocent of any crime simply on the ground that he believes he has a right to keep them and is thus not dishonest. But suppose he is enough of a lawyer to appreciate that the goods are not his but P's: he is still not guilty – while he may have *mens rea*, the subsection makes it clear that there is no *actus reus*. The result is otherwise, however, if D has not given value, as where he received the property as a gift. If, for example, C purchases the property in good faith from the thief and gives it to D who later discovers the truth and decides to keep it, D is guilty. A purchaser for value who suspects that the goods may be stolen has been held[2] by a magistrates' court to be not "acting in good faith" and so unable to rely on the subsection.

---

[1] *Adams* [1993] Crim LR 72.
[2] *Broom v Crowther* (1984) 148 JP 592, DC, discussed by Spencer [1985] Crim LR 92 and 440 and by Williams [1985] Crim LR 432. D is not guilty of handling when he only "suspects" and does not "believe" that the goods are stolen: below, para **13–41**.

2–44   The protection afforded by s. 3 (2) is limited. D may with impunity keep the goods or give them away to an innocent donee. If, however, he sells the goods to an innocent buyer he will probably be guilty of obtaining the price by the implied deception that he is entitled to sell the goods.[1] Following *Gomez*, if he is guilty of obtaining by deception, he also steals the money. If he sells or gives the thing to one who knows it is the property of a third party, the recipient will be guilty of theft (and possibly of handling) and D, it seems, of abetting him. Section 3 (2) does not seem wide enough to exempt him from liability for abetting theft or handling by another of the property.[2]

If D assumes rights over and above those which he believed himself to be acquiring, he may be guilty of theft. If C finds goods in such circumstances that he reasonably believes the owner cannot be discovered by taking reasonable steps, and sells the goods to D who knows these facts, D is aware that he is acquiring only the rights of a finder, not those of the owner. If, then, D subsequently discovers who the owner is, a later assumption of a right to keep the thing is the *actus reus* of theft.

---

¹   Cf *Wheeler* (1990) 92 Cr App Rep 279, 282, below, para **4–32**, where it is said to be arguable that there was no such representation where the sale took place in market overt, now abolished. If that were right in principle, it might apply to other situations in which a seller who has no title is able to give one.

²   Cf *Sockett* (1908) 1 Cr App Rep 101. This conclusion does not seem to be affected by the dicta of Lord Bridge in *Bloxham* (1982) 74 Cr App Rep 279, 283, which relate to liability for handling as a principal.

2–45   It should be noted that there is no similar exemption for the handler of stolen goods which have been bought in good faith. Suppose D enters into a contract to buy a picture hanging in a gallery, delivery to be made at the end of the exhibition. Unknown to D, the picture has been stolen. Before the end of the exhibition, he discovers the truth, but dishonestly takes delivery of the picture. He is not guilty of theft (s. 3 (2)) but is apparently guilty of handling the picture by receiving it knowing it to be stolen, contrary to s. 22.¹ Section 3 (2) would not exempt Ashwell.² He took the coin in good faith and for value (his promise to repay) and later (it is submitted) assumed rights of ownership which he believed himself to be acquiring when he received the coin; but his guilt would arise, not from any defect in the transferor's title, for there was none, but from a defect in his own title.

---

¹   Below, para **13–01**.
²   Above, para **2–31**.

(vii)   Can there be multiple thefts of the same property?

2–46   If D, in a supermarket, dishonestly swaps labels, he assumes a right of the owner and steals the article he dishonestly intends to buy for the lower price. If he then removes that article from the shelves he assumes another right; and when he buys the article he assumes yet a third right, ownership, which, until that moment, he, as a buyer, has acknowledged to belong to the seller. Has he committed three thefts of the same thing? If appropriation is the assumption of *a right* can there not be as many thefts of a thing as there are rights in or over it? The answer is to be found in s. 3 (1)¹ which provides that a later assumption of a right may be an appropriation when D has come by the property "without stealing it". This implies that where he has come by the property by stealing it, later assumptions of a right to it by keeping or dealing with it as owner do not amount to appropriations.² The draftsman was ensuring that a car thief does not steal the car afresh each morning when he gets into it. In *Atakpu and Roberts*,³ DD obtained cars on hire by deception in Germany and Belgium, and drove them to England, dishonestly intending to sell them here. In the pre-*Gomez* case of *Hircock*,⁴ where the facts were similar except that the whole transaction took place within the jurisdiction, a conviction for theft of a car was upheld: the fact that D had already obtained the car by deception contrary to s. 15 did not preclude a charge of stealing it by the subsequent sale. But, after *Gomez*, it is clear that Hircock stole the car when he obtained it. In *Atakpu*, it was held, reluctantly following *Gomez*, that DD had stolen the cars when they obtained them abroad and could not steal them again by the projected sale in England. *Hircock* is impliedly overruled by *Gomez*. In *Atakpu*, convictions for conspiracy to steal the cars were quashed because the plan did not involve the commission of theft of the cars within the jurisdiction of the English court. The offences of obtaining and theft in Germany would still not be triable here under the Criminal Justice Act 1993, s. 2, because no "relevant event" occurred in England and Wales; but, assuming the act was an offence under German law, the agreement in England would be an indictable conspiracy to commit those offences under the new s. 1A of the Criminal Law Act 1977: Criminal Justice Act 1993, s. 5 (1).[5]

---

[1]   Above, para **2–03**.

[2]   It is different where rights are assumed, abandoned and resumed. Where D steals property but leaves it on the owner's premises because his van will not go, his later removal of it may amount to a second theft: *Starling* [1969] Crim LR 556, CA (larceny). Cf *DPP v Spriggs* [1993] Crim LR 622, below, para **8–14**.

[3]   [1994] QB 69, [1993] 4 All ER 215, CA.

[4]   (1978) 67 Cr App Rep 278, [1979] Crim LR 184 and commentary.

[5]   Presumably even at the time of the offence Atakpu and his accomplices could have been successfully prosecuted for conspiring to obtain by deception, and therefore to steal, *the price* which they intended to get from unsuspecting purchasers of the cars in England.

(viii)   Is theft abroad "theft"?

2–47 Sullivan and Warbrick[1] argue that the court in *Atakpu* was misled by the phrase "theft abroad is not triable in England". They contend that so-called "theft abroad" is not "theft" under English law. DD had, therefore, come by the cars *without* stealing them[2] so their later assumption of a right to the cars in England would have amounted to an appropriation, a theft under English law for the first time. The cars, according to that view, were to be stolen in English law for the first time when appropriated in England. The court had relied on s. 24 (1) of the Theft Act 1968 which it is convenient to set out here and which provides that:

> "The provisions of this Act relating to goods which have been stolen shall apply whether the stealing occurred in England or Wales or elsewhere, and whether it occurred before or after the commencement of this Act, provided that the stealing (if not an offence under this Act) amounted to an offence where and at the time when the goods were stolen. . ."

Sullivan and Warbrick argue that this points to a conclusion opposite to that of the court – the subsection provides an extended definition of "stolen goods" for the purposes only of the offence of handling and it acknowledges that stealing goods outside England and Wales is "not an offence [sc. theft] under this Act". It might, however, be argued, to the contrary that the words in parentheses imply that some stealing outside England and Wales is an offence under the Act. In some jurisdictions, e.g. Canada, taking with intent *temporarily* to deprive is theft. It may be well be that these words[3] are properly construed to cover cases such as the handling in England of goods stolen in Canada by Canadian law, whether or not there was an intent permanently to deprive. It is debatable whether such conduct should be an offence under English law. The problem in *Atakpu* will disappear if Part 1 of the Criminal Justice Act 1993[4] is ever brought into force but there is no sign of that at the time of writing.

---

[1]   [1994] Crim LR 650, 659.

[2]   See s. 3 (1) of the 1968 Act, above, para **2-03**.

[3]   The words in parentheses cannot be intended to apply to stealing in England and Wales *before* the commencement of the Act, because that could never be an offence under the Act.

[4]   See above, paras **1–18** to **1–24**, Griew, *Theft*, 17–02 to 17–12.

2–48   The preceding paragraphs have implications for cases like *Shuck*.[1] D, a company director, acting within the scope of his authority, transferred the company's funds to a subsidiary in the Isle of Man, a place outside the jurisdiction of the English courts, with intent there to dispose of them dishonestly for his own benefit. It was held that he stole the property when it was disposed of by his innocent agent in the Isle of Man, presumably because D, directing operations in England, was assuming the rights of an owner here.[2] No doubt, pre-*Gomez*, it was assumed that the transfer of assets to the Isle of Man, being authorised, could not be theft. If so, we now know that that assumption was unfounded. It seems that D stole the property when he transferred it with theftuous intent. If so, even if theft abroad is theft by English law, he could not steal it again by the dispositions in the Isle of Man and he was wrongly convicted. Appropriation in the Isle of Man, directed from England,will unquestionably be capable of being theft triable here under the Criminal Justice Act 1993 – but not if the appropriator has already committed theft of the property in England.

---

[1]   [1992] Crim LR 209, CA.
[2]   See *Ex p Osman* (1990) 90 Cr App Rep 281, 289, above, para **2–34**.

(ix)   Appropriation as a continuing act[1]

2–49   An offence may be committed in an instant yet continue being committed for some time thereafter. It is often important to know how long a particular theft continued. A person may be guilty of a theft by aiding and abetting it while it is being committed by another, but he cannot aid and abet the theft once it is over. A person may be guilty of robbery if he uses force while theft is being committed but not by using force when the theft is at an end. A person may be guilty of the offence of handling stolen goods only if he does a proscribed act "otherwise than in the course of the stealing". Theft may certainly be committed in an instant, so that D could be convicted of the offence even if he was immediately arrested. It does not follow that the offence is over in an instant, though that seems to have been the opinion of the court in *Pitham*.[2] D stole P's property by inviting E to buy it. It was held that the theft was over and done with, so that, when E agreed to buy and received the property, he was receiving stolen goods "otherwise than in the course of the stealing". That is a very doubtful decision. In *Atakpu*,[3] after a careful review of the pre-*Gomez* authorities,Ward J summarised the law as follows:[4]

> "(1) theft can occur in an instant by a single appropriation but it can also involve a course of dealing with property lasting longer and involving several appropriations before the transaction is complete; (2) theft is a finite act – it has a beginning and it has an end; (3) at what point the transaction is complete is a matter for the jury to decide upon the facts of each case; (4) though there may be several appropriations in the course of a single theft or several appropriations of different goods each constituting a separate theft as in *R v Skipp*, no case suggests that there can be successive thefts of the same property . . ."

The court thought that, on a strict construction, *Gomez* left "little room for a continuous course of action" but they would not wish that to be be the law and preferred the view that appropriation continues so long as the thief can sensibly be regarded as in the act of stealing, "or in more understandable words, so long as he is 'on the job'" as it was put in Smith & Hogan.[5] It was not necessary for the court to decide the matter because no jury could have reasonably concluded that the theft of the cars in Frankfurt or Brussels in that case was continuing when the cars were brought, days later, into England. It is thought that this is the better view and that to treat appropriation simply as an instantaneous act would be inconsistent with the provisions of the Act relating to robbery and handling which pre-suppose that there can be a course of stealing.

So if D enters a house and seizes a jewellery box with theftuous intent he is guilty of theft as soon as he does so, but the theft continues while he is in the course of removing it from the premises: *Hale*,[6] where the court held that, as a matter of common sense, D was in the course of committing theft for the purposes of s. 8 and that it was for the jury to decide whether or not the act of appropriation was finished.

In *Meech*,[7] D, with P's authority, cashed P's cheque, dishonestly intending to deprive him of the money. He took it to a prearranged destination where E and F staged a fake robbery to account for its loss. The court assumed that if D had appropriated the money when he drew it from the bank (and, since *Gomez*, we know he did) the theft would have been over by the time of the rendezvous, so that E and F could not be abettors in such a theft. Whether it could be regarded as continuing probably depends on the distance in time, place and circumstance between the initial appropriation and the division of the spoils, which does not appear in the report.

---

[1]   See Williams [1978] Crim LR 69; Tunkel [1978] Crim LR 313.
[2]   Above, para **2–36.**
[3]   Above, para **2–46.**
[4]   [1994] 4 All ER 215 at 223.
[5]   7th edition 513.
[6]   (1978) 68 Cr App Rep 415, [1979] Crim LR 596. Cf *Gregory* (1981) 74 Cr App Rep 154, [1982] Crim LR 229.
[7]   [1974] QB 549. According to the report of *Anderton v Wish* in [1980] Crim LR 319, 320, Roskill LJ, approving the principle of "continuing appropriation", said that a passage of his judgment in *Meech* reading "the misappropriation only took place when the three men divided up the money at the scene of the robbery" should read "the misappropriation took place *not later than* when the three men . . . ". But this passage (though cited in the immediately preceding case of *Oxford v Peers* (1980) 72 Cr App Rep 19 where the court doubted the decision in *Anderton v Wish*) was omitted from the report (presumably revised by the judge) in (1980) 72 Cr App Rep 23.

(x)   Is an act or omission an essential element of appropriation?

2–50   A mere decision in D's mind to assume the rights of an owner is not enough to amount to an appropriation.[1] In *Eddy v Niman*,[2] it was said that "some overt act . . . inconsistent with the true owner's rights" is required; but that case must now be regarded as overruled by *Gomez*. What is now required is conduct which is, or would be, inconsistent with the owner's rights if he had not consented to or authorised it. It seems that a secret dishonest intention may now turn an authorised act into theft. Appropriation can be performed by omission as well as by act. This seems to be implicit in the provision in s. 3 (1) that a person may appropriate by "keeping . . . as owner" property which he has come by innocently. "Keeping" would not seem necessarily to involve doing any act but to be satisfied by D's omission, with the appropriate intent, to divest himself of possession.

If D's seven-year-old child brings home P's tricycle and D, knowing that the child has come by it unlawfully, does nothing about it,[3] intending that P shall be permanently deprived of the tricycle, it is submitted that this would be theft by D. This might be regarded as an assumption of ownership through the innocent agency of the child who, no doubt, would continue to act as owner. If D were to say to his wife, "Let Richard keep it," this, it is thought, would probably be sufficient assumption of ownership. Even where D does nothing at all, as where sheep stray from P's land on to D's and he simply allows them to remain there,[4] treating them as part of his own flock, he ought to be guilty. In such circumstances it may, however, be difficult or impossible to prove any intention to "keep" and the charge will then fail, not merely on the ground of lack of *mens rea*, but because there was no appropriation.

[1]   *Eddy v Niman* (1981) 73 Cr App Rep 237, DC.
[2]   (1981) 73 Cr App Rep 237 at 241.
[3]   Cf *Walters v Lunt* [1951] 2 All ER 645. Cf *Police v Subritzky* [1990] 2 NZLR 717 (mother guilty of theft by not preventing four year-old child from wheeling pushchair home from toyshop).
[4]   Cf *Thomas* (1953) 37 Cr App Rep 169.

(f)   Attempted theft

2–51   An attempt, with *mens rea*, to assume the rights of an owner, is an attempt to steal.[1] The fact that any assumption of any of the rights of an owner is an appropriation and therefore the complete crime of theft means that there is often little, if any, room for an offence of attempt. D's first dishonest act will be the complete crime. Common sense might suggest that the act of swapping the price labels in a supermarket is merely an act preparatory to obtaining an article by deception; but it is the full offence of theft of the article.[2] One of the practical effects of *Gomez*[3] is to enlarge the offence of theft to include acts which were formerly (and sensibly) held to be preparatory acts. In the *Asil Nadir* case Tucker J asked:[4]

> "If for example, a Defendant has authority to arrange the disposition of goods in a warehouse, and he places certain goods near the door so that his accomplices can come and steal them, is the Defendant's act an unauthorised act so as to amount to an appropriation and theft? Or is it merely a preparatory act?"

Following *Morris*, the authority then prevailing, Tucker J opined that this was a preparatory act. It now appears to be theft. Tucker J was posing an analogy to the allegations before him that D, a company director with authority to transfer the company's funds to a subsidiary abroad, did so with the intention of there disposing of them, not for the company's benefit but for his own private interests. He held that this was a merely preparatory act. After *Gomez*, it is theft.

A person may be guilty of an attempt although the facts are such that the commission of the offence is impossible, as where D tries to steal from a pocket, wallet, car or other place which is in fact empty. He attempts to steal a thing in action if he dishonestly draws a cheque on P's bank account which is overdrawn and has no overdraft facility. He may be guilty of attempting to steal from P property which is in fact his own if, because he is making a mistake of fact, he believes the property belongs to P. If his mistake is one of civil law, the matter is more doubtful. D's *mens rea* is the same – he intends to appropriate property belonging to another – but the case would probably be held to fall outside the terms of the Criminal Attempts Act 1981, s. 2 (1), which provides: "A person may be guilty of attempting to commit an offence . . . even though the facts are such that the commission of the offence is impossible."[5]

[1]   Criminal Attempts Act 1981, s. 1 (1).
[2]   Above, para **2–06**.
[3]   Above, para **2–09**.
[4]   *R v Central Criminal Court, ex p Director of Serious Fraud Office* [1993] 2 All ER 399, 401.
[5]   See commentary on *Huskinson* [1988] Crim LR 620 at 622, Smith & Hogan, 323.

(g) Theft only of specific property

2–52 Theft can be committed only in respect of some specific thing, tangible or intangible, described in the indictment or information. It is not necessary for the prosecution to prove that D stole the whole of the property mentioned, but the sentence should relate only to the property proved to have been stolen.[1] It follows from the need to specify the property stolen that merely to cause P to become indebted to Q, however dishonestly, is not to steal from P. In *Navvabi*[2] D, by the unauthorised use of his cheque book and cheque card, obtained gaming chips in a casino, causing his bank to become indebted to the casino for the amount of the cheques. He was convicted of theft, apparently of money, on a direction that "writing a cheque backing it with a cheque card is an appropriation of the assets of the bank". That was wrong. It was impossible to specify any property of the bank that had been appropriated. The appellant's counsel's concession that an appropriation took place when funds were transferred by the bank to the casino was doubted by the court and was surely also wrong. The "appropriation" of funds to pay the debt was the act of the bank, not that of D, nor was it done as D's agent.

Difficult to reconcile with this principle is *Monaghan*.[3] D, a supermarket cashier, received the price of goods from a customer and put the notes and coins in the till without ringing up the purchase. She was then arrested, charged with and convicted of stealing that money. She admitted that she intended to steal. At the end of her shift, or perhaps when some earlier opportunity occurred, she would have taken from the till a sum equivalent to that unrecorded. Had that occurred, she would undoubtedly have been guilty of stealing the money so taken. Since *Gomez* it is no longer an objection that she had dealt with the money exactly as her duty required by putting it in the till; but how could it be said that she had appropriated, or, if she had carried out her plan, would have appropriated, *that* money? That money may well have gone into her employer's safe, while she stole money paid by some other, as yet unascertained, customer. It was impossible to prove the appropriation of any specific money. Even after *Gomez*, this seems to be a case of a merely preparatory act.

---

[1] *Parker* [1969] 2 QB 248, [1969] 2 All ER 15, CA; *Machent v Quinn* [1970] 2 All ER 255. Cf *Levene v Pearcey* [1976] Crim LR 63, below, para **4–13**.

[2] (1986) 83 Cr App Rep 271, [1987] Crim LR 57, CA. Probably D ought to have been charged with obtaining a pecuniary advantage by deception, contrary to s. 16 (2) (b) of the Theft Act 1968, below, para **4–08**.

[3] [1979] Crim LR 673, CA, and commentary.

2–53 A case which presents even greater difficulty is *Thompson*.[1] D, a computer operator employed by a bank in Kuwait, opened accounts in his own name there. He programmed the computer to debit the accounts of wealthy customers of the bank and credit his own accounts with corresponding amounts. He then took off for England and the program operated while he was in the air. In England he opened other accounts and instructed the Kuwait bank to telex his credit balance to his English banks. The Kuwait bank obliged and D withdrew money from those accounts and spent it. He appealed against his conviction for obtaining money by deception contrary to s. 15, arguing that he obtained the property in Kuwait, outside the jurisdiction of the court. But the court held that the transaction in Kuwait was a nullity. The programming of the computer was no different in substance from forging the accounts with a pen. It was held that "the only realistic view of the undisputed facts" was that property was obtained by deception "when the relevant sums of money were received by the appellant's banks in England". But clearly no "money" in the sense of banknotes was received. Nor was any other property belonging to the Kuwait bank obtained. The credit balances at the English banks (if not void) were things in action belonging to D; and they had never belonged to anyone else.[2] Far from receiving any property, the English banks were undertaking (or thought they were undertaking) the burden of a supposed debt owed by the Kuwait bank to D. No doubt this created a corresponding indebtedness of the Kuwait bank to the English bank. Presumably the loss would fall in the end on the Kuwait bank; but, as we have seen, to cause P to become indebted to Q is not to steal from P, nor is it to obtain from him by deception. Property may have been obtained by deception when D drew on the English accounts; but this was not the offence with which he was charged.

---

[1]   (1984) 79 Cr App Rep 191, CA, criticised in [1984] Crim LR 427, 428, Griew 6.11, Arlidge and Parry, 3.07.
[2]   *Preddy*, below, para **4–60,** confirms this view of the law.

2–54   *Theft without loss.* The popular conception of theft is that the thief makes a gain and his victim suffers a corresponding loss. This was indeed the situation at common law and under the Larceny Acts; but the extended definition of stealing in the Theft Act 1968 and, particularly, its application to things in action, means that there may now sometimes be theft without loss. In *Chan Man-sin v A-G of Hong Kong,*[1] it was held that a company accountant who drew a forged cheque on the company's account stole from the company the thing in action consisting in its credit balance or its contractual right to overdraw. Yet it was settled law[2] that the honouring of the forged cheque and the debiting of the company's account was a nullity and the company, on discovering the unauthorised debit, was entitled to have it reversed. It was nothing more than an error in the books of the bank. In law, the company was never a penny worse off. Yet it was held that there was both an appropriation – because D had assumed the rights of an owner over the credit balance – and an intention permanently to deprive – because he intended to treat the thing as his own to dispose of – regardless of the company's rights.[3]

---

[1]   [1988] 1 All ER 1, [1988] Crim LR 319, PC. *Wille* (1987) 86 Cr App Rep 296 is to the same effect. See also *Hilton* (1997) Times, 18 April.
[2]   By *Tai Hing Cotton Mill Ltd v Liu Chong Hing Bank Ltd* [1986] AC 80, [1985] 2 All ER 947, PC.
[3]   Theft Act 1968, s. 6, below, para **2–127.**

B.   PROPERTY "BELONGING TO ANOTHER"

2–55   The property alleged to have been stolen must "belong to another", "Belonging to another" is, however, widely defined to include almost any legally recognised interest in property. By s. 5 (1) of the Act:

> "Property shall be regarded as belonging to any person having possession or control of it, or having in it any proprietary right or interest (not being an equitable interest arising only from an agreement to transfer or grant an interest)."

D may be guilty of stealing his own property if another person, P, has any proprietary interest in it; but if D owns the entire proprietary interest in the thing he cannot steal it; there is no property "belonging to another" for him to appropriate. No one can steal from himself.

2–56   If the property belongs to no one, it cannot be stolen. If property is abandoned there can be no theft of it. Whether an owner has abandoned his property or not is a question of the intention evinced by him in disposing of his property. If he intends to exclude others from it, he does not abandon it, though it may be clear that he intends to make no further use of it himself. So it will be theft for D to appropriate diseased carcases which P has buried on his land.[1] A householder does not abandon goods which he puts in his dustbin. Prima facie, he intends the goods for the local authority which collects the refuse, so that a dustman may be guilty of theft if he appropriates the goods knowing that he is not entitled to do so.[2] A person who loses property does not necessarily abandon it because he abandons the search for it.[3] The test is whether P has evinced an intention to relinquish his entire interest in the property, without conferring an interest on anyone else. Of course, if D mistakenly believes that P has abandoned his interest in the property, D's appropriation cannot be theft, he does not intend to appropriate property belonging to another, he has no intent permanently to deprive and he is not dishonest.[4]

If the prosecution are unable to establish the identity of the owner, a charge of stealing from a person unknown should lie.[5] It will be necessary to prove that the accused knew, or believed that by taking reasonable steps he could find out, who was the owner.[6] A mis-statement of the owner is not a material averment if the accused is not prejudiced thereby.[7]

---

[1]   *Edwards* (1877) 13 Cox CC 384. On abandonment see A.H. Hudson (1984) 100 LQR 110.
[2]   *Williams v Phillips* (1957) 41 Cr App Rep 5, DC.
[3]   Cf *Hibbert v McKiernan* [1948] 2 KB 142, DC.
[4]   *Small* [1987] Crim LR 777, CA, below, para **2–113**; *Ellerman's Wilson Line Ltd v Webster* [1952] 1 Lloyds Rep 179, DC.
[5]   Cf *Gregory* [1972] 2 All ER 861, below, para **13–42** (handling stolen goods belonging to a person unknown); *Pike v Morrison* [1981] Crim LR 492, DC (criminal damage – name of owner an immaterial averment).
[6]   See s. 2 (1) (c), below, para **2–114**.
[7]   *Etim v Hatfield* [1975] Crim LR 234, below, para **4–04**.

(a) Ownership, possession and control

2–57   Since the law protects all interests in property, where two or more persons have different interests in the same property, any one of them may steal the property from the other or others by appropriating the other's interest in it. As was the case with larceny,[1] an owner in the strict sense can be guilty of stealing his own property from one who has mere possession or custody of it. For example, D pledges his watch with P as security for a loan but takes it back again without repaying P and without his consent. This is an appropriation by D of property which belongs to P for the purposes of the section. The position is precisely the same where D bids for a car at an auction, it is knocked down to him and he then takes the car without paying the auctioneer, P, and without his (P's) consent.[2] The car became D's property on the fall of the hammer but P retained his seller's lien for the price and D has therefore appropriated P's property.

---

[1]   Cf *Rose v Matt* [1951] 1 KB 810, DC.
[2]   Cf *Dennant v Skinner and Collom* [1948] 2 KB 164, Hallett J.

2–58   The owner may steal from his bailee at will. Though he has a right to terminate the bailment at any time, he will be guilty of theft if he simply dishonestly appropriates the bailed chattel. It is only in exceptional cases that the problem will arise, because it will usually be clear that the bailor had a claim of right to recover possession. In *Turner (No 2)*,[1] however, D, who had delivered his car to P to be repaired, took it back, dishonestly intending not to pay for the repairs which P had carried out. In truth, P probably was not a mere bailee at will, having a lien on the car. But the judge directed the jury that they were not concerned with liens and so the Court of Appeal had to decide the appeal on the basis that there was no lien. An argument that P's possession as a bailee at will was insufficient was rejected. The court said there was no ground for qualifying the words "possession or control" in any way.

It looks more than a little odd that, where D has a better right to possession than P, he can nevertheless commit theft by the exercise (however dishonestly) of that "right". It might have been thought that a thing does not belong to a possessor, P, as against D who has an immediate right to take possession from him. Possibly *Turner (No 2)* may be explained by holding that a bailor has no right, even in the civil law, to take back the chattel bailed, without notice to the bailee at will.

Suppose D's car is stolen by P, and D later finds the car standing outside P's house (or the house of a bona-fide purchaser, P). D has, of course, a right to take it back. But suppose he does not know this, and thinks that a court order is necessary to enable him lawfully to resume possession. Believing that he has no right in law to do so (i.e. dishonestly), he takes the car. According to *Turner (No 2)*, he is guilty of theft. If he were convicted and the court asked to exercise its power to order the car to be restored to the person entitled to it,[2] the incongruous result would be that the car should be given to the convicted thief, who was and always had been the person entitled to it. Perhaps the decision in *Turner (No 2)* would not be pressed so far.[3]

---

[1]   [1971] 2 All ER 441, [1971] Crim LR 373, discussed in [1972B] CLJ at 215–217. Described by Williams as "one of the most extraordinary cases under the the the Theft Act": *TBCL* s. 33.8. It is hard to believe the decision represents the law. Arlidge and Parry, para 1.14, regard the decision as "absurd" because D did nothing dishonest (in the objective sense they attribute to the word, "dishonestly") however dishonest his state of mind.

[2]   See s. 28 (1), below, para **14–06**.

[3]   *Meredith* [1973] Crim LR 253 (Judge Da Cunha) seems inconsistent but right in principle (no theft of impounded car from police because police had no right to retain it).

2–59   Similar problems arise where D retains possession as well as ownership and P has the lower interest which is described as "control" in the Act. D, an employer, entrusts his employee, P, with goods for use in the course of his employment. D continues both to own and to possess the goods; but, if he dishonestly deprives P of control, he may, to the same extent as the bailor at will, be guilty of theft. It was larceny at common law for a master who had entrusted money to his servant to re-take it, intending to charge the hundred for an alleged theft. So if today an employer takes his own property from the custody of his employee, intending to claim against his insurers for its loss, he might be held to have stolen it. The more natural charge would be obtaining, or attempting to obtain, money from the insurers under s. 15 (or, since *Gomez*, of theft); but he might not yet have done anything more than merely preparatory to the commission of that offence.

2–60   Where the property belongs to more than one person, as may easily occur under s. 5 (1), and D appropriates it for himself, it follows that he may be convicted of stealing it from any one, or all, of the persons to whom it belongs. P lets a lawn-mower on hire to Q who hands it over to his employee, R, to mow the lawn. P remains the owner, Q remains in possession as bailee and R has control. If D now appropriates the lawn-mower for himself, he commits theft from all three of them. If, in order to appropriate the lawn-mower, he uses force on R, he commits robbery from P, Q and R.[1]

---

[1]   See s. 8 of the Act. At common law, it would have been robbery only from R, and similarly under the Larceny Acts. Cf *Harding* (1929) 21 Cr App Rep 166.

(b)   Equitable interests

2–61   The clear implication of s. 5 (1) is that equitable as well as legal interests are generally protected.[1] "An equitable interest arising only from an agreement to transfer or grant an interest" is the only recognised exception. Where property is subject to a trust it "belongs to" both the trustee (legal interest) and the beneficiary (equitable interest). A third party who appropriates it steals it from both of them; and the one may steal it from the other The question whether P has an equitable interest in property alleged to have been stolen from him may involve difficult issues of civil law. In *Clowes (No 2)*[2] the question was whether investors, who had subscribed money for investment in gilts by a company controlled by D, had an equitable interest in certain assets of the company. In deciding that they did, the court found it necessary to consider various Chancery decisions and to rely on the principle, inter alia, that where a trustee mixes trust money with his own, the beneficiaries have a first charge on, and therefore an equitable interest in, the mixed fund. A person dishonestly withdrawing money from the fund may therefore be guilty of stealing it from the beneficiaries. Changes in the civil law may affect the reach of the law of theft. So a decision that the payer of money under a mistake of fact retains an equitable interest in the money so paid and is not, as was previously thought, a mere creditor, means that the dishonest appropriation of the money by the payee may be theft according to general principles, removing the necessity for reliance on the tortuous provisions of s. 5 (4).[3]

The parenthesis in s. 5 (1) excludes from the protection of the law "an equitable interest arising only from an agreement to transfer or grant an interest". If D, the owner of land, enters into a specifically enforceable contract to sell it to P, an equitable interest in the land passes to P, and D is, in some respects, a trustee of the property for P. If D were to sell the land to a third party, it might have been held, but for the parenthesis, that this was theft of the land under s. 4 (2) (a).[4] If, after D has contracted to sell to P, a third party, E, enters on the land and appropriates something forming part of the land by severing it, this will be theft from D but, because of the parenthesis, it will not be theft from P. An equitable interest similarly passes to the buyer under a specifically enforceable agreement to buy shares.[5] The seller who dishonestly re-sells is protected. It does not follow that the buyer's contractual right is not a thing in action capable of being stolen.[6]

---

[1]   But cf *A-G's Reference (No 1 of 1985)* [1986] 2 All ER 219 at 226, below, para **2–79** suggesting that some equitable interests are not protected.
[2]   [1994] 2 All ER 316.
[3]   Below, para **2–81**.
[4]   Below, para **2–90**.
[5]   Gower *Modern Company Law* (3rd edn) 448, n. 25.
[6]   See [1979] Crim LR 220 at 224–225.

2–62   A contract for the sale of goods may be a sale or an agreement to sell. If it is a sale, the legal interest passes to the buyer and a re-sale by the seller who remains in possession may thus constitute theft from the buyer.[1] If, however, it is an agreement to sell, the buyer usually acquires neither a legal, nor (since contracts for the sale of goods are generally not specifically enforceable) an equitable interest,[2] so the provision will not generally be required in such cases. It may be, however, that in the exceptional case where a contract for the sale of goods is specifically enforceable, an equitable interest does pass to the buyer before the legal ownership does so. Again, the parenthesis makes it clear that there can be no theft from the buyer. The reason for the parenthesis probably is that an action for breach of contract is a sufficient sanction against a person who, having contracted to sell to X, re-sells in breach of contract to Y. Such conduct is, perhaps, not generally thought to be more reprehensible than other breaches of contract. It is probably incidental that an appropriation by a third party is not a theft from the buyer; but this is not serious since it is inevitably a theft from the seller.

---

[1]   See above, para **2–26**
[2]   *Re Wait* [1927] 1 Ch 606, CA.

(c)   Co-owners and partners

2–63   D and P are co-owners of a car, D sells the car without P's consent. Since P has a proprietary right in the car, it belongs to him under s. 5 (1). The position is precisely the same where a partner dishonestly appropriates the partnership property. Whether or not his conduct constitutes the tort of conversion, it is theft.[1]

---

[1]   *Bonner* [1970] 2 All ER 97n. The Torts (Interference with Goods) Act 1977, s. 10, amends the law of conversion. Cf *McHugh* (1988) 88 Cr App Rep 385 at 393.

(d)   Trustee and beneficiary

2–64   Conversion by a trustee was a special offence under s. 21 of the Larceny Act 1916. Now it is ordinary theft. The beneficiary, by definition, has a proprietary interest in the trust property and any dishonest appropriation of it by the trustee is theft. Section 5 (2) provides:

> "Where property is subject to a trust, the persons to whom it belongs shall be regarded as including any person having a right to enforce the trust, and an intention to defeat the trust shall be regarded accordingly as an intention to deprive of the property any person having that right."

Where the trust is a charitable one, its object is to effect some purpose beneficial to the public, rather than to benefit particular individuals. Such trusts are enforceable by the Attorney-General, and an appropriation of the trust property by a charitable trustee will, accordingly, be regarded as theft from that officer.

2–65   Trusts for the purpose of erecting or maintaining monuments[1] or maintaining animals[2] have been held valid, though unenforceable for lack of a human beneficiary or a charitable intent. If the trustee of such a trust were to appropriate the funds for himself it would seem clear that he would commit theft from anyone who was entitled to the residue. It would be no defence that he believed the residuary legatee to be undiscoverable: s. 2 (1) (c). If the trustee were himself entitled to the residue, he could not commit theft, since he would be, in effect, the absolute and exclusive owner of the property.

---

[1]   *Trimmer v Danby* (1856) 25 LJ Ch 424; *Re Hooper* [1932] 1 Ch 38.
[2]   *Pettingall v Pettingall* (1842) 11 LJ Ch 176; *Re Dean* (1889) 41 Ch D 552.

(e)   Things in or on the land

2–66   A person in possession of land has sufficient possession or control of articles in or on the land, even if he is unaware that they are there, at least if he intends to exclude trespassers from entering and taking any such thing.[1] A trespasser on a golf course was convicted of larceny from the secretary and members of the golf club regarding balls which had been lost by their owners while playing. He was not guilty of stealing from the owners unless he believed that they could be discovered by taking reasonable steps; but he certainly knew of the interest of the club in excluding him as a "pilferer" of lost balls.[2] Possibly a finder who was not trespassing – a visitor playing a round of golf or a person crossing the course under a public right of way – would have a better right than the club to the ball. If so (and it is a question of civil law), it is submitted that he could not be guilty of theft.

---

[1]   *Woodman* [1974] QB 754, [1974] 2 All ER 955, CA.
[2]   *Hibbert v McKiernan* [1948] 2 KB 142, [1948] 1 All ER 860 discussed in [1972B] CLJ at 213–215.

2–67   *Proprietary interests and treasure trove.* The question whether treasure trove, or its successor "treasure", can be stolen is of some importance. Treasure trove at common law is any article of gold or silver hidden by its owner with a view to its subsequent recovery. In the absence of its original owner and his successors in title, treasure trove belongs to the Crown. It is therefore capable of being stolen from the Crown by any person, including the owner or possessor of the land in or on which it is found. Where the treasure is in or on land which does not belong to the Crown, the Crown does not have possession or control of the treasure, but it does have a proprietary interest in it because it is the owner. In *Hancock*[1] D was charged with stealing from the Crown Celtic silver coins which he had found using a metal detector on another person's land. It was argued that the Crown's right to have the doubtful status of the coins determined was itself a "proprietary right or interest". If a finder succeeds in concealing from the the Crown his find of coins, the Crown has lost something of value – the chance that, on investigation, the find would prove to be treasure trove. It was held, however, that such a chance is not a proprietary interest. This seems right. If A and B each claims to be the sole owner of certain property, and the dispute is eventually resolved in favour of A, it would be odd to hold that B had a proprietary interest in the property up to the moment when it was determined that he had never had any interest in it.

---

[1]   (1990) 90 Cr App R 422, [1990] Crim LR 125.

2–68   When the Treasure Act 1996 comes into force, the common law of treasure trove will be abolished and replaced by a broader concept of "treasure" which will include, as well as any object which would at present be treasure trove, other specified objects at least 300 or, in some cases, 200 years old. When treasure is found it will, like treasure trove, vest in the Crown (or the Crown's franchisee). The finder of treasue trove or treasure who takes it for himself commits the *actus reus* of theft: he has appropriated property belonging to the Crown. Proof of *mens rea* is more difficult. If the only potential owner is the Crown, it must be proved that the finder knew the Crown was, or at least might be,[1] the owner, i.e., that he knew the property had the factual characteristics of treasure trove or, when the 1996 Act comes into force, some other form of treasure – e.g., that a bracelet was at least 300 years old and was made of at least 10% by weight of precious metal. But even that would not necessarily be enough. The defendant might know these facts but still be unaware of the Crown's proprietary interest because of his ignorance of the law of treasure trove.[2]

The court in *Hancock* was sceptical about the alternative course of charging the finder with theft from the owner of the land. The law has been clarified by *Waverley Borough Council v Fletcher.*[3] F, using a metal detector in a public park belonging to the council, found a mediaeval gold brooch. A coroner's inquest decided that it was not treasure trove and the coroner returned it to F. It was held that the council was entitled to a declaration that the brooch was its property. Auld LJ stated two principles of general importance in the law of theft:

"1. Where an article is found in or attached to land,the owner or possessor of the land has a better title than the finder.

2. Where an article is found unattached on land, the owner or possessor of the land has a better title than the finder only if he exercised such manifest control over the land as to indicate an intention to control the land and anything that might be found on it."[4]

In the *Waverley* case it was immaterial that the land was held by the council as a public open space to be used for various sports and recreations. Digging in the land was an act of trespass. A digger who dishonestly intended to keep anything he found for himself would be guilty of attempted theft and of stealing from the council anything he found and kept for himself.[5] The owner of the land in which articles are buried has a proprietary interest in those articles because they are in his possession or control. The property may also, if it is treasure trove, belong to the Crown. The proprietary interest of the owner of the land is much easier to prove than that of the Crown. If the intent to steal from the landowner can be proved, the way may be opened for proving theft from the Crown. Under the doctrine of "transferred malice",[6] the finder's intention dishonestly to deprive the landowner of the property may be treated as an intention dishonestly to deprive the Crown. If the property turns out to be treasure trove, the finder may be guilty of stealing it both from the landowner and from the Crown.

---

[1]   "might be" because the finder may be aware that "reasonable steps" might reveal that the find was of silver and that it had been concealed, not lost: Theft Act 1968, s. 2 (1) (c), below, para **2–114.**

[2]   Ignorance of the civil law may negative *mens rea*: Smith & Hogan, 86.

[3]   [1996] QB 334, [1995] 4 All ER 756, CA.

[4]   In *Bridges v Hawkesworth* (1851) 21 LJQB 75 the plaintiff, the finder of banknotes, apparently lost by someone on the floor of a shop, was held to have a better right to the money than the owner of the shop: "The notes were never in the custody of the defendant nor within the protection of his house, before they were found, as they would have been if they had been intentionally deposited there." In *Parker v British Airways Board* [1982] QB 1004 a passenger who found a gold bracelet in a British Airways Executive lounge was held to have a better right to it than British Airways. Even if the finder, being unaware of his rights, had taken the bracelet with a dishonest intention, he could not, presumably, have been guilty of theft, since he was doing no more than he was entitled to do; but he might then (theoretically) have been guilty of attempted theft. On the other hand in *Hibbert v McKiernan* [1948] 2 KB 142 a trespasser on a golf course was held guilty of larceny from the secretary and members of the golf club of balls lost by golfers. He was aware of the intent of the club to exclude him as a "pilferer" of lost balls, so the case is distinguishable.

[5]   In *Rowe* (1859) 8 Cox CC 139 R was convicted of larceny from a Canal Company of iron found in the bed of a canal when it was drained. The true owner of the iron was unknown but the Canal Company had a sufficient property in it. *Rowe* was followed by Chitty J in *Elwes v Brigg Gas Co* (1886) 33 Ch D 562 where an ancient boat, buried in land belonging to the

plaintiff was discovered by his lessee, the defendant, excavating the site for a gasholder. The boat was held to belong to the plaintiff. In *South Staffordshire Water Co v Sharman* [1896] 2 QB 44 two gold rings were found in the mud in the Minster Pool in Lichfield by one of a number of labourers employed to clean it out. It was held by Lord Russell of Killowen CJ that the owner of the pool had a better right than the finder. And cf. *Woodman* (1974) 59 Cr App Rep 200, CA, above, para **2–66.**

6   Smith & Hogan, 77.

(f) The property of a corporation and its controlling officers

2–69   A corporation such as a limited company is a person distinct from its members. A member can steal the property of the corporation. It is property "belonging to another". A director of a limited company can steal the property of that company. The injury is suffered by the shareholders or, if the company is insolvent, by its creditors; but the property does not belong to them and the theft is not from them but from the company. Suppose, however, that D and E are the sole directors and sole shareholders in the company ("a sole director case"). The property still "belongs to another" – the company – but, before *Gomez*, it was difficult to see that there could be an appropriation under the principle in *Morris*: the only persons who could speak for the company, D and E, had authorised and consented to the Act in question. As the majority in *Gomez*[1] said, this argument is no longer open – the consent or authority of the owner is no longer a bar to theft. They added (and here the dissenting judge, Lord Lowry, agreed)[2] that even if *Morris* had been right on this issue, the directors would still be guilty: the principle that the mind of the controlling officers is the mind of the company does not apply to offences committed against the company. There is, however, still some difficulty in understanding how it can be said that property belonging to another has been *dishonestly* appropriated.[3] Clearly the appropriator is not dishonest vis-à-vis the shareholder because he is the shareholder and therefore it is very artificial to say that he is dishonest with respect to the company which exists for the benefit of the shareholders. He may of course be dishonest vis-à-vis the company's creditors – but the property does not belong to them. They are not the victims of the alleged theft, though they will be the ones to suffer if the company becomes insolvent and the assets have been dispersed by the directors. It is clear, however, that the members of a partnership facing insolvency commit no offence under the Theft Acts if they dissipate the partnership's assets to the detriment of its creditors. They cannot steal from the partnership because they are the partnership; but their creditors are in no different situation from those of the company. It has been argued that the interests of the creditors of an insolvent or doubtfully solvent company are the interests of the company,[4] but it is not clear that this is an established principle or that it is the foundation of the cases holding that the sole director may steal the company's property.[5]

---

1   [1993] 1 All ER at p 40, per Lord Browne-Wilkinson.
2   At pp 35–38.
3   "Directors' Thefts and Dishonesty" by Professor D.W. Elliott [1991] Crim LR 732.
4   See correspondence, [1991] Crim LR at 929.
5   *A-G's Reference (No 2 of 1982)* [1984] QB 624, [1984] 2 All ER 216, CA, and *Philippou* (1989) 89 Cr App Rep 290, both approved in *Gomez*. *McHugh* (1988) 88 Cr App Rep 385 at 393 and *Roffel* [1985] VR 511 were disapproved. Cf *Pearlberg and O'Brien* [1982] Crim LR 829; *Painter* [1983] Crim LR 819, CA, and commentaries, G.R. Sullivan [1983] Crim LR 512, [1984] Crim LR 505, Dine [1984] Crim LR 387, Williams *TBCL* 811.

(g) The human body and parts of it

2–70   There could be no larceny of a corpse at common law[1] and it remains the law that there is no property in a corpse. However executors or administrators or others with the legal duty to inter a body have a right to custody and possession of it until it is properly buried. They do not "own" the corpse in the strict sense of the word but, while they have custody or possession, it appears to belong to them for the purposes of the Act, so it is at least possible that a charge of theft would lie against one who took the corpse from them. A skeleton which has been prepared for anatomical study, or a corpse which has been stuffed or embalmed, is the subject of property in the ordinary way. The snatching of the embalmed Jeremy Bentham from University College would no doubt be regarded as a serious theft. In *Dobson v North Tyneside Health Authority*,[2] where these principles were confirmed, a brain which had been removed at an autopsy was preserved in paraffin, in pursuance of an obligation to preserve material bearing on the cause of death for as long as the coroner thought fit. It was held that this (i) was not on a par with embalming and (ii) did not entitle the next of kin to the brain for burial purposes. Their civil action failed because they had neither ownership nor the right to possession of the brain. But if they had taken it from the Health Authority they could presumably have been guilty of theft.

Fluids taken from the living body are property. So a motorist has been convicted of stealing a specimen of his own urine provided by him for analysis.[3] The same rule should clearly apply to a blood sample.[4] It is probable that parts of the living body may be stolen from the living person. Thus, a magistrates' court has held a man guilty of larceny when he cut some hair from a girl's head without her consent:[5] and this seems entirely reasonable. It would be extraordinary if a woman did not own her own hair!

---

[1]   *Handyside's Case* (1749) 2 East PC 652; *Sharpe* (1857) Dears & B 160. See A.T.H. Smith "Stealing the Body and its Parts" [1976] Crim LR 622; P. Matthews "Whose Body" (1983) 36 CLP 193. For other offences which might be committed, see Williams *TBCL* 679–680. *Doodeward v Spence* (1908) 6 CLR 406, 95R (NSW) 107.
[2]   [1996] 4 All ER 474, [1997] 1 WLR 596, CA.
[3]   *Welsh* [1974] RTR 478, CA.
[4]   Cf *Rothery* [1976] RTR 550, CA.
[5]   (1960) The Times, 22 December. "For centuries human hair has been bought and sold without controversy": M.G. Bridge, *The Sale of Goods,* 26–27.

(h) P's right that D shall retain and deal with property

2–71   There are other cases which would have amounted to fraudulent conversion under the Larceny Act where there might have been doubt whether P has a proprietary right or interest. Any doubt is resolved by s. 5 (3):

> "Where a person receives property from or on account of another, and is under an obligation to the other to retain and deal with that property or its proceeds in a particular way, the property or proceeds shall be regarded (as against him) as belonging to the other."

This covers a very wide range of cases. Every bailment seems to be included. So does every trust. So where D has received property from or on account of P in the circumstances described in this subsection it will almost always (if not always) be the case that P has a legal or an equitable interest in the property or proceeds. The case then is covered by s. 5 (1) and subsection (3) is unnecessary. Even so, the provision is useful because it enables the prosecution to make out its case without the need to resort to the technical question whether P retains an equitable interest. It extends the meaning of "belonging to another" as widely as is practicable. If there is no legal obligation on D to retain and deal with the property in a particular way, it is his to do as he likes with, and it cannot be theft for him to do what he is entitled to do. But where there is such an obligation, it seems right that the property should be capable of being stolen by D. It has been held that D "receives property from" P within the meaning of the subsection when P returns a proforma bill of exchange supplied by D, signed by P as acceptor and by P's bank as guarantor, although D is the owner of the paper throughout.[1] If D then dishonestly disposes of the bill, contrary to the terms on which P had returned it to him, he commits theft of a valuable security. If D had put the proforma before P for signature while retaining possession and control, s. 5 (3) could not have applied and D could have been guilty of theft only if the circumstances were such as to give P an equitable interest in the bill.

---

[1]   *Arnold* (27 June 1997, unreported), CA. Cf *Danger*, below, para **4.57**.

2–72   It is settled that "obligation" in s. 5 (3) and (4) means a legal, not a merely moral or social, obligation.[1] Where the relevant transaction is wholly in writing, it is for the judge to decide as a matter of law whether it does create the legal obligation alleged and to direct the jury accordingly.[2] Where the obligation is alleged to have been created wholly or partly by word of mouth, or by conduct, the judge should direct them that, if they find the necessary facts (which he must specify) proved, there *is* an obligation – not that it is "open to them" to find – that there is an obligation.[3]

If D is under no legal obligation to retain and deal with property which has been delivered to him or its proceeds, he can lawfully do what he likes with it and it is incapable of being stolen. This is ordinarily the position where money is lent. Assuming that D, the borrower, received the money honestly, his subsequent decision to dispose of money loaned and never to repay it, however dishonest, cannot be theft. It is not always easy to determine whether D was under an obligation to retain and deal or at liberty to dispose of the property entirely as he wished.

The subsection applies only where the obligation exists in law and D has personal knowledge of its nature and extent.[4] The knowledge of his agents cannot be imputed to him. It is probably not enough that he is aware of the facts giving rise to that obligation, unless he also realises that it is an obligation. If he does not do so, it would be difficult to prove dishonesty.

---

[1]   *Gilks* [1972] 3 All ER 280 (s. 5 (4)); *Meech* [1974] QB 549, [1973] 3 All ER 939; *Wakeman v Farrar* [1974] Crim LR 136, DC.
[2]   *Clowes (No 2)* [1994] 2 All ER 316, holding that a brochure inviting the payment of money for investment in gilts was a contractual document creating a trust.
[3]   *Dubar* [1995] 1 All ER 781, following *Mainwaring* (1981) 74 Cr App Rep 99, CA and disapproving dicta in *Hall* [1972] 2 All ER 1009 at 1012 and *Hayes* (1976) 64 Cr App Rep 82 at 85 and 87.
[4]   *Wills* (1990) 92 Cr App Rep 297, CA.

2–73   A common occasion for the application of s. 5 (3) is that where D receives property from C for onward transmission to, or for the benefit of, E. The required obligation may be imposed on D either by D's relationship with C, or his relationship with E, or both. In *Lewis v Lethbridge*,[1] D obtained sponsorships in favour of a charity (E) and received £54 from the sponsors (C). He did not deliver the money to the charity and was convicted of theft. His conviction was quashed because the magistrates had made no finding of any rule of the charity requiring D to hand over the actual cash received, or to maintain a separate fund. It might have been different if he had been supplied with a collecting box. No consideration was given to the question whether any obligation was imposed by the sponsors. They might have been surprised to hear that they were giving money to D to do as he liked with. In *Wain*,[2] the Court of Appeal, disapproving *Lethbridge*, held that the approach was unduly narrow and that, on similar facts, D was under an obligation and accordingly guilty.

In *Lewis v Lethbridge*, the court concentrated exclusively on the relationship between D and E. In *Huskinson*,[3] by contrast, the obligation could only arise out of the relationship between C and D. D applied for, and received from the Housing Services Department, C, housing benefit to enable him to pay his rent to his landlord, E. D gave some of the money to E but, as the court thought, dishonestly,[4] spent the remainder on himself. It was held that he was not guilty of theft. No obligation to pay the money to E could be found in the statutory provisions authorising the payment of housing benefit. Housing benefit is, apparently, the tenant's money to do as he likes with.

---

[1]   [1987] Crim LR 59, DC.
[2]   [1995] 2 Cr App Rep 660.
[3]   [1988] Crim LR 620 and commentary.
[4]   His conduct was not "dishonest" in the objective sense favoured by Arlidge and Parry, above, para **2–20**, since he was entitled to do what he liked with the money. Presumably he thought he was bound to give it to E and so had a dishonest mind.

2–74   The obligation is to deal with that property or its proceeds in a particular way. The words, "or its proceeds", make it clear that D need not be under an obligation to retain particular monies. It is sufficient that he is under an obligation to keep in existence a fund equivalent to that which he has received. If the arrangement permits D to do what he likes with the money, his only obligation being to account in due course for an equivalent sum, the subsection does not apply.

Therefore the appropriation of an advance payment for work to be done by D will be theft only if the money was given with an obligation to use it for a specific purpose. In this respect, the Act seems to reproduce the old law of fraudulent conversion.[1] Suppose, for example, D agrees to paint P's house for £50 and simply asks for "an advance payment of £10". If he appropriates the £10 to his own use this will not be theft for P has no proprietary right or interest in it nor is D under any obligation to deal with that property in any particular way

The result should be different where D agrees to paint P's house and asks for £10 to buy the paint which he will use on the job. If he appropriates the £10, it is submitted that this now will be theft.[2] Similar situations arise where D employs P and requires him to deposit a sum of money as security for his honesty. If the terms of the arrangement are that D can do what he likes with the money then D cannot steal it[3] but if D has agreed to retain the money, as by depositing it at a bank,[4] then it is capable of being stolen.

Similarly where D is a debt-collector who is required by the terms of his contract to hand over the money he collects, less a certain percentage, to the creditors: if he is under an obligation to keep in existence a separate fund, then the money he receives is capable of being stolen.[5] If, however, the arrangement with the creditors is such that D is merely their debtor to the extent of the debts collected, less commission, the money he receives from the debtors is his and he is under no obligation to deal with that money in a particular way. It is a question of the construction of the contract between the debt-collector and the creditors.

---

¹   See [1961] Crim LR 741 at 797.
²   Cf *Jones* (1948) 33 Cr App Rep 11; *Bryce* (1955) 40 Cr App Rep 62; *Hughes* [1956] Crim LR 835.
³   As in *Hotine* (1904) 68 JP 143.
⁴   As in *Smith* [1924] 2 KB 194.
⁵   *Lord* (1905) 69 JP 467.

2–75   A travel agent who receives money from clients to pay for travel arrangements is under an obligation to provide tickets, etc., but not necessarily under an obligation to retain and deal with the money in a particular way. In *Hall*,[1] the agent paid the money into his firm's general trading account – a fact which was not decisive since it did not affect any interest his clients might have in the money[2] – and applied it in the firm's business. The firm failed and the clients received neither tickets nor the return of their money. Not a penny remained. In the absence of evidence of a special arrangement imposing an obligation on the agent it was held that he was not guilty of stealing from the clients. If he was entitled to use the money for the general purposes of the firm's business, he committed no theft from the clients even if he was completely profligate in its expenditure or had spent it all at the races.[3]

An insurance broker who receives premiums for a number of insurance companies on terms that the premiums will vest and remain in them is guilty of theft if he dishonestly uses the money for his own purposes. It was so held in *Brewster*,[4] notwithstanding that it was known by the principals that brokers, as a matter of general practice, did use the premium monies for the purposes of their own businesses and ultimately accounted for equivalent amounts. If the contract had been varied to allow D to use the money in this way, he would not have been guilty. The decision was based on a finding that there was no evidence of such a variation but only an "indulgence" – the companies were tolerating a breach of contract. If so, it seems that the agent using the monies without dishonest intent, was appropriating them and committing the *actus reus* of theft. There is a nice question as to the point at which D became dishonest. Presumably so long as he was confident of his ability to repay and intended to do so, a jury would be unlikely to find him dishonest. When he continued to use the money knowing that there was a risk that he might not be able to repay, a jury would probably find him to be dishonest; and they would certainly do so if he used the money knowing that he could not hope to repay it. There are also difficult questions of civil law as to the effect on the rights and duties of the parties of such an "indulgence" or waiver of contractual rights.

---

¹   [1973] QB 126, [1972] 2 All ER 1009, [1972] Crim LR 453 and commentary.
²   *Yule* [1964] 1 QB 5, [1963] 2 All ER 780.
³   In the latter case it might have been theft from his partners.
⁴   (1979) 69 Cr App Rep 375, [1979] Crim LR 798. Cf *Robertson* [1977] Crim LR 629 (Judge Rubin QC).

2–76   In *Cullen*,[1] P gave his mistress, D, £20 to buy food for their consumption and to pay certain debts. She spent the money on herself. The Court of Appeal held that this was a plain case of theft, rejecting D's argument that it was a domestic transaction not intended to create, and so not creating, legal relations.[2] The court does not seem to have answered a serious argument. If the civil courts would not regard it as even a breach of contract for a wife to spend the housekeeping money on a new hat, the criminal courts should not regard it as theft.

---

[1]   (1974) Unreported (No 968/C/74). Cf *Davidge v Bunnett* [1984] Crim LR 297.
[2]   *Balfour v Balfour* [1919] 2 KB 571 was relied on.

2–77   It is submitted that a person cannot be under a legal obligation to "retain and deal" unless a failure to retain and deal would involve him in civil liability to some third person – the victim of the alleged theft. That obligation must have been in existence at the moment of the appropriation. Property is regarded as belonging to P where D "receives property from [P] . . . and is under an obligation" to P. If D receives property from P with an obligation at the moment of receipt but the obligation is later terminated the property ceases to "belong" to P from that moment. It is thereafter no longer possible for D to appropriate property "belonging to P". In determining whether there was an obligation at the relevant time, the court must have regard to all the material facts which are proved to have existed at that time. A case which is difficult to reconcile with these principles is *Meech*, the facts of which have been given above.[1] The court held that the proceeds of the cheque "belonged to" P only through the operation of s. 5 (3). It had been argued that P was under no obligation to D because D had obtained the cheque by forgery. The court held that D assumed an obligation when he received the cheque because he was ignorant of its dishonest origin; that the cheque therefore belonged to P and that it did not cease to belong to him when D learned the truth about its origin, even (apparently) if the effect was that D was no longer under any obligation.

> "The fact that on the true facts if known [P] might not and indeed would not subsequently have been permitted to enforce that obligation in a civil court does not prevent that obligation on [D] having arisen. The argument confuses the creation of the obligation with the subsequent discharge of that obligation either by performance or otherwise. That the obligation might have become impossible of performance by [D] or of enforcement by [P] on grounds of illegality or for reasons of public policy is irrelevant. The opening words of section 5 (3) clearly look to the creation of, or the acceptance of, the obligation by the bailee and not to the time of performance by him of the obligation so created and accepted by him."[2]

It is submitted that if, in the light of all the proved facts, P would have had no civil claim to the cheque or its proceeds, s. 5 (3) was inapplicable. It is agreed that, where reliance is placed on s. 5 (3), it must be proved that D knew of the facts which gave rise to the obligation (and probably that there was an obligation, mistake of civil law being a defence here). But, while this is necessary, it is not enough. There must also be an *actus reus* as well as *mens rea*. The section says "is under an obligation", not "believes he is under an obligation".

---

[1]   Para **2–49**. See commentary [1973] Crim LR 772.
[2]   [1974] QB 549 at 554, [1973] 3 All ER 939 at 942, CA.

2–78   It is advisable to rely on s. 5 (3) where there is some doubt whether P has a proprietary interest within s. 5 (1). Where there is no such doubt, that subsection could add an unnecessary complication. A bailor of property alleged to be stolen by his bailee has a proprietary right. No question whether the bailee owes any "obligation" arises. It would be no answer that the bailor had himself stolen the property or obtained it by deception and might have difficulty in suing for it. It was clear at common law, and is clear under the Theft Act, that property may be stolen from a person who has himself stolen it from a third person. The law protects the possession even of a thief against one who would dishonestly dispossess him. P will usually have not merely possession of the property obtained, but also ownership, at least until the third person takes steps to avoid the transaction under which the property was obtained. Thus in *Meech*, P was probably the owner of the cheque which he had obtained by a forged instrument from the hire-purchase company. If the cheque had been stolen from him, there would have been no difficulty. The problem arose because there was no evidence of dishonest appropriation until after D had paid the cheque into his bank. The question was whether P could follow his interest into the proceeds. It is submitted that P could have done so under the principle of *Taylor v Plumer*;[1] where an agent converts his principal's property into another form (even wrongfully) the property in the changed form continues to belong to the principal. Since the court held that the money withdrawn by D was the proceeds of P's cheque,[2] the money belonged to P and it was unnecessary to rely on s. 5 (3).

Where reliance is placed on s. 5 (3) the property is regarded as belonging to another only "as against him", that is, the person owing the obligation. If, therefore, in *Meech* the property belonged to P only by virtue of s. 5 (3), E and F who dishonestly appropriated part of the proceeds of the cheque could not commit theft from P except as aiders and abettors of D. Only D had assumed an obligation to P. If the argument that D's theft was over and done with had been accepted, they could not have been guilty of theft at all but only of handling. If, however, P retained a proprietary interest in the proceeds then D and E were guilty of an independent theft.

---

[1]   (1815) 3 M & S 562.

[2]   This conclusion may, however, be questionable on the facts since P's "money" became mixed with D's money in D's bank account. See *Re J Leslie Engineers Co Ltd* [1976] 2 All ER 85 at 89–91 (Oliver J).

2–79   *A duty to account is not a duty to retain and deal.* A duty to account, creating a relationship of debtor and creditor, is not an "obligation . . . to retain and deal" within the meaning of s. 5 (3). It has been held that an employee who makes and dishonestly retains a profit from his misuse of his employer's property or his position as employee is bound to account for the profit, but only as debtor and so cannot steal the profit. D, the salaried manager of a public house, in breach of contract, sold his own beer instead of that of his employer and retained the takings instead of paying them into his employer's account. On an Attorney-General's reference,[1] it was held that the trial judge had rightly ruled that D had no case to answer on a charge of stealing the secret profit he had made: (i) he was under no obligation to "retain and deal with" the proceeds of sale within the meaning of s. 5 (3); (ii) he did not hold the secret profit on a constructive trust or, if he did, it was not such a trust as fell within the ambit of s. 5 (1) of the Theft Act 1968; and (iii) the employer had no proprietary interest in the secret profit. D was under an obligation in the civil law to account for the profit he had made, but this (subject to the doubt about the "constructive trust") was merely a debt. The conclusion depends on civil law and, particularly, *Lister & Co v Stubbs*,[2] where the Court of Appeal held that an agent, D, who receives a bribe in breach of his duty to his principal, P, must account to P for the amount of the bribe but is only a debtor and not a trustee. P has no proprietary interest in the money. In *A-G for Hong Kong v Reid*,[3] the Privy Council has now held that *Lister & Co v Stubbs* is wrongly decided. However it seems likely that the Court of Appeal, Criminal Division, will regard itself as bound by *Lister & Co v Stubbs* unless the English civil courts decide otherwise.[4] If the Hong Kong case is followed, it will open the possibility of a substantial enlargement of the criminal law.[5]

It will be noted, however, that the court in the *Attorney-General's Reference* thought (i) that not all constructive trusts fell within the ambit of s. 5 (1); (ii) that the profit which was the subject of any trust was not identifiable; and (iii) that there would be serious difficulties about proving dishonesty on the part of the profiteering publican. As to (i), s. 5 (1) refers to "any proprietary right or interest" and it is difficult to see why, or on what principle, some proprietary interests recognised by the civil law should be excluded. As to (ii), if D appropriates the whole, knowing that P is entitled to part, there seems to be no real difficulty in holding that D has appropriated the part belonging to P, though it is not identifiable as separate property.[6] And as to (iii), the alleged difficulties of proving dishonesty do not seem to have bothered the courts in the least in *Cooke*[7] where, in similar circumstances, it was held that employees might be convicted of conspiracy to defraud their employer. Conspiracy to defraud, no less than theft, requires proof of dishonesty. As the profiteering publican and his barman together rolled out the illicit barrels in the dead of night, there seems no reason why they should not similarly have been convicted of conspiracy to defraud.

---

1   See *A-G's Reference (No 1 of 1985)* [1986] 2 All ER 219, [1986] Crim LR 476 and commentary.
2   (1890) 45 Ch D 1. See also *Cullum* (1873) LR 2 CCR 28; *Eighth Report*, Cmnd 2977, para 38; Williams *TBCL* 756; A.T.H. Smith "Constructive Trusts in the Law of Theft" [1977] Crim LR 395; J.C. Smith (1956) 19 MLR 39, 46. It has been said that in none of the cases in which a fiduciary has been held liable to account for profits did the question arise whether the defendant was a trustee as opposed to being merely accountable: Hanbury and Maudsley *Modern Equity* (10th edn) 314.
3   [1994] 1 AC 324, [1994] 1 All ER 1, PC.
4   This is the attitude taken by the court in the law of provocation where a similar situation has arisen: *Campbell (No 2)* [1997] Crim LR 227, CA.
5   See J.C. Smith (1994) 110 LQR 180.
6   It may, however, be difficult to prove that D intended to appropriate property *belonging to another;* see 110 LQR 180 at 184 and Arlidge and Parry 3–062.
7   [1986] AC 909, [1986] 2 All ER 985, HL.

2–80   In *Lister & Co v Stubbs*, the secret profit took the form of a bribe to an agent who naturally did not account to his principal for it. Similarly where D, a turnstile operator, was improperly given £2 to admit to Wembley Stadium a person who had no ticket, it was held that D had not stolen the £2 from his employer, P.[1] No doubt, D was bound to account to P for the £2, but the relationship between them was that of debtor and creditor. In *Tarling v Government of Singapore*,[2] a majority of the House of Lords decided that evidence of an agreement by company directors to acquire and retain a secret profit for which they were accountable to the shareholders was not evidence of an agreement to defraud. Lord Wilberforce said that "the making of a secret profit is no criminal offence, whatever other epithet may be appropriate". That may require reconsideration in the light of the *Hong Kong* case.

---

1   *Powell v MacRae* [1977] Crim LR 571, DC.
2   (1979) 70 Cr App Rep 77, [1978] Crim LR 490, HL; discussed [1979] Crim LR 220.

(i) An obligation to make restoration of property

2–81 Suppose that D acquires possession of property by another's mistake and is liable (a question of civil law) to account to P for the value of the property so obtained. The ownership in the property may pass to D, or it may remain in P, depending on the character of the mistake. If the ownership remains in P, then, under the rules already discussed, D may steal the property: but if the ownership passes to D and P retains no proprietary right or interest, D can commit no offence under the provisions so far discussed. Such a case is, however, covered by s. 5 (4) which provides:

> "Where a person gets property by another's mistake, and is under an obligation to make restoration (in whole or in part) of the property or its proceeds or of the value thereof, then to the extent of that obligation the property or proceeds shall be regarded (as against him) as belonging to the person entitled to restoration, and an intention not to make restoration shall be regarded accordingly as an intention to deprive that person of the property or proceeds."

2–82 This provision is obviously apt to cover such a case as *Ashwell*.[1]

P, in the dark, gave D a sovereign in mistake for a shilling. When, some time later, D discovered that he had a sovereign and not a shilling, he at once decided to keep it for himself. Likewise with the case of *Middleton*.[2]

P, a post office clerk, referred to the wrong letter of advice and handed to D, a depositor in the Post Office Savings Bank, a sum which ought to have gone to another depositor. D took it, knowing that it was a much larger sum than he was entitled to.

In neither of these cases, however, is s. 5 (4) strictly necessary. Mistake of identity vitiates consent in the civil law. In *Ashwell*, it was implicit in the decision (and rightly so) that no property in the sovereign passed to D (a sovereign is necessarily a different coin from a shilling – it was a mistake of identity) – so D today would be guilty of appropriating property belonging to another under s. 1 (1) and s. 3 (1) of the Act.[3] The basis of *Middleton*, too, was that no property in the money passed to D because of a mistake as to the identity either of the deposit or of the depositor. If, however, *Ashwell* and *Middleton* should have been wrongly decided (because the property did pass) – and both have been criticised[4] – s. 5 (4) makes it quite clear that, under the Act, persons who act as they did should nevertheless be convicted. Even if the property in the money did pass to D in each of those cases, it is clear that D would be under an obligation to make restoration, if not of the actual property or its proceeds, at least of its value; and therefore the property would be treated as belonging to P. The only slight distinction is this: Middleton received £8 16s. 10d. and was convicted of stealing that sum – rightly on the basis of mistake of identity. He was, however, entitled to 10s. and, if the property had passed, he would under the Act be guilty of stealing only £8 6s. 10d. – the amount which he was bound to restore.

---

[1]   (1885) 16 QBD 190.
[2]   (1873) LR 2 CCR 38.
[3]   Above, paras **2–01** to **2–03**.
[4]   Russell 970–974, 979–982, 1553–1574.

2–83 The real object of s. 5 (4) (or at least of that part of it which deals with the value of the goods) was to remove the mischief (as it was seen) of the decision in *Moynes v Coopper*.[1] D, a labourer, had received most of his week's wages in advance from his employer. It was the employer's intention to tell the wages clerk to deduct the amount of the advance when paying D at the end of the week. He forgot to do so. The clerk therefore gave D a packet containing the full amount of his wages. D did not discover this until he arrived home when he opened the envelope and, knowing he was not entitled to it, decided to keep the whole sum. The Divisional Court dismissed the prosecutor's appeal on the ground that D had no larcenous intent at the time of taking as required by the Larceny Act 1916. This is no longer a problem: see s. 3 (1). The Court of Quarter Sessions (chairman, Mr Thesiger, QC), however, had acquitted Moynes on the more fundamental grounds that (a) D received ownership in the money and (b) D took the money with the consent of the owner. These were valid grounds.[2] The wages clerk, no doubt, had a general authority to pay each workman the weekly wage due to him. You do not revoke your agent's authority by deciding to do so and then forgetting about it. When the clerk handed the wages packet to D it seems clear that he transferred to him both ownership and possession in the money. In that case, it was quite impossible for D to be guilty of larceny of the money and it was really irrelevant (as Mr Thesiger decided) whether D decided to keep the money for himself at the wages table, or later when he got home. No one else (or so it was then thought) had any legal interest in the money – D was merely under a quasi-contractual obligation to repay to his employer an equivalent sum. He was in fact merely a particular kind of debtor. On such an analysis, there is a good deal to be said in favour of Moynes's acquittal; but few cases have attracted so much adverse criticism and it is hardly surprising that it was thought necessary to bring this case within the new law of theft; and s. 5 (4) (and particularly the words "or the value thereof") does so. Though the money would still be D's, a notional property in it would be vested in P for the purposes of this Act; and D's intention not to repay would be regarded as an intention to deprive P of the money.

Moynes v Coopper was concerned with tangible property. Section 5 (4) was applied to intangible property in *A-G's Reference (No 1 of 1983)*[3] where, through an error on the part of her employer, a policewoman's bank account was credited by means of a direct debit operation with £74 to which she was not entitled. There was some evidence that, when she discovered the error, she decided to say nothing about it and to keep the unexpected windfall. The judge withdrew the case from the jury. The Court of Appeal held that the thing in action – the debt of £74 due to D from her bank – belonged to her; but that she was under an obligation to make restoration (which the court thought is the same as "make restitution"). For the purposes of the law of theft, the thing belonged notionally to the employer and D would be guilty of theft if it were proved (i) that she intended not to make restoration, (ii) that she had "appropriated" the thing and (iii) that she had acted dishonestly.

---

[1] [1956] 1 QB 439, [1956] 1 All ER 450, criticised in [1956] Crim LR 516.
[2] This is implicitly recognised by the Act which, by s. 5 (4), circumvents ground (a). Ground (b) has become irrelevant with the disappearance of trespass as a constituent of stealing.
[3] [1985] QB 182, [1984] 3 All ER 369, [1984] Crim LR 570, followed in *Stalham* [1993] Crim LR 310, CA, rejecting an argument that the case could not stand with *Davis*, below, para **2–85**.

2–84 The CLRC seems to have assumed that in cases like *Moynes v Coopper* the entire proprietary interest in the property passes to D and that, in the civil law, he is a mere debtor. Subsequently, however, it was held by Goulding J in *Chase Manhattan Bank NA v Israel-British Bank (London) Ltd*[1] that, where an action will lie to recover money paid under a mistake of fact, the payer retains an equitable proprietary interest. If that is so, there is no need to rely on s. 5 (4) to attribute a "notional" proprietary interest to the payer. The property belongs to him within s. 5 (1). *Chase Manhattan* was considered by Lord Browne-Wilkinson in *Westdeutche v Islington London Borough Council*.[2] In his opinion, contrary to that of Goulding J, receipt of the moneys in ignorance of the mistake gave rise to no trust, but the fact that the payee learned of the mistake two days later "may well" have provided a proper foundation for the decision. In the meantime, *Chase Manhattan* had been applied by the Criminal Division of the Court of Appeal in *Shadrokh-Cigari*.[3] A bank in the USA, by mistake, credited the account of a child at an English bank with £286,000 instead of the £286 actually due. D, the child's guardian, procured the child to sign authority for the issue of large banker's drafts which D paid into bank accounts of his own. When D was arrested only £21,000 remained in the child's account. His conviction of theft from the English bank was upheld. Although the things in action created by the drafts did not, and could not, belong to the bank (because the "thing" was a right to sue the bank and the bank could not sue itself) the draft itself, the document or instrument, when first drawn by the bank's employee on the bank's paper, clearly belonged to the bank. When the bank delivered it under a mistake of fact, to D or the child, it parted with the legal ownership but retained an equitable interest by virtue of the principle in *Chase Manhattan* . It was not necessary to rely on s. 5 (4); but the court held that the subsection was an alternative route to the same conclusion. D got the drafts by the mistake of the bank and was under an obligation to make restoration of the proceeds or value. Since D knew of the mistake from the start, *Shadrokh-Cigari* does not seem to be affected by *Westdeutsche*.

The question whether the effect of s. 5 (4) was to convert all cases of obtaining property (other than land) by deception into theft no longer arises since *Gomez* decided that they are theft, independently of s. 5(4). Because it may be relevant for other purposes, it is submitted, as in pre-*Gomez* editions of this book,[4] that the subsection does not have this effect. Where D has obtained goods from P by deception, P has power, by rescinding the contract, to impose an obligation upon him; but the Act requires that D "*is*" under an obligation; and he is not, unless and until P rescinds, which he may never do, or attempt to do until it is too late.

---

[1]   [1981] Ch 105, [1979] 3 All ER 1025, Ch D.
[2]   [1996] 2 All ER 961 at 966, HL.
[3]   [1988] Crim LR 465.
[4]   See 6th edition, para [89].

2–85   *Whether the overpayment must be identified.* Section 5 (4) does not create any offence. It merely vests a notional property[1] in P which D might then appropriate. Only identifiable property can be appropriated. Suppose that Moynes, on his way home, had given his pay packet to a beggar without opening it and before he knew that it contained the full amount of his wages. He would presumably remain obliged to repay the excess but his failure to do so would be a mere refusal to pay a debt and no offence. He could no longer be guilty of theft because there would be no identifiable property to appropriate. It would be the same if, being unaware of the mistake, he had spent the whole of the wages on beer which was consumed by himself and his workmates. But if he had bought a bicycle with the wages and then realised that he had been overpaid, he might appropriate, and therefore steal, the bicycle in which the employer now had a "notional" (or, according to *Chase Manhattan*, a "real", equitable) proprietary interest. There is, however, a sufficient identification of the property if it is an unascertained part of an identifiable whole.[2]

In *Davis*,[3] D was entitled to housing benefit from the local authority, P. By mistake, P's computer, every month during a certain period, sent D two cheques, each for the full amount due.[4] D, dishonestly, did not return either of the duplicates but endorsed them to shopkeepers for cash or to his landlord for his rent, etc. He was convicted of theft of money. The court quashed his convictions on those counts where there was no evidence that he had received cash in exchange for the cheques. Paying the rent by endorsement and delivery of the cheque may have been theft of the cheque but it was not theft of money. Where he received cash for the cheque, his conviction was upheld. The cash was the proceeds of property (a cheque) got by another's mistake and, by virtue of s. 5 (4), was to be regarded as belonging to P. No reference was made to the case or principle of *Chase Manhattan Bank*. D was entitled to one of each pair of cheques but it was not necessary to identify one of them as that sent by mistake. When an overpayment is made, the whole sum is got by mistake within the meaning of the section, but the payee is, of course, liable to repay only the excess and may be convicted of stealing the excess if the other conditions of theft are satisfied. The court equated the case with that where an excessive number of coins is inserted in a pay packet. It is unnecessary to identify certain of the coins as having been included by mistake. It would be otherwise, however, if a cheque was properly sent and then, by a subsequent mistake, a second cheque was sent. Then, only the second cheque or its proceeds could be stolen.

---

[1] All proprietary interests are "notional" in the sense that they are legal concepts or notions existing only in the minds of men. What is meant by "notional" in this context is that the proprietary interest does not exist in the civil law, that branch of the law which properly determines the existence and extent of such interests.

[2] Below, para **2–110**.

[3] [1988] Crim LR 762.

[4] Does the malfunctioning of a machine constitute a "mistake" within the meaning of the subsection? If the computer was wrongly programmed, the mistake was that of a human mind. But if the automatic chocolate machine, because of a mechanical fault, gives me ten bars when I have paid only for one, it seems plain that property in the nine does not pass, because the owner of the machine does not intend it to pass. It is no different from the case where the machine falls apart and spills its contents on the floor. I might be convicted of theft without recourse to s. 5 (4).

2–86 Plainly, s. 5 (4) and the decision in *Chase Manhattan* extend the scope of stealing. Bringing *Moynes* within the net inevitably involves bringing in a number of others whose activities have not generally been thought of as criminal. For example, P pays money to D under the mistaken belief that the property of D has been lost through a peril insured against. D receives the money under the same belief.[1] Or P pays money to D under a contract for the sale of a fishery. In fact the fishery already belongs to P.[2] In both these cases, D discovers the truth and resolves not to make restoration. In legal analysis, D's situation is indistinguishable from that of Moynes: he has received money under a mistake and is under an obligation to make restoration of the value thereof. Plainly, then, the money (notionally under s. 5 (4) and actually under *Chase Manhattan*) belongs to P in both these cases and (if D's resolution not to repay can be regarded as dishonest) D is guilty of theft if he appropriates the money or the proceeds (e.g. the Rolls-Royce which he has bought with it). Only if the money cannot be traced into some property in his possession will he be exempt. Whether such cases are wisely brought within the net of theft is questionable but it is the inevitable result of covering the *Moynes* situation. And it can involve the criminal law in some of the finest distinctions drawn in the civil law. Suppose that P wishes to terminate the employment of his employee, D. Both P and D believe that a binding contract of service exists between them and P pays D £30,000 to be released from his obligation to continue to employ D. The parties then discover that P could (and, had he known the truth, would) have dismissed D without paying him a penny, since D had committed breaches of contract which were unknown to P and not present to D's mind when he accepted the £30,000. D then appropriates the £30,000. If, as the Court of Appeal held,[3] D was under an obligation to restore the value of £30,000, this would be the *actus reus* of theft by D; but as the House of Lords held[4] that there was no such obligation, it is no offence. It may be that all of the cases discussed in this paragraph would founder from the inability to prove a dishonest intention; yet these recipients of money are, in law, in no different situation from Moynes himself.

---

[1]   Cf *Norwich Union Ltd, Fire Insurance Society Ltd v Price* [1934] AC 455.
[2]   *Cooper v Phibbs* (1867) LR 2 HL 149. It is assumed for the purpose of this example that the contract was void.
[3]   *Lever Bros Ltd v Bell* [1931] 1 KB 557. The Court of Appeal thought the contract was void.
[4]   *Bell v Lever Bros Ltd* [1932] AC 161.

(j) The meaning of "obligation"

2–87   The word "obligation" in s. 5 (4) means a legal obligation.[1] It was so held in *Gilks*.[2] D placed bets including one on a horse, Fighting Scot. Fighting Scot was unplaced and the race was won by Fighting Taffy. Because of a mistake on the part of the clerk in the betting shop, D was paid as if he had backed the winning horse and received £117.25 instead of £10.62, winnings on other races. D took the money, knowing that he was being overpaid. The trial judge ruled that "at the moment the money passed, it was money belonging to another". But, in case his first ruling was wrong, the judge went on to consider s. 5 (4) and ruled that it was applicable if D was under an "obligation", even though it was not a legal obligation, to repay. The Court of Appeal decided that the latter ruling was wrong: "obligation" cannot be construed as meaning a moral or social obligation as distinct from a legal one. The court interpreted the judge's first ruling as meaning that "the property in the £106.63 never passed to the appellant"; and they held that the ruling, so interpreted, was right.

The difficulty over s. 5 (4) arises because of the decision of the Court of Appeal in the civil case of *Morgan v Ashcroft*.[3] It was there held that, (i) since the Gaming Act 1845 makes wagering transactions void, the court could not examine the state of accounts between a bookmaker and his client, and (ii) money paid under a mistake is recoverable only if the mistake was as to a fact which, if true, would have made the payer legally liable to pay. For both these reasons an overpayment by a bookmaker was held to be irrecoverable. Gilks, therefore, was under no legal obligation to repay the money.[4]

The decision of the court in *Gilks* that the ownership never passed was based on the decision in *Middleton*, one of the most dubious and hotly-debated decisions on the old law of larceny. It is regrettable that recourse should be had to such a case in interpreting the Theft Act; but, even if *Middleton* was rightly decided, its *ratio* was inapplicable to the facts of *Gilks*. It turned on the fact that the court held that there was a mistake of identity, either the identity of the payee or the identity of the post office deposit which was being repaid. In *Gilks*, there was no question of any such mistake. The clerk intended to pay the sum of money which he handed over to Gilks and to no one else. It is difficult to suppose that the bookmaker (or the plaintiff in *Morgan v Ashcroft*) could have successfully sued for conversion of the money. It is submitted that there is no doubt that the ownership in money does pass in these circumstances.

¹ Cf *Mainwaring* (1981) 74 Cr App Rep 99, above, para **2–72**.
² [1972] 3 All ER 280, [1972] 1 WLR 1341, CA, criticised by Arlidge and Parry (1st edn), 1.13, and in [1972B] CLJ at 202.
³ [1938] 1 KB 49, [1937] 3 All ER 92.
⁴ It is of interest to note that where a bet is placed with the "Tote" this problem does not arise. Such a bet is not a wager, since the Tote can neither win nor lose. The bet is an enforceable contract. An overpaid investor is no doubt under an obligation to repay: *Tote Investors Ltd v Smoker* [1968] 1 QB 509, [1967] 3 All ER 242, CA.

2–88 *Gilks and Gomez.* Since *Gomez*¹ it seems clear that when Gilks took the money he dishonestly appropriated property belonging to another, even if the ownership did pass to him. That looks like a plain case of theft; but there is a difficulty. He had no right to take the money (the clerk would have been justified in withholding it) but, once he had got it, he was doing no more than retaining money which he was entitled in law to retain. He could have resisted a restitution order under s. 28 of the Act on the ground that *Morgan v Ashcroft* is direct authority that the bookmaker was not a "a person entitled to recover" the money. It is arguable that a person should not be held guilty of stealing property when he has a better right to it than anyone else. Gilks had no better right to it at the moment before he took it; thereafter he had a better right to it than anyone. It seems odd to say he stole the money when he was entitled to keep it – but common sense suggests he was a thief. The defect in the law, if there is one, is with the decision in *Morgan v Ashcroft*.

The legal obligation must be to "make restoration of the property or its proceeds or of the value thereof". An obligation to pay the price for goods sold is not an obligation "to make restoration". So if P sells goods to D for £10 and, by mistake, sends a bill for £5, D does not steal if he dishonestly pays £5 and keeps the goods.²

¹ Above, para **2–09**.
² See discussion of *Lacis v Cashmarts* [1969] 2 QB 400 at 411, [1972B] CLJ at 204.

C. WHAT CAN BE STOLEN

2–89 Stealing is the dishonest appropriation of property and, by s. 4 (1):

"'Property' includes money and all other property, real or personal, including things in action and other intangible property."

It should be noted at once that this definition is highly qualified, so far as land and wild creatures are concerned, by subsections (2), (3) and (4) of s. 4.¹ Under the old law, there could be no larceny of land, things in action or other intangible property or wild creatures while at large. The point about the first two cases was that there could be no taking and carrying away. Land was regarded as an immovable and things in action had no physical existence. The difficulty with wild creatures at large was that they had no owner. Each of these items requires separate consideration.

¹ Below, paras **2–90**, **2–98** and **2–99**.

(a)   Land

2–90   Now that the requirement of taking and carrying away has disappeared from the law, the technical obstacle to land being the subject of theft has disappeared. Land was formerly a possible subject of fraudulent conversion[1] and, since fraudulent conversion has now been swallowed by theft, it was essential that land should, in some circumstances at least, be stealable. It would have been possible to leave s. 4 (1) unqualified and a perfectly workable law would have resulted. The Committee, for reasons of policy, decided against this course. Section 4 (2) provides:

> "A person cannot steal land, or things forming part of land and severed from it by him or by his directions, except in the following cases, that is to say –
>
> (a)   when he is a trustee or personal representative, or is authorised by power of attorney, or as liquidator of a company, or otherwise, to sell or dispose of land belonging to another, and he appropriates the land or anything forming part of it by dealing with it in breach of the confidence reposed in him; or
>
> (b)   when he is not in possession of the land and appropriates anything forming part of the land by severing it or causing it to be severed, or after it has been severed; or
>
> (c)   when, being in possession of the land under a tenancy, he appropriates the whole or part of any fixture or structure let to be used with the land.
>
> For purposes of this subsection 'land' does not include incorporeal hereditaments; 'tenancy' means a tenancy for years or any less period and includes an agreement for such a tenancy, but a person who after the end of a tenancy remains in possession as statutory tenant or otherwise is to be treated as having possession under the tenancy, and 'let' shall be construed accordingly."

It may be helpful to spell out the possible liability of the various categories of persons in detail.

---

[1]   Above, para **1–16**.

(i)   *Trustees, personal representatives, and others authorised to dispose of land belonging to another*

2–91   Any of these persons may steal the land or anything forming part of it by dealing with it in breach of the confidence reposed in him. So if he sells or gives away the land or any fixture or structure forming part of it, he commits theft.

(ii)   *Other persons not in possession*

Such a person may steal only by severing, or causing to be severed, or appropriating the thing after severance. A purported sale by such a person of the land would not be theft. An attempt to sever, as by starting to dig out a sapling, is an assumption which is not a sufficient appropriation, though no doubt an attempt to steal.

The rule formerly was that a person could not be convicted of stealing anything which he had severed from the realty (subject to specific statutory exceptions) unless he first abandoned and then re-took possession. Under the Act the general rule is that a person who is not in possession of land can steal fixtures, growing things and even the substance of the land itself, if, in each case, he first severs it from the realty. The following acts, which would not (or may not) have been larceny under the old law, are theft under the new:

D enters upon land in the possession of P and (i) demolishes a brick wall and carries away the bricks; (ii) removes a stone statue fixed in the land; (iii) digs sand from a sand pit and takes it away; (iv) cuts grass growing on the land[1] and at once loads it on to a cart to drive away; (v) takes away P's farm gate.[2]

Outside the law of theft remains the case where D appropriates land without severing it, as where he moves his boundary fence so as to incorporate a strip of P's land into his own.[3]

---

[1]   Cf *Foley* (1889) 17 Cox CC 142.
[2]   Cf *Skujins* [1956] Crim LR 266.
[3]   The arguments for and against making land the subject of theft are summarised in *Eighth Report*, Cmnd 2977 at pp 21–22.

(iii)   Other persons in possession as tenants

2–92   If a tenant removes a fixture – for example a washbasin or fireplace – he may be guilty of stealing it. Likewise if he removes any structure – for example a shed or greenhouse which is fixed to the land. If the structure is resting on its own weight and not a fixture then it is, of course, stealable under the general rule and there is no need to rely on s. 4 (2) (c). But the tenant will not be guilty if he digs soil or sand from the land and appropriates that. This exemption applies only to the person in possession of the land. If his wife or a member of the family were to dig and sell sand, it would seem that s. 4 (2) (b) would be applicable and theft would be committed. In such a case, there is some authority for suggesting that the husband could be convicted as an aider and abettor.[1] If the husband were the principal in the act it is possible that anyone assisting him might be held liable as an aider and abettor, even though he could not himself be convicted.[2]

Unlike s. 4 (2) (b), 4 (2) (c) does not require that the thing be severed. It appears then that if the tenant contracted to sell the unsevered fireplace in his house he would be guilty of theft, even where there was no intention to sever it, as where it is sold to the tenant's successor in the tenancy. If the tenant purports to sell the land he commits no offence and a purported sale of an ordinary house would be indistinguishable from a sale of the land. The house could hardly be held to be a "structure let to be used with the land". The phrase implies that the structure is of an ancillary nature.

---

[1]   *Sockett* (1908) 1 Cr App Rep 101.
[2]   Cf *Bourne* (1952) 36 Cr App Rep 125; *Cogan and Leak* [1976] QB 217, [1975] 2 All ER 1059; *Millward* [1994] Crim LR 257; Smith & Hogan, 155–158.

(iv)   Other persons in possession otherwise than as tenants

2–93   A person may be in possession of a land as a licensee.[1] Curiously, he is not within the terms of s. 4 (2) (c) and so is incapable of stealing the land or anything forming part of it. He thus commits no offence if he dishonestly appropriates fixtures or digs sand or ore from the land. This appears to be an oversight in the Act. He of course may be guilty of stealing structures not forming part of the land.

---

[1]   *Errington v Errington and Woods* [1952] 1 KB 290, [1952] 1 All ER 149; see Megarry & Wade (5th edn) 798–799.

2–94   It may still occasionally be important to determine whether a particular article forms part of the land. Generally appropriation will involve severance,

so non-possessors will be caught by s. 4 (2) (b) while tenants are caught by
s. 4 (2) (c). But if a licensee in possession appropriates a structure, it is vital to
know whether it forms part of the land. This is a question of the law of land
and the answer depends on the degree of annexation and the object of
annexation. The chattel must be actually fixed to the land, not for its more
convenient use as a chattel, but for the more convenient use of the land.

2–95   Incorporeal hereditaments[1] are now stealable. The most important of
these are easements, profits and rents. The main purpose of the provision would
seem to be to cover the theft of a rent-charge. No doubt this was the subject of
fraudulent conversion under the old law, and called for a provision of this
kind. But instances of theft of the other interests can only be extremely rare.
For example, P has a right of way over O's land – an easement. D executes a
deed purporting to relieve O's land of the burden of the easement. Or D, a
tenant of P's land, purporting to be the freeholder, allows O, the adjoining
landowner, to erect a building which will necessarily obstruct the flow of light
to windows on P's land which have an easement of light. These acts seem to be
appropriations of the easement which, if done with the necessary *mens rea* will
amount to theft. The most obvious instances will be those where a trustee or
personal representative disposes of an easement, profit or rent for his own
benefit. These cases are not covered by s. 4 (2) (a) but incorporeal hereditaments
can be stolen by persons generally.

It will be noted that these examples relate to existing incorporeal
hereditaments. Dishonestly to purport to create an easement in the land of
another would not seem to amount to an offence unless it is done by one of the
persons mentioned in s. 4 (2) (a). In the latter case, such an act would seem to
amount to "dealing with the land in breach of the confidence reposed in him".

---

[1]   See Megarry & Wade, 11, 813, 814.

2–96   The fact that D's efforts to dispose of an interest in P's land in these
cases would be ineffective to do so would not seem to affect the result in the
criminal law. When a bailee of goods purports to sell the goods, he is unable
(in general) to pass a good title; yet it cannot be doubted that his purporting to
do so amounts to an appropriation of the goods. The same is now true of a
person who has no proprietary or possessory interest of any sort in the goods.
The position must be the same in the case of a purported disposal of an interest
in land.[1]

It may be added that where the person purporting to dispose of the interest in
land has done so for reward, the simpler and more appropriate course will be to
charge him with obtaining or attempting to obtain by deception from the person
from whom he seeks the reward. Where D purports to dispose of the interest as
a gift, however, the only possible charge will be one of stealing the interest;
but such cases are likely to be extremely rare.

---

[1]   The problem of "intention permanently to deprive" is the same as that discussed above, para
2–54. See also *Chan Wai Lam*, below, para **4–53**, fn 1.

2–97   A rather strange anomaly resulting from the exception of incorporeal
hereditaments from the meaning of "land" is that if D, not being one of the
persons mentioned in s. 4 (2) (a), purports to dispose of the whole of P's interest
in the land (for example, the fee simple) he will not commit theft (though he
might be guilty of obtaining the price of the land by deception); whereas if, as
in the examples given, he purports to dispose of a comparatively small part of
P's interest he will be guilty of theft.

(b)   Exception of things growing wild

2–98   Things growing wild on land undoubtedly fall within the definition of property in the Act and, but for an exception, could be stolen by a person not in possession of land if he severed and appropriated them. Section 4 (3), however, provides:

> "A person who picks mushrooms growing wild on any land, or who picks flowers, fruit or foliage from a plant growing wild on any land, does not (although not in possession of the land) steal what he picks, unless he does it for reward or for sale or other commercial purpose.
>
> For purposes of this subsection 'mushroom' includes any fungus, and 'plant' includes any shrub or tree."

The effect is in general to exempt things growing wild from the law of theft. It will be theft however if:

(i) (except in the case of a mushroom) D removes the whole plant. For example, he pulls out a primrose or a sapling by the roots. This is not picking from a plant and so is not within the exception.

(ii) D removes the plant or part of it by an act which cannot be described as "picking". For example, he saws off the top of a Christmas tree growing wild on P's land, or cuts the grass growing wild on P's land with a reaper or a scythe.

(iii) D picks mushrooms or wild flowers, fruit or foliage, for a commercial purpose – for example, mushrooms for sale in his shop or holly to sell from door-to-door at Christmas. The provision is no doubt intended to be used against depredation on a fairly large scale but it would seem to cover such cases as where D, a schoolboy, picks mushrooms intending to sell them to his mother or the neighbours. It is possible, however, that such a single isolated case might be held not to fall within the law as not being a "commercial" purpose – for it will be noted that the wording of the subsection requires that sale, as well as other purposes, be "commercial". It might be argued that this requires that D, to some extent, must be making a business of dealing in the things in question.[1]

It will, of course, be theft to pick a single cultivated flower, wherever it is growing.

---

[1]   But cf Williams *TBCL* (1st edn) 683, fn 1.

(c)   Wild creatures

2–99   The distinction between wild creatures (*ferae naturae*) and tame creatures (*mansuetae naturae*) is a matter of common law.[1] Some tame animals, like dogs and cats, could not be stolen at common law; but now, all tame animals may be stolen. Wild creatures could not, while at large, be stolen at common law or under the Larceny Acts because no one had any property in them until they were taken or killed. The owner of the land on which they happened to be had an exclusive right to take them which was protected by the criminal law relating to poaching but was not protected by the heavier guns of larceny.

When the wild creature was killed or taken, the property in it vested in the owner of the land on which this was done,[2] but the thing was now in the possession of the taker who could not therefore steal it. If, however, he abandoned the thing on P's land, then possession of it vested in P and a subsequent removal of it by D was larceny. Difficult questions could arise whether D had abandoned the creature or not. If he put rabbits into bags or bundles and hid them in a ditch on P's land, he retained possession so that it was no larceny if he returned later and appropriated them;[3] whereas if he merely left the things lying on the surface of the land, this might well have constituted abandonment of the thing.[4]

Though this result was rightly criticised, it was the logical consequence of the rule of the civil law which provided that the thing was owned by no one until it was taken. Had no special provisions been made in the Theft Act for wild animals they could probably have been stolen by virtue of s. 3 (1): though there would have been no appropriation at the instant of taking (because the thing was no one's property) any subsequent assumption of ownership (as by carrying the thing away) would have been theft from the owner of the land on which it was taken.

---

[1]   See East 2 PC 607; Russell 2, 903.
[2]   *Blades v Higgs* (1865) 11 HL Cas 621.
[3]   *Townley* (1871) LR 1 CCR 315; *Petch* (1878) 14 Cox CC 116.
[4]   Cf *Foley* (1889) 17 Cox CC 142.

2–100   For reasons of policy, it was decided that it was undesirable to turn poaching generally into theft; and accordingly, s. 4 (4) provides:

"Wild creatures, tamed or untamed, shall be regarded as property; but a person cannot steal a wild creature not tamed nor ordinarily kept in captivity, or the carcase of any such creature, unless either it has been reduced into possession by or on behalf of another person and possession of it has not since been lost or abandoned, or another person is in course of reducing it into possession."

The effect of s. 4 (4) is that wild creatures cannot be stolen, except in the following cases:

(i) The creature is tamed or ordinarily kept in captivity. For example, P's tame jackdaw, the mink which he keeps in cages, the animals in Whipsnade Zoo. The eagle which escaped some years ago from London Zoo could be stolen while at large, because it was ordinarily kept in captivity. (This phrase seems clearly to refer to the specific animal and not to the species of animal.[1]) Animals like bees or pigeons which roam freely are sufficiently reduced into possession if they have acquired a habit of returning to their home (*animus revertendi*).[2] Possession is not lost because they are flying at a distance. If bees swarm, the common law rule is that the owner retains his possession only so long as he can keep them in sight and follow them. Possession is lost even though they are in sight if they have swarmed on land where he cannot lawfully follow.[3] A person who then takes them, or destroys them, does not commit theft or criminal damage. Bees could not be said to be "tamed" or "ordinarily kept in captivity".

(ii) The creature has been reduced into and remains in the possession of another person or is in the course of being so reduced.[4] For example, P, a poacher, takes or is in course of taking a rabbit on O's land. This is not an offence under the Act. D takes the rabbit from P. This is theft by D from both P and O.

Except in these two cases, wild creatures cannot be stolen; so it will not be theft to take mussels from a mussel bed on an area of the foreshore which belongs to P and which P has tended in order to maintain and improve it.[5]

---

[1]   In *Nye v Niblett* [1918] 1 KB 23, it was held that the words of s. 41 of the Malicious Damage Act 1861 (now repealed, see Criminal Damage Act 1971) " . . . being ordinarily kept . . . for any domestic purpose" referred to the species of animal; but Darling J thought the section also protected a particular animal which was kept for a domestic purpose though the class to which it belonged was not so ordinarily kept. In the present section, however, the interpretation actually

adopted in *Nye v Niblett* is untenable. Even though the great majority of animals of a particular wild species are ordinarily kept in captivity, a particular wild animal of that species which is and always has been in fact at large can hardly be stolen.

2   Blackstone Commentaries 2, 392–393.
3   *Kearry v Pattinson* [1939] 1 KB 471, [1939] 1 All ER 65, CA.
4   Section 4 (4).
5   *Howlett and Howlett* [1968] Crim LR 222, CA.

2–101   The effect is that the poacher who reduces game into possession, abandons it and later resumes possession (so that he was guilty, under the old law, of larceny from the owner of land) no longer commits any offence of theft. The creature has not been reduced into possession by or on behalf of another person. The landowner may have acquired possession when the game was left on his land[1] but it can hardly be said that the reduction into possession was by him on his behalf. Clearly, this slight narrowing of the law of stealing is of no great significance.

1   *Hibbert v McKiernan* [1948] 2 KB 142, [1948] 1 All ER 860; above, para **2–66**.

2–102   If the creature, having been reduced into possession, escapes again (and it is not a creature ordinarily kept in captivity) it cannot be stolen since possession of it has been lost. A more difficult case is that where the possession of the carcase of the creature is lost. P, a housewife, buys a pheasant and loses it from her shopping basket on the way home. D picks it up and reads her name and address on the wrapping but determines to keep it for himself. If possession of the pheasant has been lost then D is not guilty and we have a curious case of a particular kind of chattel where there can be no stealing by finding. It is very arguable, however, that even in this case, theft is committed, for the old law of larceny by finding must have proceeded on the assumption that even the person who had lost goods retained possession of them – otherwise there would not have been that trespass which was an essential element of larceny at common law.[1] If that argument is correct, however, then there is another rather anomalous distinction between the loss of a dead wild creature and the loss of a live one – for the Act clearly contemplates that it is possible to lose possession of a wild creature and, even if this is inapplicable to the carcase, it must apply at least to the living animal. This is one of very few instances where possession is important under the Act and, significantly, it presents problems.

1   "It appears clear on the old authorities that every person who takes a thing upon a finding is civilly a trespasser, except in the one case of a person who finding a thing when it is really lost takes it 'in charity to save for its owner'": Pollock and Wright on *Possession in the Common Law,* 171.

(i)   Poaching

2–103   Poaching may amount to an offence under a variety of enactments – the Night Poaching Act 1828, the Game Act 1831 as amended by the Game Laws (Amendment) Act 1960, and the Poaching Prevention Act 1862. In addition certain provisions relating to the poaching of deer and fish were dealt with in the Larceny Act 1861 and, in view of the decision to repeal the whole of that Act, these are reproduced in Schedule 1 to the 1968 Act (below, p 274) in a simplified form and with revised maximum penalties. These provisions have been put in the Schedule rather than in the body of the Act to avoid giving the impression that they are intended to be a permanent part of the law of theft.[1] The CLRC has suggested that there should be a review of the whole law of poaching followed by comprehensive legislation which would replace Schedule 1.[2]

---

[1]   *Eighth Report*, Cmnd 2977, para 53.
[2]   Ibid.

(ii)   Criminal damage

2–104   The Criminal Damage Act 1971 defines "property" in such a way as to exclude those wild creatures and those growing things which cannot be stolen; so the provisions of the Theft Act cannot be circumvented by a charge of criminal damage.

(d)   Things in action

2–105   A thing in action is property which does not exist in a physical state but which may be vindicated by a legal action. Examples are a debt, shares in a company, a copyright or a trade mark. The Patents Act 1977, s. 30, declares that a patent or an application for a patent is not a thing in action but is personal property so it is clearly "other intangible property" and is capable of being stolen. An invention for which no patent has been granted or applied for is clearly another form of intangible property,[1] whether or not it is a thing in action. So is a company's export quota if it is transferable for value.[2] Confidential information is not property so an undergraduate who unlawfully acquires and reads or makes a copy of an examination question paper may not be convicted of stealing intangible property, namely confidential information belonging to the University.[3] It follows that the wrongful acquisition and use of trade secrets is not theft.[4]

---

[1]   See Patents Act 1977, s. 7 (2) (b). See also below, para **4–56**.
[2]   *A-G of Hong Kong v Nai Keung* (1987) 86 Cr App Rep 174, PC. The strange notion to be found in *Williams and Crick* (1993) (No 91/3265/W3) that, following *Nai-Keung,* "a transfer" of property could be a thing in action, received no encouragement in *Preddy* [1996] 3 All ER 481 at 489. The export quota was "an asset capable of being traded on a market" – per Lord Goff.
[3]   *Oxford v Moss* [1979] Crim LR 119. But might he have been convicted of stealing the question paper on the ground that the "virtue" had gone out of it when he put it back? Below, paras **2–126** to **2–128** and commentary at [1979] Crim LR 120.
[4]   Griew, 2–21, 2–83; Williams *TBCL*, 688–689, 722–723.

(i)   Intent to deprive of a thing in action

2–106   It is only in exceptional cases that the thief of a chattel deprives, or intends to deprive, the owner of his ownership. Usually he deprives him, and intends to deprive him, only of possession. The thief intends to deprive the owner of all the *benefits* of ownership but he knows very well that the chattel continues to belong to his victim and that there is nothing he can do about that. He knows he is handling stolen goods and that, if he is found out, the goods will be taken from him and restored to their owner. So the intent permanently to deprive in the law of larceny referred to an intent to deprive the owner permanently of *possession*, no more. We thus encounter a difficulty when theft is extended to things in action: by definition, they do not exist in possession. An intent to deprive permanently of possession is an impossibility. Things in action are owned but not possessed. So the questions arise (i) whether, in order to amount to an appropriation, there has to be an actual deprivation of ownership; and (ii) whether there has to be an intention to deprive of ownership.

The first question is easily answered in the light of the case-law: any assumption of any of the rights of an owner amounts to an appropriation[1] and such an assumption may fall far short of a deprivation of ownership or possession. The second question also requires a negative answer in the light of s. 6 of the 1968 Act, as construed by the courts.[2] D's intention "to treat the thing as his own to dispose of regardless of the other's rights" is to be regarded as an intention permanently to deprive.

[1] *Morris* [1984] AC 320, HL, above, paras **2–04** to **2–08**.
[2] *Chan Man-sin v A-G of Hong Kong* [1988] 1 All ER 1, above, para **2–54**; *Hilton* (1997) Times, 18 April.

2–107   A credit balance in a bank account and a contractual right to overdraw the account are things in action belonging to the customer. If D dishonestly draws a cheque on P's account and causes the credit balance to be reduced or eliminated, or the overdraft facility to be reduced or exhausted, he appropriates the thing in action. In *Kohn*,[1] which decided these points, D's convictions of theft on other counts were quashed because the account on which the cheques were drawn was already overdrawn beyond the agreed limit: there was nothing in the account to steal. It would seem that today,[2] whatever the position then, D might be convicted of an attempt – it is the same in principle as attempting to steal from an empty pocket.

An objection to a conviction of theft in a case like *Kohn* is that, almost inevitably, the cheque is a forgery and it is settled law that the honouring of a forged cheque, and the consequent debiting of the customer's account, is a nullity;[3] so that (i) in fact the thing is not "appropriated", and (ii) there is (if the drawer of the cheque knows the law) no intention permanently to deprive. But the answer accepted by the Privy Council[4] is (i) that "Any assumption by a person of [a right] of an owner amounts to an appropriation" and the drawing of a cheque on the account is undoubtedly a right of the owner of the account, and (ii) D's intention to "treat the thing as his own to dispose of regardless of the other's rights" is a sufficient intention permanently to deprive.

In this type of case the theft is of a somewhat artificial nature because the victim of the theft, the owner, never loses anything. The loss falls on the bank against which no theft is committed, unless the customer has "held out" the rogue as having authority to draw the cheque. It also makes little sense to talk about an "intention" permanently to deprive in the natural meaning of the phrase because "the thief" is unlikely to have any knowledge of the effect of forgery, "holding out", or any other considerations which, in law, determine whether there will be any actual deprivation of the owner of the cheque if he carries out his intention. The intention "to treat the thing as his own to dispose of" is, however, easily recognised.

[1] (1979) 69 Cr App Rep 395, CA. Cf *Forsyth* [1997] Crim LR (August).
[2] Criminal Attempts Act 1981, s. 1. Smith & Hogan, 329–334.
[3] *Tai Hing Cotton Mill Ltd v Liu Chong Hing Bank* [1986] AC 80, [1985] 2 All ER 947, PC.
[4] *Chan Man-sin v A-G of Hong Kong*, above, para **2–54**. The Board held that the assumption of "a right" was enough, following *Morris*; but the drawer of the forged cheque assumes the right to destroy (in whole or part) the credit balance and that is surely an assumption of all the rights of the owner of the balance, or the part of it alleged to be stolen. Cf *Wille* (1987) 86 Cr App Rep 296, CA.

2–108   When does the theft of the credit balance take place? In *Kohn*, Lane LCJ said, "The completion of the theft does not take place until the transaction has gone through to completion" – i.e. when the account is actually debited.[1] But in *Navvabi*[2] his Lordship himself treated that statement as *obiter*; and in

Re Osman,[3] the Divisional Court, finding support in *Wille*[4] (which did not decide the point), held that the theft takes place when and where D issues the cheques, just as it occurs when and where D sends a telex dishonestly disposing of another's property.

Professor Griew has argued against this conclusion, pointing out that the state of P's account may be much more difficult to ascertain when the cheque is issued than when it is presented to the bank.[5] The account might be overdrawn and any overdraft facility exhausted. This certainly shows that it is more difficult to *prove* a theft if it is committed when the cheque is issued but it does not establish that it *cannot be committed* at that time if it can be proved that the account was in credit or that the overdraft facility was not exhausted. Take an analogous case. D has ostensible but not actual authority to sell P's goods which are lying in a warehouse. D dishonestly sells the goods to Q, intending to keep the proceeds of sale for himself. Because D has ostensible authority, the ownership passes to Q as soon as the contract is made. There is clearly an appropriation and D is guilty of theft. But now suppose that, when Q goes to collect the goods, it appears that they have been removed from the warehouse by P and consumed or otherwise disposed of. It is difficult to determine whether the removal and disposition occurred before or after the sale by D to Q. If it occurred after that sale, the removal and disposition cannot undo the theft which D has committed; but, if it occurred before that "sale", the theft was never committed because there was nothing to sell and nothing to steal. This is precisely the same difficulty – a problem of proof – as arises when D issues the cheque to the payee and it is uncertain whether the account is in credit or not. The difficulty of proof is no argument for holding that there cannot be theft of goods where it is possible to prove that they were in the warehouse at the time of the sale; and, equally, it is no argument for holding that there can be no theft of the thing in action represented by the credit balance or overdraft facility where it can be proved to have existed at the time of the issue of the cheque. If it could not be proved that the goods were in the warehouse or the account in credit at the material time, D could be convicted of an attempt to steal. The case is exactly analogous to an attempt to steal from a pocket when it cannot be proved that there was anything in it.

Professor Griew concedes that "A possible solution, not excluded by the cases, is to treat D's act as continuing (as an appropriation or potential appropriation) until the account is debited." The continuing appropriation theory seems right. The effect of D's act may reasonably be held to continue, no less than the carrying away of tangible property which has already been taken. If there was nothing in the account (or nothing in the warehouse) when D purported to appropriate it, the offence would be committed when the account was credited (or when the warehouse was stocked).

---

[1]   (1979) 69 Cr App Rep 395 at 407. To the same effect, see *Hilton* (1997) Times, 18 April.
[2]   Above, para **2–52**.
[3]   Above, para **2–34**.
[4]   (1987) 86 Cr App Rep 296, CA.
[5]   E.J. Griew "Stealing and Obtaining Bank Credits" [1986] Crim LR 356 at 362; Griew, *Theft*, 2–153, a passage cited in *R v Governor of Brixton Prison, ex p Levin* [1996] 4 All ER 350, 363; but it does not appear that the court's attention was drawn to the argument in this section.

2–109   It is thought that theft would not be committed by a mere breach of copyright. If D, in writing a book, were to copy out large sections of another book in which P owned the copyright, this would be a breach of copyright but it would not be theft. It is an assumption of a right of the owner and so might now be regarded as an appropriation, but there would seem to be no evidence of an intent to deprive P permanently of his property. D is not treating the thing as his own "to dispose of". It would be more analogous to making a merely temporary use of another's chattel.

(ii) The necessity for specific property

2–110 We have noted that theft can be committed only of some specified property[1] but it is not necessary that the property be "specific" in the sense in which that term is used in the Sale of Goods Act 1979.[2] It would be enough under the Theft Act that D had appropriated an unascertained part of an ascertained whole though such property would not be "specific" for the purposes of the Sale of Goods Act. If D is charged with stealing five out of a consignment of ten tins and it emerges at the trial that he was guilty of stealing all ten, he may be convicted of stealing the five.[3] Conversely, if he is charged with stealing ten tins and it emerges that he stole only five of them, he may be convicted of stealing the five. It is not an objection that it is impossible to point to the five which have been stolen. In *Tideswell*,[4] P's servant, E, weighed a quantity of ashes into trucks for D, but entered a less quantity in P's books and charged D for that less quantity. It was held that D was guilty of larceny of the balance of the ashes over those for which he had paid. D's contract with P was not to buy the whole bulk of the ashes at so much per ton, but only to buy such as he might want at that price. The court took the view that E had no authority to pass the property except in those ashes for which he charged; that the balance therefore remained P's property, and it was immaterial that it was not distinguishable from the bulk.[5] It is submitted that this is theft under the Theft Act. Indeed, it would be more accurate in such a case to charge D with theft of the whole; for it is difficult to see how property passes in any of the ashes since "Where there is a contract for the sale of unascertained goods no property in the goods is transferred to the buyer unless and until the goods are ascertained."[6] The goods appear never to have been ascertained in that case.[7] On the other hand, it may be said that, while there is an appropriation of the whole quantity (an *actus reus*), D has a claim of right in respect of the quantity for which he has paid or agreed to pay. Such reasoning was not, however, used in *Middleton*[8] where D was convicted of stealing the whole sum of money although he was entitled to a less sum.

---

[1]   *Navvabi* (1986) 83 Cr App Rep 271, above, para **2–52**.
[2]   Section 62.
[3]   Cf *Pilgram v Rice Smith* [1977] 2 All ER 658, above, para **2–37**; *Davis* [1988] Crim LR 762, CA, commentary at 765.
[4]   [1905] 2 KB 273.
[5]   In *Lacis v Cashmarts* [1969] 2 QB 400 at 411 (discussed in [1972B] CLJ at 204–208), the Divisional Court thought it an unavoidable and apparently fatal difficulty on a larceny charge that it was impossible to distinguish the goods alleged to be stolen from other goods lawfully taken. The court thought there would be no difficulty under the Theft Act. It is thought that it is as much, or as little, a difficulty for theft as for larceny; and that it is not a real difficulty in either case. The court seems to have overlooked *Tideswell*. Difficulties do arise, of course, if there is a charge of handling and the stolen goods cannot be identified.
[6]   Sale of Goods Act 1979, s. 6.
[7]   Cf *Re Wait* [1927] 1 Ch 606.
[8]   (1873) LR 2 CCR 38, above, para **2–82**.

2–111 A more intractable problem than that of *Tideswell* is presented by *Tomlin*.[1] D was the manager of P's shoe shop. Between stocktaking in March,

1953 and September, 1953 goods to the value of £420 had gone from the shop without the proceeds of sale being accounted for. D's conviction for embezzlement of that sum was upheld. The court[2] rejected the argument that there could be no conviction for embezzling a general deficiency and that embezzlement of specific sums on specific dates must be proved. Clearly in cases of this kind it is virtually impossible to prove that D took the money for a particular pair of shoes and put it straight into his pocket; and it is submitted that the defence that there can be no theft of a general deficiency would fail under the Theft Act. D has not in fact appropriated "a deficiency"; he has appropriated a sum of money, no doubt on a number of different occasions, but between specific dates. Thus far *Tomlin* should present no problems; but a further point which was not argued is not easily solved. On the evidence it is very difficult to see how the jury could have been satisfied beyond reasonable doubt that D took money and not shoes.[3] If D has appropriated shoes, it is difficult to see how he can properly be convicted on an indictment alleging that he stole money, even to the same value. If the jury are satisfied that he took the shoes or the money it may well be that, in practice, they will convict him of stealing the money if that is what he is charged with and they think it the more likely event; but strictly speaking, they ought not to do so unless satisfied beyond reasonable doubt; and, if the defence is raised, it would seem that the judge would be bound so to direct the jury.

---

[1]   [1954] 2 QB 274, [1954] 2 All ER 272.
[2]   Following *Balls* (1871) LR 1 CCR 328. In substance, such an indictment alleges an indefinite number of offences but it is not bad for duplicity: Archbold 1–144; *Cain* [1983] Crim LR 802, CA. Cf *DPP v McCabe* [1992] Crim LR 885, DC.
[3]   Or that he took the money before he put it into the till (embezzlement) and not after (larceny). As both types of appropriation are now theft, this problem need not be pursued.

2–112   There are other instances of dishonest profit-making which may be morally indistinguishable from theft but which are not punishable under the Act because of absence of an appropriation of any specific thing. For example, an employer withholds part of his servant's wages as a contribution to a pension fund and dishonestly omits to make that contribution. However, the employer may possibly now be guilty of inducing the employee by deception to forgo payment of the portion of his wages, contrary to 1978, s. 2 (1) (b).[1] Finally, there is the example discussed *obiter* in *Tideswell*:

> "Suppose the owner of a flock of sheep were to offer to sell, and a purchaser agreed to buy, the whole flock at so much a head, the owner leaving it to his bailiff to count the sheep and ascertain the exact number of the flock, and subsequently the purchaser was to fraudulently arrange with the bailiff that whereas there were in fact thirty sheep they should be counted as twenty-five and the purchaser should be charged with twenty-five only, there would be no larceny, because the property would have passed to the purchaser before the fraudulent agreement was entered into."[2]

If the property in the whole flock had passed, then it might be argued that there was no appropriation of "property belonging to another". The answer is that the owner retained his lien on the whole flock for the unpaid part of the true price, and that the bailiff appropriated it by delivering the sheep. Whether the property would have passed before the appropriation is, however, less clear than the learned judges appear to have thought; for, under the Sale of Goods Act 1979, s. 18, r 3, where "the seller is bound to weigh, measure, test, or *do some other act or thing* with reference to the goods for the purpose of ascertaining the price, the property does not pass until such thing be done, and the buyer has notice thereof ".

If the bailiff agreed to deliver the whole flock of sheep before he counted them the agreement would be a sufficient act of appropriation of P's property.[3]

When the bailiff accounted to the owner for the price of 25 sheep, he would be guilty of dishonestly inducing him by deception to forgo payment for the other five, contrary to 1978, s. 2 (1) (b);[4] and he and the purchaser would be guilty of a conspiracy to commit that offence.[5]

---

[1] Below, para **4–95**.
[2] Per Lord Alverstone CJ [1905] 2 KB 273 at 277; see to the same effect, Channell J, ibid at 279.
[3] Cf *Rogers v Arnott*, above, para **2–33**.
[4] Below, para **4–95**.
[5] Cf *Ayres* [1984] 1 All ER 619, HL.

---

2   THE MENS REA OF THEFT

2–113   The changes made by the 1968 Act in the *mens rea* of theft were less significant than the fundamental reforms of the *actus reus*. The characteristics of the old law were:

(i) The stealing need not be done *lucri causa*, that is, it was unnecessary to prove that D intended to make any kind of profit for himself or another.

(ii) It must be done "fraudulently"; and

(iii) without a claim of right made in good faith; and

(iv) with intent permanently to deprive the owner of his property.

These characteristics were broadly preserved and must be proved by the Crown. Inferences may be drawn from D's conduct but it is plain, and must be made plain to a jury, that the question is as to the state of D's mind.[1] By s. 1 (2):

"It is immaterial whether the appropriation is made with a view to gain, or is made for the thief's own benefit."

Thus (to take the facts of pre-Theft Act cases) if D takes P's letters and puts them down a lavatory or backs P's horse down a mine shaft he is guilty of theft notwithstanding the fact that he intends only loss to P and no gain to himself or anyone else. It might be thought that these instances could safely and more appropriately have been left to other branches of the criminal law – that of criminal damage to property for instance. But there are possible cases where there is no such damage or destruction of the thing as would found a charge under another Act. For example, D takes P's diamond and flings it into a deep pond. The diamond lies unharmed in the pond and a prosecution for criminal damage would fail. It seems clearly right that D should be guilty of theft.

---

[1] *Ingram* [1975] Crim LR 457, CA (defence of absent-minded taking to charge of shop-lifting). *Small* [1987] Crim LR 777, CA (D, who believes, reasonably or not, that property has been abandoned, does not intend to appropriate property belonging to another, or permanently to deprive).

A. DISHONESTY REBUTTED WHERE SECTION 2 APPLIES

2–114   By s. 2 of the Act:

"(1) A person's appropriation of property belonging to another is not to be regarded as dishonest –

(a) if he appropriates the property in the belief that he has in law the right to deprive the other of it, on behalf of himself or of a third person; or

(b) if he appropriates the property in the belief that he would have the other's consent if the other knew of the appropriation and the circumstances of it; or

(c) (except where the property came to him as trustee or personal representative) if he appropriates the property in the belief that the person to whom the property belongs cannot be discovered by taking reasonable steps.

(2) A person's appropriation of property belonging to another may be dishonest notwithstanding that he is willing to pay for the property."

(a)   Belief in the right to deprive

2–115   D is not dishonest if he believes, whether reasonably or not, that he has the legal right[1] to do the act which is alleged to constitute an appropriation of the property of another. This is in accordance with the old law of larceny. In spite of the courts' general insistence on reasonableness when defences of "mistake" were raised, it never seems to have been doubted that a claim of right afforded a defence, even though it was manifestly unreasonable.[2]

The onus is clearly on the Crown to prove a dishonest intention and, therefore, if the jury are of the opinion that it is reasonably possible that D believed that he had the right to do what he did, they should acquit.

---

[1]   It is irrelevant that no such right exists in law. A dictum to the contrary in *Gott v Measures* [1948] 1 KB 234, [1947] 2 All ER 609, is irreconcilable with the decision in *Bernhard* (below).

[2]   *Bernhard* [1938] 2 KB 264, CCA; below, para **10–31**.

2–116   The Act refers specifically to a right *in law*. This does not *necessarily* exclude a belief in a merely moral right.[1] The common law, that taking another's property is not justifiable, even where it is necessary to avoid starvation,[2] suggests that even the strongest moral claim to deprive another is not enough; but, if it is now a jury question,[3] there is no law to this effect and a jury would be likely to find that a truly starving person was not dishonest.

It is made clear that a belief in the legal right of another will negative dishonesty, just as it amounted to a claim of right under the law of larceny.[4] If D, acting for the benefit of E, were to take property from P, wrongly but honestly believing that E was entitled to it, he would clearly not be guilty of theft.

---

[1]   A belief in a moral right was not a defence to larceny: *Harris v Harrison* [1963] Crim LR 497, DC. Cf Williams *CLGP* 322.

[2]   1 Hale PC 54; *Dudley and Stephens* (1884) 14 QBD 273, CCR; *Southwark London Borough Council v Williams* [1971] Ch 734 at 744. But cf the recently discovered defence of "duress of circumstances", *Conway* [1989] QB 290, [1988] 3 All ER 1025, CA.

[3]   *Ghosh* [1982] QB 1053, [1982] 2 All ER 689, CA, below, para **2–122**. Cf *Close* [1977] Crim LR 107 (employee paying employer's debt in kind by taking employer's property without consent apparently held not to be dishonest by jury).

[4]   *Williams* [1962] Crim LR 111.

(b)   Belief that the person to whom the property belongs cannot be discovered by taking reasonable steps

2–117   Though the Act makes no reference to finding, this is obviously intended to preserve the substance of the common law[1] rule relating to finding. The finder who appropriates property commits the *actus reus* of theft (assuming that the property does belong to someone and has not been abandoned) but is not dishonest unless he believes the owner can be discovered by taking reasonable steps.

The important change in the law of finding made by the Act has already been dealt with.[2] At common law, if D's finding was innocent (either because he did not believe that the owner could be discovered by taking reasonable steps or because he intended to return the thing to the owner when he took it) no subsequent dishonest appropriation of the thing could make him guilty of larceny; but now, in such a case, he will be guilty of theft by virtue of s. 3 (1).[3]

It should be stressed that the question is one of D's actual belief, not whether it is a reasonable belief. If D, wrongly and unreasonably, supposed that the only way in which he could locate the owner of property he had found, would be to insert a full-page advertisement in *The Times*, he would have to be acquitted unless that course were a reasonable one to take, which would depend upon the value of the property and all the surrounding circumstances.

---

[1]   *Thurborn* (1849) 1 Den 387.
[2]   Above, para **2–31**.
[3]   Above, para **2–03**.

2–118   While this provision is intended mainly for the case of finding it is not confined to that case and there are other instances where it would be useful. Suppose that P arranges with D that D shall gratuitously store P's furniture in D's house. P leaves the town and D loses touch with him. Some years later D, needing the space in his house and being unable to locate P, sells the furniture.[1] This is undoubtedly an appropriation of the property of another and D is civilly liable to P in conversion; but he appears to be saved from any possibility of conviction of theft by s. 2 (1) (c).[2] Though the purchase money probably belongs to P,[3] D's immunity under the Act must extend to the proceeds of sale.

---

[1]   Cf *Sachs v Miklos* [1948] 2 KB 23, [1948] 1 All ER 67, CA; *Munro v Wilmott* [1949] 1 KB 295, [1948] 2 All ER 983.
[2]   The bailee who disposes of uncollected goods under Sch 1 of the Torts (Interference with Goods) Act 1977 will not usually be able to rely on this provision, for he will know where the owner is; but since he is "entitled . . . to sell the goods", it is submitted that there is no *actus reus*. See above, para **2–25**.
[3]   In equity, if not in law: *Taylor v Plumer* (1815) 3 M & S 562 discussed by Goode (1976) 92 LQR 360, 376 and by Khurshid and Matthews (1979) 95 LQR 79.

2–119   Where the property came to D as a trustee or personal representative and he appropriates it, he may be dishonest even though he believes that the person to whom the property belongs cannot be discovered by taking reasonable steps. The point seems to be that the trustee or personal representative can never be personally entitled to the property (unless it is specifically so provided by the trust instrument or the will) for, if the beneficiaries are extinct or undiscoverable, the Crown will be entitled to the beneficial interest as *bona vacantia*. If the trustee or personal representative appropriates the property to his own use, honestly believing that he is entitled to do so, then it is submitted that he must be acquitted. But if he knows that he has no right to do this and that the property in the last resort belongs to the Crown, he commits theft, from the beneficiaries if they are in fact discoverable and, if not, from the Crown.

(c) Dishonest appropriation, notwithstanding payment

2–120   Section 2 (2) is intended to deal with the kind of situation where D takes bottles of milk from P's doorstep but leaves the full price there. Certainly

71

D has no claim of right and he intends to deprive P permanently of his property. Doubts had, however, arisen as to whether this was dishonest.[1] This subsection resolves them. The mere fact of payment does not negative dishonesty but the jury are entitled to take into account all the circumstances and these may be such that even an intention to pay for property, let alone actual payment,[2] may negative dishonesty. The fact of payment may be cogent evidence where D's defence is that he believed P would have consented. D takes milk bottles from P's unattended milk-cart and leaves the price. He says that he assumed that P would have been very happy to sell him the milk had he been there, but that he had not time to wait for P to return. If D is believed – and the fact of repayment would be persuasive evidence – it would seem that he has no dishonest intent.

---

[1]   Cf Hawkins 1 PC c. 34, s. 7; Blackstone *Commentaries* IV 243; Russell 855–856.
[2]   *Boggeln v Williams* [1978] 2 All ER 1061, below, para **2–121**.

B.   DISHONESTY WHERE SECTION 2 DOES NOT APPLY

2–121   Section 2 provides for three situations which do not amount to dishonesty and one situation which may. But there are many other cases where it is necessary to decide whether the defendant was dishonest and the Act gives no guidance about these. A common occurrence, with which many of the leading cases are concerned, is that of an employee who takes money from his employer's till, knowing that he is forbidden to do so but intending to replace the money as soon as he can.[1] He is charged with stealing the particular notes and coins which he took from the till and there is no doubt that he has the required intention permanently to deprive his employer of these.[2] The circumstances may vary widely – the amount may be large or small, D may believe that he will be able to repay the money almost immediately, or after some longer period or he may have just a faint hope of being able to do so one day, and his purpose in taking the money may be good or bad. But the only question in each case is whether he did so "dishonestly". The meaning of this word has caused the greatest difficulty. Under the Larceny Act the taking had to be done "fraudulently and without a claim of right". It is not clear that the word "fraudulently" played any important role. Indeed, a good deal of effort was expended in trying to determine what, if anything, it added to "without a claim of right". The CLRC in their *Eighth Report*[3] seem, surprisingly, to have overlooked this fact and to have proceeded on the assumption that the word had some large though unspecified role to play. They thought that "dishonestly" was a better word than "fraudulently", not because its meaning was any different, but because it is more easily understood.

> "'Dishonestly' seems to us a better word than 'fraudulently'. The question Was this 'dishonest?' is easier for a jury to answer than the question Was this 'fraudulent'? 'Dishonesty' is something which laymen can easily recognise when they see it, whereas 'fraud' may seem to involve technicalities which have to be explained by a lawyer."

This suggests that it is for jurors to decide whether "this" is dishonest. Of course, it is for jurors to decide all questions of fact, including the state of mind of the defendant – what was his intention and belief, including his belief as to his legal rights. But, under the Larceny Act, it was probably for the judge to say whether that state of mind, when ascertained, was to be characterised in law as "fraudulent".[4] If so, the substitution of "dishonestly" for "fraudulently" led to an important change in the law. Possibly influenced by the above misleading passage in the Report, the Court of Appeal in *Feely*[5] held that it is for the jury in each case to decide, not only what the defendant's state of mind was, but also, subject to s. 2, whether that state of mind is to be categorised as dishonest.

> "Jurors, when deciding whether an appropriation was dishonest can be reasonably expected to, and should, apply the current standards of ordinary decent people. In their own lives they have to decide what is and what is not dishonest. We can see no reason why, when in a jury box, they should require the help of a judge to tell them what amounts to dishonesty."

The court was certainly much influenced by the opinion of the House of Lords in *Brutus v Cozens*[6] that the meaning of an ordinary word of the English language is not a question of law for the judge but one of fact for the jury. "Dishonestly" is such a word and so it was for the jury to attribute to it such meaning as they thought proper. A major difficulty about this view is that juries – and magistrates – are likely to give different answers on facts which are indistinguishable.[7] *Feely* at least provided a standard – that of "ordinary decent people", as understood by the jury – against which the defendant's intentions and beliefs were to be tested. Other cases, however, went further. In *Gilks*,[8] D agreed that it would be dishonest if his grocer gave him too much change and he kept it but he said bookmakers are "a race apart" and there was nothing dishonest about keeping the overpayment in that case. The judge invited the jury to "try and place yourselves in [D's] position at that time and answer the question whether in your view he thought he was acting dishonestly". The Court of Appeal thought this was a proper and sufficient direction, agreeing apparently that, if D may have held the belief he claimed, the prosecution had not established dishonesty. This applied, not the standards of ordinary decent people, but the defendant's own standards, however deplorable they might be. In *Boggeln v Williams*,[9] the court expressly rejected an argument that D's belief as to his own honesty was irrelevant and held that, on the contrary, it was crucial. D, whose electricity had been cut off, reconnected the supply through the meter. He knew that the electricity board did not consent to his doing so, but he notified them and believed, not unreasonably, that he would be able to pay at the due time. It was held that the question was whether he believed that what he did was honest.

---

[1]   *Williams* [1953] 1 QB 660, [1953] 1 All ER 1068, CCA; *Cockburn* [1968] 1 All ER 466, [1968] 1 WLR 281, CA; *Feely* [1973] QB 530, [1973] 1 All ER 341, CA.
[2]   *Velumyl* [1989] Crim LR 299 and commentary.
[3]   Para 39.
[4]   *Williams* [1953] 1 QB 660, CCA; *Cockburn* [1968] 1 All ER 466, CA.
[5]   [1973] QB 530, [1973] 1 All ER 341, [1973] Crim LR 193, CA and commentary.
[6]   [1973] AC 854, [1972] 2 All ER 1297, HL.
[7]   Cf *Sinclair v Neighbour* [1967] 2 QB 279, [1966] 3 All ER 988, CA.
[8]   Above, para **2–87**; [1972] 3 All ER 280 at 283.
[9]   [1978] 2 All ER 1061, [1978] Crim LR 242 and commentary.

2–122   A further complexity was introduced in *McIvor*,[1] where the Court of Appeal said that the test of dishonesty in conspiracy to defraud was different from that to be applied in theft. The leading case is now *Ghosh*.[2] The Court of Appeal rejected the distinction between conspiracy and theft. The same test of dishonesty is to be applied in both. *Ghosh* itself was a case of obtaining by deception contrary to s. 15 of the 1968 Act; so it is now reasonably clear that the same principle applies throughout the Theft Acts and the common law of conspiracy to defraud as well as other statutory offences such as fraudulent trading under the Companies Act 1985. The test is twofold.

(i) Was what was done dishonest according to the ordinary standards of reasonable and honest people? If no, D is not guilty. If yes –

(ii) Did the defendant realise that reasonable and honest people regard what he did as dishonest? If yes, he is guilty; if no, he is not.

This gets away from the extreme and unacceptable subjectivism of *Gilks* and *Boggeln v Williams*. D is no longer to be judged by his own standards; but there are other difficulties.

Lord Lane CJ thought that this formula would dispose of the "Robin Hood defence", but it is not clear that it does so.[3] The defendant would have to be acquitted "if the jury think *either* (a) that what Robin Hood did (rob the rich to feed the poor) was not dishonest *or* (b) that Robin Hood thought the plain man would not consider what he did as dishonest". The same might be said of a more modern example, that of the member of an animal's welfare association who takes beagles from a research laboratory because he knows they are being used in experiments. He would certainly not regard his own conduct as dishonest and so would escape under the rule as stated in *Gilks*. He might still do so under *Ghosh*. A jury of animal lovers would be likely to agree with him; and it might be difficult to satisfy any jury that the defendant did not believe that all right-thinking people would agree with him. Members of animal welfare organisations probably do so believe. But this surely should be theft. One who deliberately deprives another of his property should not be able to escape liability because of his disapproval, however profound and morally justified, of the lawful use to which that property was being put by its owner. In deciding whether a certain state of mind should be regarded as dishonest it is not irrelevant to consider how the matter will be regarded by the ordinary decent citizen who is the victim of the offence. The owners of the beagles will certainly consider that their property has been stolen, even though they are fully aware of the state of mind of the takers. The law fails in one of its purposes if it does not afford protection to a person against what he quite reasonably regards as a straightforward case of theft.

The Court of Appeal has frequently stressed that it is not necessary to give a *Ghosh* direction to the jury in every case. If there is any evidence to suggest that D's attitude was, "Whatever others may think, *I* did not consider this dishonest", the direction must be given. Where there is no such evidence it is probably unnecessary.[4]

---

[1]   [1982] 1 All ER 491, [1982] 1 WLR 409, CA.

[2]   [1982] QB 1053, [1982] 2 All ER 689.

[3]   Elliott "Dishonesty in Theft: A Dispensable Concept" [1982] Crim LR 395 at 398.

[4]   *Price* (1990) 90 Cr App Rep 409; *Brennen* [1990] Crim LR 118 (handling); *Ravenshad* [1990] Crim LR 398, CA; *Miles* [1992] Crim LR 657 (fraudulent trading).

2–123   Before *Ghosh*, the Supreme Court of Victoria had refused to follow *Feely*, when construing the identical provision in Victorian legislation. In *Salvo*,[1] Fullagar J, with whom Murphy J seems to have agreed in substance, held that it was the duty of the judge to explain to the jury what "dishonestly" meant; and he should tell them that it means "with disposition to defraud, i.e. with disposition to withhold from a person what is his right". There are two difficulties about this interpretation. The first is that it seems to add nothing to what is expressly stated in s. 2 (1) (a) – i.e. a person who has a claim of legal right is not dishonest – and leaves no function for the word "dishonestly".[2] Secondly, it seems too narrow as a matter of policy.[3] It leads to the conviction of D who, knowing that he has no right to do so, takes P's money with intent to spend it but with the certainty (in his own mind) that he will be able to replace it before it is missed, so that P will never know anything about it and suffer no detriment whatever.

1   [1980] VR 401.
2   Williams *TBCL* 730.
3   Elliott [1982] Crim LR at 406.

2–124   Elliott's solution is to dispense with the word "dishonestly" altogether but to add a new subsection (3) to s. 2:

"No appropriation of property belonging to another which is not detrimental to the interests of the other in a significant practical way shall amount to theft of the property."[1]

This solution would require legislation and that seems very unlikely. A reconsideration by the House of Lords is, however, a practical possibility and so many diverse views have now been expressed about the concept of dishonesty, in both judgments and academic writings, that the House might well be disposed to look at the matter *de novo*. It would be possible to reinterpret "dishonestly" to mean "knowing that the appropriation will or may be detrimental to the interests of the owner in a significant practical way". It should be for the jury to determine whether the result foreseen by the defendant was "detrimental" or not. The words, "in a significant practical way", might be regarded as no more than an application of the well-known *de minimis* principle to the law of theft.

Unlike Elliott's proposal, this would excuse a person who wrongly supposed that his appropriation would have no practical effect; but that is consistent with the subjective meaning which "dishonestly" is plainly intended to bear and, it is submitted, is desirable in principle. It would result in the conviction of Robin Hood, the beagle-taker and the fraudulent sub-postmistress[2] who knew she was taking a risk by "borrowing" the post office's money. It would let out the employee who "borrows" £5 from the till when closing the shop on Saturday afternoon, having no doubt that he will be able to replace it when he opens up on Monday morning, only to be robbed and rendered penniless on his way home from the pub on Saturday night. This proposal goes back substantially to the explanation offered many years ago for the meaning of "fraudulently" in the Larceny Act 1916[3] and to that made in the first two editions of this book.[4]

1   [1982] Crim LR at 410.
2   *Williams* [1953] 1 QB 660, [1953] 1 All ER 1068.
3   "The Fraudulent Sub-Postmistress" [1955] Crim LR 18.
4   1st edn, 41–44.

C.   THE INTENTION OF PERMANENTLY DEPRIVING THE OTHER

2–125   The Theft Act preserves the rule of the common law and of the Larceny Act 1916 that appropriating the property of another with the intention of depriving him only temporarily of it is not stealing.[1] English law, in general, recognises no *furtum usus* – the stealing of the use or enjoyment of a chattel or other property. This is subject to two exceptions which are considered below. The first exception concerns the removal of articles from places open to the public[2] and is a creation of the 1968 Act. The second exception, in so far as it relates to motor vehicles, has existed in the Road Traffic Acts since 1935, but the extension to other "conveyances" is new.[3] Outside these cases the law seems to remain substantially unchanged; so that, if D takes P's horse without authority and rides it for an afternoon, a week or a month, he commits no offence under the Act and, probably, no offence against the criminal law (though a civil trespass) if he has an intention to return the horse at the end of this period.[4]

---

1   *Warner* (1970) 55 Cr App Rep 93.
2   Section 11, below, para **7–01**.
3   Section 12, below, para **8–01**.
4   *Neal v Gribble* [1978] RTR 409, below, para **8–07**.

(a)   Deprivation of persons with limited interests

2–126   Theft may be committed against a person having possession or control of property or having any proprietary right or interest in it.[1] The element of permanence relates to the deprivation of P, not to the proposed benefit to D. It would seem clear, therefore, that where P has an interest less than full ownership, an intention by D to deprive him of the whole of that interest, whatever it might be, is sufficient. If, as D knows, P has hired a car from Q for a month, and D takes it, intending to return it to Q after the month has expired, this must be theft from P, for he is permanently deprived of his whole interest in the property, but it is not theft from Q for he, plainly, is not permanently deprived. It should be stressed that the question is always one of intention; so if, in the above example, D, when he took the car, believed P to be the owner, he would apparently not commit theft even though P was, in fact, deprived of his whole interest.

This is capable of producing rather odd results where the interest of the person deprived is a very small one. O writes a letter and gives it to P to deliver by hand to Q. D intercepts P and takes the letter from him. Having read it, he delivers it (as he always intended) to Q. This could be theft of the letter from P (though not from O or Q) since P is permanently deprived of his possession or control of it. If the letter is taken by force or threat of force, it will be robbery from P.

---

1   Section 5 (1), above, para **2–55**.

(b)   Section 6 and the common law

2–127   The draft bill proposed by the CLRC contained no definition or elaboration of the phrase "intention of permanently depriving". The Committee were well aware of the existing case-law and must have assumed that it would continue to be applied. The government had other ideas and introduced a clause which, after much amendment, became s. 6.[1] At common law and under the Larceny Acts the phrase was held to include the cases where –
   (i) D took P's property with intention that P should have it back only by paying for it – e.g. he took P's property so that, pretending that it was his own, he could sell it to P.[2]
   (ii) D took P's property intending to return it to P only when he had completely changed its substance – e.g. D, being employed by P, to melt pig iron, took an axle belonging to P and melted it down in order to increase his output and consequently his earnings;[3] or D wrongfully fed P's oats to P's own horses;[4] or took P's horse intending to kill it and to return the carcase.[5]
   (iii) D took P's property and pawned it, intending to redeem and restore it to P one day but with no reasonable prospects of being able to do so.[6]

Section 6 was apparently intended to cover these cases and no more. But they all related, inevitably, to deprivation of possession of chattels and no consideration was given to the difficulty of applying the concept of intent to deprive to things in action which, by definition, are not possessed.

The section is expressed to apply only to the offence of theft, but obtaining by deception contrary to s. 15 also requires an intent permanently to deprive. Section 15 (3) provides that s. 6 shall apply for the purposes of s. 15, with the necessary adaptation of the reference to appropriating, as it applies for the purposes of s. 1. As virtually all cases under s. 15 are, prima facie, also cases of theft, it would be highly unsatisfactory if different tests were applicable.

As Professor Spencer has written,[7] and the Court of Appeal was inclined to agree,[8] s. 6 "sprouts obscurities at every phrase". Section 6 (1) provides:

> "A person appropriating property belonging to another without meaning the other permanently to lose the thing itself is nevertheless to be regarded as having the intention of permanently depriving the other of it if his intention is to treat the thing as his own to dispose of regardless of the other's rights, and a borrowing or lending of it may amount to so treating it if, but only if, the borrowing or lending is for a period and in circumstances making it equivalent to an outright taking or disposal."

[1]   See J.R. Spencer "The Metamorphosis of Section 6 of the Theft Act" [1977] Crim LR 653.
[2]   *Hall* (1849) 1 Den 381.
[3]   *Richards* (1844) 1 Car & Kir 532.
[4]   *Morfit* (1816) Russ & Ry 307.
[5]   Cf *Cabbage* (1815) Russ & Ry 292.
[6]   *Phetheon* (1840) 9 C & P 552; *Medland* (1851) 5 Cox CC 292. Cf *Trebilcock* (1858) Dears & B 453 and *Wynn* (1887) 16 Cox CC 231 which are inconclusive on the point.
[7]   Spencer, fn 1.
[8]   *Lloyd* [1985] QB 829 at p 834, CA.

2–128   In *Lloyd*,[1] the Court of Appeal approved academic opinions that s. 6 need be referred to in exceptional cases only and then the question for the jury should not be "worded in terms of the generalities" of the section but be related to the particular facts. The court cited the opinion of Edmund Davies LJ,[2] that "Section 6 . . . gives illustrations, as it were, of what can amount to the dishonest intention demanded by section 1 (1). But it is a misconception to interpret it as watering down section 1", and concluded, "we would try to interpret the section in such a way as to ensure that nothing is construed as an intention permanently to deprive which would not prior to the 1968 Act have been so construed". But before and since *Lloyd* courts have given the words of the section its wider ordinary meaning. In *Downes*,[3] the Court of Appeal held that D committed theft when, being in possession of vouchers belonging to the Inland Revenue and made out in his name, he sold them to others who, as he knew, would submit them to the Revenue so as to obtain tax advantages. The primary reason for the decision was that the document when returned would be in substance a different thing; but the court also held that s. 6 was to be given its ordinary meaning – D intended to treat the vouchers as his own to dispose of regardless of the Revenue's rights. Subsequently, in *Chan Man-sin*'s case,[4] the Privy Council held that, where a company accountant drew a forged cheque on the company's account, there was "ample evidence" of intention permanently to deprive the company of its credit balance, even on the assumption that D contemplated that the fraud would be discovered and the company would lose nothing. He intended to treat the balance as his own to dispose of regardless of the company's rights. *Re Osman*,[5] another case of "theft without loss", is similar. In *Bagshaw*,[6] the Court of Appeal said that the restrictive view taken in *Lloyd* was *obiter* and that "there may be other occasions on which s. 6 applies". Thus the current opinion seems to be that s. 6 is to be given its ordinary meaning (whatever that may be) and is not necessarily restricted to the scope of the common law meaning of the concept. The concept certainly has to be applied to situations which did not arise at common law like the theft of a thing in action. It seems inevitable that it must equally apply to treating a chattel, like the refrigerator in *Bloxham,*[7] as one's own to dispose of, thus extending theft beyond anything contemplated by the CLRC who had no idea that s. 6 was going to be introduced. They contemplated that same concept would be applicable to both s. 1 and s. 15, as was held under the Larceny Act 1916.

1   [1985] QB 829, [1985] 2 All ER 661, CA.
2   *Warner* (1970) 55 Cr App Rep 93 at 97.
3   (1983) 77 Cr App Rep 260, [1983] Crim LR 819, CA and commentary.
4   Above, para **2–54**.
5   Above, para **2–34**.
6   [1988] Crim LR 321.
7   (1943) 29 Cr App Rep 37. Above, para **2–35**.

(c)   Conditional intention to deprive

2–129   In *Easom,*[1] the Court of Appeal said that "a conditional appropriation will not do". The difficulty of supporting this proposition is that all intention is conditional, even though the condition be unexpressed and not present to the mind of the person at that time. D picked up a woman's handbag in a cinema, rummaged through the contents and put it back having taken nothing. The handbag was attached by a thread to a policewoman's wrist. D's conviction for stealing the handbag and the specified contents – tissues, cosmetics, etc. – was quashed because D never had any intention of permanently depriving P of any of those things. It followed that he was not guilty of attempting to steal any of them. No doubt he intended to steal things which were not there – presumably money – and might have been convicted of attempting to steal on a suitably-worded indictment.[2] There was no intention permanently to deprive. Consequently, he was not guilty of attempting to steal the handbag, or the specified contents either. As the chattels were rejected as soon as they were identified, it may be better to say that there was no appropriation, not even a conditional one.

1   [1971] 2 QB 315 at 319, [1971] 2 All ER 945 at 947, CA.
2   See para **2–130**, below.

2–130   In *Husseyn,*[1] DD opened the door of a van in which there was a holdall containing valuable sub-aqua equipment. They were charged with attempted theft of the equipment. The judge directed the jury that they could convict if DD were about to look into the holdall and, if its contents were valuable, to steal it. The Court of Appeal, following *Easom*, held that this was a misdirection: "it cannot be said that one who has it in mind to steal only if what he finds is worth stealing has a present intention to steal". In *Re A-G's References (Nos 1 & 2 of 1979),*[2] the Court of Appeal held these words were applicable only to an indictment which alleged an intent to steal a specific object, such as sub-aqua equipment. It would have been different if the indictment had charged an attempt to steal "some or all of the contents of the holdall" or, in *Easom*, of the handbag. Yet, in *Husseyn*, the sub-aqua equipment *was* the contents of the holdall – there were no other contents; so, according to the court, D was not guilty of attempting to steal the equipment if it was described as such, but he was guilty if it was described as the "contents of the holdall". At that time it was clear law that there could be no conviction for attempting to steal a thing that was not there – it was the sub-aqua equipment or nothing. Since the Criminal Attempts Act 1981,[3] this is no longer so. A person looking for money in an empty handbag might now be convicted of attempting to steal money. The only problem in cases of this kind is one of the form of the indictment. The formula approved in the *A-G's References* is not satisfactory because, in these cases, the defendant did not intend (or it was not proved that he intended) to steal any of the contents. But he undoubtedly intended to steal something – something which was *not* "all or any of the contents".[4] The indictment would be accurate if it alleged simply that D attempted to steal from the handbag, or holdall.[5] This is so whether or not there is anything there that D would have stolen. D's intention to steal anything he finds which he thinks worth stealing is a present intention to steal, at least so far as the law of attempts is concerned. The failure to specify any subject matter cannot be an objection since the 1981 Act.[6]

---

[1] (1978) 67 Cr App Rep 131n, [1978] Crim LR 219, CA and commentary; discussed at [1978] Crim LR 444 and 644.
[2] [1980] QB 180, [1979] 3 All ER 143, [1979] Crim LR 585, CA and commentary.
[3] Smith & Hogan, 304.
[4] Cf *Bayley and Easterbrook* [1980] Crim LR 503, CA and commentary.
[5] Cf *Smith and Smith* [1986] Crim LR 166, CA and commentary; Archbold, 21–82.
[6] Similarly with the law of burglary. Below, para **11–27**. It may be different where the charge is theft. A lorry-driver was held (in a civil action) not guilty of theft of the goods loaded on his lorry when he drove off intending to steal the load "if and when the circumstances were favourable": *Grundy (Teddington) Ltd v Fulton* [1983] 1 Lloyd's Rep 16, CA; but he had assumed a right of the owner (cf *Gomez*) and the only question is whether the conditional intention was enough.

2–131   It is submitted that the better view is that an assumption of ownership, which is conditional because there is an intent to deprive only in a certain event, is theft. For example, D takes P's ring intending to keep it if the stone is a diamond, but otherwise to return it. He takes it to a jeweller who says the stone is paste. D returns the ring to P. It is submitted that he committed theft when he took the ring. The fact that he returned it is relevant only to sentence. In *Easom*,[1] the court said, "if a dishonest postal-sorter picks up a pile of letters intending to steal any which are registered, but, on finding that none are, replaces them, he has stolen nothing". If the postal-sorter were authorised to sort through the letters there would at that time have been no appropriation but he might now be convicted of an attempt to steal registered letters. If he did some unauthorised act, such as taking the letters home, intending to keep any which was registered, it would seem to be the same as the case of the ring.

A similar problem may arise where D takes the property of P, say a ring, intending to claim a reward from P for finding it. If he intends to return the ring in any event and hopes to receive the reward, he is not guilty of stealing the ring though he is about to attempt to obtain by deception – and so to steal – the reward. But if he intends to retain the ring unless he receives the reward, he seems to be in substantially the same situation as the taker who sells the property back to the owner. It might be said, however, that in this example, the taker is not treating the property as his own. There are two possible answers to this: the assertion of a better right to possession might be regarded as treating the property as one's own; or, s. 6 not providing an exclusive definition, this might be regarded as an analogous case falling within the same general principle.

---

[1] Above, para **2–129**.

(d)   Disposition of the property as one's own

2–132   The attribution of an ordinary meaning to the language of s. 6 presents some difficulties.[1] It is submitted, however, that an intention merely to use the thing as one's own regardless of the other's rights is not enough. It adds nothing to "appropriates" since appropriation consists in an assumption of the right of an owner.   The words, "dispose of," are crucial and are, it is submitted, not used in the sense in which a general might "dispose of" his forces but rather in the meaning given by the *Shorter Oxford Dictionary*: "To deal with definitely; to get rid of; to get done with, finish. To make over by way of sale or bargain, sell."[2] In *DPP v Lavender*,[3] however, the Divisional Court seems to have held D's intention to treat the thing as his own, regardless of the owner's rights, as crucial and to have minimised the importance of "to dispose of". D surreptitiously removed two doors from another property belonging to his council landlord to replace doors in the council property he occupied. Did he not in fact treat the doors as the property of the council, like the rest of the premises he occupied? If a secretary surreptitiously swaps her typewriter for the similar model operated by a colleague (because she believes it works better), does she steal the typewriter from her employer? She may well steal it from her colleague whom she does intend to lose her limited interest for ever.

---

[1]   See *Harjindel Atwal* [1989] Crim LR 293 (Judge Fricker QC) and commentary.
[2]   This passage was cited in *Cahill* [1993] Crim LR 141, CA.
[3]   [1994] Crim LR 297.

2–133   It is submitted that, on a similar basis, there is no reason why there should not be a conviction for theft in a case like that of the taker of the Goya from the National Gallery: "I will return the picture when £X is paid to charity." Substantially, the taker is offering to sell the thing back and his case is, in principle, the same as those contemplated by s. 6 (1). Nor should it make any difference that the price demanded is something other than money. "I will return the picture when E (who is imprisoned) is given a free pardon" – this should be sufficient evidence of an intent permanently to deprive.

The general principle might be that it is sufficient that there is an intention that P shall not have the property back unless some consideration is supplied by him or another; or, more generally still, unless some condition is satisfied.

(e)   Borrowing or lending

2–134   Where money or any thing which is consumed by use – like petrol – is "borrowed", the dishonest "borrower" has an intention permanently to deprive even though he intends to replace the money or the article with another which is just as good. He intends to deprive the owner of the specific thing he has appropriated.[1] In the case of a true borrowing it appears that there can be no theft, however dishonest the borrower may be, because, by definition, he does intend to return the specific thing taken. Yet by s. 6 (1), if the borrowing "is for a period and in circumstances making it equivalent to an outright taking . . . ", the borrower may be regarded as having the intention of depriving the owner permanently. This is a rather puzzling provision, because it would seem, prima facie, that borrowing cannot be an "outright taking". Clearly, however, this part of the subsection is intended to do something and, therefore, certain borrowings are to be treated as the equivalent of outright takings. Once this is accepted, it is not difficult to divine the kind of borrowings which are intended to be covered: they are those where the taker intends not to return the thing until the virtue is gone out of it. D takes P's dry battery, intending to return it to P when it is exhausted; or P's season ticket, intending to return it to P when the season is over. Similar in principle are those cases where D intends to return the thing only when it is completely changed in substance.[2]

---

[1]   *Velumyl* [1989] Crim LR 299.
[2]   See cases cited above, para **2–127**. Dicta in *Bagshaw* [1988] Crim LR 321 concerning the "virtue" test seem inappropriate to the facts of that case.

2–135   Where property belonging to another has been entirely deprived of an essential characteristic, which has been described as its "virtue", the matter seems reasonably clear. But what if the virtue has not been entirely eliminated – but very nearly? D takes P's season ticket for Nottingham Forest's matches intending to return it to him in time for the last match of the season. Is this an "outright taking" so as to amount to theft of the ticket? If it is, is it theft if D intends to return the ticket in time for two matches? – or three, four, five or six – where should the line be drawn? The difficulty of drawing a line suggests that it should not be theft of the ticket unless D intends to keep it until it has lost *all* its virtue.[1] This means, of course, that if D takes P's car and keeps it for ten years, he will not be guilty of theft if, when, as he intended all along, he returns it to P, it is still a roadworthy vehicle, though the proportion of its original value which it retains is very small. If it can no longer be described as a car, but is scrap metal, then, if D intended to return it only when it was reduced to this state, he has stolen it.

---

[1]   The difficulty might satisfactorily be overcome in this particular case by holding that the right to see each match is a separate thing in action, of which P is permanently deprived once that match is over. Cf *Chan Wai Lam v R* [1981] Crim LR 497.

2–136   The provision regarding lending appears to contemplate the situation where D is in possession or control of the property and he lends it to another. If D knows that the effect is that P will never get the property back again, he clearly has an intent permanently to deprive. Similarly if D knows that, when P gets the property back again, the virtue will have gone out of it, this is equivalent to an outright disposal. The examples of the dry battery, season ticket, etc.[1] are applicable here, though they seem less likely to arise in the context of lending than of borrowing.

---

[1]   Above, para **2–134**.

(f)   Parting with property under a condition as to its return

2–137   Section 6 (2) provides:

"Without prejudice to the generality of subsection (1) above, where a person, having possession or control (lawfully or not) of property belonging to another, parts with the property under a condition as to its return which he *may not* be able to perform, this (if done for purposes of his own and without the other's authority) amounts to treating the property as his own to dispose of regardless of the other's rights."

This is clearly intended to deal with the kind of case which gave difficulty under the old law, where D, being in possession or control of P's goods, pawns them. If D had no intention of ever redeeming the goods, there was no problem – he was guilty of larceny and he would now clearly be guilty of theft, apart from s. 6 (2). But what if D does intend to redeem? The answer now is that if he knows that he may not be able to do so, he is guilty of theft. The subsection does not seem to permit of a distinction between the case where D knows that the chances of his being able to redeem are slight and the case where he believes the chances are high; in either case, the condition is one which he knows he may not be able to perform.

2–138   The common law cases suggested that it was theft, notwithstanding an intention to redeem, if the pawner had no reasonable prospects of being able to do so.[1] It is submitted, however, that the question under the Theft Act is a purely subjective one: D must *intend* to dispose of the property regardless of the other's rights, and s. 6 (2) merely describes what he must intend. If then D is in fact *convinced*, however unreasonably, that he will be able to redeem the property, he does not come within the terms of s. 6 (2) because he intends *to dispose of it under a condition which he will be able to perform.*

This is not necessarily conclusive, however, for subsection (2) is without prejudice to the generality of subsection (1); and it might reasonably be argued that even the pawner who is convinced of his power to redeem intends to treat the thing as his own to dispose of, regardless of the other's rights. This would be equally true if the pawner in fact had power to redeem; and, since pawning is not "lending", there is no need to prove that it was equivalent to an outright disposal. The difficulty about this interpretation is that it makes it very difficult to see why s. 6 (2) is there at all; if D's disposition of property under a condition which he is able to perform is theft under subsection (1), why refer specifically to the case of a condition which he may not be able to perform? On the whole it would seem that the better approach is to hold that one who is certain of his ability to redeem does not have an intent permanently to deprive. Such a person, in some circumstances, may well be found by the jury not to be dishonest. For example D, a tenant for a year of a furnished house, being temporarily short of money, pawns the landlord's clock, knowing that he will certainly be able and intending to redeem it before the year expires. A prosecution for theft of the clock should fail on the grounds both that he is not dishonest and that he has no intent permanently to deprive. The case might formerly have been dealt with as one of unlawful pawning.[2]

---

[1]   *Phetheon* (1840) 9 C & P 552; *Medland* (1851) 5 Cox CC 292. *Trebilcock* (1858) Dears & B 453 and *Wynn* (1887) 16 Cox CC 231 are inconclusive.

[2]   Pawnbrokers Act 1872, s. 33 was repealed from 1 August 1977, and not replaced by the Consumer Credit Act 1974.

(g)   Abandonment of property

2–139   Early nineteenth-century cases on the taking of horses decided that there was no intent permanently to deprive, although D turned the horse loose some considerable distance from the place where he took it.[1] In the conditions of those times it might be supposed that D must have known that there was a substantial risk that P would not get his property back. This lenient attitude may be contrasted with that adopted in the pawning cases,[2] and the right course would seem to be to attach no importance to these old decisions in the interpretation of the Theft Act.

The case where the property is abandoned is not within s. 6 (2) for D does not part with the property under a condition. He might, however, be regarded as having an intention to treat the thing as his own to dispose of regardless of the other's rights. If D borrows the thing and then leaves it where he knows the owner or someone on his behalf will certainly find it, he clearly does not have an intent permanently to deprive. But if he abandons the thing in circumstances such that he knows that it is quite uncertain whether the owner will ever get it back or not, then it would not be unreasonable to hold that he has an intention to treat the thing as his own to dispose of regardless of the other's rights. By analogy to the pawning case discussed above, it would seem that it should be immaterial whether D believes that the chances of P's getting the property back are large or small; it is sufficient that he intends to risk the loss of P's property. Suppose, for example, that D, being caught in the rain when leaving a restaurant in London, takes an umbrella to shelter him on his way to the station and abandons it in the train on his arrival at Nottingham. He should be guilty of theft.

---

[1]   *Phillips and Strong* (1801) 2 East PC 662; *Crump* (1825) 1 C & P 658; *Addis* (1844) 1 Cox CC 78.
[2]   Above, para **2–138**.

(h)   Stealing or obtaining cheques

2–140   Since the 1968 Act, the requirement of an intent permanently to deprive has been thought to cause peculiar difficulty in relation to the stealing and obtaining of cheques. Before 1968 the courts seem to have had no difficulty in holding that a person could steal a cheque or obtain it by false pretences.[1] Since 1968 courts and commentators alike have tended to consider the question of obtaining cheques primarily as one of obtaining a thing in action, apparently losing sight of the fact that cheques were undoubtedly the subject of theft and obtaining by false pretences before there was any possibility of committing an offence by stealing or obtaining a thing in action as such.[2] Most judges and writers have treated the cheque as either a thing in action or "a piece of paper"; but the "valuable security" referred to in (inter alia) ss.13 (larceny in dwelling-houses), 14 (larceny from the person) and 32 (false pretences) of the Larceny Act 1916, though not a thing in action but something tangible (something that could be stolen from the person or from a house), was not a mere piece of paper, any more than a key is just a piece of metal or a swipe card is a piece of plastic, or a theatre or railway ticket a piece of pasteboard. The physical thing was one which had special properties.[3] It is not any piece of paper which will cause, say, a bank clerk to hand over £1,000; but a cheque will do that. Of course the cheque *is* (i) a piece of paper which (ii) *creates* a thing in action but it is also (certainly if given for value) (iii) a valuable security. The Theft Act 1968 does not specifically refer to valuable securities as property which may be stolen or obtained, any more than it refers to title deeds to land, or dogs, or other things which the Larceny Acts had to mention expressly because they could not be stolen at common law. There is no longer any need to refer to any of these, because they are all "property", as widely defined for the purposes of theft and obtaining by s. 4 (1) of the 1968 Act. Just as a dog or title deeds may now be stolen, or obtained, so may a valuable security; and that means, not the thing in action, nor a mere piece of paper, but the instrument, the physical thing with certain writing on it. And, if it may be stolen, it may also be obtained by deception. It is certain that the wide definition of property in the Theft Act 1968 was intended to include anything which could be stolen or obtained under the Larceny Acts or at common law.

---

[1]   *Pople* [1951] 1 KB 53, sub nom *Smith* [1950] 2 All ER 679. See also *Essex* (1857) 7 Cox CC 384, CCCR (conviction quashed on other grounds); *Hudson* [1943] KB 458, CCA and *Arnold* (27 June 1997, unreported), CA.

²   This trend seems to have begun with *Duru* [1973] 3 All ER 715 and continued through the decision of the House of Lord in *Preddy* [1996] AC 815, [1996] 3 All ER 481, below, para **4–60**. The House at last rejected the erroneous notion that D obtains a thing in action from P when he induces him to draw a cheque in his favour; but it did not (and was not called on to) recognise that, though D does not obtain a thing in action from P, he obtains something more than a piece of paper from him.

³   "A cheque is not a piece of paper and no more. . . . It is a piece of paper with certain special characteristics" *Kohn* (1979) 69 Cr App Rep 395 at 409, per Lord Lane CJ.

2–141   It is important to note that not all cheques do create things in action. An action on the cheque will lie only if it is given for valuable consideration – i.e., any consideration sufficient to support a simple contract or an antecedent liability.¹ If D induces P to make him a gift of a cheque for £50, that cheque does not create any thing in action – but it is still a cheque and, it is submitted, a valuable security.² Unless P stops it, the cheque will enable D to deprive P of £50. When D gets his hands on it, he has a valuable, tangible thing in his possession. It is worth noting that, because a cheque need not be a thing in action, it is immaterial that the drawer's promise is voidable for fraud.³ The cheque remains a valuable security because it is an effective key to the drawer's bank account. When D obtains the document he has acquired a tangible thing which is of real value to him, and to P, who has parted with it. In *Kohn*⁴ the Court of Appeal held that where D dishonestly drew a cheque on a company's account for his own purposes he was guilty of two thefts – (i) of the cheque and (ii) of the thing in action consisting in the company's bank account which the honouring of the cheque destroyed in whole or in part.⁵

¹   Bills of Exchange Act 1882, s. 27 (1). Is a cheque paying housing benefit or other social security payment a thing in action? Cf. *Davis* (1988) 88 Cr App R 347, [1988] Crim LR 762, CA.

²   In *Yates* (1827) 1 Moody 170 it was held that an unstamped order was not a valuable security because it would have been illegal for the drawer to pay out on it; but there is nothing illegal in honouring a cheque given without consideration. A document *authorising* the payment of money, which such a cheque does, is a valuable security: Theft Act 1968, s. 20 (3).

³   In *Danger* (1857) 7 Cox CC 303 (below, para **4–57**) Lord Campbell CJ said at p 309: "We should not have given weight to the argument, that even in the prisoner's hands it was not a valuable security by reason of the fraud which would prevent him from enforcing it."

⁴   (1979) 69 Cr App Rep 395.

⁵   Arlidge and Parry, 3–010, criticise the case because "the court appears to have treated the cheques as *intangible* property"; but it is submitted that Lane CJ distinguished clearly between the "cheque counts" and the "thing in action counts" (p 410). The relevance, for the former counts, of the paper ceasing "to be a thing in action" was that the tangible thing, the paper, changed its character on being stamped, so that the thing appropriated was (like a melted-down key) not the thing returned to the owner. While both thefts are undoubtedly committed where P's account is in credit, it would be wrong to punish D twice for what is, in substance, a single offence. If P's account is overdrawn, this in no way impairs the conviction for theft of the cheque.   The real value of the valuable security is the factor which ought to be taken into account in sentencing, not the value of a mere piece of paper.

(i)   Theft of P's bank balance (or right to overdraw)

2–142   When D has dishonestly obtained a cheque from P, he usually acquires a voidable right of action against P on the cheque. When he presents the cheque and it is honoured, any right of action he had against P terminates. If his account is overdrawn and the cheque merely reduces his indebtedness, the property is extinguished. If his account is in credit he has converted his own property (his right of action against P) into another form. The indebtedness of D's bank to D has been increased by the amount of the cheque and D's thing in action is now his right to sue his own bank for the credit balance represented by the cheque. This new thing in action belongs, in law if not in equity, to D.

Whether P has an equitable interest in it is considered below. But, P's own bank balance, a thing in action belonging to him, is debited with the amount of the cheque. D has not obtained anything from P[1] but it seems that, by his use of the cheque – the key to P's bank balance – he has appropriated that balance, or P's right to overdraw, as the case may be. Since *Gomez*, it is no longer an objection that D's dealing with the cheque signed by P was authorised by P. It is theft.

---

[1]   This is the effect of *Preddy* [1996] 3 All ER 481, HL, below, para **4-60.**

2–143   *Where D procures a transfer of funds by telegraphic transfer or CHAPS order.* It is convenient to consider here whether the procuring of such a transfer might amount to theft. There are two possible properties of P of which theft might be committed.

(i) As we have noted in connection with cheques, the credit balance in P's account at the beginning of the transaction is undoubtedly property belonging to P. When the transfer takes place, that thing in action belonging to P, to the value of £X, has not gone *anywhere*, as *Preddy* decides, but it has, nevertheless, gone for ever – it is extinguished. If it is a loan transaction, as most of the pre-*Preddy* cases were, D may have had an intention to repay, but that would have been an intention to create a new thing in action. Where a loan of cash is obtained by deception, the intention of the borrower to repay may possibly negative dishonesty but it does not negative the intent permanently to deprive. The principle is the same whether we are concerned with cash or things in action. The difficulty lies in finding an appropriation. If D or his agent caused the diminution in that balance, it is submitted that D stole it. As argued above, if D was paid by a cheque which he presented and which was honoured, it seems clear that he did appropriate P's balance. Unless the processing of the cheque was fully automated, the actions of one or more persons would intervene, but these were in effect innocent agents. The position is the same where funds are transferred by telegraphic transfer or CHAPS order, if the process is initiated by D as in *Hilton*[1] where D had direct control of a bank account belonging to a charity and he gave instructions for the transfer of the charity's funds in order to settle his personal debts. It was held that D stole the thing in action when the funds were transferred. The position is less clear where D does not have control of the bank account and does not personally initiate the process by which P's account is debited, as in the usual mortgage fraud situation. D, by deception, induces P to agree to lend him £X and P does so by instructing his bank to transfer the funds by telegraphic transfer or CHAPS order. True, D has procured the whole course of events by his deception but the voluntary intervening acts of P break the chain of causation. D may not even be aware of the process by which the transfer of funds is effected.[2]

(ii) The second property is the credit balance acquired by D. This could not be property belonging to P before the deception because it did not exist. It does not follow that it did not become property belonging to P at the moment of its creation. This question was not in issue in *Preddy*. D is the primary owner of the thing in action but it does not follow that no one else has any proprietary interest in it. In *West Deutsche Landesbank Grozentrale v Islington London Borough Council*[3] Lord Browne-Wilkinson said, "Although it is difficult to find clear authority for the proposition, when property has been obtained by fraud equity imposes a constructive trust on the fraudulent recipient: The property is recoverable and traceable in equity." The thing in action is the proceeds of P's property. In *Governor of Brixton Prison, ex p Levin,*[4] D, a dishonest computer operator, caused P's bank account in the United States to be debited and the account of D's accomplice, E, with a different US bank to be credited. The question was whether E's drawing on this credit would have amounted to theft if done in England. Beldam LJ said[5] that the property appropriated was not thing in action consisting in P's bank balance but different property; yet P retained, until the balance was restored, an interest in the funds representing it. If so, in a case like *Preddy* D has, in the words of s. 3(1) of the 1968 Act, "come by the property (innocently or not [in this case, not!]) without stealing it" and therefore "any later assumption of a right to it by keeping or dealing with it as owner" amounts to an appropriation of property belonging to P. It does not appear whether any argument on these lines as canvassed in *Preddy* but, if it is right, it is possible that a conviction for theft could have been substituted in some of cases.

---

[1]   Unreported, No 96/6490/Y5 (7 March 1997, CA).
[2]   Cf *Caresana* [1996] Crim LR 667 and commentary and *Naviede* [1997] Crim LR (September): "We are not satisfied that a misrepresentation which persuades the account holder to direct payment out of his account is an assumption of the rights of the owner such as to amount to an appropriation of his rights within s.3 (1) of the 1968 Act".
[3]   [1996] 2 All ER 961 at 996,
[4]   [1994] 4 All ER 350, DC.
[5]   P 364.

(j)   Things to be returned – but for a price

2–144   A problem similar to that of the cheque arises with the theft of a railway ticket or any other ticket which entitles the holder to services or goods when he returns it. If D takes the ticket from another passenger, P, there is no difficulty. D intends to deprive P permanently not only of the ticket but also of the thing in action (the contractual right to travel) which it represents; but if he takes the ticket from the railway company intending to use it, he probably intends to give it up at the end of the journey. The railway company own the piece of paper but they cannot own the contractual right to travel. As with the cheque, it may be said that D intends to return a different thing, a cancelled ticket. That should be enough

Moreover, D intends that the railway company shall have the ticket only by paying for it – through the provision of a ride on the train. He has a conditional intent to deprive. This explanation has the advantage that it extends to things which are intended to be returned (but only for value) in an unchanged form. For example, D takes milk tokens from a dairy intending to return them in exchange for milk; or gaming chips from the proprietor of a gaming club, intending to return them in exchange for the right to play.[1] In all these cases there is probably a conditional intention permanently to deprive in the literal sense. The cheque, ticket, tokens and chips will probably not be returned at all if the taker realises that he is not going to receive the value they represent.

---

[1]   Cf correspondence in [1976] Crim LR 329 and commentary on *Pick* [1982] Crim LR 238 which should be read in the light of the Gaming Act 1968, s. 16, which was overlooked.

CHAPTER 3
Robbery

3–01   Robbery was a common law offence and was never defined in the Larceny Acts. A definition is now contained in s. 8 (1) of the Theft Act 1968:

"A person is guilty of robbery if he steals, and immediately before or at the time of doing so, and in order to do so, he uses force on any person or puts or seeks to put any person in fear of being then and there subjected to force."

Both robbery and assault with intent to rob, contrary to s. 8 (2), are punishable with life imprisonment.

A.   ROBBERY AN AGGRAVATED FORM OF THEFT

3–02   Robbery is an aggravated form of stealing. Proof of the commission of theft is essential to secure a conviction. Surprisingly, the court in *Forrester*[1] treated as open the question whether the word "steal" in s. 8 is to be regarded as subject to the definition of theft in s. 1. It is submitted that there is no doubt that it is to be so regarded and that whenever the Act refers to "theft", "thief", "steal" or "stolen" it is referring to theft contrary to s. 1. If it were otherwise there might be difficulty in treating theft as an "included offence" on an indictment for robbery for the purposes of s. 6 (3) of the Criminal Law Act 1967.

It follows from the fact that theft is an element of robbery that robbery is not committed if any element of theft cannot be proved. Accordingly, it is not robbery if D has a claim of right to the property which he takes by force, even if he knows he has no right to use force, because the claim of right negatives theft.[2]

---

[1]   [1992] Crim LR 792.
[2]   *Skivington* [1968] 1 QB 166, [1967] 1 All ER 483 (a case under the Larceny Act); *Robinson* [1977] Crim LR 173, CA. In *Forrester* (above) D admitted that he had no claim of right; but a person without a claim of right is not necessarily "dishonest".

3–03   It is necessary to prove that there has been an appropriation[1] of the property of another by force or threat of force. The wider concept of appropriation approved in *Gomez*[2] has a correspondingly broadening effect on robbery. Taking hold of the property with intent to steal it is enough, whereas under the Larceny Act this might have constituted only an attempt. If D by threats of force induced P to lay down property with the intention of taking it up,[3] or if he snatched at a lady's earring but failed to detach it from her ear,[4] the robbery would be complete. Where a handbag is dragged by force from a lady's grasp so that it falls to the ground, there is an appropriation and a robbery: *Corcoran v Anderton*[5] where the court thought (and *Gomez* now confirms) that forcible tugging at the handbag would have been a sufficient appropriation, even if the lady had managed to retain control.[6] If D were pursuing P with intent to take his purse by force and P were to throw away the purse in order to escape,[7] this would not be theft until D did some act to appropriate the purse; but, even before he did so, he might be guilty of attempted robbery, for his pursuit of P would probably be more than a merely preparatory act and he might also be guilty of an assault with intent to rob.

---

1   See above, para **2–03**.
2   [1993] 1 All ER 1, above, para **2–09**.
3   Cf *Farrell* (1787) 1 Leach 322n (robbery held not complete).
4   Cf *Lapier* (1784) 1 Leach 320 (held robbery, because the earring was detached).
5   (1980) 71 Cr App Rep 104.
6   At 108.
7   Cf Hale 1 PC 533. It is different if the purse is thrown down at D's direction for then he has assumed the rights of the owner.

B.   USE OR THREAT OF FORCE

3–04   The aggravating factor is the use, or the threat of the use, of force against the person. The term "force" was preferred to "violence", which was used in the Larceny Act 1916 to designate an aggravated form of robbery. Though the difference, if any, between the words is an elusive one, it is probable that "force" is a slightly wider term. Thus it might be argued that simply to hold a person down is not violence but it certainly involves the use of force against the person. Force denotes any exercise of physical strength against another whereas violence seems to signify a dynamic exercise of strength as by striking a blow. In *Dawson*,[1] it was held that, where D nudges P so as to cause him to lose his balance and enable D to steal, it is a question of fact for the jury whether the nudge amounts to "force". It is submitted that it would be better if the law gave an answer to the question – preferably in the affirmative.

---

1   [1976] Crim LR 692, CA, and commentary.

3–05   The force must be used or threatened in order to steal.[1] So, if D is attempting to commit rape on P and she offers him money to desist, which he takes, he is not guilty of robbery (even assuming that there is theft of the money) whether he in fact desists, or continues and completes the rape.[2] Similarly if D knocks P down out of revenge or spite and, having done so, decides to take, and does take, P's watch, he does not commit robbery. Such cases can, however, be adequately dealt with by charging rape or an offence under the Offences Against the Person Act 1861, as well as theft.

---

1   *Shendley* [1970] Crim LR 49, CA. If the jury are satisfied that D stole, but not satisfied that he used force for the purpose of stealing, they should acquit of robbery and convict of theft.
2   Cf *Blackham* (1787) 2 East PC 555, 711.

3–06   At common law the prosecution had to prove that D's force was directed against P's person in order to overpower him or make him give up the property.[1] It was not enough that force was used on the property to get possession of it, as where force was used to detach P's watch chain from his waistcoat pocket. The CLRC[2] did not intend to alter this rule – it was not their intention to turn "bag-snatching" into robbery – but the rule was not spelt out in their draft bill or in the 1968 Act. In *Clouden*,[3] where D wrenched P's shopping basket out of her grasp and ran off with it, the Court of Appeal held that "the old distinctions have gone" and that it was rightly left to the jury to say whether D used "force on any person" in order to steal. Thus the bag-snatcher will usually be guilty of robbery – because "snatching" will involve some force on the person – whereas the pickpocket usually will not because he acts with stealth, not force.

1   *Gnosil* (1824) 1 C & P 304.
2   *Eighth Report*, Cmnd 2977, para 65.
3   [1987] Crim LR 56, CA, following *Dawson and James* (1976) 64 Cr App Rep 170, CA.

3–07   Though the Act omits the word "wilfully", which was included in the draft bill proposed by the CLRC,[1] it is submitted that the force or threat must be used intentionally or at least recklessly; so that for D accidentally to cause P to fall and injure himself while picking his pocket or accidentally to cut him while slitting his pocket to get his money would not be robbery.

1   *Eighth Report*, Cmnd 2977 at 102.

C.   IMMEDIATELY BEFORE OR AT THE TIME

3–08   The force or threat must be used immediately before or at the time of stealing, and, in the case of a threat, it must be of force "then and there". Thus there can be no robbery or attempted robbery by letter or telephone, except in the most unlikely circumstances – for example, D telephones P that if P does not hand over certain property to E (D's innocent agent who has called at P's house) D will detonate an explosive charge under P's house. Where the threats seek to secure a transfer of property at some time in the future the proper charge would be blackmail, contrary to s. 21.

3–09   To use force when a theft has been, but is no longer being, committed – for example, in order to escape – does not constitute robbery. This raises the question which arises in other contexts under the 1968 Act of how long a theft continues.[1] It is submitted that this question should receive a uniform answer in these different contexts. In the context of robbery, *Hale*[2] decides that, where D has assumed the ownership of goods in a house, the "time of" stealing is still continuing while he is removing the goods from the premises so that he is guilty of robbery if he uses force to get away with the goods. Whether he is guilty of robbery if he uses force when running down the garden path or driving off in the getaway car are, it seems, questions which the court will leave to the common sense of the jury.[3] Was D still "on the job"?[4] There comes a point when no reasonable jury could find the thief to be still in the course of stealing and this must surely be not later than the time when the expedition is complete.

1   Above, para **2–49**, below, para **13–34**.
2   (1978) 68 Cr App Rep 415, CA, criticised by A.T.H. Smith, *Property Offences,* 14–31 to 14–32. *Hale* is unaffected by *Gomez*: *Lockley* [1995] Crim LR 656.
3   *Hale,* above.
4   *Atakpu* [1994] QB 69, [1993] 4 All ER 215, CA.

3–10   Where an act of force has occurred after the theft is over, it would, of course, be proper to charge D both with theft and with the appropriate crime under the Offences against the Person Act 1861.[1] Where a mere threat has been used after the theft is over this will generally not constitute a separate offence unless it is a threat to kill,[2] because a threat to do some lesser degree of harm is not an offence unless it amounts to an assault.[3]

1   Offences against the Person Act 1861, s. 16.
2   Ibid.
3   See Smith & Hogan 388.

D.   FORCE OR THREAT AGAINST A THIRD PERSON

3–11   It is clear that, under the Theft Act, force used against any person will constitute robbery when it is used in order to commit theft. Similarly a threat to use force against any person aimed at putting that person in fear of being then and there subjected to force is enough. So if D, being about to commit theft from P, is interrupted by a passer-by, Q, and repels Q's attempt to interfere, either by actual force or the threat to use force, he is guilty of robbery if he completes the theft. It is immaterial that no force or threat is used against P from whom the theft is committed. It would seem that in such a case the indictment would properly allege robbery from P, for clearly there was no robbery from Q.

3–12   The case put above may be an extension of the common law of robbery; but there is another respect in which the Act may have narrowed the law. Suppose that D threatens P that, if P will not hand over certain property to D, D will use force on Q. This was probably robbery at common law.[1] It is difficult if not impossible, however, to bring such a case within the words of the Act since D does not seek to put any person in fear of being then and there subjected to force in order to commit theft. He does not put P in such fear because the threat is to use force on Q. He does not put Q in fear because the threat is not addressed to him. Such cases should again be treated as blackmail contrary to s. 21.

---

[1]   *Reane* (1794) 2 East PC 734 at 735–736, per Eyre CB, *obiter*.

3–13   It might be different in the example put in the previous paragraph if the threat were addressed to Q as well as to P or overheard by Q. If it were D's object to cause Q to intercede with P to hand over the property, so as to save himself from D's threatened force, this would be robbery.

3–14   At common law, the theft had to be from the person or in the presence of the victim. In *Smith v Desmond*[1] the House of Lords, reversing the Court of Criminal Appeal,[2] put a wide interpretation upon this rule, holding that it was satisfied if the force or threat of force was used on a person who had the property to be stolen in his immediate personal care and protection. D was therefore guilty of robbery when he overpowered a nightwatchman and a maintenance engineer in a bakery and then broke into a cash office some distance away and stole from a safe. Though the victims did not have the key to the office or the safe they were in the building to guard its contents which were, therefore, in their immediate personal care and protection.

---

[1]   [1965] AC 960, [1965] 1 All ER 976.
[2]   [1964] 3 All ER 587.

3–15   Such a case is obviously within the terms of the Theft Act. Indeed, it follows from what has been said above that there is no longer any necessity to prove that the property was in the care and protection of the victim of the force or threat. It is enough that the force or threat was directed against any person so that, if in *Smith v Desmond* the persons overpowered had been mere passers-by who happened to have interfered with D's plans, this would be enough under the Theft Act, though not at common law.

CHAPTER 4
Criminal Deception

4–01   The Theft Acts create eight offences of dishonestly getting something by deception. They are:
1.   Obtaining property: 1968, s. 15.
2.   Obtaining a money transfer: 1968, s. 15A.
3.   Obtaining a pecuniary advantage: 1968, s. 16.
4.   Procuring the execution of a valuable security: 1968, s. 20 (2).
5.   Obtaining services: 1978, s. 1.
6.   Securing the remission of a liability: 1978, s. 2 (1) (a).
7.   Inducing a creditor to wait for or to forgo payment: 1978, s. 2 (1) (b).
8.   Obtaining an exemption from or abatement of liability: 1978, s. 2 (1) (c).
Though the Acts use four verbs, "obtain", "procure", "secure" and "induce", the offences all contain a common element in that D must achieve the proscribed result by deception. It is convenient to consider this and the other elements common to all these offences together. The word "obtain" is used for this purpose, to include the other three verbs. The common elements are:
1.   The meaning of "obtaining by deception".
2.   The meaning of "any deception".
3.   The meaning of "dishonestly".

A. THE COMMON ELEMENTS IN OBTAINING OFFENCES

(a) Obtaining by deception

4–02   The obtaining must be *by deception*.[1] It must be proved that D's conduct actually deceived P and caused him to do whatever act is appropriate to the offence charged. It follows that the deception must precede the relevant act. If, after D, a motorist, has had his tank filled by an attendant, P, and the entire proprietary interest in the petrol has passed to him, he falsely convinces P that it will be paid for by his firm, he does not obtain the petrol by that deception.[2] It would be otherwise if the seller, P retained a lien on the petrol[3] – as he possibly would if the petrol were in a can in D's car. If P was still in possession of the petrol it continued to "belong to" him, and would be obtained from him when he was induced to surrender his lien by allowing D to take the petrol away. If D was dishonest from the start, he might be convicted of obtaining the petrol by the implied representation that he had a present intention to pay. This course will not be open where self-service is invited and D dishonestly helps himself, unless it can be proved that P pressed the button releasing the petrol to the pump in reliance on a representation by D that he intended to pay, implicit in his driving on to the forecourt.[4]

If then P knows that D's statement is false,[5] or if he would have acted in the same way even if he had known it,[6] or if he does not rely on the false statement but arrives at the same erroneous conclusion from his own observation or some other source,[7] or, of course, if he does not read or hear the false statement, D is not guilty of obtaining. In each of these cases, however, D may be convicted of an attempt to obtain by deception.[8] The onus is on the prosecution to prove that the representation was effective. Probably it is unnecessary to go so far as to prove that P believed the statement to be true; it is enough that, though he had his doubts about it, he acted in reliance on it – he would not have so acted if it had not been made.

The principle that deception must be the cause of the obtaining seems to have been stretched in *Miller*.[9] D induced P to ride in his car by falsely representing that it was a taxi. P probably knew that he had been deceived by the time a grossly excessive fare was demanded but paid because he was afraid. An argument that it must be proved that P paid because he believed the lie to be true was rejected. It was sufficient that the lie was a cause of the payment; and, but for the lie, P would never have entered the car. It may be that where D, by deception, causes P to incur a legal obligation, the act of performing that obligation is obtained by deception, even though, when P performs it, he knows that it is false.[10] But that was not so in *Miller*; P was not, and it is unlikely that he supposed he was, under an obligation to pay the excessive sum to the bogus taxi-driver. Since *Gomez*, a better charge would be theft.[11]

The normal way of proving that a deception was relied on is to call P to say that he relied on it.[12] Like any other allegation, however, this may be proved by inference from other facts without direct evidence.[13] Where more than one false representation is alleged, it is sufficient to prove that one of them was operative; but the jury must, subject to the majority verdict provisions, be agreed on the one. It is not sufficient that some are satisfied only as to one representation and the remainder only as to another.[14] Whether a representation was made is a question of fact for the jury. Whether it was false usually depends on the meaning intended or understood by the parties and that too is a question for the jury, even where the statement is made in a document. Where – in this context, exceptionally – the issue is as to the legal effect of a document, it is for the judge to decide.[15]

---

[1] See, generally, A.T.H. Smith "The Idea of Criminal Deception" [1982] Crim LR 721.

[2] *Collis-Smith* [1971] Crim LR 716, CA. But he may be guilty of making off without payment, below, Chapter 5.

[3] He almost certainly does not because he has parted with possession as well as ownership of the petrol. *Cf Edwards v Ddin* [1976] 3 All ER 705, 1 WLR 942.

[4] *Coady* [1996] Crim LR 518, CA. D may, however be guilty of theft of the petrol, above, para **2–07,** and of evading his liability to pay the price by deception, contrary to s. 2 (1) (b) of the Theft Act 1978, below, para **4–87**.

[5] *Ady* (1835) 7 C & P 140; *Mills* (1857) Dears & B 205; *Hensler* (1870) 11 Cox CC 570; *Light* (1915) 11 Cr App Rep 111.

[6] *Edwards* [1978] Crim LR 49, CA. See commentary at 50.

[7] *Roebuck* (1856) Dears & B 24. Cf the similar principle which applies to misrepresentation in relation to the law of contract: *Attwood v Small* (1838) 6 Cl & Fin 232; *Smith v Chadwick* (1884) 9 App Cas 187, HL.

[8] *Hensler* (1870) 11 Cox CC 570.

[9] (1992) 95 Cr App R 421, [1992] Crim LR 744, discussed by Griew, *Theft*, 8–55 to 8–57, A.T.H. Smith *Property*, 17–125.

[10] Below, para **4–05**.

[11] See above, para **2–41**.

[12] *Laverty* [1970] 3 All ER 432, CA; *Tirado* (1974) 59 Cr App Rep 80 at 87, CA.

[13] *Tirado* (above) at 87.

[14] *Brown* (1983) 79 Cr App Rep 115, CA. *Price* [1991] Crim LR 465. See J.C. Smith "Satisfying the Jury" [1988] Crim LR 335.

[15] *Adams* [1994] RTR 220, [1993] Crim LR 525 and commentary. (Commentary approved in *Page* [1996] Crim LR 821). Cf. *Deller*, above, para **2–24**.

4–03   A case that is difficult to reconcile with these principles is *Sullivan*.[1] D represented that he was the "actual maker" of dartboards. The representation was untrue and it was held that he was guilty of obtaining by false pretences from customers who sent him the price of a board although they said in evidence that they parted with their money "because I wanted a dartboard". No one said that he paid because he thought D was the "actual maker". The court apparently thought that there could be no other conceivable reason for their doing so. This seems doubtful. As Sullivan was unknown to them, it probably mattered not at all whether he was the actual maker, so long as he supplied a satisfactory dartboard.

In *Laverty*,[2] a case under s. 15, D changed the registration number-plates and chassis number-plate of a car and sold it to P. It was held that this constituted a representation by conduct that the car was the original car to which these numbers had been assigned; but D's conviction for obtaining the price of the car by deception from P was quashed on the ground that it was not proved that the deception operated on P's mind. There was no direct evidence to that effect – P said he bought the car because he thought D was the owner – and it was not a necessary inference.[3]

---

[1]   (1945) 30 Cr App Rep 132.
[2]   [1970] 3 All ER 432. Cf *Talbot* [1995] Crim LR 396.
[3]   If the only flaw in the prosecution's case was that the representation did not influence P, the court had power to substitute a conviction for an attempt. They did not do so, possibly because there was also insufficient evidence that D intended to deceive P into buying the car by this representation. The purpose of changing the plates may well have been not to deceive the buyer, but to deceive the police, the true owner and anyone else who might identify the vehicle. It would seem that the prosecution would have been on stronger ground had they alleged that D had made a representation by conduct that he had a right to sell the car.

4–04   In *Etim v Hatfield*,[1] where D produced to a post office clerk a false declaration that he was entitled to supplementary benefit and was granted £10.60, but no post office employee gave evidence, it was held that D was rightly convicted because there was no conceivable reason for the payment other than the false statement. In *Laverty*, the court stated that the principle in *Sullivan* should not be extended; but *Sullivan* was followed and *Laverty* distinguished in *Etim v Hatfield*. *Etim*'s case is defensible as one where it was a necessary inference that P acted on the representation; but such a conclusion is hard to justify in the case of *Sullivan*.

Equally difficult to reconcile with principle and more significant is *DPP v Ray*.[2] D, having consumed a meal in a restaurant, dishonestly decided to leave without paying, waited until the waiter went out of the room and then ran off. The House of Lords, Lords Reid and Hodson dissenting, held that the waiter was induced to leave the room by D's implied and continuing representation that he was an honest customer intending to pay his bill. It does not appear that the waiter was ever called in evidence; and it would seem, on the facts, very far indeed from being a necessary inference that the waiter acted on the alleged representation. A doubtful application of a fundamental principle, even by the House of Lords, does not, however, impair the validity of the principle itself; and it remains necessary in every case to prove beyond reasonable doubt that P was deceived by, and acted upon, the representation.

---

[1]   [1975] Crim LR 234.
[2]   [1974] AC 370, [1973] 3 All ER 131, [1974] Crim LR 181 (see commentary). The prosecution was brought under 1968, s. 16 (2) (a) which has now been repealed, but the case remains an authority on this point.

4–05 So far we have used the traditional term, "representation," to mean what D did. It has been argued that, under the Theft Acts, this is no longer appropriate. The CLRC preferred the term, "deception" to "false pretence" because (i) "deception" includes the effect on the mind of P, whereas "false pretence" does not; and (ii) deception "seems more apt in relation to deception by conduct".[1] Point (i) is obviously correct, but when we compare the phrases, "obtains by deception" and "obtains by a false pretence", the difference disappears because the latter necessarily implies that the false pretence has deceived. Point (ii) suggest no more than a better description of the same thing. It is argued,[2] however, that the effect may have been to make a change of substance and an extension of the law, because it is no longer necessary to prove a "representation". But the authors are unable to find any case in which it is not "at least arguable, and usually clear, that [D's] conduct did amount to a misrepresentation".[3] And their conclusion that the law requires proof that D's words or conduct caused P to believe in, and act on a "proposition" which he knew to be false[4] does not seem to be materially different from the traditional view. Words or conduct intended to induce belief in a proposition is a representation, express or implied. It seems that we may safely continue to adhere to the traditional terminology.

---

[1] *Eighth Report*, Cmnd 2977, para 101 (iv).
[2] Arlidge and Parry, 4–003 to 4–025.
[3] Para 4–012.
[4] This necessarily brief summary of the authors' conclusion does not, of course, do full justice to it.

(i) Obtaining by deceiving a third party

4–06 In *Kovacs*[1] it was held that s. 16 (1) of the 1968 Act does not require that the person deceived should suffer any loss arising from the deception. The deception might be practised on one person with the result that the pecuniary advantage was obtained from another. All that was necessary was that there should be a causal connection between the deception and the obtaining. If this is true for s. 16, it must be true for the other obtaining offences. *Kovacs* was applied by the House of Lords in *Charles* and *Lambie*, considered in the next paragraph.

The principle seems to be that where D deceives O into doing an act which imposes a legal liability upon P to do something else, D may be held to have obtained by deception the act which P does, not because he is deceived, but because he is bound to do it.[2] If P has "held out" D to O as having authority to contract on P's behalf – e.g. P has led O to believe that D has authority to buy goods for him – and D makes a contract with O in P's name, within the scope of this ostensible authority, P is bound by the contract even though D had not, and knew he had not, P's actual authority to make it. If D has bought the goods within the scope of the ostensible authority, P is bound to pay O and, though P has never been deceived, the price has been obtained from him by D's false representation that he had authority to make it. *Kovacs*, *Charles* and *Lambie* are all suspect decisions on other grounds, but that suspicion does not necessarily extend to this principle.

---

[1] [1974] 1 All ER 1236, 58 Cr App Rep 412, CA.
[2] *Beck*, below para **6–18**, is a doubtful decision because there was only a commercial, not a legal, obligation.

(ii) Obtaining by using a cheque card or credit card

4–07 The principle that the representation must cause the obtaining has created problems where something is obtained by one who uses a cheque backed by a cheque card, or a credit card. The cheque card in issue in these cases contained an undertaking by the bank that, if the conditions on the card were satisfied, the cheque would be be honoured. The position with credit cards was similar. The bank issuing the card entered into contracts with tradesmen, agreeing to pay the tradesman the sum shown on a voucher signed by the customer when making a purchase, provided that the conditions were satisfied. In the case of credit cards, the contract between the bank and the tradesman preceded the purchase by the customer, whereas in the case of the cheque card that contract was made when the tradesman accepted the customer's cheque, relying on the card which was produced.[1] This distinction is not material for present purposes.

The conditions on both types of card may be satisfied although the holder is exceeding his authority – i.e. the cheque card-holder's bank account is overdrawn or even closed, and the credit card-holder is exceeding the credit limit which the bank has allowed him. The tradesman accepting either type of card will usually do so simply because the conditions on the card are satisfied. He will neither know nor care whether the customer is exceeding his authority and using the card in breach of contract with the bank. He will get his money in any event – and that is all he will be concerned with. This is neither immoral nor unreasonable. The whole object of these cards is to dispense the tradesman from concerning himself in any way with the relationship between the card-holder and his bank. The tradesman is perfectly entitled to take advantage of the facility which the banks offer him.

---

[1]   *First Sport Ltd v Barclays Bank plc* [1993] 3 All ER 789, [1993] 1 WLR 1229, CA (Civ Div), holding, Kennedy LJ dissenting, that the bank was bound even though the cheque was a forgery. Lord Roskill's opinion in *Lambie* (all their Lordships concurring) that the customer was making a contract as agent for the credit card company is powerfully criticised by Bennion, 131, NLJ 431. See also Williams *TBCL* 779 discussing *Charles* and cheque cards: "The card-holder is the bearer of the offer, but need no more be regarded as the bank's agent to contract than was the newspaper that carried the celebrated advertisement by the [Carbolic Smoke Ball Co], or the newsagent who sold the copy of the newspaper to [Mrs Carlill], an agent for [the smoke ball company]." (*Carlill v Carbolic Smoke Ball Co* [1893] 1 QB 256, CA, is obviously the case to which Professor Williams intended to refer.) The courts continue to treat the person producing the card as an agent with the ostensible authority of the bank but, on this issue, it is submitted that the dissenting judgment of Kennedy LJ in *First Sport Ltd v Barclays Bank plc* [1993] 3 All ER 789 at 797, d-f, above, is to be preferred.

4-08   In *Charles*,[1] D obtained gaming chips at a gaming club by the use of cheques and a cheque card, knowing that his account was overdrawn and that he had no authority to overdraw. The conditions on the card were satisfied so that the representation usually implied on the drawing of a cheque,[2] i.e. that the facts are such that the cheque will be met, was true. The representation alleged was that he was entitled and authorised to use the cheque card. If such a representation was made, it was untrue and he knew it was untrue. He was convicted of obtaining a pecuniary advantage, namely increased borrowing by way of overdraft, by the deception that he was entitled and authorised to use the card. The manager, Mr Cersell, said, "If there is a cheque card we make no inquiries as to [D's] credit-worthiness, or as to the state of his account with the bank. All this is irrelevant unless the club has knowledge that he has no funds, or the club has knowledge that he has no authority to overdraw."[3] Notwithstanding this forthright statement (and others) the House of Lords held that there was evidence that Mr Cersell had been induced to give the gaming chips by D's implied representation that he was entitled and authorised to use the cheque card.[4]

---

[1] *Metropolitan Police Comr v Charles* [1977] AC 177, [1976] 3 All ER 112.
[2] Below, para **4–20**.
[3] See [1976] 1 All ER 659 at 663–664.
[4] The holding that there is an implied representation of authority to use the card is suspect. If the relationship between D and his bank is irrelevant, as it surely is, why should D be taken to be saying anything about his authority? If Q actually asks him, D can answer, "It is none of your business – you are only concerned with the conditions on the card." Representations, like terms in contracts, should only be implied under the compulsion of necessity.

4–09 In the light of the evidence quoted, this finding seems, with respect, to be almost perverse; but *Charles* was followed in *Lambie*.[1] D was the holder of a Barclaycard. She had exceeded her credit limit and been asked to return the card but had not done so. She bought goods in a shop and tendered the card. The assistant, Miss Rounding, having checked that the conditions were satisfied, allowed her to take the goods. D was convicted of obtaining a pecuniary advantage from the bank by the false representation that she was entitled to use the card. Her conviction was quashed by the Court of Appeal which thought, wrongly, that there was a material distinction between cheque cards and credit cards. The House of Lords restored the conviction. Miss Rounding was as emphatic as Mr Cersell that she was totally uninterested in the state of account between the customer and her bank. "From my experience I or my shop is not any more worried about accepting a Barclaycard as accepting the same number of pound notes . . . We will honour the card if the conditions are satisfied whether the bearer has authority to use it or not." It seems to have been recognised on all hands that the state of the card-holder's account with his bank is a matter of complete indifference to the representee. Since the authority to use the card depends on the state of the account, it is difficult to see how one can be indifferent to the one without being equally indifferent to the other. Apparently in the teeth of her own testimony, the House of Lords held that there was evidence that Miss Rounding had been induced to accept the card by the alleged false representation by D that she was entitled to use it.

---

[1] [1981] 1 All ER 332, CA; revsd [1982] AC 449; [1981] 2 All ER 776, [1981] Crim LR 712, HL, and commentary. Since the repeal of s. 16 (2) (a) of the 1968 Act, Lambie's conduct could not constitute obtaining a pecuniary advantage; but it is probably obtaining services, contrary to 1978, s. 1, below, para **4–75**.

4–10 It is clear that if Mr Cersell or Miss Rounding had been aware that the bearer of the card had no authority to use it, neither would have entered into the transaction. They would then have been parties to a fraud on the bank. They did not care whether D had authority or not but they would have cared if they had known he had no authority. In both cases the House attached great importance to this fact but it seems irrelevant. However dubious the reasoning, these decisions establish, for all practical purposes, that one who dishonestly uses a cheque or credit card in excess of his authority is guilty of obtaining a pecuniary advantage, or services, from the bank.

Yet, notwithstanding *Charles* and *Lambie*, it appears that prosecutors have had difficulties in obtaining convictions in similar cases where the tradesman has admitted that the deception did not operate on his mind. It seems that this was the reason why the prosecution resorted unsuccessfully in *Navvabi*[1] to a charge of theft, though the facts were remarkably close to those of *Charles*; and in *Kassim*,[2] it was said to be the reason for the proliferation of charges of procuring the execution of a valuable security, contrary to 1968, s. 20 (2). It is not at all surprising that the honest tradesman should say, "I didn't care whether D had authority to use the card or not" but it is surprising that he would also say, "And I would still have accepted the card even if I had known he had no authority to use it." Unless he is prepared to go so far,[3] *Charles* and *Lambie* assert that he has been deceived; but the indictment alleges that he was induced to accept the card by D's false statement that he had authority to use it and the truth is that it did not matter to him whether D had authority or not.[4] It may be that juries prefer the truth to legal fiction, even fiction written by the House of Lords.

Since it is the tradesman who is deemed to have been deceived, it follows that the goods or services are obtained from him by the same "deceptions". In *Lambie*, the House criticised the justices for dismissing a charge of obtaining goods from the shop, contrary to s. 15 of the 1968 Act. It may be, however, that the justices observed that D caused no loss to the seller, who got his money from the bank, and it may be that D neither intended nor foresaw any loss to the seller. They may, therefore, have held that so far as the seller of the goods was concerned, as opposed to the bank, there was no evidence of dishonesty.

---

[1]   Above, para **2–52**.
[2]   (1988) 152 JP 405 at 417, [1988] Crim LR 372, CA; revsd, [1992] 1 AC 9, [1991] 3 All ER 713. See Lord Ackner at p 721.
[3]   According to the Law Commission, shop assistants and others "will often give evidence that they had no interest in [D's] relationship with his bank and would still have accepted the payment in question had they known the truth". Law Com No 228 (Conspiracy to Defraud), 1944, para 438.
[4]   See the model cross-examination suggested at [1981] Crim LR 716.

(iii)   Obtaining for a corporation

4–11   Where D is charged with obtaining a cheque from a limited company, it was held in *Rozeik*[1] that it must be proved that a person whose state of mind was that of the company was deceived. The managers who signed the cheques were the proper persons to do so but they were not deceived because they knew that the representations were false – though, on the unusual facts of the case, they were not parties to the fraud. Only the managers could undertake the legal obligation involved in drawing a cheque; the managers *were* the company for the purpose of issuing cheques, so the company was not deceived. The decision was based on the then prevailing view that D was obtaining a thing in action belonging to the company. That view has since been exploded.[2] It is only as a tangible thing, a "valuable security", that the cheque can be obtained from its drawer. It is sufficient that D obtains possession or control of such a thing, so, if he deceives a secretary, or a messenger employed by the company to hand over the cheque he has obtained it by deception. It is just as if he had deceived the janitor employed by the company into handing over the keys of the safe by the representation that he was the managing director.

---

[1]   [1996] 1 Cr App Rep 260, [1996] Crim LR 271, CA.
[2]   *Preddy*, below, para **4–60**.

(iv)   Obtaining and machines

4–12   The prevailing opinion is that it is not possible in law to deceive a machine.[1] It would be unreal to treat an automatic chocolate machine as deceived when it is activated by a foreign coin or washer. "To deceive is . . . to induce a man to believe that a thing is true which is false, and which the person practising the deceit knows or believes to be false."[2] Deceit can be practised only on a human mind.[3] Where D obtains property or a pecuniary advantage as the result of some dishonest practice on a machine, without the intervention of a human mind, he cannot be guilty of an obtaining offence. It was held to be larceny (and, implicitly, not obtaining) to get cigarettes from a machine by using a brass disc instead of a coin.[4] The owner of the machine intends to pass ownership and possession of the goods to anyone who inserts the proper coin.[5] There is no difference, so far as the law of theft is concerned, between operating the machine by the use of a foreign coin and causing it to disgorge its contents by the use of a screwdriver. If a tradesman makes a dishonest claim on the appropriate form for the repayment of VAT input tax and the claim, without being read by anyone, is fed into a computer which automatically produces a cheque for the sum claimed, this may be regarded as indistinguishable from obtaining the cigarettes by the foreign coin.[6] The clerks who feed the document into the machine and put the cheque in the envelope are innocent agents – like an eight-year-old child, told to put the foreign coin in the machine and bring home the cigarettes. It has been held[7] that since VAT returns are processed by computer, a person making a false return does not have an intent to deceive for the purposes of s. 39 (2) (a) of the Value Added Tax Act 1983; but this assumes that D knows that no person is going to act on the false statement. If he believes that a person will be deceived, he is attempting to commit the offence.

There is a similar problem where the machine does not produce goods but provides a service.[8] If the service is dishonestly obtained without deceiving a human being, there can be no obtaining offence.[9] If D, by using a foreign coin, operates the washing machine in P's launderette, he is not guilty of obtaining the service by deception but may be convicted of the offence of abstracting electricity, perhaps of stealing the hot water, and possibly of making off without payment contrary to 1978, s. 3 (1).[10]

---

1   Griew, *Theft*, 8–12, thinks this "appears now to be universally accepted." See also Williams, *TBCL* 794 and A.T.H. Smith, *Property Offences*, 11–02. Arlidge and Parry, 4–054, however are more doubtful. Some devices used to operate machines are now "instruments" for the purposes of the law of forgery. Difficulties to which this may give rise are discussed in Smith & Hogan, 683–686, Arlidge and Parry, 5–012.
2   *Re London and Globe Finance Corpn Ltd* [1903] 1 Ch 728 at 732.
3   See (1972) Law Soc Gaz 576 and Law Commission Working Paper No 56, p 51.
4   *Hands* (1887) 16 Cox CC 188. Cf *Cooper and Miles* [1979] Crim LR 42 (Judge Woods), *Goodwin* [1996] Crim LR 262, CA.
5   Just as a newsvendor who leaves papers in the street for customers to pay for and take.
6   This may, however, amount to forgery. See Forgery and Counterfeiting Act 1981, s. 10 (3), discussed, Smith & Hogan, 674–676.
7   According to Arlidge and Parry, 4–054, by the trial judge in *Moritz* (17–19 June 1981) unreported. The problem regarding VAT is dealt with by the Finance Act 1985, s. 12 (5), which provides, as an alternative *mens rea* to "intent to deceive", "intent to secure that a machine will respond to the document as if it were a true document".
8   Below, para **4–75**.
9   Below, para **4–76**.
10   Below, para **5–01**.

(v)   Obtaining too remote from deception

4–13   Under the old law of false pretences it was held in *Clucas*[1] that, if D induces P by deception to accept bets on credit and D backs a winning horse, the money paid by P to D is not obtained by deception; the effective cause of the obtaining is not the deception but the fact that D backed a winner. Similarly it was held in *Lewis*[2] that D who obtained employment as a teacher by deception did not obtain the salary paid at the end of the month by deception; the salary was paid for the work done, not in consequence of the deception. Both of these cases are now expressly provided for in 1968, s. 16 (2) (c) and constitute an offence of obtaining a pecuniary advantage by deception.[3] In *King and Stockwell*,[4] convictions for attempting to obtain property by deception were upheld where DD persuaded P to employ them to cut down P's trees by falsely stating that the trees were dangerous. The court rejected the argument that, if the money had been paid, it would have been paid because the work had been done, not because of the deception. The question whether the deception would have been an operative cause of the obtaining of the money was one of fact for the jury. This casts some doubt on *Clucas*[5] and still more on *Lewis*. In the case of many contracts of service, however, it is obvious that there does come a point when the salary or wage is paid solely because the work has been done and any deception by which the employment was obtained has become inoperative. It would be absurd to suggest that D, who obtained his job by deception 30 years ago, obtained last month's salary by that deception. Even in that case, however, D might be convicted under s. 15 where he is paid a higher salary if his employer still believes the false representation he made on appointment that he holds a particular qualification which entitles him to be on a higher salary scale. The deception then appears to be the direct and continuing cause of his obtaining the additional money.[6]

---

[1]   [1949] 2 KB 226, [1949] 2 All ER 40, CCA, distinguished in *Miller*, above, para **4–02**.
[2]   (1922) Somerset Assizes, per Rowlatt J: Russell, *Crime* 1186n.
[3]   Below, para **4–65**.
[4]   [1987] QB 547, [1987] 1 All ER 547, [1987] Crim LR 398, CA and commentary.
[5]   It may be noted that in *Clucas* the two defendants were convicted of conspiracy to defraud. This may seem inconsistent because if P paid out only because the punter had backed a winning horse he was not defrauded; but perhaps a bookmaker is "defrauded" when he is induced to take the bet.
[6]   Cf *Levene v Pearcey* [1976] Crim LR 63 and commentary (taxi-driver obtaining excessive fare by telling passenger normal route blocked).

(b)   Any deception

4–14   By s. 15 (4):

"For purposes of this section 'deception' means any deception (whether deliberate or reckless) by words or conduct as to fact or as to law, including a deception as to the present intentions of the person using the deception or any other person."

The definition in 1968, s. 15 (4) applies to 1968, ss. 15, 15A, 16 and 20 (2) and to 1978, ss. 1 and 2.

(i)   Proof of falsity

4–15   It must be proved that D made a false statement.[1] If his statement was true he cannot be guilty of the offence (though he may now be guilty of an attempt),[2] even though he believed it to be false and was completely dishonest. Where this rule requires the prosecution to prove a negative and the affirmative fact which, if it exists, will establish the truth of the statement, is within the knowledge of the accused, there may be an onus on him, not to prove anything, but at least to introduce some evidence of the affirmative fact. In *Mandry and Wooster*,[3] street traders selling scent for 25p said, "You can go down the road and buy it for 2 guineas in the big stores." The police checked on certain stores but it was admitted in cross-examination that they had not been to Selfridges. It was held that it was not improper for the judge to point out that it was impossible for the police to go to every shop in London and that "if the defence knew of their own knowledge of anywhere it could be bought at that price . . . they were perfectly entitled to call evidence". Since no evidence was called to show that the perfume was on sale at Selfridges or anywhere else, the convictions were upheld.

---

1   Cf *Banaster* [1979] RTR 113.
2   Criminal Attempts Act 1981.
3   [1973] 3 All ER 996; cf *Silverman* (1987) 86 Cr App Rep 213.

(ii)   Deliberate or reckless

4–16   A deception is deliberate if D knows his statement is false and will or may be accepted as true by P. A deception is reckless if he is aware that it may be false and may be accepted as true by P; or if he is aware that it is ambiguous and may be understood by P in the false sense.[1] Carelessness or negligence is not enough.[2] If D believes his statement to be true, he is not reckless, however unreasonable his belief may be; but the more unreasonable D's alleged belief, the more likely is it that the court or jury will be satisfied that the belief was not really held. The *Caldwell*[3] test of recklessness, though it was at one time stated to be of general application,[4] is inappropriate and has not been followed[5] in the context of reckless statements.

If then D says to P, "This watch chain is solid gold", not knowing whether it is solid gold or not and, either not caring a jot whether the statement is true or false or hoping that the statement will turn out to be true, he is guilty of an offence under s. 15 (1) if the statement turns out to be untrue and, in consequence, P is induced to pay money for the chain.

---

1   *Dip Kaur v Chief Constable for Hampshire* [1981] 2 All ER 430, above, para **2–17**.
2   *Staines* (1974) 60 Cr App Rep 160, CA. This is the rule in the tort of deceit – *Derry v Peek* (1889) 14 App Cas 337 – and it would be remarkable if deception in the criminal law were held to be wider than deceit in the civil.
3   [1982] AC 341, [1981] 1 All ER 961, [1981] Crim LR 392, HL and commentary; Smith & Hogan 64–70.
4   *Seymour* [1983] 2 All ER 1058, HL. See now *Reid* [1992] 3 All ER 673, HL.
5   *Large v Mainprize* [1989] Crim LR 213, DC.

(iii)   By words or conduct

4–17   By s. 15 (4) of the 1968 Act (which is applicable as well to ss. 15A, 16 and 20 (2) and to deception offences under the 1978 Act), deception means any deception by words or conduct. In *Barnard*,[1] D went into an Oxford shop wearing a fellow-commoner's cap and gown. He induced the shop-keeper to sell him goods on credit by an express representation that he was a fellow-commoner; but Bolland B said, *obiter*, that he would have been guilty even if he had said nothing. In an Australian case,[2] the wearing of a badge was held to be a false pretence when it indicated that the wearer was entitled to take bets on a racecourse. Offering a car for sale, knowing that the odometer has been set back by a previous owner is a false representation. Similarly where a buyer tenders an article in a supermarket, knowing that the proper price has been altered by a mischievous label switcher or misapplied by a careless assistant.[3] The cashier is no less deceived as to the price at which the goods are for sale than where the label is switched by D himself.

Where D knows that P is or may be under a misapprehension, anything whatever done by D to confirm P in his error is capable of amounting to a deception. Positive steps taken by a seller to conceal from a buyer defects in the goods may amount to fraud in the civil law and would seem to be capable of being deception under the Theft Acts. If P inspected the goods and, because of the concealment, failed to detect the fault, the offence would be complete. If P omitted to inspect the goods and so was not deceived,[4] D would be guilty of an attempt. To display a picture with a collection belonging to a particular seller may amount to fraud and seems to be capable of being a deception, if it is known that the price will be enhanced by the fact that the picture appears to belong to that collection.[5]

It has been held to be fraud in the civil law for the seller of a ship to remove her from the ways where she lay dry and where it might be seen that the bottom was eaten and her keel broken, and to keep her afloat so that these defects were concealed by the water.[6] This would seem to amount to deception. Suppose, however, that the ship was already in the water before any sale was in prospect. Would it be an offence for the seller to leave her there when viewed by the buyer and say nothing about the defects? It would seem not; there are no "words or conduct" here and presumably the seller might not even be civilly liable in such a case.

---

[1]   (1837) 7 C & P 784.
[2]   *Robinson* (1884) 10 VLR 131.
[3]   Contra, A.T.H. Smith, *Property Offences*, 17–26. Cf *Dip Kaur v Chief Constable for Hampshire* [1981] 2 All ER 430, DC, [1981] Crim LR 259 and commentary, above, para **2–14**.
[4]   Cf *Horsfall v Thomas* (1862) 1 H & C 90.
[5]   Cf *Hill v Gray* (1816) 1 Stark 434, a doubtful decision, since it is not clear that the seller induced the buyer's mistake.
[6]   *Schneider v Heath* (1813) 3 Camp 506, approved by the Court of Appeal in *Ward v Hobbs* (1877) 3 QBD 150 at 162, CA.

4–18   *Conduct and omissions.* In commercial transactions D, though under a duty to do nothing to confirm any misunderstanding by P, has no duty to correct it even though he is fully aware of it. "The passive acquiescence of the seller in the self-deception of the buyer does not entitle the buyer to avoid the contract."[1] *A fortiori*, it cannot amount to a criminal offence. It may be different, however, if D is under a duty to speak. In *Firth*,[2] a consultant was held to have deceived a hospital, contrary to 1978, s. 2 (1), by failing to inform the hospital that certain patients were private patients, knowing that the effect would be that they would be exempted from liability to make a payment. The court made no reference to the statutory definition, presumably regarding an omission in breach of duty as "conduct".

---

[1]   *Smith v Hughes* (1871) LR 6 QB 597, above, para **2–23**.
[2]   (1989) 91 Cr App Rep 217, CA; [1990] Crim LR 326, CA and commentary, criticised in Archbold, 21–348. Cf *Shama* [1990] 2 All ER 602, 1 WLR 661, CA.

(iv)   Deception by implied statement

4–19   The most difficult question is as to how far statements should be held to be implied in words or conduct. It is established that one who enters a restaurant and orders a meal impliedly represents that he intends to pay for the meal before leaving[1] and probably also represents, in the absence of an agreement for credit, that he has the money to pay.[2] A person who registers as a guest in a hotel represents that he intends to pay the bill at the end of his stay.[3] A wine waiter employed at a hotel impliedly represents that the wine he offers is his employer's, not his own.[4] A motor trader who states that the mileage shown on the odometer of a second-hand car "may not be correct" represents that he does not know it to be incorrect.[5] A bookmaker, it is submitted, represents, when he takes a bet, that he intends to pay if the horse backed wins.[6] One who takes a taxi represents that he intends to pay, and has the means of paying, at the end of the ride.[7] A customer in a supermarket who tenders goods to the cashier represents that the price label on the goods is that which he believes to be authorised by the management,[8] so that there is a deception if he knows that the label has been "switched" by himself or another. These are all representations of present fact.

Where there has been an express representation, there will usually be ample evidence that the representee actually had the misrepresented fact in mind. In the case of implied representations, this may not be so. When a customer in a restaurant orders food, it is unlikely that the waiter actually thinks, "He is saying that he has the means to pay for this meal." The buyer of a car may not consciously reflect that the seller is asserting that he is the owner, or that he has the right to sell the car.[9] In each case, it is something that goes without saying. The waiter would not take the order if he knew that the customer had no means of paying for it. Moreover in each of the cases put it matters to the representee (unlike the representees in *Charles* and *Lambie*) that the representation is true. The waiter, for example, is not content to deal with the customer whether he has the means to pay or not – whereas the representees in *Charles* and *Lambie* were quite content to deal with their customers, whether they had authority to use their cards or not (so long as they did not know the customers had no authority). Unlike the waiter, they knew they would be paid anyway.

[1]   *DPP v Ray* [1974] AC 370 at 379, 382, 385, 388, 391, [1973] 3 All ER 131, HL.
[2]   Ibid, at 379, 382.
[3]   *Harris* (1975) 62 Cr App Rep 28, CA.
[4]   *Doukas* [1978] 1 All ER 1061, [1978] Crim LR 177, CA. The decision is to be preferred to *Rashid* [1977] 2 All ER 237, CA.
[5]   *King* [1979] Crim LR 122.
[6]   Cf *Buckmaster* (1887) 20 QBD 182.
[7]   Cf *Waterfall* [1970] 1 QB 148, [1969] 3 All ER 1048, CA.
[8]   Cf *Morris*, above, para **2–06**.
[9]   Cf *Wheeler* (1990) 92 Cr App Rep 279, 282, CA (seller in market overt (now abolished) probably represents only that he transfers such title as he has).

(v)   Representations implied on drawing cheques

4–20   From *Hazelton* (1874)[1] until *Metropolitan Police Comr v Charles* (1976)[2] it was thought to be settled law that a person tendering a cheque impliedly makes three representations: (i) that he has an account on which the cheque is drawn; (ii) that he has authority to draw on the bank for that amount; and (iii) that the cheque as drawn is a valid order for that amount. In *Charles*, the House of Lords cast doubt on the second of these representations,[3] saying that in substance there is only one representation – that the facts are such that, as far as can reasonably be foreseen, the cheque will be honoured on presentment. Lord Edmund-Davies quoted with approval the words of Pollock B in *Hazelton*[4] that the representation is that "the existing state of facts is such that in the ordinary course the cheque will be met". In *Gilmartin*, the Court of Appeal thought that "this terse but neat epitome of the representation . . . should properly be regarded as an authoritative statement of the law".[5] It is the same where the cheque is post-dated as where it is not. Such a representation is complete only if the facts include a certain intention and belief of the drawer.

As the court points out, whether the cheque is post-dated or not, it may be the drawer's intention to pay in sufficient funds to meet it before presentation. Alternatively, he may believe that a third party is going to pay in such funds – as where he draws a cheque, knowing that his account is overdrawn but confidently expecting that he will have an ample credit balance tomorrow when his monthly pay is paid into his account by his employer. There being no express representation, the drawer must be taken to be saying that either, (a) there are sufficient funds in the account to meet the cheque; or, (b) he intends to pay in sufficient funds; or, (c) he believes that a third party will do so. Each is a representation of fact, not a mere promise, and so is sufficient to amount to a deception.[6]

---

[1]   LR 2 CCR 134, the source of the proposition in Kenny *Outlines* 359, adopted in *Page* [1971] 2 QB 330 at 333.

[2]   [1977] AC 177, [1976] 3 All ER 112, HL.

[3]   But see [1977] Crim LR at 616.

[4]   (1874) LR 2 CCR 134 at 140.

[5]   (1983) 76 Cr App Rep 238 at 244.

[6]   In *Charles* [1976] 3 All ER 112 at 116, Viscount Dilhorne said, "Until the enactment of the Theft Act 1968 it was necessary in order to obtain a conviction for false pretences to establish that there had been a false pretence of an existing fact." This is misleading. It is still necessary to prove a representation of an existing fact or of law: *Beckett v Cohen* [1973] 1 All ER 120, [1972] 1 WLR 1593, DC; *British Airways Board v Taylor* [1976] 1 All ER 65, HL. All that the 1968 Act did was to make clear that certain statements of fact – i.e. present intentions – were for the future to be treated as such. The implication of Viscount Dilhorne's statement was not accepted by Lord Diplock (p 113) or Lord Edmund-Davies (p 121) or by the court in *Gilmartin*.

4–21   In *Greenstein*,[1] DD made a practice of applying for very large quantities of shares, sending a cheque for an amount far in excess of the money in their bank accounts. They had no authority to overdraw but they expected to be allotted a relatively small number of shares and to receive a "return cheque" for the difference between the prices of the shares applied for and the shares allotted. By paying the return cheques into their accounts they enabled the cheques drawn by them to be honoured, on most occasions on first presentation, on other occasions after, apparently, a very short interval, on second presentation. It was alleged that DD had obtained shares by "*Hazelton*" representations (the case being decided before *Charles*), that they had authority to draw the cheques and that they were good and valid orders. In some cases, where DD had given an undertaking required by the issuing houses that "the cheque sent herewith will be paid on first presentation", there was an allegation of a further representation to that effect. Since all the cheques were met on first or subsequent presentation, no one lost a penny but some applicants who might have got shares if DD had made more modest applications did not get them because, as DD anticipated, there were not enough to go round.

It was held that DD had no authority, either from banking practice or the particular facts proved, to draw the inflated cheques; and that they were not valid orders because they could be met only by paying in the return cheques. There was, therefore, a deception. The deception was effective because the issuing houses would not have entertained the application had they known that their own return cheques were going to be used to fund it. The jury's verdict implied that DD were reckless whether their cheques would be honoured on first presentation; and, on the facts, the jury "were entitled if not bound to infer that the deception was deliberately dishonest".

It would seem then that *Greenstein* was correctly decided in the light of *Charles*. DD did not have the belief which they impliedly represented they had. As in Viscount Dilhorne's speech in *Charles*,[2] there is a disturbing and, it is submitted, unwarranted suggestion that a representation as to something other than present fact will do.

The court distinguished the dicta of Buckley J in *Re London and Globe Finance Corpn Ltd* [3] on the ground that Buckley J "did not have in mind a case where the thing in which a person is induced to believe is a future state of affairs which comes about by a lucky chance, or as here by the act of the very person who was induced by the deception to do it". With respect, the inducing of a belief "in a future state of things" is incapable of being a deception. The deception must be as to present facts, including D's present intention or belief; and, so long as it is understood that "believe" does not require complete conviction [4] and that P sufficiently believes if he relies on the truth of the representation though he is not completely convinced it is true, [5] there should be no qualification of Buckley J's proposition that there can be no deception unless a person is induced to believe that a thing is true which is false in fact.

---

[1]   [1976] 1 All ER 1, 61 Cr App Rep 296, CA.
[2]   See para **4–20**, fn 6, above.
[3]   [1903] 1 Ch 728 at 732, above, para **4–12**.
[4]   Cf Griew in Glazebrook *Essays* 69 et seq.
[5]   See [1977] Crim LR at 621.

4–22   It is certainly not enough to establish an implied deception that there is an implied term for the purposes of the law of contract and that the party bound by the term knows that it is unfulfilled. [1] Suppose, for example, that the seller of goods, in circumstances in which the law implies an undertaking on his part that the goods are of "satisfactory quality", knows that the goods are not "satisfactory" but says nothing. It will be necessary to prove that the seller knew that he was being taken by the buyer to be making a particular assertion and that he knew the assertion to be false or that he did not believe it to be true. An obvious example of a sufficient deception is where the seller induces a sale of an inferior article by producing a sample of superior quality. [2] Though he does not say so in terms, the seller inevitably knows [3] that the buyer understands him to assert that the bulk corresponds with the sample in quality.

An apparently innocent act may constitute deception when considered in the light of a previous course of conduct. D laid before P a number of bars of metal of little value, saying "Eight ounces at four shillings an ounce". The fact that he had previously pledged ingots of silver, which were similar in appearance to the bars now produced, established fraud. [4]

---

[1]   For a discussion of the controversial case of *Berg v Sadler and Moore* [1937] 2 KB 158 and of the implications for the criminal law of *Smith v Hughes* (1871) LR 6 QB 597, see fourth edition of this book, pp 86–89.
[2]   *Goss* (1860) Bell CC 208.
[3]   The question must still be left to the jury – "Did this seller know?": Criminal Justice Act 1967, s. 8.
[4]   *Stevens* (1844) 1 Cox CC 83.

(vi)   Can an omission to undeceive be a deception?

4–23   Where D's statement is true at the time it is made but later to his knowledge becomes false, he will be guilty of obtaining by deception if P acts on the false statement by tendering property or a pecuniary advantage which D dishonestly accepts. In *DPP v Ray*, [1] the statement was D's implied representation that he intended to pay for his meal. This statement was true when made and continued true until the end of the meal, but when D changed his mind it became false. It was held that the waiter acted on the false statement by leaving the room, when he would not have done so had he known the truth, that D intended to leave without paying. If D had changed his mind during the meal, it is clear that any part of the meal served and any service performed by the waiter thereafter would have been obtained by deception. It is essential to prove that P acted on the false representation and that the result of P's so acting was that D obtained the property or the service as the case may be. It was accepted that, if D had decided not to pay and made off while the waiter was out of the room, he would not have committed the offence. On the particular facts, D's continued presence was essential to the prosecution's case. Whether continuing conduct is required as a matter of principle is a different matter. Lord Pearson said:

> "By 'continuing representation' I mean in this case not a continuing effect of an initial representation, but a representation which is being made by conduct at every moment throughout that course of conduct. .."

---

[1]   [1974] AC 370, [1973] 3 All ER 131, HL; *Nordeng* (1975) 62 Cr App Rep 123 at 129, CA.

4–24   Is this a material distinction? Suppose that D sends a written order to D for a book, promising to pay the price within 10 days of delivery. If (i) D does not intend to pay, he will obtain the book by deception. Suppose (ii) that D does intend to pay when he posts the order, but changes his mind before P reads it. Again, it seems clear that D will obtain the book by deception. The representation is false when communicated. It is quite immaterial that D and P are not in each other's presence. Suppose (iii) that D's change of mind occurs just after P has read the order but before he acts on it by appropriating a book to the contract and sending it. Here we have only "the continuing effect of an initial representation". One view[1] is that this would be materially different; there has been no deception "by words or conduct", as required by s. 15(4), only a mere omission to undeceive. However, P *is* deceived from the moment of D's change of mind, no less than in *Ray*. It was not self-deception. What deceives him if it is not D's overall "conduct" – the representation and the omission to correct it? The distinction between cases (ii) and (iii) seems immaterial.

Whatever the true position in those cases, it seems that the same result must follow in the case where the statement is false when made but believed by D to be true, if D discovers that the statement is false and thereafter accepts property or a service from P who, as D knows, is acting on the false statement.

This is not to argue that criminal liability should be imposed in all cases where the civil law imposes a duty to speak. This is a highly technical matter and there are instances where it would not be obvious to the layman that to remain silent would be tantamount to deception. Such cases may be unsuitable for the imposition of criminal sanctions. The point is that criminal liability should not be imposed where the civil law imposes no duty to speak. Where it does impose such a duty then the act may reasonably be held criminal but only if the words of the Act may fairly be said to cover the case.

---

[1]   Cf Arlidge and Parry, 4–015 to 4–018; Griew, *Theft*, 8–34, A.T.H. Smith, *Property Offences*, 17–92, Williams, *TBCL* 787, speaking of the "fiction of continuing representation". But why is it a fiction? P sends the book only because he continues to rely on P's representation that he intends to pay for it. This is decidedly less fictitious than that deduced from Ray's continuing to sit at the cafe table.

(vii)   As to fact or law

4–25   In the old law of false pretences the books unanimously stated that the misrepresentation must be as to a matter of fact.[1] They then went on to contrast representation of fact with representation of opinion or intention. No discussion is to be found of representations of law and no authority is cited to show that a misrepresentation of law would not have been a sufficient false pretence. Indeed there appears to be no authority to that effect. On the other hand there is no authority to show that a misrepresentation of law was enough. It is thus uncertain to what extent the express inclusion of deception as to a matter of law extends the law. Certainly it seems desirable that misrepresentations of law should be within the terms of the Act. Consider the following cases:

(i) D and P are reading a legal document and D deliberately misrepresents its legal effect. This would seem to be misrepresentation of law since the construction of documents is a question of law. If D does so with the object of leading P to believe that D has some right over P's land so as to induce P to pay money for the release of that right, this would seem to amount to obtaining by deception.

(ii) P and his wife, D, have entered into a separation agreement whereby P covenanted to pay D an annual sum "free of any deduction whatever". D, knowing that the true legal construction of the document is to the contrary,[2] represents to P that this prevents P from deducting income tax. This is a misrepresentation of law and it would seem that D is guilty of obtaining the money (or at least that portion of it which represents the tax which ought to have been deducted) by deception.

---

[1]   Archbold (36th edn) 1945; Russell 1171; Smith & Hogan (1st edn) 408; Kenny 358.
[2]   *Ord v Ord* [1923] 2 KB 432.

4–26   In the cases just considered, it has been assumed that the law is quite clear and definite and D knows what it is. Many legal disputes arise, of course, where the law is uncertain. In these instances it is most unlikely that an offence could be committed under the Act. It must often happen that counsel make submissions as to the law in court which do not accord with, or are in direct opposition to the proposition which the same counsel would formulate if he were writing a textbook on the matter. The nature of his submission where the law is uncertain is governed by the interests of his client. A solicitor making similar submissions so as to exact money by way of compromise could not be said to be committing an offence because it is impossible to prove that the statement is (or was at the time) false – the law, *ex hypothesi*, being uncertain.

4–27   The following proposition formulated by Street[1] for the law of the tort of deceit is probably equally true of deception under s. 15:

"If the representations refer to legal principles as distinct from the facts on which those principles operate and the parties are on an equal footing, those representations are only expressions of belief and of the same effect as expressions of opinion between parties on an equal footing. In other cases where the defendant professes legal information beyond that of the plaintiff the ordinary rules of liability for deceit apply."

---

[1]   *Torts* (8th edn) 111–112.

(viii)   Deception as to intention

4–28 Deception includes a deception as to the present intentions of the person using the deception or any other person. A representation as to present intention may be expressed or implied. Several examples of implied representations have been considered above.[1]

It must be proved in these cases that D had no intention of carrying out his promise at the time he made it or at the time it was acted on. If he intended to carry out his promise at those times but later changed his mind he is guilty of a breach of contract but of no criminal offence. It has long been recognised that a misrepresentation as to present state of mind will found a civil action for deceit and this is no more difficult to prove in the criminal than in the civil case – though the standard of proof is, of course, higher. Evidence as to the circumstances in which the promise was made, or as to a systematic course of conduct by D or, of course, as to a confession are examples of ways in which a jury might be convinced beyond reasonable doubt that D was deceiving P as to his present intentions.

---

[1]   Para **4–19**.

4–29 Deceptions as to the present intentions of another person seem to be rare. Examples would be where an agent obtains property for his principal by representing that the principal intends to render services or supply goods, well knowing that the principal has no such intention, or where an estate agent says that a particular building society is willing to advance half the purchase price of a house, knowing that this is not so, and thus induces a purchaser to pay a deposit.

(ix)   Statements of opinion

4–30 A statement of opinion was not a sufficient false pretence under s. 32 of the Larceny Act 1916. The leading case, *Bryan*,[1] carried this doctrine to extreme lengths. There D obtained money from P by representing that certain spoons were of the best quality, equal to Elkington's A, and having as much silver on them as Elkington's A. These statements were false to D's knowledge.[2] Nevertheless ten out of twelve judges[3] held that his conviction must be quashed on the ground that this was mere exaggerated praise by a seller of his goods to which the statute was not intended to apply. Erle J said, "Whether these spoons . . . were equal to Elkington's A or not, cannot be, as far as I know, decidedly affirmed or denied in the same way as a past fact can be affirmed or denied, but it is in the nature of a matter of opinion." This can hardly be true, however, of the statement that the spoons had as much silver on them as Elkington's A. This seems to be no less a misrepresentation of fact than that a six-carat gold chain is of fifteen-carat gold which has subsequently been held to be a sufficient false pretence.[4] It has been held[5] that it is a misrepresentation of fact for the accused to state "that they [had] effected necessary repairs to a roof [which repairs were specified] that they had done the work in a proper and workmanlike manner and that [a specified sum] was a fair and reasonable sum to charge for the work involved". The evidence showed that nothing needed to be done to the roof, what had been done served no useful purpose and it could have been done for £5, whereas £35 was charged. Even an excessive quotation for work to be done may be a sufficient deception where a situation of mutual trust has been built up between D and his customer so that D must be taken to be saying dishonestly that he is going to make no more than a modest profit, when he knows that the profit, if the quotation is accepted, will be very large.[6]

1   (1857) Dears & B 265.
2   D's counsel said: "I cannot contend that the prisoner did not tell a wilful lie . . . ".
3   Willes J *dissentiente* and Bramwell B *dubitante*.
4   *Ardley* (1871) LR 1 CCR 301.
5   *Jeff and Bassett* (1966) 51 Cr App Rep 28, CA. Cf *Hawkins v Smith* [1978] Crim LR 578 ("Showroom condition throughout" a false trade description of a car which has interior and mechanical defects).
6   *Silverman* (1987) 86 Cr App Rep 213, [1987] Crim LR 574, CA.

4–31   The Theft Act gives no guidance as to whether a misrepresentation of opinion is capable of being a deception. In principle there is no reason why it should not be, where the opinion is not honestly held. A vendor's description of his tenant as "a most desirable tenant" when the rent was in arrears and, in the past, had only been paid under pressure was held by the Court of Appeal to be a sufficient misrepresentation to found an action in deceit.[1]

> "In a case where the facts are equally well-known to both parties, what one of them says to the other is frequently nothing but an expression of opinion. . . . But if the facts are not equally well-known to both sides, then a statement of opinion by one who knows the facts best involves very often a statement of a material fact, for he impliedly states that he knows facts which justify his opinion."[2]

The way seems open to the courts, if they so wish, to hold that "deception" extends to this kind of case. The use of that term frees them from the fetters of false pretences. A view of commercial morality very different from that of the majority of the judges in *Bryan* now prevails and deliberate mis-statements of opinion would today be generally condemned as dishonest, no less dishonest, indeed, than mis-statements of other facts – for whether an opinion is held or not is a fact – and the law should follow the changed attitude. It may, moreover, be a significant fact that at the time *Bryan* was decided, it was not possible for the prisoner to give evidence in his own defence.[3]

Against this view, it might be argued that, since the Act has expressly removed one limitation on false pretences (representations as to intention) and has said nothing about this limitation, Parliament's intention is to allow it to continue. It is submitted that this would be a quite unjustifiable assumption. Parliament, in fact, has left it to the judges and, by the use of new terminology, given them a more or less free hand. The question now ought to be not "Is it a matter of opinion?" but, "If it is a matter of opinion, was it D's real opinion?" If the opinion is not honestly held there is, in truth, a misrepresentation of fact for the accused's state of mind is a question of fact. The Act indeed recognises this by holding false promises to be deception. If "I intend . . . " (not intending) is a deception, is not "I believe . . . " (not believing) equally a deception?

1   *Smith v Land and House Property Corpn* (1884) 28 Ch D 7.
2   Ibid, at 15, per Bowen LJ.
3   In *Ragg* (1860) Bell CC 208 at 219, Erle CJ, referring to *Bryan*, said " . . . if such statements are indictable a purchaser who wishes to get out of a bad bargain made by his own negligence, might have recourse to an indictment, on the trial of which the vendor's statement on oath would be excluded, instead of being obliged to bring an action where each party would be heard on equal terms".

4–32   *Deception inducing performance of a binding contract*. It seems that no offence is committed if D and P have entered into an enforceable contract and D deceives P into performing that contract. In *Wheeler*[1] D, a bona-fide purchaser of a stolen medal, one morning sold the medal to P. Delivery was to be in the afternoon. D was not dishonest before or at the time of the sale. The medal belonged to its original owner until D sold it but, because the sale was in market overt,[2] the ownership immediately passed to P. Before delivery D was informed that the medal had been stolen. P inquired whether the medal was on a police list of stolen property. D dishonestly said that it was not. P then paid the price and took delivery of the medal. He would not have done so had he not been deceived. D's conviction for obtaining the price by falsely representing that he was the lawful owner and entitled to sell it was quashed on the ground that the particulars in the indictment were not made out.   Since the medal already belonged to P, the court said that D could not and did not make that representation. This seems to assume that D understood the law of sale of goods including the doctrine of market overt. D may very well have supposed that the sale was not complete until delivery; and P may have supposed that he was entitled to refuse to accept and pay for the medal if it had been stolen. In the morning D believed he was the owner and entitled to sell. He would not have been entitled to sell in the afternoon because he knew the medal was stolen but it had already been sold. The court attached much importance to the fact that P had no right to rescind the contract of sale. He was bound to take delivery and pay the price. The fact seems to be that D induced P to pay the price by deception; and unless the case turns on the fact that the deception was wrongly described, it may be that it decides that it is not an offence by deception to induce the performance of an act which the other is bound to do.

---

[1]   (1990) 92 Cr App Rep 279, CA. Cf para **2–44** above and the discussion by Griew, *Theft*, 8–40 to 8–41. If D is entitled in law to recover the price of goods from P, can his obtaining it be an offence under s. 15 or theft contrary to s. 1? Cf *Talbott* [1995] Crim LR 396.

2   The doctrine of market overt was abolished by the Sale of Goods (Amendment) Act 1994.

(c)   Dishonestly

(i)   Where there is or may be a claim of right

4–33   The deception must also be done "dishonestly". Dishonesty is a subjective concept. The jury must assess D's actual beliefs, whether reasonable or not. The reasonableness or otherwise of the alleged belief is relevant only to the question whether it is actually held or not.[1] Section 32 of the Larceny Act 1916 required an "intent to defraud" and the Court of Criminal Appeal said repeatedly that this meant "dishonestly"[2] so the law would appear to be unchanged. The Court of Appeal has said,[3] however, that "dishonestly" has a wider ambit without indicating the respects in which it is wider. D may deceive deliberately or recklessly, yet not obtain dishonestly.[4] "Dishonestly" is a separate element in the *mens rea*. The jury should always be directed that they must be satisfied that the deception was done dishonestly; though the absence of direction on this point may not be fatal where dishonesty is, in the particular circumstances, an inevitable inference from a deliberate deception.[5] There is no definition of dishonesty for the purposes of this section and the partial definition in s. 2 (1) applies only for the purposes of s. 1 of the Act. The judge must now direct the jury in accordance with *Ghosh*[6] and in *Woolven*[7] the Court of Appeal thought that this direction was wide enough to embrace the occasions on which there might be a claim of right. If this is true for obtaining, it is equally true for theft; and s. 2 (1) (a) of the Act is in effect redundant. If every jury would inevitably find that a person with a claim of right is not dishonest under the *Ghosh* test, there is no need for a claim of right direction. Where the charge is theft, the premise is probably well-founded; but where obtaining by deception is charged it is less clear. Dishonesty then comes into question only where D has made a deliberate or reckless deception. A jury might well think a person dishonest who had practised a deliberate deception even where he did so to get something to which he thought he was entitled.[8]

It is submitted that a claim of right is as inconsistent with dishonesty under s. 15 and other obtaining offences, as it is for theft. It is submitted that the statement of the Court of Apeal in *Lightfoot*[9] that "The defendant's knowledge of the law, whether the criminal law or the law of contract, is irrelevant", must be qualified at least to the extent that a mistake of civil law giving rise to a claim of right is a defence. Because theft and obtaining property by deception overlap – indeed, since *Gomez*, all obtaining, except of land, is theft – it would be inconvenient and unjust if it were otherwise. If D believes the property to be his own, whether through a mistake of fact or a mistake of law, he has a defence if the charge is brought under s. 1. It would be wrong that he should have no defence if the charge is brought under s. 15. If the judge has to direct the jury expressly on the theft charge that claim of right is a defence (and it is submitted that he should), then it is desirable that he should also have to do so on the obtaining charge, instead of leaving the jury to deduce this from the general *Ghosh* direction.[10]

---

[1]   *Lewis* (1975) 62 Cr App Rep 206, [1976] Crim LR 383, CA.
[2]   *Wright* [1960] Crim LR 366.
[3]   *Potger* (1970) 55 Cr App Rep 42 at 46, CA.
[4]   See *Wright* (above), *Griffiths* [1966] 1 QB 589, [1965] 2 All ER 448 and *Talbott* [1995] Crim LR 396.
[5]   *Potger* (above), fn 3; but see also *McVey* [1988] Crim LR 127 and commentary.
[6]   Above, para **2–122**. See *Melwani* [1989] Crim LR 565, CA.
[7]   (1983) 77 Cr App Rep 231, [1983] Crim LR 623, CA.
[8]   In *Falconer-Atlee* (1973) 58 Cr App Rep 348 at p 358, a case of theft, the judge's direction on dishonesty was held to be defective because he omitted to tell the jury that s. 2 (1) (a) expressly provided that a person with a claim of right was not dishonest. Yet, since D's mistake, if any, was a mistake of fact, the direction does not seem to have been necessary or, indeed, appropriate. The court in *Woolven* distinguished that case, not because it was a case of theft but, apparently, on the ground that the direction in the instant case did, in effect, if not in so many words, tell the jury to acquit if they thought D might have a claim of right.
[9]   (1992) 97 Cr App Rep 24, [1993] Crim LR 137, CA. Cf. *Bernhard* [1938] 2 KB 264 and Theft Act 1968, s. 2 (1) (a).
[10] In *Parker* (1910) 74 JP 208 Ridley J held that a claim of right was no answer to a charge of demanding money upon a forged document with intent to defraud. In *Woolven*, the court thought that case was not a decisive authority against a claim of right defence under s. 15; and *Parker* has been overruled by the Forgery and Counterfeiting Act 1981, s. 10 (2). Cf Smith & Hogan 682–683 and the fourth edition of this book, paras 181–183.

4–34   If this be correct, D would have a defence in the following case:

D's car has been obtained from him by X who gave a cheque drawn on a bank where he had no account and who never paid the price. X has sold the car to a bona-fide purchaser, P. P refuses to give up the car to D. D, believing that he is entitled to have the car back, recovers possession by pretending to be a mechanic from P's garage collecting the car for servicing.

Here D has no actual right to recover possession of the car; he is certainly guilty of a deliberate deception; but if he genuinely believes he is entitled to possession of the car, it is submitted that the jury should be told that he is not "dishonest" for the purposes of the section.

Probably the same result must follow where D's belief relates not to any specific property but to the repayment of debt:

D, a Hungarian woman, has been P's mistress. On the termination of the relationship, P promises to pay D £100. Later he declines to do so. D is advised by a Hungarian lawyer that she is entitled to the money. By a deliberate deception she causes P to pay her £100.[1] In such a case there was, and no doubt is, a sufficient claim of right to negative an "intent to steal"; and, if so, there should equally be a defence to obtaining by deception.

A more difficult case is that where D obtains something other than the thing to which he has a claim of right.

D's employer, E, cannot pay D's wages because he cannot obtain payment of a debt owed by P to E. D, by deception, obtains some of P's property and delivers it to E, hoping thereby to enable E to procure the payment of the debt – and the means to pay D's wages.

In such a case[2] Coleridge J thought that the facts negatived an intent to defraud; and in a subsequent case[3] Pollock CB put this on the ground that D must have thought he had some right to obtain the property which he did obtain. Of course, he had no right in law so to do, in which case the decision on these facts must depend on the state of D's mind in the particular case. Did he, or did he not, believe he had, or that E had, a legal right to act in this way? Looked at in this way, it would seem rather unlikely that a claim of right could often be made out. D had a claim of right to his wages; E had a claim of right to payment by P of the debt (both being actual rights) but the question is whether D had a claim of right to the particular property he obtained by the deception. Few people would suppose today that they have a right to take the property of a debtor to compel him to pay his creditor.

---

[1] Cf *Bernhard* [1938] 2 KB 264, below, para **10–31**.
[2] *Williams* (1836) 7 C & P 354. Cf *Close* [1977] Crim LR 107, CA.
[3] *Hamilton* (1845) 1 Cox CC 244.

(ii) Where there is no claim of right

4–35 Prior to *Feely*[1] the courts were inclined to decide as a matter of law that certain common types of conduct were dishonest. In *McCall*,[2] the Court of Appeal decided that to obtain a loan by deception was dishonest even though D intended to repay. D's submission that such conduct "is not necessarily tainted with dishonesty" was rejected. There was "an unanswerable case" against him. In *Halstead v Patel*,[3] D knowingly overdrew on a Giro account, intending to repay at some future date when a strike was over. It was held, relying on decisions which were not followed in *Feely*, that the "pious hope" of repaying at some future date was no defence; the justices were bound to convict. In *Potger*,[4] where D induced P to subscribe for magazines by the false representation that he was a student taking part in a points competition, it was no answer that magazines worth the money would have been delivered in due course. The Court of Appeal came close to giving a definition of dishonesty in obtaining cases:

" . . . once the jury had come to the conclusion that these were deliberate lies intended to induce the various persons to do acts which would benefit[5] the appellant and that they were or would have been induced so to act by those lies, it was inevitable that the jury should reach the conclusion at which they did arrive."

---

[1] Above, para **2–121**.
[2] (1970) 55 Cr App Rep 175. In *Melwani* [1989] Crim LR 565, CA, it was said that *McCall* "cannot really survive the decisions in *Feely* and *Ghosh*"; and this may be true of the other cases cited in this paragraph.
[3] [1972] 2 All ER 147, 1 WLR 661. The judgment is clearly wrong in so far as it refers to a "belief based on reasonable grounds". See [1972] Crim LR 236; *Lewis* [1976] Crim LR 383, CA.

⁴   (1970) 55 Cr App Rep 42.
⁵   But should not the emphasis have been on prejudice to P rather than benefit to D? Cf *Welham v DPP* [1961] AC 103, [1960] 1 All ER 805, HL.

4–36   *Feely*, as modified in *Ghosh*,¹ applies in an obtaining offence as in theft. In *Feely*, Lawton LJ contrasted the case of the man who takes money from a till intending to repay (presumably before it is missed); and the man who obtains cash by passing a cheque on an account with no funds, intending to pay funds in to meet the cheque when it is presented. According to *Cockburn*² (overruled in *Feely*) the first man was dishonest in law whereas:

> "the man who passes the cheque is deemed in law not to act dishonestly if he genuinely believes on reasonable grounds that when it is presented to the paying bank there will be funds to meet it."

Lawton LJ commented:

> "Lawyers may be able to appreciate why one man should be adjudged to be a criminal and the other not; but we doubt whether anyone else would."

The man passing the cheque would be acquitted of an obtaining offence on the ground that he does not intend to deceive,³ so the question of dishonesty would be unlikely to arise. If it did, it would now be a matter for the judgment of the jury in accordance with *Ghosh*. But the cases are not indistinguishable for the raider of the till intends to commit a legal wrong – a trespass against, or a breach of contract with, the owner – whereas the passer of the cheque has no such intention.

Feely was followed in an obtaining case, *Greenstein*,⁴ the first prosecution brought in respect of a particular method of "stagging". The judge told the jury:

> " . . . this is the first prosecution. It has not yet been decided if what they did did amount to a dishonest criminal deception and it will be you who will decide the answer to that question."

But the answer given by the jury is of no authority in any future case, even on exactly similar material facts. Surely the law should supply the answer to the question whether this practice is lawful or not – just as the law should say whether it is or is not lawful to obtain a loan by deception with intent to repay in due course. It is not the function of the jury to make law.

¹   Above, para **2–122**.
²   [1968] 1 All ER 466, [1968] 1 WLR 281, CA.
³   Above, para **4–20**.
⁴   [1976] 1 All ER 1, [1975] 1 WLR 1353, CA above, para **4–21**.

4–37   Though, since *Ghosh*, the question for the jury would be formulated differently, *Greenstein* remains the authority that it is not necessarily a defence to a charge of dishonesty that D did not intend anyone to suffer financial loss. Where D, who has no money in his bank account and no authority to overdraw, obtains goods by using a cheque card, he knows that the person from whom the goods are obtained will suffer no financial loss – the loss will fall on the bank. For this reason, it may be that a charge of obtaining services from the bank will be preferred to one of obtaining goods from the seller; but it appears that there is evidence of dishonesty towards the seller as well, if he was induced by the deception to part with his property.¹

¹   See the discussion of cheque card frauds, above, para **4–07**.

4–38   Suppose that D, by making false statements as to his assets, persuades his bank manager to allow him to borrow by way of overdraft. Section 16 (2) (b) of the 1968 Act says that he is to be regarded as having obtained a pecuniary advantage. It is now for the jury to decide whether it is a defence that D intended (and was able) to repay the loan with interest in the agreed time. In a sense he has not obtained a "pecuniary advantage" at all, since he is going to give a full economic return for what he gets, but that is not necessarily an answer.[1] If D, aged 48, applies for an appointment for which the maximum age is 45, stating that he is 44, he commits the *actus reus* of the offence if he is appointed (and of an attempt if he is not). It is for the jury to decide whether he is dishonest if he can say truthfully, "I was the best qualified candidate and would have earned every penny of my salary if appointed." It is true that s. 16 (2) (c) defines only "pecuniary advantage" and the advantage must be obtained "dishonestly"; but it is thought that it would defeat the intention behind s. 16 (2) if the meaning given to "dishonestly" excluded these cases.

---

[1]   Below, para **4–67**.

B.   OBTAINING PROPERTY BY DECEPTION

4–39   By s. 15 of the 1968 Act:

"(1) A person who by any deception dishonestly obtains property belonging to another, with the intention of permanently depriving the other of it, shall on conviction on indictment be liable to imprisonment for a term not exceeding ten years.

(2) For purposes of this section a person is to be treated as obtaining property if he obtains ownership, possession or control of it, and 'obtain' includes obtaining for another or enabling another to obtain or to retain."

(a)   The obtaining

(i)   For one's self

4–40   It must be proved that property was in fact obtained. Evidence that, following the representation, the property would have been transferred to D in the normal course, is not enough. It is not sufficient to prove that D made dishonest applications to the Department of Employment for unemployment benefit, that the Department's system was that, in response to applications, Girocheques produced by computer were sent to the applicants, and that D had never complained of not receiving a Girocheque: *Bogdal v Hall*,[1] where the court thought it would be unsafe to draw an inference that D had received any of the cheques – but there was prima facie evidence of an attempt to obtain. There is a sufficient obtaining if D obtains ownership, possession or control.[2] If D is lawfully in possession of P's goods, for example, as a bailee, and he dishonestly by deception induces P to sell him the goods, the offence is complete when the ownership passes to D. Conversely if D by deception induces P to enter into an unconditional contract to sell to D specific goods which are in a deliverable state, the offence is complete although the goods never leave P's possession. The ownership in the goods passes as soon as the contract is made and it is immaterial that the time of payment and of delivery is postponed.[3] Similarly if D, by deception, induces P to transfer to him a bill of lading in respect of goods which are at sea, he will be guilty of obtaining not merely the bill of lading but also the goods which it represents, for title to them passes on indorsement and delivery of the bill. It may be that, in these cases, P will suffer no loss; but it is right that such conduct should be criminal since it puts P's property at risk. D has probably obtained a voidable title to it and, if he can re-sell to a bona-fide purchaser before P succeeds in avoiding the contract, the bona-fide purchaser will get an unimpeachable title to the property and P will be permanently deprived of it.

---

[1]   [1987] Crim LR 500, DC.

[2]   It is unnecessary to prove that D obtained the whole of the property mentioned in the information or indictment, but the sentence should relate only to property proved to have been obtained: *Levene v Pearcey* [1976] Crim LR 63, above, para **4–13**, fn 6.

[3]   Sale of Goods Act 1979, s. 18, r. 1.

4–41   It follows that if D, being in a foreign country, say France, sends a letter to England deceiving P into selling him goods which are in England, D is guilty of obtaining by deception in England as soon as the property passes to him. It is immaterial that he never sets foot within the jurisdiction. If the letter arrives within the jurisdiction but does not deceive P, D is liable to conviction in England for an attempt. This is so even if the letter is lost before it reaches these shores. Though nothing whatever has happened in England, D intended consequences to occur here and it is to the consequences intended that we have regard when dealing with attempts (and conspiracy or incitement). The Criminal Justice Act 1993 will codify this rule when it is brought into force.[1]

---

[1]   Section 3 (3) and para **1–19** above. For earlier authorities see *Baxter* [1971] 2 All ER 359 at 362, CA, per Sachs LJ. *DPP v Stonehouse* [1978] AC 55, [1977] 2 All ER 909, [1977] Crim LR 544, HL and commentary.

4–42   The converse case is where D, in England, sends a letter to P in France, deceiving P into transferring property in goods to D in France. It was held in *Harden*,[1] a prosecution for obtaining by false pretences under the Larceny Act 1916, that the English courts had no jurisdiction: the prohibited result did not occur in England. *Harden* was doubted by Lord Diplock in *Treacy v DPP*.[2] Lord Diplock thought that the question would call for re-examination when it arose under s. 15 of the 1968 Act: subject to any contrary intention of Parliament, the only limitations on the jurisdiction of the courts of the United Kingdom were those imposed by international comity. The question did arise, apparently for the first time, in *Smith*.[3] It was held that, even if the obtaining (the transfer of funds from one bank account in New York to another[4]) occurred only in New York, the court had jurisdiction on the ground that all the relevant acts were done in London – the representor and the representee were both here, the representation was made and the representee was deceived here. Though it was not necessary to decide the point, the court favoured the opinion that, while possession of the property may have been obtained only in New York, ownership and control were obtained in England where the transferee was. Proximity may be necessary for control of a physical object but not of intangible property like a bank account. Possession has a physical element but ownership is intangible, a bundle of rights which may be held to go wherever the owner goes. These problems will disappear if and when Part I of the Criminal Justice Act 1993 is brought into force.

---

[1]   [1963] 1 QB 8, [1962] 1 All ER 286.

[2]   [1971] AC 537, [1971] 1 All ER 110.

[3]   [1996] 2 Cr App Rep 1, 16–21, [1996] Crim LR 329, CA.

[4]   In the light of *Preddy*, below, para **4–60**, the case is probably wrongly decided but this does not affect its authority on the jurisdiction point.

4–43   It may happen that ownership in goods passes from seller to buyer when the goods are "appropriated to the contract" but the buyer does not get possession until the goods are delivered. The transfer of both ownership and delivery may be induced by the same deception. It was argued in the sixth and earlier editions of this book that even if, because of *Harden*, the transfer in France of ownership was not an offence triable in England, the subsequent delivery of possession in England was. Whatever the merits of that argument at the time, it seems unlikely that the delivery of possession, albeit obtained by deception, can now be regarded as a separate offence. Obtaining the ownership is theft of the goods and *Atakpu*[1] shows that they cannot be stolen twice. There is no second theft when possession is obtained. Equally, it is thought, the goods cannot be obtained twice. Though the offence may be committed by obtaining ownership or control, it is an offence of obtaining *the property*; and, once obtained, it cannot be obtained again. It is desirable that there should be consistency between the offences of theft and obtaining property.

---

[1]   [1994] QB 69, [1993] 4 All ER 215, CA, above, para **2–46**.

4–44   It is enough that D obtains control. So if D, an employee, by deception induces his employer, P, to entrust goods to D for use in the course of D's employment, D may be guilty of the offence though he has obtained not possession of the goods but control or "custody" as this particular relation to goods is sometimes called.

(ii)   For another

4–45   "'Obtain' includes obtaining for another or enabling another to obtain or retain."[1] So if D, by deception, induces P to make a gift of goods to E, D is guilty. That would be a case where D obtained for another. An instance of D's enabling another to obtain would be where E is negotiating with P for the sale of goods by E to P and D deceives P as to the quality of the goods so as to induce him to enter into the contract with and pay the price to E. Of course E, in these examples, would also be guilty if he was a party to D's fraud.

---

[1]   Section 15 (1). *DPP v Stonehouse* [1978] AC 55, [1977] 2 All ER 909, [1977] Crim LR 544, HL.

4–46   The meaning of "enabling another . . . to retain" presents more difficulties. If E is in possession of P's goods and D, by deception, induces P to agree to transfer the ownership in the goods to E, this would be "obtaining for another" and not "enabling another to retain". The latter provision must be intended to apply to the situation where D induces P to allow E to retain some interest which E already has, for, if P is induced to transfer any new interest, this is obtaining for another. There seem to be three possible cases:
   (i)   E is P's bailee at will and D, by deception and with the appropriate intent, induces P not to terminate E's possession.
   (ii) E is P's employee and has custody of P's goods. D, by deception, induces P not to terminate that custody, again with the appropriate intent.
   (iii) E has obtained the ownership of property from P under the terms of a contract voidable by P. P is proposing to rescind that contract. D, by deception, induces him to refrain from doing so. It is clear that D has enabled E to retain ownership and therefore he is to be "treated as" obtaining property.
   In case (iii), however, D is probably not guilty of an offence because he did not enable E to retain property "belonging to another". P has neither ownership, possession nor control. The question is whether property can be said to "belong

to" a person for the purpose of the section where he has nothing more than the right, by rescinding a contract, to resume ownership of it. The answer to this question seems to be in the negative: P has no proprietary right or interest in the property.[1] It is true that s. 15 (2) gives an extended meaning to the words "obtains property" – D is, in the specified circumstances, to be "treated as obtaining property", whether he does so or not – but it does not, in terms, extend the meaning of the equally important phrase, "belonging to another".[2] A right to rescind, it is submitted, is not a proprietary interest.

---

[1] Cf s. 5 (1), above, para **2–55**.
[2] The meaning given to this phrase by s. 5 (1) (and 4 (1)) applies for the purposes of the Act generally: s. 34 (1)

4–47 It will be noticed that the Act makes no provision for the case where D by deception retains goods for himself. In most cases this will clearly fall under theft contrary to s. 1 so there will be no problem. In examples (i) and (ii), above, E, if he has *mens rea*, will be guilty of theft by "keeping [the property] as owner",[1] and D of aiding and abetting him: whereas if E has no *mens rea*, D will be guilty of theft through an innocent agent. But it is improbable that D or E is guilty of theft in example (iii).

If D is in possession or custody of P's property and, by deception, he induces P to allow him to retain that possession or custody as the case may be, with the intention of permanently depriving P of the property, D will be guilty of theft. If, however, D has acquired ownership and possession of the property from P before deception, it is difficult to see how he can be said to have appropriated the property of another. Suppose that D has acquired ownership and possession of P's property under a contract voidable by P for an innocent misrepresentation committed by D. P is about to rescind the contract and thus regain his ownership in the goods. D by deception induces him to refrain from doing so, intending to keep the goods permanently for himself. D can hardly be said to have appropriated the property of another since P has no interest, legal or equitable, in the property at this time; nor is this obtaining under s. 15 (1).

---

[1] Section 3 (1), above, para **2–03**.

(iii) Necessity for specific property

4–48 D cannot be guilty of enabling E to retain, unless there is some specific property which is the subject of the retention. So if D, E's accountant, deceives the Inland Revenue Inspector whereby E's liability to tax is reduced by £50, no offence is committed under this section. In a sense, of course, D has, by deception, enabled E to retain property; but it is not the property of another. It is submitted that the provision cannot have been intended to apply to the mere non-payment of a debt which is all that this is. D would, however, be guilty of an offence under 1978, s. 2 (1) (b).[1]

---

[1] Below, para **4–95**.

(b) Property

4–49 By s. 34 (1) the broad definition in s. 4 (1) applies, and the limitations for the purposes of theft by s.4 (2)–(4) are inapplicable, to deception. It seems clear, then, that s. 15 extends far beyond the "chattel, money or valuable security" which could be the subject of obtaining by false pretences under the

Larceny Act 1916, s. 32. Non-larcenable chattels which were not the subject of false pretences[1] may be obtained by deception. Other cases require more detailed consideration.

---

[1] *Robinson* (1859) Bell CC 34.

(i) Land

4–50 Land presents peculiarly difficult problems because of the nature of interests in land and the fact that the terminology of the Theft Act is geared to the traditional subject matter of obtaining by false pretences, namely goods. Under English law, ownership subsists not in the land itself but in an abstract entity called "an estate". The freeholder owns not the land but the fee simple estate in the land, and the leaseholder has a leasehold estate. The land itself may, however, be possessed. The offence may be committed therefore by obtaining the ownership of an estate in the land or by obtaining possession or control of the land, provided that there is an intention to deprive the victim permanently of his interest, whatever it is.

4–51 *Where P parts with his estate.* There is little difficulty where the owner is induced to convey his whole estate to the rogue. For example, P, the owner of the freehold, is induced to convey the fee simple to D; or a lessee is induced to assign his whole leasehold interest to D. An obvious case is where an imposter procures the transference to himself of trust property or a deceased person's estate. But there are other cases. Suppose D induces P to sell him land for use as a coach-station, by agreeing that he will purchase all the petrol he needs for his coach-business from P. D never has any intention of honouring his promise. If the legal estate in the land is conveyed to D, or if D is given possession before conveyance, it seems clear that the offence is complete. It may be thought, however, that the offence is complete, at an earlier stage. The general rule is that when A contracts to sell land to B, an equitable interest in the land passes at once to B. This arises from the fact that a decree of specific performance will normally be granted for a contract for the sale of land and "equity looks on as done that which ought to be done". If the contract is not specifically enforceable, no interest passes.[1] When there has been deception, it seems inevitably to follow that the contract is voidable for fraud by the vendor and thus not specifically enforceable against him.[2] If the transaction has got no further than the contract, it seems, then, that D could not be convicted of the full offence, though he might be convicted of an attempt.

---

[1] Megarry and Wade *Law of Real Property* (4th edn) 582.
[2] Ibid 585.

4–52 *Where P creates a smaller estate.* The main difficulty arises out of the necessity for an intention permanently to deprive the owner of the property. Such an intent may be difficult or impossible to discover where the owner is induced not to part with his whole estate, but to carve some smaller estate out of it. Suppose that D, by deception, induces P, the owner of the freehold, to grant him a lease of the land for two years. Clearly D does not intend to deprive P permanently, or indeed at all, of the property which belongs to him – i.e. his freehold interest. Nor, if he intends to vacate the property after two years, does he intend to deprive P permanently of possession of the land. The position would be the same if P were himself a lessee whose lease had three years to run and he granted D a sub-lease for two years. These cases look much the same as

117

that of the owner of a ship who charters it for two years. If the charterer has induced the charter by deception but intends to comply with its terms, he does not commit an offence, because of his lack of intention permanently to deprive. There is a possible answer to this analogy. A lease of land differs from the letting of a chattel in that an estate in land is created by the granting of the lease. That estate is regarded in law as a separate piece of property; and D intends that P shall never have that particular piece of property. The snag about this is that it is impossible to say that the leasehold estate ever "belonged to", or could belong to P, the owner of the freehold.[1] If it were surrendered to P it would cease to exist as a separate piece of property and merge in P's larger interest. The leasehold interest does not exist until the lease is granted – and then it belongs to D. This case may, however, now be dealt with as an obtaining of services contrary to 1978, s. 1.[2]

---

[1]   *Chan Wai Lam* [1981] Crim LR 497 (Court of Appeal of Hong Kong) and commentary; cf *Preddy*, below, para **4–60**.
[2]   Below, para **4–75**.

4–53   *Where P retains his estate but D obtains possession.* What is the effect of obtaining possession of land by deception? If P's only interest in the land is his possession of it, then, clearly the offence may be committed. For example, P is a squatter on the land with no title to it other than his actual possession. Even where P has a good title to the land which he does not lose through the deception, it is thought that the offence will be committed if he is to be deprived of possession for a period coincident with this interest. For example, D deceives P, who is a lessee of land for two years, to allow him into possession as a licensee for those two years. P's leasehold estate continues unimpaired. What then of the case where D obtains from P, the freeholder, a lease of the land for 99 – or 999 – years? P has not been deprived of his freehold interest but, fairly clearly, D has an intention to deprive him of possession of the land for the rest of his natural life.[1] Is it an answer that the land will some day revert to some remote successor in title? It is submitted that when the Act speaks of permanently depriving "another", it means the living person whose property is taken or obtained; so that if he is never to have it back in his lifetime, this element of the offence is made out. (So it would be theft if D were to take P's property, intending to restore it to P's executor after his death.) Even if this argument is correct, it provides no answer to the case of the man who obtains a short lease by deception and there is an awkward question as to where the line is to be drawn; but this too may be treated as a case of obtaining services contrary to 1978, s. 1.[2]

---

[1]   In *Chan Wai Lam* [1981] Crim LR 497 (Court of Appeal of Hong Kong) D was held to have no intent permanently to deprive where he obtained from the Hong Kong government a lease which would have expired three days before the end of the lease of the New Territories held by the government. Had the lease obtained been three days longer, it is submitted that there would have been evidence that D would have obtained possession with intent permanently to deprive. Otherwise he might have been held liable on the *de minimis* principle – but the courts are properly reluctant to invoke that principle in criminal cases.
[2]   Below, para **4–75**.

4–54   *Where P parts with a portion of his estate.* The position is thought to be different where P is induced to transfer to D parts of his fee simple or other interest. For example, to convey to D the fee simple in the shooting-rights, or the minerals or to grant D an easement or profit a prendre. Here there is evidence that D does intend to deprive P permanently of a portion of his freehold interest.

If D is granted only a lease of the mineral rights, then there is the same difficulty as with grants of other leasehold interests; but may he be convicted of obtaining the actual minerals which he removes from the land? He certainly intends to deprive P permanently of these. The difficulty here might be that he is entitled by virtue of the estate which he holds, albeit an estate voidable for fraud, to take the minerals. The problem is essentially one of remoteness, and some authorities[1] suggest that the obtaining of the minerals may be too remote from the deception. It might well be otherwise, however, in a case where D by deception obtains not a lease but a mere contractual licence to take the minerals. This would not differ in principle from the common case of obtaining by deception, where D obtains the property in pursuance of a contract voidable for fraud.

---

[1] See above, para **4–13**.

4–55 *Where the freeholder obtains from the lessee.* It has been seen that the offence is committed if a lessee is induced to assign his lease. What if he is induced to surrender it to his landlord? P is permanently deprived of his interest, so there is no difficulty on that score. But is it possible to say that D has obtained property, when P's estate has simply ceased to exist? It certainly looks very odd, however, that D, the landlord, should commit no offence when anyone else in the world who persuaded P to transfer his estate would be so guilty. Perhaps the answer is that D has obtained possession of the land with intent and P shall have it no more and that is enough. It would be theft, if s. 4 did not exclude theft of land.

(ii) Things in action

4–56 Things in action and other intangible property (e.g. patents) are clearly property so that D commits an offence under s. 15 (1) if, by deception, he causes P to transfer his book debts, his copyright or patent to him.

An equitable assignment of a thing in action requires no formality.

> "Where there is a contract between the owner of a chose in action and another person which shows a clear intention that such a person is to have the benefit of the chose, there is without more a sufficient assignment in the eye of equity."[1]

Although, as with land, this result is said to follow from the principle that equity looks on as done that which ought to be done,[2] it does not depend on the availability of specific performance, for it is immaterial that no consideration is given by the assignee.[3] The assignment will be complete and the thing obtained by deception, notwithstanding the fraud. A purported assignment of a future thing in action can operate only as a contract to assign. One who, by deception, induces such an "assignment" will be guilty of an attempt to obtain by deception. If he gave consideration then, on the thing coming into existence, the full offence will be complete.

---

[1] Cheshire, Fifoot and Furmston *Law of Contract* (12th edn) 507. "Chose" is a synonym for "thing".
[2] Ibid 506.
[3] Ibid 511–514.

4–57 *Cheques.*[1] If Q draws a negotiable cheque in favour of P for consideration supplied by P, P owns the thing in action represented by the cheque. If D then deceives P into negotiating it to him, D has obtained the thing in action. The right to sue Q on the cheque has been transferred from P to D. If , on the other hand, D deceives P into drawing a cheque in D's favour, he cannot be guilty of obtaining the thing in action.[2] It never belonged to P – he could not sue himself – it was a new item of property which, from the moment of its creation, belonged to D.[3]

The fact that D is not guilty of obtaining the thing in action does not, however, mean that he cannot be convicted of obtaining the cheque. The piece of paper on which the cheque is written will, as D presumably knows, be returned to P's bank when, as D intends, he presents it. But the cheque, the tangible thing, is more than a mere piece of paper. It is a valuable security, property which could be obtained by false pretences under the Larceny Act 1916 before there was any possibility of committing an offence by obtaining things in action or other intangible property. The cheque, whether it creates a thing in action or not,[4] is a valuable thing because it is, in effect, a key to the drawer's bank balance. When it is presented and cancelled, it ceases to be a valuable security. Even if D does not intend to deprive P permanently of the piece of paper, he *does* intend to deprive him permanently of the valuable security. The old case of *Danger*,[5] however, appears to decide that nothing has been obtained from P. D produced to P a bill of exchange, duly stamped, signed by himself as drawer and payable to himself and, by false pretences, induced P to accept the bill by writing his name across it. It was held that P had no property in the document as a security or even in the paper on which it was written, so D had not obtained property belonging to another. Later cases,[6] however, suggest, or are explicable only on the basis, that the crucial fact was that P had no property in, or probably even possession of, the piece of paper. All that Danger obtained was the act of signing the paper, and a signature could not be described as property. Where the bill paper or cheque form belongs to P – he owns it or is in possession of it – and is signed and delivered by P, D obtains a tangible thing belonging to P – a valuable security.

---

[1] See J.C. Smith, "Obtaining Cheques by Deception or Theft," [1997] Crim LR 396, and para **2–140**, above.

[2] He is probably guilty of procuring the execution of a valuable security. Below, para **6–14**.

[3] *Preddy* [1996] AC 815, [1996] 3 All ER 481, HL, below, para **4–60**. Issuing the cheque is not an assignment of part of the thing in action consisting in the debt owed by P's bank to P, because the holder of a cheque cannot sue the bank on the cheque; Bills of Exchange Act 1882, s. 53 and *Schroeder v Central Bank of London Ltd* (1876) 34 LT 735.

[4] Cheques create things in action only if given for valuable consideration – i.e. any consideration sufficient to support a simple contract or an antecedent liability: Bills of Exchange Act 1882, s. 27 (1). A cheque given without consideration – a birthday present – does not create a thing in action but is, it is submitted, a valuable security – it gives access to the drawer's bank balance.

[5] (1857) 7 Cox CC 303, discussed by J.C. Smith [1997] Crim LR 401.

[6] *Governor of Brixton Prison, ex p Stallmann* [1912] 3 KB 424, DC; *Pople* [1951] 1 KB 53, sub nom *Smith* [1950] 2 All ER 679; *Rozeik* [1996] 1 Cr App Rep 260, CA; *Caresana* [1996] Crim LR 667, CA, to name but a few.

4–58 *Obtaining a cheque from a corporation.* It was held in *Rozeik*[1] that where it is alleged that D obtained a cheque from a limited company, it must be proved that a person whose state of mind was that of the company was deceived. This goes too far. The only question is whether the property was obtained in consequence of the deception of any person.[2] Possession may be obtained from any person who has possession, whether he is the owner or not. Ownership may be obtained from a person who has, or who has power to give, ownership. A thing in action can be obtained only from a person who has the power to transfer a thing in action. In *Rozeik* the managers who signed the the company's cheques were the proper persons, and the only persons with authority, to do so and they were not deceived because they knew that the representations were false.[3] The case was decided before the decision of the House of Lords in *Preddy*, so the assumption (which we now know to be wrong) was that the thing in action which D obtained from the company was property "belonging to" the company. The only persons who could grant the thing in action were not deceived so it was not obtained by deception. It was irrelevant for this purpose that other employees might have been deceived into putting the cheques before the managers for signature or preparing inaccurate accounts.[4] After *Preddy*, the question now, it is submitted, is whether D obtained the valuable security – the instrument, a tangible thing – by deception. If it was handed to him by the managers, he did not. But if he deceived any other employee, for example, a receptionist or messenger, into handing over the cheques, he obtained them by deception, just as he would if he obtained any money or chattel belonging to the company in that way. It is immaterial that the person giving possession had no authority to do so.[5]

---

[1]   [1996] 1 Cr App Rep 260, [1996] Crim LR 271, CA, doubted by Blackstone's CP, B5.18.
[2]   Arlidge and Parry, 4–104 to 4–108.
[3]   Surprisingly, they were not, or had to be treated as if they were not, parties to the fraud.
[4]   Archbold, 21–198a takes a different view: "it was critical to the success of his scheme that all the employees in the chain thought that they were processing ordinary bona-fide applications, i.e., that they were deceived." Certainly, but no property was obtained until the managers signed the cheque – and they knew the truth. The obtaining was not the result of those deceptions. The intervention of the managers broke the chain of causation. It would be different if the manager was unaware of the falsity. Cf Arlidge and Parry, 4–106. It is unlike *Kovacs* (1974) 58 Cr App Rep 412, CA where, because O is deceived, an obligation to deliver is imposed on P. No obligation was imposed on the managers.
[5]   The statement in Smith & Hogan, 569–570, requires qualification.

(c)   Belonging to another

4–59   Property "belongs to another" for the purposes of this section if the other has possession or control of it or any proprietary right or interest in it except an equitable interest arising only from an agreement to transfer or grant an interest.[1] Thus, the owner may be guilty of obtaining his own property by deception where, by deception, he dishonestly induces another to give up his lawful possession or control of that property. Suppose that D has pledged his clock with P as security for a loan and, by deception, he induces P to let him have the clock back again, intending neither to restore it nor to repay the loan.[2] The case where D, by deception, induces his servant, P, to surrender custody of D's goods is more doubtful. Even if D has a dishonest intention – for example, to charge P with having stolen the goods[3] – he may be guilty of no offence because he has a right to require P to return the goods at any time.

If D is entitled under the civil law to have his property back again, but P declines to deliver it, it is submitted that D commits no offence by recovering possession by deception. Suppose D has made P a bailee at will. He terminates the bailment by demanding the return of the property. On P's refusal to restore it, D obtains it by deception. In most cases, of course, D will have a claim of right which will negative dishonesty; but, even if he does not, it is submitted that it ought to be held that there is no *actus reus* in such a case. It would generally be incongruous that a man should be guilty of an offence under the criminal law in obtaining property which, by the civil law, he is entitled to have.[4] It is true that the manner of exercising such a right has been held to justify the intervention of the criminal law formerly, where a right of entry on to premises was exercised by violence or threats,[5] in blackmail,[6] and demanding property on a forged instrument contrary to s. 7 of the Forgery Act 1913.[7] Though the attempt to recover property is an essential part of these offences, it is evidently the use of the force, of the menace and of the forged instrument which is the gist of the offence. It might be argued that deception should fall into the same category. Deception, however, is less socially dangerous than force and does not attract that revulsion which nowadays attaches to blackmail. Demanding on forged instruments is less easily distinguishable; but like blackmail, it is an offence the gist of which is the demand. In the present case, the gist of the offence is the obtaining of property belonging to another: and, as against D, it ought not to be said that property belongs to P merely because P is in possession of it, if D is entitled to recover possession from him.

If, in the example given above, D had not terminated the bailment, the answer might be different. If he were then to recover possession by deception and with a dishonest intent – for example, intending to charge P with having lost the property – he should be guilty.[8]

---

[1]   The definition of "belonging to another" in s. 5 (1) (above, para **2–55**) applies to s. 15: see s. 34 (1), below, p 273.
[2]   Cf *Rose v Matt* [1951] 1 KB 810, [1951] 1 All ER 361, above, para **2–57**.
[3]   Cf *Anon (undated)* 2 East PC 558; *Smith* (1852) 2 Den 449.
[4]   Cf *Wheeler*, above, paras **2–44, 4–32**.
[5]   Criminal Law Act 1977, Part II, Smith & Hogan 801 (6th edn) 812.
[6]   Below, para **10–15**.
[7]   *Parker*, above, para **4–33**, fn 10. See Smith & Hogan 682.
[8]   Cf the corresponding case in theft, and *Turner (No 2)*, above, para **2–58**.

(d)   Something belonging to D must be transferred to P

4–60   The offence is not committed unless something which belongs to P before the deception is transferred to D in consequence of it. In *Preddy*,[1] the House of Lords, reversing the Court of Appeal, held that where D dishonestly and by deception procures a transaction whereby P's bank account is debited by £X and, consequently, D's bank account is credited by £X, D is not guilty of obtaining property "belonging to" P. The effect is exactly the same as if D had obtained £X belonging to P but, in law, nothing which formerly belonged to P now belongs to D. A thing in action[2] belonging to P (the indebtedness of P's bank to P) has been diminished (or perhaps extinguished) and a different thing in action (the indebtedness of D's bank to D) has been enlarged (or perhaps created). This is the effect when funds are transferred between bank accounts, as is now common, by telegraphic transfer or CHAPS order. The decision caused consternation because of the many frauds, particularly "mortgage frauds", which had been and were being prosecuted, it now appeared wrongly, under s. 15. The Law Commission speedily produced a Report and draft Bill[3] which rapidly became the Theft (Amendment) Act 1996, filling the lacuna exposed by *Preddy* with a new s. 15A of the 1968 Act creating an offence of obtaining a money transfer by deception.[4]

---

[1]   [1996] AC 815, [1986] 3 All ER 481, HL.
[2]   Cf para **2–105**, above.
[3]   *Offences of Dishonesty: Money Transfers*, Law Com No 243 (1996).
[4]   See below, para **4–64**.

(e)   The mens rea of obtaining property

4–61   The constituents of the *mens rea* are:
(i)   Deliberation or recklessness in making the deception.[1]

(ii) Dishonesty.[2]

(iii) Intention permanently to deprive.[3]

(iv) An intention, with or without a view to gain, to obtain property.

Constituents (i) and (ii) have been sufficiently examined above. Of (iii), it need be added only that the s. 6 meaning of the term applies for the purposes of s. 15 with the necessary adaptation of the reference to appropriation.[4]

---

[1]   Above, paras **4–15** to **4–16**.

[2]   Above, paras **4–33** to **4–38**.

[3]   Above, paras **2–125** to **2–144**.

[4]   Section 15 (3).

4–62   There is no provision corresponding to that for theft that "it is immaterial whether the appropriation is made with a view to gain . . . ".[1] It can hardly be doubted, however, that no further element of this nature is required in addition to the elements of *mens rea* described above. The draftsman perhaps took the view that the intention to obtain property, which is implicit in the subsection, in itself constituted a view to gain so[2] that any further express requirement would be superfluous. The terms of the Act make it clear that if D appropriates P's diamond and throws it into a deep pond, intending to deprive both P and himself permanently of it, he is guilty of theft. It does not, in express terms, say that D is guilty of deception if he obtains the ownership in or possession of P's diamond by deception with the intention of throwing the diamond into the pond and depriving P and himself permanently of it. It is submitted, however, that the obtainer of the diamond would be guilty of obtaining by deception. It is desirable that the same principles should govern s. 15 as s. 1.

---

[1]   Section 1 (2), above, para **2–113**.

[2]   See below, para **4–63**.

4–63   It is submitted that an intention to obtain property for oneself or another is a constituent of the *mens rea*. The *actus reus* of the offence is not committed where D, dishonestly and by deception, causes P to be deprived of his property but neither D nor anyone else obtains it. An intention to deprive another of property is therefore not a sufficient *mens rea* for the offence.

If D dishonestly tells P that a work of art owned by P is obscene, that it is being looked for by the police and that the best thing he can do is to burn it, D is not guilty of an offence under the section if P complies.[1] Suppose then, that D's object is to cause loss to one person, but that this will, incidentally, bring profit to another. For example, D induces P to exclude E from his will by telling P false stories of E's misconduct. D does not know or care who will profit as a result of E's exclusion from the will. Someone almost certainly will. Suppose that P, having substituted S's name for E's, dies and the executors pay the legacy to S. There is no doubt that D has dishonestly obtained property by deception for S. The *actus reus* is complete. Is it a defence for D to say that he did not intend to obtain property for anyone, that his only intention was to ensure that E did not benefit and that he would have been perfectly content with the outcome if P had decided to spend all his money in his lifetime?

It is arguable that the essence of the offence is the obtaining of property; that, in this example, the obtaining of the advantage is merely incidental to the fulfilment of D's plan and that, accordingly, D should not be guilty. If he were to be convicted, the iniquity of his conduct (when he came to be sentenced) would be found to lie in his malicious deprivation of E; but that is not an offence. This argument requires the adoption of the narrowest possible definition of "intention" – but there is precedent for it in other offences.[2]

---

[1]   D might be guilty of criminal damage through an innocent agent.
[2]   Smith & Hogan 57–63.

C.   OBTAINING A MONEY TRANSFER BY DECEPTION

4–64   Section 15A of the 1968 Act provides:

"(1) A person is guilty of an offence if by any deception he dishonestly obtains a money transfer for himself or another.
(2) A money transfer occurs when—
    (a) a debit is made to one account,
    (b) a credit is made to another, and
    (c) the credit results from the debit or the debit results from the credit.
(3) References to a credit and to a debit are to a credit of an amount of money and to a debit of an amount of money."

This very specific provision describes what Preddy did and enacts that it is an offence. The Law Commission rejected the apparently obvious course of amending s. 15, finding that this could be done only by an undesirable amount of "deeming". The new offence seems to fill the lacuna very effectively but it is not, of course, retrospective, so only money transfers obtained after 18 December 1996 may be prosecuted under s. 15A. Subsection (3) limits the offence to "money", meaning an obligation to pay money, notably the obligation of a banker to his customer. It would not therefore apply to transfers of other things in action, such as bonds and securities.[1] Subsection (4) (below, p 264) anticipates and excludes possible unmeritorious defences. This is not an exclusive list, as the words, "in particular", are intended to make clear. There are many matters which a court may properly hold to be immaterial, though they are not listed in the subsection.

Obtaining a money transfer by cheques. Preddy also settled[2] that where D induces V to draw and deliver a cheque in favour of D, D is not guilty under s. 15 of the 1968 Act of obtaining by deception the thing in action represented by the cheque. That thing in action was never "property belonging to" V. From the moment it came into existence, it belonged to D. When D presents the cheque and it is honoured a debit is made to V's account and a corresponding credit to D's, so a money transfer as defined in s.15A (1) occurs. Arguably, in such a case, the *transfer* has not been obtained by deception but by D's presentation of the cheque (as where a key is obtained by deception and used to open a safe and steal: the money taken from the safe has been stolen, not obtained by deception). Subsection (4) (b) appears to assume that the transfer has been obtained by deception and, for practical purposes, probably puts the matter beyond all doubt. Even so, the new offence will not be committed until the cheque is honoured. D will, however, clearly be guilty of an attempt to commit that offence when he presents, or attempts to present, the cheque. Until he does so, he has probably done no act which is more than merely preparatory to the commission of the s. 15A offence. Nor will D be guilty of obtaining a transfer of funds if he negotiates the cheque to E for cash. P's account has not yet been debited and no account has been credited. The offence will be committed only when E, or some subsequent holder of the cheque presents it, and it is honoured. It is therefore almost as important as it was before the Theft (Amendment) Act 1996 to know whether D has obtained the cheque, as a valuable security, contrary to s. 15.[3]

1   This limitation was criticised by Lord Donaldson of Lymington, whose amendments designed to broaden the ambit of the offence were not accepted by the House of Lords: Hansard, HL, vol. 576, col. 796.
2   Following *Danger* (1857) 7 Cox CC 303, CCR and overruling *Duru* [1973] 3 All ER 715, [1974] 1 WLR 2, sub nom *Asghar* [1973] Crim LR 701, CA.
3   See above, para **4–57**.

D.   OBTAINING A PECUNIARY ADVANTAGE BY DECEPTION

4–65   The draft bill proposed by the CLRC's *Eighth Report* would have created two offences of (i) obtaining credit by deception and (ii) inducing an act by deception with a view to gain. Part of the proposal did not commend itself to Parliament. Instead, a new clause, which became s. 16, was introduced to create the offence of obtaining a pecuniary advantage by deception. Section 16 (2) (a) proved to be so obscure that it amounted to "a judicial nightmare"[1] and it was repealed by the 1978 Act. Section 16, as amended, provides:

"(1) A person who by any deception dishonestly obtains for himself or another any pecuniary advantage shall on conviction on indictment be liable to imprisonment for a term not exceeding five years.

(2)   The cases in which a pecuniary advantage within the meaning of this section is to be regarded as obtained for a person are cases where—

   (a)   . . .

   (b)   he is allowed to borrow by way of overdraft, or to take out any policy of insurance or annuity contract, or obtains an improvement of the terms on which he is allowed to do so; or

   (c)   he is given the opportunity to earn remuneration or greater remuneration in an office or employment, or to win money by betting.

(3)   For the purpose of this section 'deception' has the same meaning as in section 15 of this Act."

1   *Royle* [1971] 3 All ER 1359 at 1363, CA, per Edmund Davies LJ.

4–66   Section 16 creates only one offence.[1] Subsection (2) merely describes the various types of pecuniary advantage the obtaining of which will amount to an offence, just as s. 4 describes the property which may be stolen under s. 1. It is, however, important that the particulars of the offence should specify precisely what is the pecuniary advantage which the accused is alleged to have obtained. "If you indict a man for stealing your watch, you cannot convict him of attempting to steal your umbrella";[2] and, equally, a man who is charged with obtaining a pecuniary advantage of one sort should not be convicted of obtaining a pecuniary advantage of a completely different sort. So a conviction was quashed where D was charged with obtaining a pecuniary advantage within the meaning of s. 16 (2) (a) (now repealed) and the court held that he had obtained a pecuniary advantage, not within that provision, but within s. 16 (2) (c).[3]

1   *Bale v Rosier* [1977] 2 All ER 160, [1977] 1 WLR 263.
2   *McPherson* (1857) Dears & B 197 at 200, per Cockburn CJ.
3   *Aston and Hadley* [1970] 3 All ER 1045, [1970] 1 WLR 1584, CA.

(a)   Pecuniary advantage

4–67   The meaning of this term is limited to the cases set out in the two remaining paragraphs of s. 16 (2). In these cases a pecuniary advantage is deemed to have been obtained. If the facts proved are within one of the paragraphs, it is no defence that D obtained no pecuniary advantage in fact.[1] Conversely, it is no offence to obtain a pecuniary advantage in fact, if the facts proved are not within one of the paragraphs. The pecuniary advantage may be obtained by the person practising the deception for himself, or it may be obtained for another. The words, "for a person" in subsection (2), refer not only to D but also to the other person referred to in subsection (1).[2] The following paragraphs[3] deal with the obtaining by D of a pecuniary advantage for himself; but it should be borne in mind that, in all cases, it is an offence to obtain a similar pecuniary advantage for another.

---

[1]   *Turner* [1974] AC 357, HL, per Lord Reid; below, para **4–87**. See criticism by Waters (1974) 37 MLR 562.
[2]   *Richardson v Skells* [1976] Crim LR 448 (Recorder Self).
[3]   Paras **4–68** to **4–74**.

(i)   Section 16 (2) (b)

4–68   It has been held that a person "is allowed to borrow by way of overdraft" when the overdraft facility is granted to him, though he never draws on it.[1] The judge pointed out that the subsection says, "is allowed to borrow", not "borrows"; that the alternative, "or obtains an improvement of the terms", plainly refers to the agreement: and (he thought) that actually borrowing might be an offence of obtaining property by deception, contrary to s. 15.[2]

---

[1]   *Watkins* [1976] 1 All ER 578 (Judge Paul Clarke).
[2]   Possibly the obtaining of the money might be held to be too remote by analogy to the employment and betting cases (above, para **4–13**), the obtaining of the overdraft facility corresponding to the obtaining of employment; but it is thought this would not be a good analogy.

4–69   D is "allowed to borrow by way of overdraft" when, in breach of contract, he uses a cheque card with which he has been entrusted by his bank, so that the bank is legally bound to honour the cheque and so grant or extend an overdraft.[1] It appears that the bank is held to have "allowed" a course of action which it has in fact expressly forbidden. In *Bevan*,[2] the court sought to explain this on the ground that the honouring of the cheque, though an act that the bank was legally and commercially obliged to do, was nevertheless "an act of will" – it might have refused to honour its obligations – so the bank "allowed" the borrowing when it honoured the cheque. This wades deeper into the mire. If honouring the cheque is the "allowing", the allowing, i.e. the pecuniary advantage, is not obtained by deception because the bank is now in full possession of the facts. It is the trader who honours the cheque card, and he alone, who is held (however artificially)[3] to have been deceived, so the obtaining must result from something that he does in consequence of the deception. What he does, of course, is to impose the obligation on the bank by accepting a cheque in reliance on the card. If a pecuniary advantage is obtained by deception (and the courts say it is) that advantage must logically be the imposition of that obligation, not the honouring of it by the bank.

It has been cogently argued[4] that the words "by way of overdraft" would not extend to a bank loan effected by crediting some other account in the same or another bank. If money were obtained there would probably be an offence under s. 15. If no money were obtained, there would be an offence of obtaining services by deception, contrary to 1978, s. 1, the payment for the service being the interest to be charged on the loan. That section would indeed seem to cover virtually all cases under s. 16 (2) (b).

---

[1]   *Waites* [1982] Crim LR 369, CA and commentary. Cf Williams *TBCL* 883, fn 1.

²   (1986) 84 Cr App Rep 143, [1987] Crim LR 129, CA and commentary.
³   Above, paras **4–06** to **4–08**.
⁴   Griew 10–07.

4–70   It may be that insurance and annuity contracts were singled out because they are cases where the insurer is peculiarly dependent on the assured's good faith, since the special facts which affect the risk lie peculiarly within the latter's knowledge. It may, therefore, have been thought that the insurer needs special protection against the assured's fraud. Even if the increased sum were actually paid, the payment might be too remote[1] from the deception to constitute an offence under s. 15.

Contracts of insurance are contracts *uberrimae fidei*, so that, under the civil law, there is an obligation to make disclosure of any material circumstance. Failure to do so renders the contract voidable. No action will lie for damages, however – i.e. the non-disclosure is not "deceit" – and it is submitted that a mere non-disclosure will not amount to a deception ("by words or conduct") for the purposes of s. 16, unless the non-disclosure makes, and is known by the accused to make, the words or conduct which have been used positively misleading.[2]

¹   See above, para **4–13**.
²   *Lord Kylsant* [1932] 1 KB 442. A case where " . . . a document has been put forward . . . in such a form that though it stated every fact correctly, fact by fact, and everything was correctly stated by the card, yet the true effect of what was said was completely false and completely misleading".

(ii)   Section 16(2)(c)

4–71   Obtaining an office or employment by false pretences did not amount to an offence under the Larceny Act 1916 and some cases held that the obtaining of the wage or salary was too remote from the false pretence to be an offence.[1] Those cases may be wrongly decided;[2] but, whether or not that is so the matter is now specifically dealt with. D commits an offence if he obtains employment by stating that he has a qualification which he does not possess; or if he obtains employment at a higher salary by stating that he has that qualification. The offence is also committed by one who obtains employment, or employment on better terms, for another in a similar way.

¹   *Lewis* (1922) Russell on Crime (12 ed) p 1186, above, para **4–13**.
²   See para **4–13**, above.

4–72   It is not an offence under the section to obtain the opportunity to earn remuneration otherwise than in "an office or employment". A person who, by deception, obtained the tenancy of a public house did not commit the offence. The tenancy was not an "office" or "employment".[1] D sought the tenancy in order to obtain a justices' licence in order to obtain remuneration. It may be that the holder of a justices' licence does hold an office; but D had not yet obtained, or attempted to obtain, such a licence. Getting the opportunity to obtain the justices' licence did not amount to getting the opportunity to earn remuneration in that office.

The words, "office or employment" are not defined, but in *Callendar*[2] it was held that they are not confined to the narrow limits of a contract of service. D, who held himself out as a self-employed accountant, was "employed" by his clients and, having practised a deception to gain that employment, was guilty of an offence. So it seems that a freelance author is employed by his publishers, and a solicitor by his client, for the purposes of the subsection. "Employment" is not a technical term but is to be given its ordinary meaning.

As noted above,[3] it was held that no offence was committed under the Larceny Act when D induced P to take bets on credit by false pretences and that a payment made by P to D when D backed a winning horse was too remote from the false pretence which induced P to accept the bet. Whether or not this is still the position regarding obtaining property, s. 16 (2) (c) deals specifically with the case. D would be guilty of this offence whether he was allowed to bet on cash or on credit terms.

---

[1]   *McNiff* [1986] Crim LR 57, CA.
[2]   [1993] QB 303, [1992] 3 All ER 51, CA.
[3]   Above, para **4–13**; *Clucas* [1949] 2 KB 226, [1949] 2 All ER 40.

(iii)   The mens rea of obtaining a pecuniary advantage

4–73   The constituents of the *mens rea* are:
(1)   Intention or recklessness in making the deception.[1]
(2)   Dishonesty.[2]
(3)   An intention to obtain a pecuniary advantage.
Constituents (1) and (2) have been sufficiently examined above. Constituent (3) requires further discussion.

---

[1]   Above, paras **4–15** to **4–16**.
[2]   Above, paras **4–33** to **4–38**.

4–74   Causing a pecuniary disadvantage to another is not necessarily the same thing as obtaining a pecuniary advantage for oneself or another. An exactly similar argument to that employed in relation to obtaining property by deception[1] may be relied on here. Suppose that D's object is to cause loss to one person, but that this will, incidentally, bring a pecuniary advantage to another. For example, E is a candidate for an appointment with P. D sends to P a reference containing false statements, so as to ensure that E will not be appointed. D does not know who the other candidates are, but, if his deception is the reason why E is not appointed, one of them will obtain a pecuniary advantage as the direct result of D's deception. Suppose that the deception is successful and, consequently, S is appointed and E is not. There is no doubt that D has dishonestly obtained a pecuniary advantage by deception for S. The *actus reus* is complete. Is it a defence for D to say that he did not intend to obtain a pecuniary advantage for anyone, that his only intention was to ensure that E did not obtain a pecuniary advantage and that he would have been perfectly content with the outcome if P had decided not to make an appointment at all?[2]

It is arguable that the essence of the offence is the obtaining of the advantage; that, in this example, the obtaining of the advantage is merely incidental to the fulfilment of D's plan and that, accordingly, D should not be guilty.

---

[1]   Above, para **4–63**.
[2]   Cf *DPP v Luft* [1977] AC 962, [1976] 2 All ER 569, HL.

E.   OBTAINING SERVICES BY DECEPTION

4–75   A person's labour is something of economic value. It is the principal means by which most people acquire property but it is not in itself property. To cause another by deception to do certain work is not an offence of obtaining property even though the deceived person has suffered an economic loss and the deceiver has made a corresponding gain as a result of the deception. The mischief is very much the same as where property is obtained but it is only since 1978 that this fact has been expressly recognised by the law. Where D induced P to render services in advance of payment, this might have been treated as an obtaining of credit by fraud contrary to the Debtor's Act 1869 (many sections now repealed) or possibly the obtaining of a pecuniary advantage through the deferment of a debt by deception contrary to s. 16 (2) (a) of the Theft Act 1968 (also repealed). These offences did not, however, relate to the gist of the offence which was that P had been wrongly caused to expend his labour and thereby suffered an economic loss.

Section 1 of the Theft Act 1978[1] provides:

"(1) A person who by any deception dishonestly obtains services from another shall be guilty of an offence.

(2) It is an obtaining of services where the other is induced to confer a benefit by doing some act, or causing or permitting some act to be done, on the understanding that the benefit has been or will be paid for.

(3) Without prejudice to the generality of subsection (2) above, it is an obtaining of services where the other is induced to make a loan, or to cause or permit a loan to be made, on the understanding that any payment (whether by way of interest or otherwise) will be or has been made in respect of the loan."

---

[1] See CLRC Working Paper, *Section 16 of the Theft Act* (1974), *Thirteenth Report* (1977), Cmnd 6733; Spencer [1979] Crim LR 24; Leng (1979) 143 JP 16 & 33; Syrota, Annotations in *Current Law Statutes* and 42 MLR 301; Williams [1979] CLJ 4.

(a) By deception

4–76   The service must be obtained by deception. D does not commit the offence where he succeeds in dishonestly enjoying the service without deception as where he secretly enters a cinema or cricket ground or where he induces a taxi-driver to carry him by threats. As in the case of other obtaining offences,[1] it must be proved that a person was deceived and did, or caused or permitted the act conferring the benefit in consequence of the deception.

Section 5 (1) provides that "deception" has the same meaning as in s. 15 of the 1968 Act. This has been considered above[2] and only one matter calls for comment here. Because s. 1 requires that P must do the act, or cause or permit the act to be done, on the understanding that it has been or will be paid for, it might be argued that the deception must relate to D's intention to pay. It is submitted that this is not so. The function of the words, "on the understanding that the benefit has been or will be paid for", is to exclude from the operation of the section services which are rendered gratuitously. If D induces his neighbour, P, to mow D's lawn as an act of friendship by falsely stating that he has sprained his ankle, no offence is committed. If D makes the same false statement and, at the same time, offers P £10 to do the job, an offence is committed if P mows the lawn on the understanding that he will be paid and because he believes the story of the sprained ankle, even though D always intends to pay and does pay. The lie is clearly a deception within s. 15 of the 1968 Act and it induces P to confer a benefit on the understanding that it will be paid for. Clause 1 of the Committee's draft bill and the bill first introduced into Parliament were restricted to "a deception going to the prospect of payment being duly made".[3] There is no such restriction in s. 1 of the Act and no warrant in the words used for implying it. The effect is that the section is rather wider than one might expect in a Theft Act. The offence may be committed where no economic loss is contemplated or caused. An example is the case where D induces P to let him have the hire of a car for the day by falsely stating that he has a driving licence. D may intend to pay or even have paid in advance but he is still guilty of an offence under the section. The result is consistent with s. 15 of the 1968 Act as applied in *Potger*.[4] A possible answer to this view is that the jury might not find D's conduct to be dishonest where he intends no economic loss. While the courts continue to leave a wide discretion to juries in deciding whether conduct is or is not dishonest, it is impossible to state the law with any degree of certainty; but if the conduct envisaged is not dishonest, then Potger was wrongly convicted.

---

[1]   Above, paras **4–02** to **4–38**.
[2]   Para **4–14**.
[3]   Cmnd 6733, p 23. The point was decided in *Naviede* [1997] Crim LR (September).
[4]   (1970) 55 Cr App Rep 42, CA; above, para **4–35**.

(b)   Services

4–77   The difficulty of defining "services" deterred the CLRC from proposing an offence of obtaining services by deception.[1] The CLRC thought that services would have to be defined to include any act and that this would not be materially different from the offence proposed in Clause 12 (3) of the draft bill attached to the *Eighth Report* which had proved to be unacceptable to Parliament. The Committee therefore proposed a narrower offence of "Deception as to the prospect of payment".[2] This was included in the bill introduced by the government but this time Parliament took a different view. A preference was expressed for an offence of obtaining services, widely defined, and, after reference back to the CLRC, the provision which became s. 1 emerged. Under s. 1 "services" may be:

  (i)   any act done by P provided that
    (a)   it confers a benefit on someone other than P and
    (b)   it is done on the understanding that the benefit has been or will be paid for; or
  (ii)   any act which P causes or permits to be done, whether by D or another, provided that
    (a)   it amounts to a benefit to, or confers a benefit on, someone other than P and
    (b)   it is caused or permitted on the understanding that the benefit has been or will be paid for.

---

[1]   Cmnd 6733, para 7.
[2]   Cmnd 6733, p. 23.

(c)   Some act

4–78   It is submitted that any act which satisfies the conditions stated is enough. If this is right there is a substantial overlap with ss. 15 and 16 (2) (b) and (c) of the 1968 Act. To give property is undoubtedly to confer a benefit and in most cases under s. 15 the property is to be paid for. To allow D to borrow by way of overdraft or to take out a policy of insurance is to confer a benefit and the benefits are to be paid for by the interest on the overdraft and the payment of the premiums. The fact that the transfer of property is not ordinarily described as "services"[1] is not sufficient, it is submitted, to take the case out of s. 1 since subsection (2) states positively, "It is an obtaining of services where . . . ". It is true that 1978, s. 3, distinguishes between the supply of goods and the doing of a "service"; but it is clear that "services" in s. 1 is intended to include some types of supply of goods, for example, hire; and it is thought that there is no sufficient ground for distinguishing between one type of supply and another. Contrary to this view was the decision in *Halai*[2] that a mortgage advance is not a service. The court may have thought that obtaining a mortgage advance by deception was an offence under s.15 and that the two offences are mutually exclusive – an opinion with which Lord Goff in *Preddy*[3] was not unsympathetic. But the CLRC intended this to be a very broad offence, "loosely described as 'obtaining services'",[4] a phrase which they did not use in their proposed offence, either in the Working Paper or later Report . The phrase is a drafting device and should not be allowed to have any limiting effect. The CLRC were well aware of, and unperturbed by, the overlap with other Theft Act offences. The Court of Appeal has now accepted that s. 1 has this broad meaning and has overruled *Halai*.[5] In the meantime, Parliament, on the recommendation of the Law Commission, had dealt with the matter by enacting the new subsection (3), set out above (para **4–75**). That subsection does not apply to anything done before 18 December 1996. The overruling of *Halai* – deciding that the case never was the law – is therefore of practical importance, expecially in enabling the Court of Appeal, in appropriate cases, to substitute convictions under s. 1 of the 1978 Act for convictions which have to be quashed in the wake of *Preddy*.

---

[1]   Cf Spencer [1979] Crim LR 24 at 28.
[2]   [1983] Crim LR 624, CA.
[3]   [1996] 3 All ER 481 at 495.
[4]   CLRC *Working Paper on Section 16 of the Theft Act 1968,* August 1974, para 27.
[5]   The opinion in *Graham* [1997] 1 Cr App Rep 302 at 317 that *Halai* should no longer be followed may have been obiter but the matter is put beyond doubt by *Cooke* [1997] Crim LR 436, *Cumming-John* [1997] Crim LR (September), *Hilton* (7 March 1997, CA) and *Naviede* [1997] Crim LR (September).

4–79   P must be induced to do or to cause or permit some *act*. A mere omission will not do. This is not likely to be a serious limitation on the operation of the section. Even where D seeks to induce P to refrain from doing something, it is probable that this will require some act, or the causing or permitting of some act. P, a bank manager, has stated that he proposes to withdraw D's overdraft facility. D, by deception, persuades him not to do so. It is probable that P will do such acts as giving instructions to his staff and writing to D to confirm that the facility is still available; and P will, of course, permit D to draw further cheques on the bank though his account is overdrawn. What, however, if D, while recumbent in a deck chair at the seaside, falsely tells the attendant that he has paid the hire? The attendant permits D to continue to lie motionless in the chair. That is a benefit, but can it be described as an act? If a case of this kind, serious enough to deserve prosecution, should arise, it would be better dealt with under s. 2 (1) (b).[1]

---

[1]   Below, para **4–95**.

4–80   The offence is not complete until the act which confers the benefit and which is to be paid for, is done. If, by deception, D obtains a high place on the local authority waiting list for council houses, he may well be said to have obtained a benefit but that benefit is not to be paid for. If, in due course, he is granted the tenancy the continuing deception has induced an act for which it is understood that he will pay through the rent and the offence is now complete. Obtaining a high place on the list should, however, be regarded as a more than merely preparatory act so as to amount to an attempt to commit the offence, contrary to the Criminal Attempts Act 1981. Where, on the other hand, D obtains a contract under which he is to render services for payment, for example, to paint P's house, it seems that there is no offence under s. 1. The contract is not to be paid for. It might be argued that P has been induced by deception to cause or permit an act to be done, namely the performance of the contract by D, and that act is to be paid for – it is to be paid for by P himself. This argument is fallacious because it is the causing or permitting the act which is the benefit and which must be done on the understanding that it will be paid for. P's causing or permitting D to paint his house is not to be paid for. The case may be contrasted with that where a car-hire firm is induced by deception to cause a car to be delivered to D or to permit D to take the car. Here it is the causing or permitting which is to be paid for, not the taking of the car by D, and the case is covered by s. 1. When P does the act or causes the act to be done it is clear that the offence is complete only when the act has been done. It is less obvious when the allegation is that P permitted the act to be done. It might be argued that the offence is complete when P gives permission.[1] It is submitted that the better view is that the act conferring the benefit must be done in all cases. Only then are services obtained. If P has given permission for the act to be done, D will be guilty of an attempt.

---

[1] Cf *Watkins* [1976] 1 All ER 578, above, para **4–68** where "allowed" in 1968, s. 16 (2) (b) was held to mean the act of allowing; but that depended on the context.

(d) A benefit

4–81 The act must be done, or caused or permitted, by P but it is sufficient that it is a benefit to anyone, not necessarily to D.[1] The offence might be committed where, for example, D obtains education at a school or university for his son, beauty treatment for his wife, lodging for his mistress, the transfer of a centre-forward to his favourite football club or the cleaning of his employer's offices. A survey of a building by a building society is for the benefit of the prospective mortgagor since he cannot obtain a mortgage without it.[2] There is unlikely to be much difficulty in determining that the act confers a benefit where it is done on the understanding that it has been or will be paid for. Men do not generally pay for acts of others unless they will be beneficial. There may, however, be occasional cases which give rise to difficulty.

---

[1] *Nathan* (1997) Archbold News, 5 June.
[2] *Halai* [1983] Crim LR 624, CA.

(e) "A benefit" – in whose eyes?

4–82 In the great majority of cases the "benefit" will be something of economic value. D need not be financially enriched, as he is in the case where he obtains property. The service might be, for example, a massage which makes him feel better or a haircut which makes him look smarter. It is submitted that the effect of the service does not fail to be a benefit because the person acting or the jury, or persons generally, would not regard it as beneficial. Suppose D instructs the barber to shave his magnificent head of hair; the woodcutter to fell a splendid tree; the painter to respray his new Rolls-Royce in shocking pink.[1] In each case P protests at what he regards as an act of barbarity but is finally persuaded by the offer of money to do the act. It would be quite inappropriate that D's liability should depend on the subjective judgment of others as to whether the act was beneficial. It is submitted that it is sufficient that it was a benefit to D's eyes.

In these examples, the act done – hair-cutting, tree-felling, painting – is a service in the ordinary commercial sense. It is probably immaterial that the transaction is contrary to public policy – the services of a prostitute are presumably "a benefit" to the customer.

---

[1]   But what if the tree or Rolls-Royce belongs to D's estranged wife, E, who is horrified at what is done? Is the satisfaction of D's malice against E a benefit to him? D should be charged with criminal damage.

4–83   Where the act done, or caused or permitted, has no apparent commercial value, it may be argued that it is incapable of being a benefit within the Act. It is submitted that, again, it is a sufficient answer that D was willing to pay, or expressed a willingness to pay, for the act in question. D promises P £100 if P will walk to York. It is well recognised in the law of contract that P's walking to York is such a "benefit" to D as to amount to a sufficient consideration to make D's promise enforceable. To borrow (and modify) the facts of a well-known case in the law of contract:[1] D says to P, the owner of certain boilers: "Let me weigh your boilers and I will pay you £100." D has no intention of paying but, on the understanding that he will be paid, P allows him to weigh the boilers. In the actual case, the court appears to have had no idea why D had this strange wish to weigh someone else's boilers (and generations of law students have puzzled in vain over the matter) but they had no doubt that P had given consideration to D by allowing him to do so. It is submitted that in such a case P has conferred a benefit on D. This does not necessarily mean that the words "to confer a benefit" are deprived of all meaning, as the following examples show.

---

[1]   *Bainbridge v Firmstone* (1838) 1 Per & Dav 2.

4–84   Can the act be a benefit where the doing of it amounts to a criminal offence? The answer may depend on the purpose for which the offence was created. If the object of the law is to protect D (or the third party on whom the alleged benefit is conferred) against the act in question, it is arguable the doing of it cannot be regarded as a benefit.[1] If D, aged 17, induces P to tattoo him by falsely representing that he intends to pay, P is prima facie guilty of an offence under the Tattooing of Minors Act 1969. P could not, of course, recover the price of the tattooing from D but, as is shown below,[2] that is not in itself enough to rule out an offence under s. 1. However, the object of the law is to protect minors from being tattooed. Since the law regards this as an evil to be prevented. arguably it cannot consistently regard it at the same time as a benefit. If P can show that he believed and had reasonable cause to believe that D was over 18, then he is not guilty of the tattooing offence; but the act which has been done is nevertheless one that the law aims to prevent.

Also falling into this category is the case where the act is done to D and is an act to which he cannot effectively consent. He promises to pay P if she will whip him so as to inflict bodily harm upon him. P (it seems) is guilty of an offence against D, notwithstanding his consent.[3] A rather more likely example, perhaps, is that where D, a pregnant woman, promises to pay P to perform an illegal abortion on her. This is unlikely to be regarded as a benefit to D in law, whatever view she may take of it. All this, however, depends on whether it is held that "benefit" is a meaningful word or, as the majority of commentators think, a mere drafting device without substantive meaning.

[1]   Arlidge and Parry, 4–149, Griew, 9–06, and A.T.H. Smith, *Property Offences*, 18–22 and 18–27 to 18–28, all think this is reading too much into the word "benefit", which is merely a drafting device. But see also Spencer [1979] Crim LR 24 at 27.
[2]   Para **4–85**.
[3]   *Donovan* [1934] 2 KB 498.

4–85   Where the object of the law is something other than the protection of D, the forbidden act will clearly amount to a benefit to D although it is an offence. Where D obtains the hire of a car by falsely representing that he has a licence he commits an offence by driving it, but there seems to be no reason why the use of the car should not be regarded as a benefit to him. The law requiring a licence is not for the protection of the driver (or at least not primarily for his protection). If D obtained a television set on hire-purchase terms without paying the deposit at one time required by the law, the whole transaction was illegal but the use of the set appears to be plainly a benefit to D. There are cases where the act done is a grave crime yet an undoubted benefit to D, as where he hires P to kill X who is blackmailing D or who stands between D and a vast inheritance. To be free of the blackmailer, to inherit the great estate, is undoubtedly a benefit to D.

(f)   The understanding

4–86   Where D is induced by deception to render for nothing a service for which he would normally charge, it is impossible to contend that the act has been done on the understanding that it has been or will be paid for and thus there is no offence against s. 1. For example, D, by a false hard-luck story, induces P, a taxi-driver, to give him a free ride. This is a gratuitous service and so not within the terms of s. 1. D is, however, probably guilty of the offence of obtaining exemption from liability to make a payment, contrary to 1978, s. 2 (1) (c).[1] Probably a contingent liability to pay – as with a credit card the use of which is "free" only so long as the account is settled promptly – is enough.

The understanding is that someone, not necessarily P, has been or will be paid. It will, for example, commonly be the case that P, an employee, will confer a benefit on the understanding that his employer has been or will be paid. The understanding may be that the payment will be made not by D but by a third party. For example, D represents that his firm will pay his hotel bill.

The understanding is that of P. D must know that P understands that payment has been or will be made. It should be irrelevant that P's understanding is unreasonable if D knows that it exists.[2] The understanding will usually amount to a contract but it is not necessary that it should be so.

Sections 2 and 3 of the 1978 Act are both confined to cases in which there is an enforceable liability. No such limitation is expressed in s. 1 and there is no ground for implying it. The prostitute cannot sue for the price of her services but they may be obtained from her by deception. Suppose that D, a minor, by falsely representing that he intends to pay the fee of £100, induces P to give him flying lessons. P will probably be unable to sue successfully for the fee because it is most unlikely that flying lessons will be held to be necessary for a minor. P has, however, undoubtedly conferred a benefit on D and D is guilty of an offence of obtaining services by deception. The case is much the same in principle as that where D, a minor, obtains non-necessary goods from P by deception. P is unable to sue D for the price of the goods but he can prosecute him to conviction for an offence under s. 15 of the 1968 Act.

[1]   Below, para **4–97**.
[2]   Contra, Syrota, Current Law Statutes.

(g) Paid for

4–87   In the great majority of cases, the benefit will be paid for in money – whether in cash or by cheque. The CLRC intended the offence in Clause 1 of their draft bill to be –

"... essentially an offence of dishonestly obtaining by deception services on which a monetary value is placed ..."[1]

Where D induced a building society to open an account in his favour by drawing a bad cheque, he did not commit the offence, according to *Halai*,[2] because (i) no benefit is conferred on him, and (ii) the "service" is not to be paid for. The first reason we now know to be wrong but the second is sound where the building society makes no charge for its services.

The Committee relied on the word "payment" to confine the offence to services on which a monetary value is placed. Section 1 is different from the draft clause in important respects but in this respect it appears to be the same, "paid for" having the same effect as "payment". The question is whether "paid for" might include "payment" by goods or services instead of money. For example:

D agrees with P that, if P will paint D's house with D's paint, D will put a new engine in P's car when it has done 60,000 miles. P paints the house. D, as he intended all along, refuses to supply the engine. Or:

D promises P that, if P will dig D's garden, D will give him a night's lodging. P digs the garden and D, as he intended all along, refuses to give him the lodging.[3]

In these cases, it could scarcely be said that a monetary value had been placed on the services in question and, if "paid for" does indeed require the fixing of a monetary value, no offence is committed. Clearly, however, D's acts are within the mischief at which the section is aimed, and it is by no means impossible for "paid for" to be construed to include "payment" by goods or services.[4] It is submitted that it should be so construed.

"Paid for" does not imply a payment appropriated to this particular service. D commits the offence if he induces P to repair his television by falsely representing that he has an annual maintenance contract with P's employer or if he borrows books from a University library by falsely representing that he is a student, thus implying that he has paid or will pay the fees which entitle him to this service; or if he induces an AA scout to repair his car by pretending that he is a member who has omitted to bring his membership card with him.

---

[1]   *Thirteenth Report*, para 9.

[2]   [1983] Crim LR 624, CA, now overruled on this point. Above, para **4–78**. The court equated a bank account with a building society account. But, arguably, a bank account is a service to be paid for either by bank charges or the maintaining of a minimum balance.

[3]   See the second edition of this work, paras [268] to [269], where these examples were considered in relation to 1968, s. 16 (2) (a). They amounted to offences only if the word "charge" were to be construed broadly so as to include "obligation". The point was never decided. See third edition, para [208].

[4]   Cf *White v Elmdene Estates* [1959] 2 All ER 605 at 610–611, per Lord Evershed MR, below, para **5–08**.

F.   EVASION OF LIABILITY BY DECEPTION

4–88   Section 2 of the Act probably creates three offences.[1] There are material differences in both *mens rea* and *actus reus* between the three paragraphs, (a), (b) and (c), and the section does not contain the common unifying element which enabled the court to hold that s. 16 of the 1968 Act creates only one offence.[2] The offences are probably not mutually exclusive.[3] For instance, D who secures the remission of a liability contrary to para (a) and who has an intent to make permanent default is almost certainly also guilty of inducing his creditor to forgo payment contrary to para (b). If D has no intention to make permanent default, he may be guilty under (a) but not under (b); and if he induces P merely to forgo payment (as distinct from remitting the liability – whatever that distinction may be) with intent to make permanent default, he is guilty under (b) but not under (a). The three offences overlap but it must be assumed that they are not coincident and that no one of them includes the whole of another. The offences are triable either way and punishable on indictment with five years' imprisonment.

---

[1]   In *Holt* [1981] 2 All ER 854, CA, the court referred to "the three offences" in s. 2 (1).
[2]   *Bale v Rosier* [1977] 2 All ER 160, above, para **4–58**.
[3]   *Holt* (above); *Jackson* [1983] Crim LR 617.

(a)   Securing the remission of a liability

4–89   Section 2 (1) (a) provides that a person is guilty of an offence where, by any deception, he:

> "dishonestly secures the remission of the whole or part of any existing liability to make a payment whether his own liability or another's."

This provision is limited to cases where there is an existing debt though it may have been created only seconds beforehand, as where a motorist buys petrol and then secures remission of his liability to pay for it. It does not apply to the case where D by deception induces P to agree to render a service without charge or at a lower price than he would have charged in the absence of the deception. That case is covered by para (c).[1] It applies only to legally enforceable liability. It has no application to a "debt" which is unenforceable because it arises out of a transaction which is illegal because it contravenes a statute,[2] or which, as in the case of a wagering debt, is declared void by statute or which, as in the case of money promised to a prostitute[3] for her services, is treated as illegal in the law of contract.[4]

---

[1]   Below, para **4–97**.
[2]   Cf *Garlick* (1958) 42 Cr App Rep 141.
[3]   Cf *Caslin* [1961] 1 All ER 246, [1961] 1 WLR 59.
[4]   Cheshire, Fifoot & Furmston *Law of Contract* (12th edn) Ch 11.

4–90   Section 2 (2) provides: "subsection (1) shall not apply in relation to a liability that has not been accepted or established to pay compensation for a wrongful act or omission." The CLRC explained that this subsection would prevent the offence being committed where, for example, "a person lies about the circumstances of an accident in order to avoid the bringing of civil proceedings for negligence against him".[1] The reason is that the Committee could see no justification "for extending the criminal law to cases where the existence of any liability is disputed"; "the claimant can launch civil proceedings if he thinks he has been deceived when he absolved the other party from liability". They thought, however, that "the dividing line is reached where liability is not disputed even though the amount of that liability is. On this basis it would be an offence . . . for an antique dealer to lie about the age and value of jewellery sent to him for valuation which had been lost as a result of his admitted negligence". It may seem strange that D should be liable if he dishonestly induces P to reduce his claim from £500 to £100 but not liable if he induces him to drop the claim altogether. The latter seems a greater offence. The difference, perhaps, is that the former may result in a compromise and, while the compromise would be voidable for fraud, the onus would be on P to establish the fraud. Liability may sometimes be accepted or established before the quantum is agreed[2] but more often negotiations will lead to a single agreement covering both. If, in the course of such negotiations D tells lies which cause P to settle for £500 when otherwise he would have pursued his claim for £1,000, no offence is committed for no liability has been accepted or established until the agreement is concluded. Nor is it by any means completely clear that the section fulfils the intention of the CLRC. Suppose that liability but not quantum has been accepted; that the true measure of damages is £1,000 and that D deceives P into accepting £500. It is difficult to see that any liability to pay £1,000 has been accepted or established so as to be capable of being remitted in part.

---

[1]   *Thirteenth Report*, para 16.
[2]   *Tomlin v Standard Telephones and Cables Ltd* [1969] 3 All ER 201, [1969] 1 WLR 1378, CA.

(b) Remission

4–91   The words, "secures the remission of . . . any existing liability", must be read in the light of the fact that it is an offence under para (b) to induce a creditor to forgo payment with intent to make permanent default. Paragraph (a) does not require any intention to make permanent default. Plainly a difference is intended between remitting liability and forgoing payment. The obvious difference seems to be that forgoing payment does not affect the existing liability whereas remitting liability does. Similarly para (c)[1] seems to be concerned with a deception which affects the legal relationship between two persons, whereas, quite clearly, (b) does not require any modification of the legal relationship but only a forbearance to enforce unchanged rights. A remission of a liability, like an exemption from or abatement of a liability, suggests some change in legal rights and duties. In *Holt*,[2] the court said that it found great difficulty in introducing these concepts into the construction of the subsection. They added, "Thus the differences between the offences relate principally to the different situations in which the debtor–creditor relationship has arisen." This is difficult to follow. Both paras (a) and (b) with which the court was concerned simply assume an "existing liability" which, apparently, may have arisen in any way whatsoever. The differences relate to the manner in which the parties treat the existing liability, not to the way in which it arose.

Nothwithstanding this dictum, then, it remains arguable that remission is some act of the creditor which has the effect in law of wiping out the legal liability; that the defendant must intend to secure remission and therefore intend the legal liability to be wiped out.[3] This would explain the absence of the words "with intent to make permanent default" in (a) and in (c). If a person intends that something shall cease to exist he intends to deprive the owner of it for ever. By securing remission, D deprives P permanently of his right; and that is sufficient to constitute the offence even though D may not intend to "make permanent default" in that he intends to pay the appropriate sum one day.

---

[1]   Below, para **4–97**.
[2]   [1981] 2 All ER 854, [1981] 1 WLR 1000, CA.
[3]   Griew, *Theft*, 10–12, fn 15, writes "It does not seem credible that s. 2 (1) (a) should be as narrow as this view would make it." Cf A.T.H. Smith, *Property Offences*, 20–35. But Arlidge

and Parry, 4–177, point out that "Forgoing payment is a more drastic step than merely waiting for payment, and remitting the liability is more drastic than both."

4–92   Where D, the holder of a credit card, dishonestly and by deception induces his creditor, P, to accept "payment" by credit card he secures the remission of an existing liability because his liability to P is unconditionally extinguished.[1] In *Jackson*,[2] the card was tendered in payment not by the holder but by a thief. It was held that D had secured the remission of his liability. The trader would forthwith look, not to D, but to the credit card company for payment and, if the conditions on the card were satisfied, the company would be bound to pay and the trader could not recover the debt twice. If payment by cheque backed by a cheque card is merely conditional, the position is less clear; but it may be regarded as a remission, though subject to revival in the unlikely event of the failure of the bank to meet its obligations.

A mere agreement by a creditor that he will not enforce a legal liability does not destroy the debt in law.[3]

" . . . it is a daily occurrence that a merchant or tradesman, who is owed a sum of money, is asked to take less. The debtor says he is in difficulties. He offers a lesser sum in settlement, cash down. He says he cannot pay more. The creditor is considerate. He accepts the proffered sum and forgives him the rest of the debt. The question arises: is the settlement binding on the creditor? The answer is that, in point of law, the creditor is not bound by the settlement. He can the next day sue the debtor for the balance, and get judgment."[4]

---

[1]   *Re Charge Card Services Ltd* [1987] Ch 150, [1986] 3 All ER 289 (Millett J), affd [1988] 3 All ER 702, CA. Payment by credit card is an absolute and not merely conditional payment. That decision is based on a close examination of the nature of the various contractual relationships involved and does not necessarily apply to payment by cheque backed by a cheque card. Millett J said, *obiter*, [1986] 3 All ER at 301 h–j, that payment by cheque is conditional, even when acompanied by a cheque card. The point was left open in the Court of Appeal [1988] 3 All ER at 711. Arlidge and Parry, 4–157, fn 65, suggest that the cases are indistinguishable in principle.

[2]   [1983] Crim LR 617, CA.

[3]   *Jorden v Money* (1854) 5 HL Cas 185, HL; *D & C Builders Ltd v Rees* [1966] 2 QB 617, [1965] 3 All ER 837, CA.

[4]   [1966] 2 QB 617 at 623, [1965] 3 All ER 837 at 839, 840, per Lord Denning MR. There is no question of the debt being remitted in equity. Equity will not assist D because of his fraud.

4–93   If the debtor's statement of his difficulties is a lie, he has dishonestly and by deception induced his creditor to forgo payment but he has not induced him to remit the debt. Suppose, however, that the debtor, D, meets all his creditors who agree together and with D to accept a dividend of 50 per cent – that is, to forgive D one half of each of the debts he owes. Because each creditor is supplying consideration to the others by agreeing to surrender one-half of his debt, this agreement is enforceable in law and D's debt has been remitted in part. If he has practised a dishonest deception, he is guilty of an offence under (a). It is immaterial that D does not intend to make permanent default because he intends to deprive P permanently of his legal thing in action, his property. If D does not intend to make permanent default – he intends one day to pay up – this is a defence only if the jury find that it negatives dishonesty. The case is very much the same as of the person who, without authority, takes money from a till, intending to spend it but hoping that one day he will be able to repay the owner. In both types of case D intends to deprive the owner of his property permanently and, if he is dishonest, that is sufficient to entail liability.

4–94   Others[1] think that the paragraph has a wider operation and this was, indeed, the opinion of the CLRC:

> "An example would be where a man borrows £100 from a neighbour and when repayment is due, tells a false story of some family tragedy which makes it impossible for him to find the money; this deception persuades the neighbour to tell him that he need never repay."[2]

Has the man secured the remission of the liability to pay £100 when the liability continues unimpaired throughout? The neighbour may, of course, have intended to remit the liability but in law he did not do so. If, next week, the man had won half a million on the pools, the neighbour would no doubt have expected to recover his £100 and would presumably have been entitled to do so. The draftsman used a strong word, "secured", and it is difficult to see that it has been satisfied. On the other hand, there is no doubt that the neighbour has been induced to forgo payment (of the existing, unremitted, debt) and, if the debtor intends to make permanent default, this is an offence under para (b).

Another case which has been thought to come within para (a) is that of a seller, P, who believes the buyer's, D's, false story that certain goods were never delivered and are not now needed and cancels the invoice which was sent. If the goods were delivered in fact, the debt exists throughout. There has been no rescission nor, indeed, any intention to rescind. P had no intention of remitting any debt because he had been led to believe that no debt existed. This again seems to be better regarded as a case of forgoing payment.

The effect would be that para (b) would have a much wider sphere of operation than para (a). This would be contrary to the expectations of the Committee. However, criminal sanctions are imposed on defaulting debtors sparingly and it is not inappropriate that they should be applicable only where D causes P actually to give up his legal right or where he has an intent to make permanent default.[3] The limitation on the combined effect of paras (a) and (b) would not be a serious one. If, however, a construction similar to that suggested for para (a) were applied to para (c), the latter paragraph would also be rendered largely though not entirely inoperative. This might be thought more serious because (c) is the only provision which extends to prospective as well as existing liability.[4] Unless a lot of weight is put on the use of the word "secures" in (a) as contrasted with "obtains" in (c), it would be difficult to construe (a) so as to require an effect on liability in law and (c) so as not to do so; and, in order to salvage (c), it may be argued that the right interpretation is to construe "secure the remission" in (a) to mean "secure an agreement to remit"[5] and to accept that the words "or to forgo payment" in (b) are inoperative. Even so, it is submitted that the offence would be committed only where P knows that there is a liability and intends to remit it.[6] If he is deceived into believing that there is no liability he is induced to forgo payment but not to agree to remit anything. It is argued below that the consequences of a strict and (it is submitted) true construction of (c) are by no means disastrous; and it is submitted that the right course is to construe "secure the remission of liability" to mean what it says.

---

[1]   Cf Syrota *Current Law Statutes*; Griew 9–10, fn 14.

[2]   *Thirteenth Report*, para 13.

[3]   Since the Criminal Attempts Act 1981 it is arguable that, even if D has not secured the remission of a liability, he is guilty of an attempt to do so. If he mistakenly believes that the debt is remitted, he has the intent to commit the offence. A mistake of civil law might be equated with a mistake of fact. See Smith & Hogan 83–85, 323 and commentary on *Huskinson* [1988] Crim LR 620 at 622–623.

[4]   Though even here s. 1 would fill much of the function intended by the CLRC for para (c) – where a person obtains services at a reduced rate: see *Thirteenth Report*, Cmnd 6733, para 14.

(c)   Inducing creditor to wait for or forgo payment

4-95   Section 2 (1) (b) provides that a person commits an offence where, by any deception, he:

> "with intent to make permanent default in whole or in part on any existing liability to make a payment, or with intent to let another do so, dishonestly induces the creditor or any person claiming payment on behalf of the creditor to wait for payment (whether or not the due date for payment is deferred) or to forgo payment . . . "

The only person who can make default on any existing liability is of course the person under liability. If D is not under a liability he can be guilty of the offence only if he makes the deception with intent to allow another person who is under a liability to default.[1] There may be an existing liability although the liability is unenforceable without the order of a court.[2]

This offence may be committed where the liability is neither remitted nor postponed. D remains liable to pay throughout but the creditor is induced to refrain from taking steps to enforce that liability for the time being or at all. The paragraph is concerned with the "stalling debtor". It was held in *DPP v Turner*[3] that it was an offence under s. 16 (2) (a) of the 1968 Act where D, by deception, secured relief from the claims of his creditor for only a short period. D, being pressed one Saturday for the payment of £38, gave his creditor a cheque for that sum knowing that it would not be honoured. It was dishonoured on Monday. It was held that the debt had been "evaded". All that D got, or could have hoped to get, from his deception was relief from the demands of his creditor for a day or two. This should certainly not be a serious offence and it is now not criminal at all, in the absence of an intent to make permanent default. If, as soon as P goes off with the worthless cheque, D moves to another town, leaving no forwarding address, he may now be guilty of an offence if the court or jury is satisfied that he intended never to pay.

It is presumably not necessary that the creditor should agree to wait for or forgo payment. He may be induced to wait or forgo because he is led to believe that he has no choice in the matter. For example, D, seeing the rent-collector at the door sends his small son to say, "Daddy's out." If the disgruntled rent-collector goes away, he has been induced to wait for payment even though his present claim to the money is not waived for an instant. Similarly, where a tradesman is induced to write off the liability as a bad debt because he is persuaded, falsely, that D will never have the means to pay.

1   *Attewell-Hughes* [1991] 4 All ER 810, [1991] Crim LR 437, CA.
2   *Modupe* [1991] Crim LR 530, CA.
3   [1974] AC 357, [1973] 3 All ER 124, HL, above, para **4–67**; cf *Smith v Koumourou* [1979] Crim LR 116 and commentary.

4-96   Section 2 (3) provides:

> "For purposes of subsection (1) (b) a person induced to take in payment a cheque or other security for money by way of conditional satisfaction of a pre-existing liability is to be treated not as being paid but as being induced to wait for payment."

Apart from this provision, acceptance of a cheque amounts to a conditional payment of a pre-existing debt which suspends the creditor's remedies until the cheque has either been met or dishonoured. In the absence of the provision, then, a creditor who had accepted as valid a worthless cheque might well have been held neither to have waited for nor to have forgone payment. The effect of s. 2 (3) is that D commits an offence under para (b) if, having honestly bought and received goods at a shop, or honestly enjoyed the services of a hotel, he pays by a cheque which he knows to be worthless and goes off leaving a false address, intending never to pay.[1]

---

[1]   He is probably also guilty of an offence under s. 3; below, para **5–01**.

(d)   Obtaining exemption from or abatement of liability

4–97   Section 2 (1) (c) provides that a person commits an offence where, by any deception, he:

"dishonestly obtains any exemption from or abatement of liability to make a payment."

Whereas paras (a) and (b) are confined to existing liabilities, (c) applies simply to "liability to make a payment" which, in the context, must include, though it is not confined to, a prospective liability. Like para (a) and unlike (b) it is expressed to be concerned with an effect on liability. If the Act were strictly construed, the offence would not be committed where P makes a wholly inoperative agreement to grant D an exemption from or abatement of liability to make a payment. It was intended to apply to the case where D dishonestly obtains a rate rebate or a reduction in his rent for the future.[1] Probably D's legal liability is unaffected in either case. In the case of the rates his liability will be for the full rateable value of the property as it is, not as he has misrepresented it to be; and the reduction of the rent is likely to be inoperative because of the lack of consideration rather than the fraud which would render a contract for the reduced rent voidable but not void. Paragraph (b) cannot be invoked because there is not yet an existing liability. However, a day will come when there will be an existing liability. The rates or rent fall due. P demands the lesser sum. He does so because the deception is continuing. If D intends to make permanent default has he not now induced P to forgo payment of an existing liability? It is submitted that he has. Thus, the effect of giving para (c) its strict and, it is submitted, true, construction, is that (i) para (c), like para (a), is confined to a small number of cases; and (ii) in other cases guilt is limited to those where there is an intent to make permanent default and (iii) is postponed until the time when an actual liability exists and is forgone. The consequences are not serious and may indeed be held to be a very proper limitation on criminal liability. In *Sibartie*,[2] however, it was held that "flashing" an inapplicable season ticket to an inspector on the underground railway was an attempt to obtain exemption from a liability. It appears that persuading a person that there is no existing liability is to be regarded as obtaining exemption from liability: but it is submitted that it is more properly regarded as a case of forgoing. If the attempt had succeeded, the inspector would not have intended to remit any liability because he would have been persuaded that there was no liability to remit and D's liability to pay the proper fare would unquestionably have continued unremitted.

---

[1]   *Thirteenth Report*, Cmnd 6733, para 15.
[2]   [1983] Crim LR 470, CA.

4–98   Another type of case to which (c) was intended to apply is that where D induces P to provide him with goods or services at a cheap rate by falsely stating that he belongs to a particular organisation or that he is an old age pensioner. Probably the offence is committed in these cases. There is a voidable contract to supply the goods or service at the reduced rate so that, arguably, liability, *pro tem*, has abated. If P actually supplies the goods or service he could no doubt recover the full value in an action in quasi-contract[1] but, until he does so, his only rights are to be paid the price agreed or to rescind the contract for fraud. Even if there is no offence under (c) at the time of the agreement, however, an offence would be committed under (b) so soon as P supplied the goods or service and forbore from demanding the balance of the price because of the continuing deception. These acts will also amount to offences against 1968, s. 15, and 1978, s. 1, depending on whether it is goods or services which are obtained, but a charge under s. 2 (1) (c) more accurately describes the gist of the offence. What D has really done wrong is not to get the thing at all but to get it more cheaply. Where D obtains goods for nothing he is again guilty under both 1968, s. 15, and para (c); but where he obtains services for nothing, the only charge is under para (c). He is not guilty under 1978, s. 1, because there is no understanding that the services will be paid for.

---

[1]   See [1971] Crim LR 448 at 453 et seq.

(e)   Evasion of the liability of another

4–99   All the offences under s. 2 may be committed in respect of the liability of another. Under s. 2 (1) (a) the liability remitted may be "his own liability or another's". Under s. 2 (1) (b) the intent may be to let another make default on an existing liability. Section 2 (4) provides:

> "For purposes of subsection 1 (c) 'obtains' includes obtaining for another or enabling another to obtain."

So an offence may be committed by an accountant who secures the remission of a client's existing liability, a wife who persuades her husband's creditor to forgo payment of the husband's debt or a company secretary who obtains exemption of the company from liability to make a payment.

CHAPTER 5
Making off without Payment

5–01 The Theft Act 1978,[1] s. 3 (1) provides:

"Subject to subsection (3) below, a person who, knowing that payment on the spot for any goods supplied or service done is required or expected from him, dishonestly makes off without having paid as required or expected and with intent to avoid payment of the amount due shall be guilty of an offence."

This section deals with cases such as that of the customer in the restaurant or at the petrol station who departs without paying but it is not possible to prove that he had a dishonest intention permanently to deprive the owner at the time when he received the food or the petrol as the case may be.[2] In *DPP v Ray*,[3] such a case was held to be the offence of evading a debt by deception contrary to s. 16 (2) (a) (now repealed) of the 1968 Act; but the deception found by the court was of a highly artificial character and in many other similar cases it would be impossible to discern any deception at all.

---

[1] See CLRC Working Paper, *Section 16 of the Theft Act,* (1974) and *Thirteenth Report* (1977).
[2] If he had such an intention he is guilty of theft: *Gomez* [1993] 1 All ER 1, HL, above, para **2–09**, and, probably of obtaining property by deception contrary to 1968, s. 15.
[3] [1974] AC 370, [1973] 3 All ER 131 above, para **4–04**.

(a) *Makes off*

5–02 It is the dishonest departure from the spot which is the offence. An attempt to depart from the spot is an attempt to commit it. "The spot" will usually, but not necessarily, be the premises of the creditor. It may be a place on the highway on which the shoe-shine boy has cleaned D's shoes, or the mechanic has repaired his car in expectation of immediate payment. In *McDavitt*,[1] it was held that the spot was a restaurant and that D, who had made for the door, might be convicted, not of the full offence, but of an attempt to commit it. The words in *Brooks and Brooks*,[2] "passing the spot where payment is required", suggest that the spot is the cash point rather than the restaurant, so that D would be guilty of the full offence if he were stopped between the cash point and the door. In *Moberly v Allsop*,[3] it was held that a traveller on the London Underground was still "on the spot" when going through the exit barrier at his destination. "The spot" may change. In the case of a taxi-ride it is the agreed destination; but if D, the passenger, declines to pay at that point and the driver thereupon drives him towards the police station, D commits the offence if he alights and makes off en route.[4] The requirement and expectation of the fare due continue throughout the journey so it seems that the "spot" is in motion.

Can the offence be committed after D has left the spot without any dishonest intention? He absent-mindedly walks out of the restaurant without paying his bill. As soon as he is outside the door, he realises what he has done, but continues on his way, intending to avoid payment. Possibly his innocent departure becomes a dishonest making off at that moment. If, on the other hand, he arrives home before he realises that he has not paid, he is clearly incapable of committing the offence.[5]

143

An offence committed on leaving the premises probably continues so long as D can be said to be "making off" in the ordinary meaning of those words. If D is fleeing from the restaurant down the street, he is doing just that. If it were otherwise, an arrest by a waiter ten yards from the door would be unlawful because the power of arrest given by s. 3 (4) applies only while D is committing or attempting to commit the offence.[6]

The phrase "makes off" has a pejorative connotation, lacking in such verbs as "leaves" or "departs". It means "decamps", and is clearly apt in the case of a person who slips away secretly or runs or drives off at top speed. The phrase can hardly be limited to departure in haste.[7] It could surely also apply to a dishonest customer who, by force or threats of force, compelled a waiter to stand aside and allow him to go. It has been argued that making off is departing without the creditor's consent but this also is too narrow without, at least, some qualification. For example, at the end of a long taxi-ride, D says he is just going into the house to get the fare and disappears into the night, never to return.[8] Again, if D tells a restaurateur that he has forgotten his wallet and gives a false name and address ("Sir George Bullough, St James's Square") and is allowed to go, there is authority for saying that he goes with consent; but the case seems clearly to fall within the mischief at which the section is aimed. Professor J. R. Spencer[9] argues cogently that it means "disappearing: leaving in a way that makes it difficult for the debtor to be traced". This would cover the dishonest taxi-passenger and the impersonator. It would also apply to D who leaves a cheque signed in a false name. It would not apply to the regular customer of known address who gets away by stealth, force or fraud, or to the person who leaves a worthless cheque with his true name and address. These persons are certainly avoiding payment of a debt but the intention behind the section was not to make the debtor liable to arrest and punishment merely because he defaulted. The mischief at which it was aimed was the escape without trace of the "spot" debtor.

---

[1]   [1981] Crim LR 843.
[2]   (1982) 76 Cr App Rep 66 at 70, CA.
[3]   (1992) 156 JP 514.
[4]   *Aziz* [1993] Crim LR 708, CA.
[5]   Cf *Drameh* [1983] Crim LR 322.
[6]   Cf ibid.
[7]   Cf Bennion, [1980] Crim LR 670, A.T.H. Smith, *Property Offences*, 644-645.
[8]   Cf *Drameh* [1983] Crim LR 322.
[9]   [1983] Crim LR 573.

(b)   Goods supplied or service done

5–03   The words "goods supplied or service done" might be taken to suggest that the supply or service must precede the requirement of payment; but in *Moberly v Allsop*[1] it was held that the traveller on the Underground committed the offence on passing the exit barrier although payment was required and expected before the journey began. No doubt the requirement continues in the case of a passenger who has avoided payment of the fare and he is certainly expected to pay before he leaves the premises.

It is not sufficient that D has become indebted unless that debt arose from the supply of goods or the doing of a service. A shop-lifter who carries off the shop-keeper's property is liable to pay the price but, if the shop is not a self-service store, no goods have been "supplied" to him and he does not commit this offence when he makes off. It is submitted, however, that a self-service establishment is different and that goods are "supplied" by P to D where P has made them available to be taken and they are taken by D.[2] If it were not so, the section would fail to cover those cases at which it is primarily aimed. The customer who honestly fills up his car and then dishonestly makes off has been "supplied" with petrol. Even after *Gomez*,[3] he is probably not guilty of theft because there is no "property belonging to another" when he forms the dishonest intention. If he was dishonest from the start, he stole the petrol but it is submitted that he is also guilty of making off. Any argument that he could not at the same moment steal and be supplied is untenable. The sale of goods in *Gomez* did not cease to be a sale (or supply) of goods because the House decided that it was also theft. There is a substantial overlap of theft contrary to 1968, s. 1 with 1978, s. 3.

There is no definition of goods or of service. "Service" is not the same as the "services" of s. 1 and perhaps bears a narrower meaning. It has been suggested by Professor Williams[4] that, "The tenant of an unfurnished flat or house who bilks his landlord of the rent has not obtained a service." It is submitted, however, that the landlord, whether of furnished or unfurnished premises, does supply a service to his tenant but that the tenant is not guilty of the offence for the second reason offered by Professor Williams: " . . . and anyway there is no requirement in an ordinary lease that the rent be paid on the spot". The CLRC was anxious that the non-payment of rent should not become a criminal offence. The letting of goods is clearly the supply of goods or a service which is presumably why Williams distinguishes unfurnished premises.

The service must be "done", presumably by P or his agents. Is a service "done" where D takes advantage of a proffered facility? For example, he parks his car in an unmanned car park and leaves by lifting up the barrier and driving off without paying. Probably the custody of the car by the proprietor of the park while it was left there would be regarded as a "service done". It might be otherwise, however, if D were to leave his car in a street parking bay and drive off without putting money in the meter. The highway authority could not be said to have custody of the car, but it is arguable that the provision of a parking space on the highway is a service. Even so that case is more appropriately dealt with under the relevant regulations.

---

1   (1992) 156 JP 514, above, para **5–02**.
2   Griew 13–07, thinks goods exposed for sale are not goods supplied. Certainly; but is this not an offer to supply which becomes "supply" when the goods are removed? Griew agrees, 13–08, that permitting the use of a tennis court or a boat is a "service done" and this seems indistinguishable in principle. See also Williams *TBCL* 878 and A.T.H. Smith [1981] Crim LR 590, who argues that the self-service shop is different from the self-service petrol station. There is a "supply" in the latter case because the motorist acquires ownership on taking the petrol, but ownership does not pass when the shop-lifter takes goods. However the transfer of possession or custody may constitute "supply": cf *Greenfield* (1983) 78 Cr App Rep 179n, [1983] Crim LR 397, CA (supplying drugs).
3   [1993] 1 All ER 1, [1993] Crim LR 304, HL, above, para **2–09**.
4   *TBCL* 879.

5–04   Section 3 (2) provides:

"For the purposes of this section 'payment on the spot' includes payment at the time of collecting goods on which work has been done or in respect of which service has been provided."

It is not clear that this provision is really necessary. The cases to which it applies are probably adequately covered by the words of subsection (1). It is made clear beyond all doubt that D may commit the offence where he makes off with his clothes which have been cleaned, his shoes which have been repaired or his car which has been serviced. The existence of subsection (2) may, however, cast doubt on another type of case. D makes off without paying the shoe-shine boy who has cleaned his shoes. Work has been done on the goods but D was not "collecting" them. "Collecting" seems to imply that D is acquiring possession of the goods. He has never parted with possession of his shoes. Similarly where D calls a mechanic to repair his car which is broken down by the roadside. In no sense does the motorist "collect" his car when he drives off. It is submitted that these cases, though not within s. 3 (2), are adequately covered by s. 3 (1). If so, subsection (2) is indeed superfluous.

(c)   Unenforceable debts

5–05   Section 3 (3) provides:

> "Subsection (1) above shall not apply where the supply of the goods or the doing of the service is contrary to law, or where the service done is such that payment is not legally enforceable."

The CLRC explained this provision on the ground that "the new offence is essentially a protection for the legitimate business".[1] The offence is thus not committed where D makes off from a prostitute's flat, a brothel, a disorderly house, an obscene performance in a night-club, a drug-pedlar's premises or a betting shop, without paying for the principal service or goods provided therein. If some goods or service has been legitimately provided – for example, drinks in the night-club – the answer will depend on whether the vice of the principal service infects collateral transactions, which it may do where it amounts to illegality but should not do where the principal transaction is merely void, as in the case of the wager in the betting shop.

Where the transaction is "contrary to law", there is no distinction between goods and a service, but where it is merely "not legally enforceable", services only are affected. Thus subsection (3) applies where there is a merely void contract for services – for example, the wager – but it seems that it does not apply where there is a merely void contract for the supply of goods. If an impecunious minor has her hair done at the most expensive salon in London and walks off without paying it seems she commits no offence under s. 3 because the service done was not "necessary" and payment for it is unenforceable. If, however, the same impecunious minor dines on caviar and champagne she may be guilty of making off without payment even though – as is most probable – these expensive items cannot be proved to be necessaries for her. There is nothing contrary to law in supplying non-necessary goods to a minor. A seller may properly do so if he chooses but he will not be able to recover the price. Since goods and not services are involved, it is immaterial that payment is not legally enforceable.

---

[1]   *Thirteenth Report*, para 19.

(d)   Without having paid as required or expected

5–06   It is implicit in the section that P requires or expects payment on the spot and that the payment is due in fact and law. If a taxi-driver, in the course of a journey, commits a breach of contract entitling his passenger to rescind the contract, the passenger does not commit an offence by making off.[1] Where the money is due, does a person who gives a worthless cheque in "payment" of the debt commit the offence? Since s. 2 (3) applies only to the offence under s. 2 (1) (b) it is arguable that, for the purposes of other offences under the Act, a person who takes a cheque by way of conditional satisfaction of a pre-existing liability is to be treated as being paid.[2] As D will be guilty of the more serious offence under s. 2 (1) (b), the question may not be of great importance. In the one reported case[3] in which the matter has arisen the judge ruled that the offence was not committed because a worthless cheque was not the same as counterfeit money and that D was not making off because he departed with P's consent. The true answer may well be that D is guilty because he has not paid "as required or expected". P requires and expects payment in legal tender or by a good cheque. Payment by a worthless cheque no more satisfies his requirement or expectation than payment in counterfeit money. If, however, the cheque is backed by a cheque card, then, depending on the conditions of its issue, D may have paid as required or expected although his authority to use the card has been withdrawn or even if it has been stolen.[4] Similarly with payment by credit card.[5] If the bank is bound to honour the cheque or card, a question of civil law, P has been paid.

---

[1] *Troughton v Metropolitan Police* [1987] Crim LR 138, DC.
[2] Syrota, Current Law Statutes.
[3] *Hammond* [1982] Crim LR 611 (Judge Morrison).
[4] Cf *First Sport Ltd v Barclays Bank plc* [1993] 3 All ER 789, CA (Civ Div).
[5] Cf *Re Charge Card Services Ltd* [1988] 3 All ER 702, [1988] 3 WLR 764, CA above, para **4–92**.

(e)   Mens rea

(i)   Dishonestly[1]

5–07   D must be dishonest when he makes off. He may have been dishonest from the start (in which case he will also be guilty of theft or obtaining property or services by deception) or have formed the dishonest intention only after the goods were supplied or the service done. Whether D was dishonest or not is a question for the jury but it seems clear that he could not be held to be dishonest if he believed that payment was not due (even though required and expected by P) because, for example, the goods supplied or service done was deficient in some fundamental respect. If D were prepared to leave his name and address, that would be cogent evidence of honesty whereas secret departure or flight would be strong evidence of dishonesty. If D is E's guest in a restaurant and E leaves without paying, D will probably be liable to pay, at least for his own food, unless it ought to have been clear to the restaurateur that E was contracting to pay for both meals.[2] If D makes off, his criminal liability will depend on whether he believed he had no legal liability to pay the bill. His mistake of law might negative dishonesty.[3]

---

[1] Above, paras **2–114** to **2–124**.
[2] *Lockett v A & M Charles Ltd* [1938] 4 All ER 170.
[3] Cf *Brooks and Brooks* (1982) 76 Cr App Rep 66, CA.

(ii)   Knowing that payment on the spot . . . is required or expected from him

5–08   Clearly D is not guilty if he wrongly supposes that the goods have been supplied or the service done on credit and that he is going to receive a bill through the post; or if, for example, he is under the impression that his firm has arranged to pay his hotel bill. D's belief that he has been given credit, whether reasonable or not, is inconsistent with the *mens rea* required. Is "payment on the spot . . . required or expected" where the trader has indicated in advance that he will accept payment by credit card? He is no longer entitled to require or expect payment in cash. It now seems clear that the answer is yes. Acceptance by the trader of the credit card discharges the liability of the debtor[1] so he pays as required or expected, either by paying cash or by signing the sales voucher. If he dishonestly makes off without doing either, he commits the offence.

A similar question arises when P has indicated that he will take a cheque. Here the debtor's obligation is discharged only conditionally on the cheque being honoured but, in modern usage, a cheque is frequently treated as the equivalent of cash.[2] It is common to speak of payment by cheque. Presumably then, the trader who is willing to take a cheque (whether or not backed by a cheque card) requires or expects payment on the spot.

---

[1] " . . . the word 'payment' in itself is one which, in an appropriate context, may cover many ways of discharging obligations . . . ": *White v Elmdene Estates Ltd* [1960] 1 QB 1, [1959] 2 All ER 605 at 610–611, per Lord Evershed MR.
[2] *D and C Builders Ltd v Rees* [1965] 3 All ER 837 at 843, per Winn LJ.

(iii) With intent to avoid payment

5–09 It is now settled that an intent permanently to avoid payment is required. An intent to delay or defer payment is not enough.[1]

---

[1] *Allen* [1985] AC 1029, [1985] 2 All ER 641, HL, criticised by Griew, 12–18.

CHAPTER 6

Other Offences involving Fraud

1   FALSE ACCOUNTING

6–01   Section 17 of the 1968 Act replaced ss. 82 and 83 of the Larceny Act 1861 and the Falsification of Accounts Act 1875. It provides:

"(1) Where a person dishonestly, with a view to gain for himself or another or with intent to cause loss to another, –

(a) destroys, defaces, conceals or falsifies any account or any record or document made or required for any accounting purpose; or

(b) in furnishing information for any purpose produces or makes use of any account, or any such record or document as aforesaid, which to his knowledge is or may be misleading, false or deceptive in a material particular; he shall, on conviction on indictment, be liable to imprisonment for a term not exceeding seven years.

(2) For purposes of this section a person who makes or concurs in making in an account or other document an entry which is or may be misleading, false or deceptive in a material particular, or who omits or concurs in omitting a material particular from an account or other document, is to be treated as falsifying the account or document."

A.   *ACTUS REUS*

(a)   The account or record

6–02   The section is confined to records or documents "made or required for any accounting purpose". In the context, this plainly means accounting in the financial sense. The wording is wide enough to cover an account produced by mechanical means, as in the case of a taximeter[1] or a turnstile at the entrance to a football ground.[2] Falsifying the gas-meter or electricity-meter would seem to be an offence within the section. On the other hand, dishonestly to falsify the odometer of a car with a view to gain would not normally be an offence under this section since the odometer of a car is not usually a record made or required for any accounting purpose. It would be otherwise, however, if the odometer reading were used to calculate a mileage allowance due to the driver. It would then be indistinguishable from the taxi-meter case. The information in the document may be furnished for other purposes in addition to accounting. It is sufficient that accounting is one of the purposes for which it is required. So a hire-purchase agreement was held to be a document within the section.[3] The "material particular" need not be one which is directly connected with the accounting purpose. If it is required for an accounting purpose, it is sufficient that it is "false in some respect that matters".[4]

In *A-G's Reference (No 1 of 1980)*,[5] it was held than an application addressed to a finance company for a personal loan to pay for goods, though not "made" for an accounting purpose is required for one if the company intends to use the information supplied in its accounts in the event of the application being successful. The decision has been criticised[6] as going too far in holding that it is enough that the document is "required for an accounting purpose as a subsidiary consideration". That, however, does not seem a valid objection if the maker knows that the addressee requires it for, inter alia, an accounting purpose because he then knows that an account will be falsified if his application is accepted; but there does not appear to have been evidence that D did know this. Whether such knowledge is required is considered below.

---

1   Cf *Solomons* [1909] 2 KB 980.
2   *Edwards v Toombs* [1983] Crim LR 43.
3   *Mallett* (1978) 67 Cr App Rep 239, CA.
4   Ibid.
5   *A-G's Reference (No 1 of 1980)* [1981] 1 All ER 366, [1981] Crim LR 41, CA and commentary.
6   By Arlidge and Parry at 5–059 to 5–060 who cogently argue that "'made' refers to the intentions of the person making the document whereas 'required' refers to those of the person for whom it is made"; but it does not follow that accounting must be the only purpose or, indeed, the principal purpose, of either party. In *Cummings-John* [1997] Crim LR (September) it was held that a "Report on Title" was required by a building society "for an accounting purpose", but in *Okanta* [1997] Crim LR 451 the court was satisfied that a letter containing false information which induced a mortgage advance was so required. The difference is not obvious.

(b)   The falsification

6–03   A person making an account or record may, as s. 17 (2) makes clear, falsify it by omitting material particulars. But *Shama*[1] goes much further. D, an international telephone operator, was required to fill in for each call a "charge ticket" which was then used for accounting purposes. He connected certain subscribers without filling in a charge ticket so that they were not charged. The prosecution could not, therefore, produce any document which they alleged to be falsified. Upholding his conviction, the court said that failure "to complete a charge ticket by omitting material particulars from a document required for an accounting purpose" constituted the offence. But can a person who has entirely omitted to make a document which it was his duty to make properly be said to have "omitted material particulars" from it? The omission of material particulars seems necessarily to imply the existence of a document from which those particulars are omitted. If, however, a bundle of charge sheets, handed in at the end of the day as a complete record of the day's calls, were held be a single document, then, of course, it would be falsified. But that was not the decision.

---

1   [1990] 2 All ER 602; [1990] Crim LR 411, CA. Also criticised by Arlidge and Parry, 5–070, but accepted by Griew, 12–03, as "a robust decision" which avoided an absurdity. A better course might have been to charge the securing of the remission of a debt or (preferably) inducing the creditor to forgo the payment of a debt, contrary to s. 2 of the 1978 Act. Above, para **4–95**. When the operator handed in the forms there was presumably an implied, if not an express, representation that there was a form for each call.

6–04   The section does not in terms require any duty to account. It appears to be sufficient that the account is in fact made with the requisite intent and is false. Where there is a duty to account, however, the extent of the duty will be relevant in determining whether the account is "false". If D has accounted for everything that he is obliged to account for, his omission of other items will not in itself render the account false.[1]

Subsection (2) does not provide an exclusive definition of falsification. An act not falling within the subsection but amounting to a falsification within the ordinary meaning of the word would be within the section. Where a turnstile operator allowed A and B to enter and recorded the entry of only one of them he falsified the record, if not within the meaning of subsection (2) then within the meaning of the word, "falsifies".[2]

¹   *Keatley* [1980] Crim LR 505 (Judge Mendl) and commentary.
²   *Edwards v Toombs* [1983] Crim LR 43.

B.   THE *MENS REA*

6–05   The act must be done:
(i)   dishonestly,
(ii)   with a view to gain for himself or another or with intent to cause loss to another and,
(iii)   in the case of s. 17 (1) (b), with knowledge that the document is or may be misleading, false or deceptive in a material particular. Recklessness is sufficient.

(a)   An intention to cause the actus reus?

6–06   Must the defendant intend to cause, or at least be reckless whether he causes, the *actus reus* of the offence? If, e.g. he is charged under s. 17 (1) (a) must he know that the thing he is destroying is, or may be, a "a record or document made or required for any accounting purpose"? The ordinary principles of *mens rea* suggest that such knowledge is required. In *Graham*,¹ however, the court said "we are not for our part persuaded that knowledge of the purpose for which any record or document is made or required forms any part of the *mens rea* of the offence". But to convict of dishonest false accounting a person who had no idea that his conduct had anything to do with accounts is to impose strict liability as to an essential element of the offence and seems objectionable.

Dishonesty. Reference may be made to the discussion of this element in other crimes.² Similar problems arise here. For example, the bookmaker's clerk may "borrow" his employer's money to place bets (with a view to gain) and falsify the accounts to cover up his action but with every intention and expectation of replacing the money before it is missed. Is he dishonest?

¹   (1997) 1 Cr App Rep 302, [1997] Crim LR 340 (Transcript No 95/2171/Z2, 25/10/96, p 16).
²   Above, paras **2–121** to **2–124** and **4–33** to **4–38**.

(b)   A view to gain or intent to cause loss

6–07   For the purposes of the 1968 Act – "(i) 'gain' includes a gain by keeping what one has, as well as a gain by getting what one has not; and (ii) 'loss' includes a loss by not getting what one might get, as well as a loss by parting with what one has"¹

In blackmail, it seems that a person may have a "view to gain" where he is seeking nothing more than he is entitled to – e.g. the payment of debt which is due in law – but using an unwarranted threat.² In *Lee Cheung Wing*,³ however, the Privy Council held that D had a view to gain for the purposes of s. 17 only because he was *not* entitled to the money he sought to gain. He was an employee of a company offering facilities for dealing in futures. Employees were not allowed to use these facilities. D, in breach of his contract of employment, opened an account in the name of a friend, X. The transactions were profitable and D signed withdrawal slips in X's name. The question was whether the slips were made with a view to gain. D's defence, that he was withdrawing money to which he was entitled, was rejected on the ground that he was not entitled to the money – he would have been bound to account to his employer for a profit made by the improper use of his position as an employee. The court added that an action by D to recover the profits would probably have been defeated by a plea of *ex turpi causa non oritur actio*. The case is not decisive because it was not necessary to decide whether D would have been guilty had he been entitled to keep the money. It is not easy to see why the words should bear a different meaning in s. 17 from that which they bear in s. 21.

Suppose D falsifies the accounts so as to deceive his employer into thinking that D's department is more profitable than it really is, in order to ensure that D's employment will not be terminated.[4] It may be argued that D has no view to gain in such a case, since he intends to give full economic value for the wages he receives;[5] but, whether or not this is a sound argument (and it is probably not) he perhaps has an intent to cause loss in that he knows that the effect of his deception will be that his employer will keep open an uneconomic department. This, however, is only an "oblique" intention[6] and it is arguable that a direct intention must be proved.

---

[1]   See the discussion of these elements in connection with other crimes, below, paras **10–12** to **10–22**.
[2]   Below, para **10–15**.
[3]   (1991) 94 Cr App Rep 355, PC.
[4]   Cf *Wines* [1953] 2 All ER 1497, [1954] 1 WLR 64.
[5]   See below, paras **10–15** to **10–17**.
[6]   Smith & Hogan 57–63.

6–08   Has D a view to gain or an intent to cause loss[1] where he falsifies an account in order to conceal losses or defalcations which have already occurred? In the light of s. 34 (2) (a) above it seems that the answer ought to be in the affirmative. At least one of the objects which D will have in view will be that of avoiding or postponing making restitution – "keeping what one has" – and preventing P from getting what he might. The Court of Appeal has said in *Eden*[2] that putting off the evil day of having to pay is a sufficient gain. In *Goleccha and Choraria*,[3] on the other hand, it was held that a debtor who dishonestly induces a creditor to forbear from suing for his debt does not have a "view to gain" within the meaning of the section. But why does not the debtor have a view to gain by keeping what he has? A "deed of postponement", postponing the priority of a registered charge in favour of another obligation, does "cause loss".[4]

If D's sole object is to avoid prosecution, it is arguable that he is not guilty of the offence.[5] Telling lies to avoid prosecution, whether in an account or elsewhere, if it is to be a crime, would more naturally find a place in the offence of perverting the course of justice[6] than in the Theft Act. If D is penniless, there may be a difficulty in proving that he intended to do more than avoid prosecution; but, if he is employed, he may find it difficult credibly to deny that one of his objects was the continuance of his wages; and, as has been seen, this is almost certainly enough. Gain need not be D's sole object.

---

[1]   Below, para **10–12**.
[2]   (1971) 55 Cr App Rep 193 at 197, CA.
[3]   (1990) 90 Cr App R 241; [1990] Crim LR 865 and commentary. See also Griew, 12–07, and Arlidge and Parry, 4–181, 4–182.
[4]   *Cummings-John* [1997] Crim LR (September).
[5]   If D has an intent to make permanent default he is guilty of evading liability by deception, contrary to 1978, s. 2 (1) (b), above, para **4–95**.
[6]   Smith & Hogan (6th edn) 751–758.

2   LIABILITY OF COMPANY OFFICERS FOR OFFENCES UNDER SECTIONS 18 AND 19

6–09   Section 18 of the Act provides:

"(1) Where an offence committed by a body corporate under section 15, 16 or 17 of this Act is proved to have been committed with the consent or connivance of any director, manager, secretary or other similar officer of the body corporate, or any other person who was purporting to act in any such capacity, he as well as the body corporate shall be guilty of that offence, and shall be liable to be proceeded against and punished accordingly.

(2) Where the affairs of a body corporate are managed by its members, this section shall apply in relation to the acts and defaults of a member in connection with his functions of management as if he were a director of the body corporate."

An offence can be committed by a body corporate only through one of its responsible officers.[1] In every case where a corporation is guilty of an offence, then, there must be at least one of the officers referred to in the section who consented or connived. If he is unidentifiable, then only the corporation may be convicted; if he can be identified, he will, in the great majority of cases, be guilty of an offence under ss. 15, 16 and 17 independently of s. 18, either as a principal offender or as a secondary party. Connivance or an express consent to an offence, if it amounts to encouragement, would seem sufficient to found liability under the general law,[2] apart from s. 18. The section is intended to go farther than this:

"The clause follows a form of provision commonly included in statutes where an offence is of a kind to be committed by bodies corporate and where it is desired to put the management under a positive obligation to prevent irregularities, if aware of them. Passive acquiescence does not, under the general law, make a person liable as a party to the offence, but there are clearly cases (of which we think this is one) where the director's responsibilities for his company require him to intervene to prevent fraud and where consent or connivance amounts to guilt."[3]

---

[1]   Smith & Hogan 183–190; *Tesco Supermarkets Ltd v Nattrass* [1972] AC 153, [1971] 2 All ER 127, HL.
[2]   Smith & Hogan 126–137.
[3]   *Eighth Report*, Cmnd 2977, para 104. Notwithstanding *Wilson* [1997] Crim LR 53, applying the corresponding provision in the Insurance Companies Act 1982, s. 18, does not create an offence and no one could be charged under it. It is submitted that it is simply an extension of the ordinary law of secondary participation which is automatically applicable.

6–10   The "positive obligation" clearly does not go so far as to impose liability for negligence; you cannot consent to that of which you are unaware[1] and "connivance" involves turning a blind eye, which has usually been regarded as equivalent to knowledge.[2] Even "passive acquiescence" has sometimes been held sufficient to found liability as a secondary party, under the general law, but probably only on the ground that inactivity was a positive encouragement to others to commit the unlawful act in question.[3] Section 14 may go a little beyond this, though that is not entirely clear and the provision does not seem yet to have been interpreted by the courts.[4] At least it eases the Crown's task to the extent that they have proved their case if they prove consent and they do not have to go on to establish that the consent amounted to an aiding and abetting, etc.

---

1 *Re Caughey, ex p Ford* (1876) 1 Ch D 521 at 528, CA, per Jessel MR and *Lamb v Wright & Co* [1924] 1 KB 857 at 864.
2 Edwards *Mens Rea in Statutory Offences* 202–205; Williams *CLGP* 159; Smith & Hogan 107.
3 Smith & Hogan 136.
4 Cf the draconian provision in the Borrowing (Control and Guarantees) Act 1946, s. 4 (2), criticised by Upjohn J in *London and Country Commercial Property Investments Ltd v A-G* [1953] 1 All ER 436 at 441.

---

3 FALSE STATEMENTS BY COMPANY DIRECTORS, ETC.

6–11 Section 19 (see p 266, below) replaced s. 84 of the Larceny Act 1861. It is wider than the earlier provision in that it applies to officers of unincorporated as well as incorporated bodies – for example, the chairman of a club. It is narrower in that:

(i) there must be an intent to deceive members or creditors, whereas the earlier provision extended to an intent to induce any person to become a shareholder or partner, or to advance money, etc.;

(ii) the written statement or account must be about the body's affairs.

Examples of the kind of case to which the section is intended to apply are:

"A prospectus might include a false statement, made in order to inspire confidence, that some well-known person had agreed to become a director. It might also include a false statement, made in order to appeal to persons interested in a particular area, that a company had arranged to build a factory in that area."[1]

1 *Eighth Report*, Cmnd 2977, para 105. Under the Financial Services Act 1986, s. 200 (1) a person commits an offence if, in purported compliance with any requirement imposed on him by the Act, he furnishes information which he knows to be false or misleading in a material particular or recklessly furnishes information which is false or misleading in a material particular.

6–12 The *mens rea* consists in:

(i) an intent to deceive;

(ii) knowledge that the statement is or may be misleading, false or deceptive in a material particular.

Though no intent to defraud is required, the effect seems to be much the same, since the statement must be false in a material particular. A particular is hardly likely to be held to be material unless the person to whom it is addressed is likely to take action of some kind on it and, thus, almost invariably, to be defrauded in the wide meaning now given to "fraud".[1]

As the Criminal Law Revision Committee thought, statements made recklessly will be within the section.[2] It is enough that D knows that the statement is or may be false, etc.

1 *Welham v DPP* [1961] AC 103, [1960] 1 All ER 805, HL.
2 *Eighth Report*, Cmnd 2977, para 104.

4 SUPPRESSION, ETC., OF DOCUMENTS

6–13 Section 20 (1)[1] replaced an elaborate group of offences in ss. 27–30 of the Larceny Act 1861. These offences had been little used in recent times and the Criminal Law Revision Committee had doubts as to whether any part of them should be retained, but s. 20 (1) was included because:

"It seemed to us that it might provide the only way of dealing with a person who, for example, suppressed a public document as a first step towards committing a fraud but did not get so far as attempting to commit the fraud."[2]

It should be noted that the subsection does not apply to local government documents, the Committee being of the opinion that these were adequately protected by existing statutory provisions.

The main constituents of the offence are considered in connection with other offences.[3]

---

[1] Below, p 266.
[2] *Eighth Report*, Cmnd 2977, para 106.
[3] As to "dishonestly", see above, paras **2–114** to **2–124** and **4–33** to **4–38**; "with a view to gain" and "with intent to cause loss", see below, paras **10–02** to **10–22**.

---

5   PROCURING THE EXECUTION OF A VALUABLE SECURITY

6–14 By s. 20 (2):[1]

"(2) A person who dishonestly, with a view to gain for himself or another or with intent to cause loss to another, by any deception procures the execution of a valuable security shall on conviction on indictment be liable to imprisonment for a term not exceeding seven years; and this subsection shall apply in relation to the making, acceptance, indorsement, alteration, cancellation or destruction in whole or in part of a valuable security, and in relation to the signing or sealing of any paper or other material in order that it may be made or converted into, or used or dealt with as, a valuable security as if it were the execution of a valuable security.

(3) For purposes of this section 'deception'[1] has the same meaning as in section 15 of this Act, and 'valuable security' means any document creating, transferring, surrendering or releasing any right to, in or over property, or authorising the payment of money or delivery of any property, or evidencing the creation, transfer, surrender or release of any such right, or the payment of money or delivery of any property, or the satisfaction of any obligation."

---

[1] As to "deception" see above, paras **4–02** to **4–32**; and as to the other constituents of the offence see para **6–13**, fn 3.

6–15 The history of s. 20 (2) begins in 1857 with the case of *Danger*,[1] where it was held that D was not guilty of obtaining a valuable security by false pretences when he produced to P a bill of exchange, duly stamped, signed by himself as drawer and payable to himself and, by deception, induced P to accept the bill by writing his name across it: a valuable security, to be the subject of obtaining by false pretences, had to be the property of someone other than D. P had no property in the document. The thing in action, and even the paper on which it was written, belonged to D. The paper was probably never even in P's possession or control, being merely put in front of him for signature. His signature was all that was obtained.[2] Parliament acted quickly. An "Act to amend the Law of False Pretences" of 1858[3] made it an offence to obtain by any false pretence the signature of any person to a bill of exchange, promissory note, or any valuable security. Section 20 (2) is directly descended from that Act. It was replaced by a more elaborate provision in s. 90 of the Larceny Act 1861, which was re-enacted without substantial change in the Larceny Act 1916, s. 32 (2). The CLRC, which gave very little consideration to the matter, stated that the subsection of the clause in their draft bill which became s. 20 (2) reproduced the substance of 1916, s. 32 (3).[4] This change of form was at one time held to have resulted in an important change of substance; but in *Kassim*[5] the House of Lords held that the 1968 Act was not intended to make any change in the law. The typical instance of this offence is that where

D, by deception, procures P to draw a cheque in D's favour. The offence is complete on the cheque being signed. It avoids all the problems involved in attempting to bring the case within s. 1 or s. 15 of the 1968 Act.

---

[1]   (1857) 7 Cox CC 303. See commentary on the decision of the Court of Appeal in *Kassim* [1988] Crim LR 374 and J.C. Smith, "Obtaining Cheques by Deception or Theft," [1997] Crim LR 396.
[2]   See above, para **2–140**.
[3]   21 & 22 Vict, c.47.
[4]   *Eighth Report*, para 107.
[5]   [1992] 1 AC 9, [1991] 3 All ER 713, HL.

6–16   Woolf LJ said in the Court of Appeal in *Kassim* that "a valuable security is 'executed', properly speaking, only by its making". That court was obliged to give the terms a wider meaning but it now seems clear that they are to be interpreted in the proper sense. "Execute, make, accept, endorse" apply only to writing on a document or doing some other act which makes the document the "valuable security" in question. The words have the same meaning as in the law relating to bills of exchange. The offence does not extend to giving effect to, or carrying out the terms of, a valuable security which has already been executed. In this respect *Beck*[1] was wrongly decided. D acquired travellers' cheque forms which had been stolen in transit between the printer and an English bank. He forged the cheques and cashed them in France. The bank knew that the cheques were forged but felt obliged to honour them. It was held, wrongly, that the act of honouring the cheques constituted the execution of a valuable security in England. A similar wrong result was reached in respect of the use in France of a stolen credit card in that it was held that the voucher signed by D was a valuable security, executed when the card company in England paid the bill.

---

[1]   [1985] 1 All ER 571, [1985] 1 WLR 22, CA.

6–17   It was held in *King*[1] that a "CHAPS" (clearing house automated payment system) order was a valuable security, even though the primary "executor" was the defendant himself, because it was also signed by bank officials and their signatures were obtained by deception. This was decided before the House of Lords decision in *Kassim* and, though their lordships accepted it as right, this is not completely clear. Witnesses to the promisor's signature on a promissory note do not "execute" it; but perhaps the counter-signature of the bank officials had a more substantive effect on the validity of the CHAPS order. In *Bolton*,[2] the judge's direction that a telegraphic transfer of funds was capable of being a valuable security was held to be wrong in the absence of any evidence of how such a transfer works. In *Manjdadria*,[3] it was held that neither the telegraphic transfer nor the computerised ledger account of the solicitors making it was a valuable security. The court was somewhat sceptical about *King*, "a case in which perhaps the extreme boundaries of a valuable security were canvassed".

---

[1]   [1992] QB 20, [1991] 3 All ER 705, CA.
[2]   (1991) 94 Cr App Rep 74, CA. Woolf LJ suggested at 78–79 that the problems of mortgage frauds might be overcome by charging the procuring of the execution of the mortgage deed; but it appears that this is executed only by the procurer himself.
[3]   [1993] Crim LR 73, CA.

6–18   "Procures". The execution of the valuable security must be "procured" by deception. In *Beck*, it was argued that the execution by the bank was not so procured because the bank, knowing that the travellers' cheques were forged, paid out on them when they knew they were not legally bound to do so. The court rejected the argument, holding that, by deceiving the trader in France, D had brought about a situation in which for "legal and/or commercial reasons" the bank had no alternative but to pay. The court appears to have approved the trial judge's direction that "procured" is only another word for "caused".[1] The deception of the trader in France caused the bank to pay out in England. It was the same with the credit card company. On those facts, after *Kassim*, the question no longer arises, but it would arise where a person signed a cheque, after seeing through a deception but feeling bound to do so for legal or commercial reasons. This aspect of *Beck* gains some support from *Miller*.[2] Yet, in the similar situation arising in *Bevan*[3] it was held that the bank, which was under a legal obligation to pay, "allowed" borrowing by way of overdraft because payment by the bank was "an act of will" and consensual. These decisions are not easily reconcilable.

It is submitted that it is not sufficient that D in fact caused a valuable security to be executed unless he knew that, or at least was reckless whether, this would be the effect of a successful deception. If he contemplated the execution of a particular type of valuable security it should, however, be immaterial that the deception resulted in the execution of a valuable security of a different type. This is covered by, or by analogy to, the general principle of transferred malice.[4]

---

[1]   In other contexts "procure" has been more narrowly construed. "To procure means to produce by endeavour": *A-G's Reference (No 1 of 1975)* [1975] 2 All ER 684 at 686, CA, per Widgery LCJ. See, however, *Blakely and Sutton v DPP* [1991] RTR 405, [1991] Crim LR 763, DC.

[2]   Above, para **4–02**.

[3]   Above, para **4–61**.

[4]   Smith & Hogan 77. Cf *Mensah* [1996] Crim LR 203, CA, a case of conspiracy. If the indictment specifies a conspiracy to procure a particular type of security, then of course it must be proved that D conspired to procure the execution of a security of that type.

6–19   Valuable security. In *Benstead and Taylor*,[1] it was held that an irrevocable letter of credit was a "valuable security" within the meaning of the subsection, apparently on the ground that it was a document creating a right in property. This is a questionable interpretation of the provision. The words, "any right to, in or over property", seem to assume some existing property, a right to, in or over which is created, transferred, surrendered or released. In the case of a letter of credit there is no existing property to, in or over which a right is created. The letter of credit no doubt creates a right, but it is not a right to, in or over property. It is no answer to say that the thing in action created by the letter of credit is itself property because the subsection does not include a document creating property. If the decision is taken to its logical conclusion, any written contract is a valuable security because, being an enforceable contract, it creates a thing in action.[2] In *King*,[3] the court thought that, whether or not this criticism was justified, it did not affect that case because there was property in existence and the document evidenced both the creation and the transfer of a right. It was always hard to see how it could be both and *Preddy* now establishes that no right is transferred. The X Bank was induced by a fraudulent valuation to credit A's account with £81,000. The CHAPS order, signed by A and officials of the X Bank, authorised the transfer of that sum to the account of D's firm of solicitors with the Y Bank. The effect was that A's thing in action (his right to sue the X bank) was extinguished and a new thing in action (D's right to sue the Y Bank) created. A's thing in action was not "transferred"; D's thing in action was "created"; but it was new property, not a right in any existing property, as the section seems to require.

Documents "authorising the payment of money" which would include cheques and bills (and probably a letter of credit) are expressly included. But promissory notes (which were expressly mentioned in the 1858 Act)[4] neither create any right in existing property nor "authorise" the payment of money. Clearly promissory notes ought to be valuable securities; but this badly drafted subsection seems to exclude them.

[1]   (1982) 75 Cr App Rep 276, [1982] Crim LR 456, CA and commentary.
[2]   Above, para **4–56**.
[3]   [1992] QB 20, [1991] 3 All ER 705, [1991] Crim LR 906, CA and commentary.
[4]   Above, para **6–15**.

CHAPTER 7
Removal of Articles from Places open to the Public

7–01   By s. 11 of the Theft Act:

"(1) Subject to subsections (2) and (3) below, where the public have access to a building in order to view the building or part of it, or a collection or part of a collection housed in it, any person who without lawful authority removes from the building or its grounds the whole or part of any article displayed or kept for display to the public in the building or that part of it or in its grounds shall be guilty of an offence.

For this purpose 'collection' includes a collection got together for a temporary purpose, but references in this section to a collection do not apply to a collection made or exhibited for the purpose of effecting sales or other commercial dealings.
(2) It is immaterial for purposes of subsection (1) above, that the public's access to a building is limited to a particular period or particular occasion; but where anything removed from a building or its grounds is there otherwise than as forming part of, or being on loan for exhibition with, a collection intended for permanent exhibition to the public, the person removing it does not thereby commit an offence under this section unless he removes it on a day when the public have access to the building as mentioned in subsection (1) above.
(3) A person does not commit an offence under this section if he believes that he has lawful authority for the removal of the thing in question or that he would have it if the person entitled to give it knew of the removal and the circumstances of it.
(4) A person guilty of an offence under this section shall, on conviction on indictment, be liable to imprisonment for a term not exceeding five years."

7–02   It has been seen that an intention permanently to deprive is an essential constituent of theft, as it was of larceny. The CLRC considered the matter and came down against either (i) extending theft to include temporary deprivation, or (ii) creating a general offence of temporary deprivation of property.

"The former course seems to the Committee wrong because in their view an intention to return the property, even after a long time, makes the conduct essentially different from stealing. Apart from this either course would be a considerable extension of the criminal law, which does not seem to be called for by an existing serious evil. It might moreover have undesirable social consequences.

Quarrelling neighbours and families would be able to threaten one another with prosecution. Students and young people sharing accommodation who might be tempted to borrow one another's property in disregard of a prohibition by the owner would be in danger of acquiring a criminal record. Further, it would be difficult for the police to avoid being involved in wasteful and undesirable investigations into alleged offences which had no social importance."[1]

---

[1]   *Eighth Report*, Cmnd 2977, para 56.

7–03   The question whether temporary deprivation should be criminal attracted more attention than any other issue, both in and out of Parliament, during the passage of the Theft Bill;[1] but the government stuck firmly to the view expressed by the Committee. In two instances, the Committee found that there was a case for making temporary deprivation an offence, though not theft. These two cases are the subjects of this and the following chapter.

---

[1]   See Samuels 118 NLJ 281; Hadden 118 NLJ 305; Smith 118 NLJ 401; Parl. Debates, Official Report (HL) vol 289, cols 1305–1325, 1480–1485, vol 290, cols 51–71, 1390–1421, vol 291, cols 59–71; (HC) Standing Committee H cols 3–18. For further consideration, see Glanville Williams "Temporary Appropriation should be Theft" [1981] Crim LR 129.

7–04   Section 11 undoubtedly owes its existence to one particular and very unusual case – the removal from the National Gallery of Goya's portrait of the Duke of Wellington. The portrait was returned after a period of four years. There was evidence that the taker tried to make it a condition of his returning it that a large sum should be paid to charity. It has been argued above[1] that this should constitute a sufficient intent to deprive, but the accused was acquitted of larceny of the portrait, though convicted of larceny of the frame which was never recovered. The CLRC referred to two other cases, both of a very unusual nature.

> " . . . an art student took a statuette by Rodin from an exhibition, intending, as he said, to live with it for a while, and returned it over four months later. (Meanwhile the exhibitors, who had insured the statuette, had paid the insurance money to the owners, with the result that the statuette, when returned, became the property of the exhibitors.)[2] Yet another case was the removal of the coronation stone from Westminster Abbey."

It may well be doubted whether these instances amounted to a case for the creation of a special offence but the government acted on the Committee's suggestion and produced a clause which, after much debate and amendment, became s. 11. The object of the section is to protect things which are put at hazard by being displayed to the public. Where, however, the purpose of the display is "effecting sales or other commercial dealings", it was thought reasonable to expect the person mounting the exhibition to bear the resulting hazards and to take adequate precautions against them.

---

[1]   See para **2–133**.
[2]   If this had been foreseen by the taker then he might have been held to have an intention permanently to deprive; but this kind of foresight could probably only be attributed to a lawyer!

A.   THE *ACTUS REUS*

7–05   The ingredients of the offence are as follows:

(a)   The public must have access

So the contents of a building will not be protected where only a particular small class of persons is permitted to have access; as where the owner opens the building to the members of a club, school or similar body.

(b)   The public must have access to a building in order to view

7–06   The purpose is that of the invitor, not the invitee.[1] If the public have access to the building for this purpose, then articles in the grounds are protected.

If the public do not have access to the building or have access only for some purpose other than viewing, articles in the grounds to which they do have access in order to view are not protected. If an exhibition of sculpture is put on in the grounds of a house, it will not be an offence to "borrow" an item unless the public are also invited into the house for the purpose of viewing. If one piece of sculpture is displayed in the hall, then the fifty pieces in the grounds will also be protected. If, however, the public are invited into the house only for some purpose other than viewing – for example, to have tea – none of the articles will be protected. It follows, of course, that exhibitions in streets and squares are not protected.

---

¹   *Barr* [1978] Crim LR 244 (Deputy Judge C.S. Lowry).

(c)   The article must be displayed or kept for display

7–07   "Displayed" means exhibited in the sense in which an art gallery exhibits a painting. A cross placed in a church solely for devotional purposes is not "displayed".¹ If D, while touring the art gallery, removes the fire extinguisher, he commits no offence against this section. If the article is in a store, it may be "kept for display" though not presently displayed.

---

¹   *Barr*, above.

(d)   If the article is displayed in a building, it must be removed from the building

7–08   If it is displayed in the grounds of the building, it must be removed from the grounds. Presumably it would be enough to take the article from the grounds into the building. If D is apprehended in the course of removing the article either from the grounds or the building then, no doubt, he is guilty of an attempt.

(e)   The thing taken must be an article

7–09   The meaning of the word depends on its context. The expression, "any article whatsoever", in the Public Health Act 1936 was held not to include a goldfish, the court evidently taking the view that the word did not cover animate things.¹ On the other hand, a horse has been held to be an article for the purposes of a local Act dealing with exposure for sale at a market.² Bearing in mind the mischief at which the section is aimed, it is submitted that, if the other conditions are satisfied, any thing is protected, from an elephant in the London Zoo to a flower growing in the grounds of a stately home to which the public have access.

---

¹   *Daly v Cannon* [1954] 1 All ER 315, [1954] 1 WLR 261.
²   *Llandaff and Canton District Market Co v Lyndon* (1860) 8 CBNS 515.

---

*(f)   Where the article is in the building or its grounds as forming part of, or being on loan for exhibition with, a collection intended for permanent exhibition to the public, the offence may be committed at any time*¹

7–10   A collection is "intended for permanent exhibition to the public" if it is intended to be permanently available for exhibition to the public. It may be so intended though the pictures are exhibited in rotation and kept in store when not exhibited.[2] So the offence may be committed during the night when the building is closed, or on Sunday, even though the public are not admitted on Sunday, or in the middle of a month when the building is closed for renovation. Where this condition is not satisfied, then the article is protected only on a day when the public have access to the building. If P opens his stately home to the public on Easter Monday, then for the duration of that day only, articles displayed to the public in the building or its grounds are protected by the section. If D hides in the building until after midnight and removes an article on Tuesday he commits no offence under this section.

[1]   Section 11 (2).
[2]   *Durkin* [1973] QB 786, [1973] 2 All ER 872, CA.

(g)   If the public are admitted to view the building or part of it, then anything displayed is protected

7–11   If they are not admitted to view the building or part of it, then articles are protected only if a collection or part of a collection is displayed. Where a cathedral is open to the public to view and D removes an article which is displayed there, it is immaterial whether a collection is displayed or not. The term "collection" was used because it helps to indicate the intended purpose of the section – to protect articles assembled as objects of artistic or other merit or of public interest. It seems clear that it is not necessary that the contents should have been brought together for the purposes of exhibition in order to amount to a collection. If that were so, the contents of the stately home would be excluded from protection, for they were brought together for the edification of the collector, not for exhibition. It is no doubt sufficient that articles are preserved together. A single article could hardly constitute "a collection"; but, if it were on loan from a collection, might it not be "part of" a collection? A single article, not forming part of a collection, which was displayed to the public, would not be protected unless the public were admitted to view the building in which it was housed, as well as the article. Thus, if it were exhibited in a Nissen hut, it would not be protected, but it might be otherwise if the surroundings were more elegant.

(h)   If the public are admitted to view a collection made or exhibited for the purpose of effecting sales or other commercial dealings, the articles will not be protected[1]

7–12   If the public are admitted to view the building, it would seem that articles will be protected even though they do form part of an exhibition for the purpose of effecting sales or commercial dealings. This will be so even where the public are admitted for the dual purpose of viewing the building and the collection; when the public are admitted to view a building, any article which is displayed is protected.

[1]   Section 11 (1).

7–13   The definition of "collection" excludes not only commercial art galleries but also shops, salerooms and exhibitions for advertising purposes. Had it not been for this limitation, it is obvious that the scope of the section would have been immensely wider than is necessary to deal with the narrow class of cases at which the provision is aimed. Of course, a particular collection may be protected if the conditions of the section are satisfied, even though it is housed in a sale room, as where Christie's gave an exhibition in their sale room of articles which had been purchased from them and were lent by public galleries all over the world.

(i)   It should be emphasised that the protection of the section is not lost because the articles displayed are for sale

7–14   It is a question of the purpose of the exhibitor in inviting the public to attend. Thus, it is clear that the pictures displayed at the Royal Academy exhibitions are protected, even though they are for sale. Neither sale nor any other commercial dealing is the purpose of the Royal Academy in mounting the exhibition – though it may be the purpose of individual artists. There may be a difficult question where the exhibition has a dual purpose. Perhaps this is a case where it would be proper to have regard to the dominant purpose.

It is also clear that articles do not lose the protection of the section because a charge is made for admission with the object of making money in excess of the cost of upkeep. The sale or commercial dealing which is contemplated is one which is consequent upon the viewing of the exhibition.

B.   THE *MENS REA*

7–15   The *mens rea* of the offence is an intention to remove the article, knowing that there is no lawful authority for doing so and that the owner would not have authorised removal had he known of the circumstances. This closely follows the *mens rea* required for taking conveyances under s. 12. If the building were on fire and D removed a picture from it, he might well suppose that P would have authorised him to remove the picture had he known of the circumstances. The onus is, of course, on the Crown, once D has laid a foundation for such a defence, to prove beyond reasonable doubt that D did not so believe.

7–16   As with s. 12, "dishonesty" is not a constituent of the offence. Where students borrow some article for the purpose of a "rag", it might be debatable whether they are dishonest or not; but the question need not be considered on a charge under s. 11; it is enough that they know that the removal is not and would not have been authorised by the owner had he known of it.

CHAPTER 8
Taking a Motor Vehicle or other Conveyance without Authority

8–01 Section 12 of the Act replaced the offence under s. 217 of the Road Traffic Act 1960. Section 12 (1) provides:

> "Subject to subsections (5) and (6) below, a person shall be guilty of an offence if, without having the consent of the owner or other lawful authority, he takes any conveyance for his own or another's use or, knowing that any conveyance has been taken without such authority, drives it or allows himself to be carried in or on it."

An offence under this section was originally triable either way and punishable on indictment with three years' imprisonment but, by s. 37 (1) of the Criminal Justice Act 1988, it is now triable only summarily and punishable by a fine not exceeding level 5 on the standard scale, or by six months' imprisonment, or by both. When a jury acquits of theft of a conveyance it may convict of an offence under s. 12, whereupon the offender is punishable as he would have been on summary conviction. Section 12 appears to create two offences and it is convenient to treat them separately.

1   TAKING A CONVEYANCE

A.   TAKES

8–02 A person "takes" if he assumes possession or control of the conveyance and moves it or causes it to be moved.[1] It does not matter how small the movement is. One who fails to move a car which he intends to take is guilty of an attempt. Where a vehicle is taken but possession is then abandoned and then resumed, there is a second taking when the vehicle is moved again.[2] If a vehicle is taken by X without the consent of the owner, P, and D, being unaware that the vehicle has been so taken, takes it from X without X's consent, D is guilty of taking it without the consent of P.[3]

The Theft Act omits the words "and drives away" which were in the Road Traffic Acts.[4] The object of this omission was not to bring the mere acquisition of possession within the ambit of the offence but to include the case where the conveyance is removed without being "driven" or, in the case of an aircraft "flown", a boat "sailed" and so on. So the offence was committed where a man took an inflatable rubber dinghy from outside a lifeboat depot, put it on a trailer and drove it away.[5] The essence of the offence is not stealing a ride but depriving the owner, though only temporarily, of his conveyance.[6]

In the Larceny Acts the word "takes" connoted merely the acquisition of possession and the requirement of "asportation" rested upon the further words, "and carries away". In *Bogacki*,[7] it was held that, because "takes" is not a synonym of "uses", it imports a requirement of some degree of movement. A courting couple, occupying the back seat of a parked car as trespassers do not "take" it. If D takes possession of P's motorised caravan and lives in it for a

164

month without moving it he does not commit this offence. This is not unreasonable. It is not different in substance from making use of P's bungalow. The section is, after all, concerned with conveyances and the essence of a conveyance is that it moves.

1   *Bogacki* [1973] QB 832, [1973] 2 All ER 864. *Webley v Buxton* [1977] QB 481, [1977] 2 All ER 595. It is not enough that movement is caused accidentally: *Blayney v Knight* (1975) 60 Cr App Rep 269, DC.
2   *DPP v Spriggs* [1994] RTR 1, [1993] Crim LR 622, DC, below, para **8–14**. Cf *Starling* [1969] Crim LR 556, CA.
3   Commentary on *Spriggs* [1993] Crim LR 622, above. If necessary, reliance may be placed on the doctrine of transferred malice: Smith & Hogan 77. If D, knowing that the vehicle has been taken by X, drives the vehicle with X's consent, he is guilty, not of taking, but of driving a taken vehicle: below, para **8–13**.
4   The words were included in the Bill presented to Parliament but deleted so as to cover, e.g. the case of a boat which is towed away: HL Deb vol 291, col 106.
5   *Bogacki* [1973] QB 832, [1973] 2 All ER 864.
6   According to the Criminal Law Revision Committee, under the old law, " . . . the essence of the offence is stealing a ride" (*Eighth Report*, Cmnd 2977, at para 84); but there was more to it than that, as appears if the offence is compared with that of unlawful riding on public transport, where the authority is not deprived of the vehicle.
7   Fn 1, above.

8–03   Where an employee has control, in the course of his employment, of a vehicle belonging to his employer, possession of the vehicle in law remains in the employer and the employee's control is known as custody. If the employee, without authority, so alters the character of his control of the vehicle that he no longer holds as employee but for his own purposes, he "takes" by assuming possession in the legal sense.[1] If, in the middle of the working day, he were to decide to drive his employer's van away for a fortnight's holiday, he would "take" it as soon as he departed from his authorised route with intent to control the vehicle for his own purpose. On the other hand, a lorry-driver who diverted briefly from his authorised route merely to visit a favourite cafe would probably continue to hold as employee. The journey, though by an unnecessarily roundabout route, might still be in substance the journey he was employed to make. It is a question of degree. In *McKnight v Davies*,[2] a lorry-driver was held guilty when, instead of returning the lorry to his employer's depot, as was his duty, he drove it to a public house, drove three men to their homes, back to another pub and then to his house, returning the vehicle to the depot the following morning.

While a deviation in the course of the working day raises a question of degree, it seems clear that when the working day is over and the driver resumes control over the vehicle for a purpose of his own, he commits the offence.[3]

1   *McKnight v Davies* [1974] RTR 4, [1974] Crim LR 62, DC.
2   Above. *Mowe v Perraton* [1952] 1 All ER 423, DC, appears to be wrongly decided.
3   *Wibberley* [1966] 2 QB 214, [1965] 3 All ER 718.

8–04   It is clear that a hirer in possession of a conveyance under a hire-purchase agreement cannot commit the offence because he is the "owner" for this purpose.[1] Other bailees, however, may commit the offence. A bailee, unlike a servant, has possession of the thing entrusted to him; yet if he operates the conveyance after the purpose of the bailment has been fulfilled, that subsequent use may be held to amount to a taking, though he has never given up possession. In *McGill*,[2] D borrowed a car to take his wife to the station on the express condition that he brought it straight back. He did not return it that day and the following day drove it to Hastings. It was held that his use of the car after the purpose of the borrowing was fulfilled constituted a taking. Once the conveyance has been taken by D, however, subsequent movement of it does not constitute a fresh taking,[3] unless he has abandoned and then resumed possession; though it may be an offence under the second limb of the section.[4]

---

[1]   Section 12 (7) (b), below, p 263.
[2]   [1970] RTR 209, 54 Cr App Rep 300, CA. See commentaries at [1970] Crim LR 291 and 480 and *Whittaker v Campbell*, below, para **8–09**.
[3]   *Pearce* [1961] Crim LR 122.
[4]   Below, para **8–12**.

8–05   The requirement of the Road Traffic Act that the vehicle be "driven away" led to some very subtle distinctions. It was held that, for example, a vehicle was not being driven where D released the handbrake so that it ran down a hill or where it was being towed or pushed by another vehicle. It would seem that there is a taking in each of these cases and convictions would now be possible, if the other constituents of the offence were present.[1]

---

[1]   In *Roberts* [1965] 1 QB 85, [1964] 2 All ER 541, the court thought it "possible" that D's releasing the handbrake and allowing the vehicle to run down the hill amounted to a taking. It would clearly be sufficient taking for the purposes of larceny – suppose D had had an intent permanently to deprive, as by allowing the vehicle to run over a cliff into the sea; and it is thought that the requirements of this section should not be more stringent.

B.   FOR HIS OWN OR ANOTHER'S USE

8–06   The CLRC considered the essence of the offence they proposed in their draft bill to be "stealing a ride" but material amendments were made to the draft bill in Parliament which affect the nature of the offence. The words "and drives away" were omitted from the draft bill and the words "for his own or another's use" were inserted. These words were intended to exclude from the offence one who let the conveyance run away, or float away, out of malice. In *Bow*,[1] the Court of Appeal thought "use" meant "use as a conveyance"; but the actual taking need not involve the use of the conveyance at all – as in *Pearce*[2] where the conveyance, a rubber dinghy, was carried away on a trailer. An intention to use in the future may be enough and the court may have fairly assumed that D intended to use the dinghy for its normal purposes. If, however, he had intended to use it only as a paddling pool for his children he would not (according to *Bow*) have been guilty of the offence, though the injury to the owner would have been the same. In *Bow*,[3] D parked a vehicle in a private lane, allegedly for the purpose of poaching. P, a gamekeeper, blocked his exit with a Land-Rover and sent for the police. When P declined to move the Land-Rover, D got into it, released the handbrake and coasted 200 yards to allow his vehicle to be driven away. D's appeal, on the ground that he did not take the Land-Rover "for his own use", was dismissed: the taking necessarily involved the use of the Land-Rover "as a conveyance" and D's motive – to remove an obstruction – was immaterial. If D had pushed the vehicle without getting into it, the answer would presumably have been different. Thus in *Stokes*,[4] there was held to be no "use" where D, as a joke, pushed P's parked car around the corner so as to make P believe that it had been stolen. It would have been an offence, apparently, if D had got into the car while it was moved; but, even on those facts, or the actual facts of *Bow*, it seems doubtful whether the taking is properly regarded as "use as a conveyance"; for the purpose of the taking is not to convey any person or thing.[5] But to push a car with the intention of subsequently going for a ride in it is taking it for use as a conveyance.[6]

1   (1977) 64 Cr App Rep 54, [1977] Crim LR 176, CA and commentary.
2   [1973] Crim LR 321, CA. Cf *Dunn and Derby* [1984] Crim LR 367.
3   (1976) 64 Cr App Rep 54, [1977] Crim LR 176, CA.
4   [1983] RTR 59, [1982] Crim LR 695, CA.
5   *Bow* is also open to criticism on the ground that P had no right to detain D: Williams *TBCL* 721–722. Presumably he had no right to detain D's vehicle either.
6   *Marchant and McCallister* (1984) 80 Cr App Rep 361, CA following *Pearce*, above, fn 2. The jury convicted of an attempt although the evidence was that DD had pushed it two or three feet which amounts to the full offence.

C.   CONVEYANCE

8–07   By s. 12 (7) (a) of the Act:

"'conveyance' means any conveyance constructed or adapted for the carriage of a person or persons whether by land, water or air, except that it does not include a conveyance constructed or adapted for use only under the control of a person not carried in or on it, and 'drive' shall be construed accordingly."

Thus conveyances for the carriage of goods are excluded, but only where the conveyance has no place for a driver. A lorry is clearly within the protection of the Act, since it is constructed for the carriage of at least one person. A goods trailer, however, would not be so protected, nor a barge with no provision for a passenger. A vehicle, such as some milk floats, which is operated by a man walking beside it, is expressly excluded. A horse-drawn carriage is clearly a conveyance, but a horse is not.[1] A conveyance evidently means something that is manufactured. Moreover, it has been held that attaching a halter or bridle to the horse is not "adapting" it but only making it easier to ride.[2]

The elimination of the requirement of "driving" may bring within the section (or, at least, the first part of it) certain conveyances which otherwise would be outside it – that is any conveyance with accommodation for a passenger or passengers which has no means of self-propulsion and so cannot be driven but must be towed.

1   *Neal v Gribble* [1978] RTR 409, [1978] Crim LR 500.
2   Ibid. See commentary [1978] Crim LR 500–501.

8–08   Pedal cycles are expressly excluded by s. 12 (5):

"Subsection (1) above[1] shall not apply in relation to pedal cycles; but, subject to subsection (6) below,[2] a person who, without having the consent of the owner or other lawful authority,[3] takes a pedal cycle for his own or another's use, or rides a pedal cycle knowing it to have been taken without such authority, shall on summary conviction be liable to a fine not exceeding [level 3 on the standard scale]."

1   Above, para **8–01**.
2   Below, para **8–11**.
3   Below, para **8–09**.

D.   WITHOUT HAVING THE CONSENT OF THE OWNER OR OTHER LAWFUL AUTHORITY

8–09   If the owner had not given his consent at the time of the taking, his later declaration that he would have done so if asked is not a defence.[1] It would seem clear that a consent extracted by intimidation would not amount to a defence.[2] In *Whittaker v Campbell*,[3] the Divisional Court held that a consent obtained by fraud is consent for the purposes of the section even though it might not be so regarded in other branches of the law, such as the law of contract. D found a driving licence belonging to E and obtained the hire of a motor vehicle from P by producing the licence and representing that he was E. The *ratio decidendi* is that, even if this was a mistake of identity so fundamental as to preclude the existence of a contract between D and P, it did not "vitiate" P's consent to D's taking the car. The court recognised that it might have decided the case on a narrower ground, i.e. that P was dealing with the person in his presence, D, believing that his name was E and that he was the owner of the licence produced – errors, not as to identity but as to attributes, which would result in a merely voidable contract with D.[4] It is submitted that, in a true case of mistaken identity – which will be rare – there is no consent in fact and the law should not say there is. Suppose that P has two friends, E, in whom he has the utmost confidence, and D whom he would not trust with a tricycle. When P is away from home, D telephones, says he is E and asks for permission to borrow P's car. P, addressing him as E, tells him where to find the keys. If D then takes the car, it is submitted that he does so without the consent of the owner.[5] Apart from principle, the *ratio* (though not the facts) of *Whittaker v Campbell* is difficult to reconcile with *McGill*[6] but gains some support from *Peart*.[7] D induced P to lend his van, for a payment of £2, by representing that he wanted to drive to Alnwick and would return the van by 7.30 p.m. Instead, as presumably he intended all along, he drove to Burnley where he was found at 9 p.m. It was held that there was no taking; the misrepresentation did not vitiate P's consent. The court reserved the question whether a misrepresentation can ever be so fundamental as to vitiate consent for the purposes of this crime. If, when a conveyance has been borrowed for a particular purpose, it is "taking" to use it for a quite different purpose after the declared purpose has been fulfilled, it is difficult to see why it is not "taking" to use it immediately for a purpose quite different from that declared. It is submitted that *McGill* is to be preferred to *Peart*. If D gets P's permission to drive P's car around the corner to buy a newspaper and immediately drives off on the Monte Carlo rally, it is submitted that this is properly regarded as a taking without consent. *Peart* and *Whittaker v Campbell* were distinguished by the Court of Appeal (Civ Div) in *Singh v Rathour (Northern Star Insurance Co Ltd, third party)*.[8] A borrower of a vehicle, being aware of an implied limitation as to the purpose for which it was to be driven, did not have the consent of the owner to drive it for a purpose outside that limitation and consequently was not insured in respect of such driving.

---

[1]   *Ambler* [1979] RTR 217, CA.
[2]   *Hogdon* [1962] Crim LR 563.
[3]   [1984] QB 318, [1983] 3 All ER 582, [1983] Crim LR 812 and commentary.
[4]   Cheshire, Fifoot & Furmston, *Law of Contract* (12th edn) Ch 8.
[5]   An argument on these lines is said by A.T.H. Smith (*Property Offences*, 9–23) to involve a fallacy because "The person who is deceived intends to deal both with the owner of the voice and with the person he has in mind . . . since he believes that these two persons are one and the same." However, the one person whom P has in mind is certainly E and no one else.
[6]   [1970] RTR 209, CA, above, para **8–04**.
[7]   [1970] 2 QB 672, [1970] 2 All ER 823, CA.
[8]   [1988] 2 All ER 16, [1988] 1 WLR 422, CA.

8–10   "Other lawful authority" would apply to the removal of a vehicle, in accordance with a statutory power such as the regulations made under reg. 20 of the Removal and Disposal of Vehicles Regulations 1986, where the vehicle has been parked in contravention of a statutory prohibition, or in a dangerous situation, or in such circumstances as to appear to have been abandoned.

It would also cover any removal of a vehicle in pursuance of a common law right such as that of abating a nuisance,[1] or of a contractual right such as that of a letter under a hire-purchase agreement to resume possession in certain circumstances.

---

[1]   Cf *Webb v Stansfield* [1966] Crim LR 449.

E.   THE *MENS REA*

8–11   Section 12 (6) provides:

"A person does not commit an offence under this section by anything done in the belief that he has lawful authority to do it or that he would have the owner's consent if the owner knew of his doing it and the circumstances of it."

Once D has raised the issue, the prosecution must prove that he did not believe that he had lawful authority or that he would, in the circumstances (presumably the circumstances which D believed to exist) have had the owner's consent.[1]

If an unlicensed and uninsured garage employee who has driven a customer's car asserts that he believed he had lawful authority to do so, it must be left to the jury to decide whether they are satisfied that he had no genuine belief that the owner had consented, or would have consented, to his doing so.[2] The more unreasonable the alleged belief, the more likely is the jury to be satisfied that it was not really held.

---

[1]   *MacPherson* [1973] RTR 157, [1973] Crim LR 457, CA; *Briggs* [1987] Crim LR 708, CA.
[2]   *Clotworthy* [1981] RTR 477, [1981] Crim LR 501, CA.

---

2   DRIVING OR ALLOWING ONESELF TO BE CARRIED BY A "TAKEN" CONVEYANCE

A.   THE ACTUS REUS

8–12   Where a conveyance has been unlawfully taken, D does not commit an offence of "taking" by driving with the consent of the taker or allowing himself to be carried in or on the taken conveyance.[1] Special provision was made to meet this case in the Road Traffic Act 1962, s. 44 and reproduced in s. 12 of the Theft Act. At least one offence, separate and distinct from taking a conveyance, is created; and there are two such offences if driving[2] and allowing oneself to be carried cannot be regarded as alternative modes of commission of a single offence. Such an offence is hereafter designated a "secondary offence".

---

[1]   *Stally* [1959] 3 All ER 814, [1960] 1 WLR 79; *D (infant) v Parsons* [1960] 2 All ER 493, [1960] 1 WLR 797.
[2]   "Driving" now includes the activity of a person who sets in motion and controls an aircraft, hovercraft, boat or any other conveyance: s. 12 (7) (a). It is conceivable that the old technicalities of what is "driving" might arise again here. It is submitted that D is driving when he is in or on the vehicle and is in control of its forward or backward motion. Cf *Wallace v Major* [1946] KB 473, [1946] 2 All ER 87; *Saycell v Bool* [1948] 2 All ER 83; *Shimmell v Fisher* [1951] 2 All ER 672; *Spindley* [1961] Crim LR 486; *Roberts* [1965] 1 QB 85, [1964] 2 All ER 541; *Arnold* [1964] Crim LR 664.

(a)   Driving a "taken" vehicle

8–13   A person who drives a taken vehicle with the consent of the taker is guilty of the secondary offence of driving the taken vehicle. He is not guilty of the primary offence of taking, probably because possession of the conveyance, though unlawful, is now in the taker, not the owner. Where, however, a person drives a taken vehicle without the consent of the taker, the position is less clear.

If (a) he is unaware that the vehicle has been taken, he cannot be guilty of the secondary offence, so, if he is not guilty of the primary offence, he gets off scot-free. That can hardly have been intended. Unlike the person who drives with the consent of the first taker, he is assuming possession of the vehicle and he is certainly doing so without the consent of the person entitled to possession, the owner. The owner, not the first taker, is the victim of the offence.

If (b) he is aware that the vehicle has been taken and he drives it without the consent of the taker (or, of course, the owner) he too must (if (a) above is right) be guilty of the primary offence, for he too is assuming possession without the consent of the owner. Yet it is clear that he is guilty of the secondary offence. Assuming that there are indeed two offences, can he be guilty of both? Or does his plain guilt of the secondary offence imply that he cannot be guilty of the primary offence?

8–14   This speculation is prompted by the decision in *DPP v Spriggs*.[1] But that case is relatively straightforward. The first taker abandoned the car and thus gave up possession of it. It thereupon either reverted to the possession of the true owner or was in no one's possession. In either event D, when he drove the car, was assuming possession of, and therefore "taking" the car and committing the primary offence.

---

[1]   [1993] Crim LR 622.

(b)   Allowing oneself to be carried

8–15   If, when D allows himself to be carried, he is aiding and abetting the taking of the conveyance, he may be convicted of the primary offence as a secondary party. But if the "taking" has come to an end, the primary offence has ceased and it is no longer possible to aid and abet it. Moreover, "allow" is probably a word of wider ambit than "aid, abet, counsel or procure". If D allows himself to be driven by a person who, as he knows, would drive the car whether D was there or not, he may neither assist or encourage, nor intend to assist or encourage, the driver.[1] He is not aiding and abetting the driving but he is allowing himself to be carried. The fact that D allows himself to be carried is some evidence of secondary participation in the driving offence, but no more.[2]

---

[1]   Cf Smith & Hogan 137–141.
[2]   *C (a minor) v Hume* [1979] Crim LR 328. Cf *D (infant) v Parsons* [1960] 2 All ER 493; *Boldizsar v Knight* [1980] Crim LR 653.

8–16   It has been held that a person is not "carried" in a conveyance merely because he is present in it. Carriage imports some movement. A person is not carried in a stationary launch though he is borne by its buoyancy.[1] It would presumably be no different where the boat rises or falls with the waves or the tide. This is not distinguishable from the movement of a stationary car on its springs as people get in or out. The slightest vertical motion of a hovercraft, however, should suffice. D does not "allow" himself to be carried in a taken vehicle merely by agreeing to take a ride and sitting in the vehicle. He does so only when the vehicle moves off.[2] If, in the course of the journey a passenger learns for the first time that a vehicle has been unlawfully taken, he is, it seems, under a duty to require the driver to put him down as soon as he reasonably can.[3]

"Drives" similarly seems to import movement. One who starts up a vehicle and engages the gear has reached the stage of an attempt but has not yet committed the offence.

---

¹   *Miller* [1976] Crim LR 147, CA. Similarly, presumably, where D climbs up a rope into a tethered airborne balloon.
²   *Diggin* (1981) 72 Cr App Rep 204, [1980] Crim LR 656, CA and commentary.
³   *Boldizsar v Knight* [1980] Crim LR 653, where D pleaded guilty to allowing himself to be carried.

8–17   The vehicle must actually have been taken; one cannot know a thing to be so, unless it is so.¹

The secondary offence is intended to deal with persons other than the original taker, but is not expressly limited to such persons. Unless such a limitation is to be implied, the taker appears to commit another offence on each subsequent occasion when he drives the vehicle or allows himself to be carried in or on it. Where the original taking is not an offence because of lack of *mens rea*, a subsequent driving of it may make the taker liable. For example, D takes P's car, wrongly supposing that P consents to his doing so. The car has been taken without P's consent but no offence has been committed. Having learnt that P does not consent to his having the car, D continues to drive it. He appears to commit the offence though it is arguable that a "taken" conveyance is one taken with *mens rea*.

---

¹   D might now be guilty of an attempt where he wrongly thought he knew that the vehicle had been taken: Criminal Attempts Act 1981, s. 1.

B.   THE *MENS REA*

8–18   It must be proved that D knew that the conveyance had been taken without authority when he drove it or allowed himself to be carried in or on it as the case may be. Probably "wilful blindness" would be enough as in the case of other statutes.¹ Such a state of mind is, however, barely distinguishable from that of belief that the conveyance had been so taken. The Criminal Law Revision Committee thought that belief was not knowledge for the purpose of the old law of receiving² and made special provision for that state of mind in the new offence of handling.³ It is inevitable that comparison will be made between s. 12 (1) and s. 22, with the implication that belief will not do in the case of s. 12; but it is submitted that such an argument should not be accepted.⁴

---

¹   Smith & Hogan 107; Edwards *Mens Rea in Statutory Offences* 202–205; Williams *CLGP* 159.
²   *Eighth Report*, Cmnd 2977, para 134; below, para **13–41**.
³   See s. 22 (1), below, para **13–01**.
⁴   Below, para **13–41**.

---

3   AGGRAVATED VEHICLE TAKING

8–19   Public concern at the risks of death and injury to the person and damage to property caused by so-called "joyriders" led to the enactment of the Aggravated Vehicle-Taking Act 1992.

This Act inserts after s. 12 of the Theft Act 1968 a new s. 12A which creates an aggravated form of the offence under s. 12, punishable on indictment with imprisonment for two years or, if death is caused, five years. A person is guilty of the new offence if:

   (i)   He committed an offence under s. 12 (the "basic offence") in relation to a mechanically propelled vehicle.

(ii) After the vehicle was unlawfully taken (whether by him or another) and before it was recovered it was driven, or injury or damage was caused, in one or more of the following circumstances:

(a) the vehicle was driven dangerously (as defined in s. 1 (7) of the 1992 Act) on a road or other public place;

(b) owing to the driving of the vehicle an accident occurred by which injury was caused to any person;

(c) owing to the driving of the vehicle an accident occurred by which damage was caused to any property other than the vehicle;

(d) damage was caused to the vehicle.

It is a defence for the defendant to prove either:

(i) that the driving, accident or damage in (a), (b), (c) or (d) above occurred before he committed the basic offence; or

(ii) that he was neither in, nor in the immediate vicinity of, the vehicle when that driving, accident or damage occurred.

8–20 Section 12A is a peculiar provision in that, once the basic offence has been committed, liability for the aggravated offence depends simply on whether something – (a), (b), (c) or (d) above – happens. Anyone who commits the basic offence takes the chance that, without his doing anything more, he may become liable for the aggravated offence. Under (b) it is not necessary to prove that the vehicle was being driven dangerously; and it has been held that "owing to the driving of the vehicle" does not imply any fault in the driving of the vehicle. If, when the car is being driven with perfect care, a child runs in front of it and is inevitably injured, it seems that this has occurred "owing to the driving of the vehicle".[1] Under (d) the damage need not be caused by the driving and may apparently be caused by some third party. D may have merely allowed himself to be carried in the taken vehicle (the basic offence). If he is then standing beside it (in the "immediate vicinity" of it) when a third party runs into it and damages it, it appears that he commits the aggravated offence. This is strict liability of the most severe kind and difficult to justify in principle. The message to the "joyrider" is that he acts at his peril and if anything goes wrong, it will end not in joy but tears. Whether it will be effective remains to be seen.

---

[1] *Marsh* [1997] Crim LR 205.

CHAPTER 9
Abstracting of Electricity

9–01   The Larceny Act of 1916 made special provision for the stealing of electricity because, no doubt, it was not capable of being taken and carried away. The notion of appropriation in the Theft Act might perhaps have been applied without incongruity to the abstraction of electricity but the unique nature of this kind of property was thought to call for a special provision. It has now been held that electricity is not "property" within s. 4 of the Act and that it is not appropriated by switching on the current.[1] Section 13 of the Act provides:

> "A person who dishonestly uses without due authority, or dishonestly causes to be wasted or diverted, any electricity shall on conviction on indictment be liable to imprisonment for a term not exceeding five years."

Thus the offence would be committed by an employee who dishonestly used his employer's electrically-operated machinery without authority; by a householder who, having had his electricity supply cut off, dishonestly[2] reconnected it or who by-passed the meter; and by a tramp who, having trespassed into a house to obtain a night's shelter, turned on the electric fire to keep himself warm. If the tramp found the electric fire already burning, would he "use" the electricity by warming himself in front of it? Probably not. "Use" implies some consumption of electricity which would not occur but for the accused's act.[3] It is not necessary to prove that there has been any tampering or interference with the meter.[4] If squatters switch on the electricity, not intending to pay for it, they use it dishonestly. Suppose that D subsequently joins them and enjoys the heat and light provided. He appears to be a party to the dishonest use which is taking place.

Where two people are living in a house, it is not sufficient to prove that a meter has been improperly disconnected and that D is the registered consumer; nor that the disconnection must have been done either by D or by D2 unless it can be shown that they were acting in concert.[5] A person who knew that a meter had been disconnected to avoid payment would, prima facie, commit an offence each time he switched on an electrical apparatus; but it would be for the jury or magistrates to decide whether he did so dishonestly.

---

[1]   *Low v Blease* (1975) 119 Sol Jo 695, [1975] Crim LR 513.
[2]   See *Boggeln v Williams* [1978] 2 All ER 1061, above, para **2–121** and *Ghosh*, above, para **2–122**.
[3]   This sentence was approved in *McCreadie and Tume* (1992) 96 Cr App Rep 143, CA.
[4]   Ibid.
[5]   *Collins and Fox v Chief Constable of Merseyside* [1988] Crim LR 247, DC, and commentary; *Swallow v DPP* [1991] Crim LR 610.

9–02   The tramp who turned on the fire would not be guilty of burglary, since abstracting electricity is not one of the ulterior offences specified in s. 9 (1) (b).[1] Yet, oddly, it would seem that the person who did the acts described in the previous paragraph would be guilty of theft if it were gas he consumed, instead of electricity; so the tramp would be a burglar, if it were a gas fire. Not a very happy result.

173

---

[1] Below, para **11–02**.

9–03   There is nothing in the section to suggest that the electricity must come from the mains. Therefore it is probable that D commits the offence if he borrows my flashlight or portable radio and uses the dry battery.[1] Is the offence committed then by the dishonest "borrower" of a conveyance, such as a motor car, which consumes electricity from the battery when it is operated? If so, we have the incongruous result that the – merely incidental – use of the electricity is a more serious offence than the use of the vehicle as a whole.[2] It might be argued that if, as will usually be the case, the battery is charging properly, there will be as much electricity stored in it at the end of the journey as the beginning; and that, therefore, the use is not dishonest. An analogy might be drawn with the case where D takes P's coins, intending permanently to deprive him of them but to replace an equivalent sum from D's own money, not causing any injury to P.[3] It is not a fair analogy, however. In the case of the coins, the replacements are D's property; in the case of the electricity, the replacement is generated by the use of P's petrol and P's machinery and belongs to P as much as the electricity consumed. It seems likely, therefore, that the dishonest borrower of a motor vehicle (or motor boat, aircraft, etc.) does commit an offence against s. 13.[4]

---

[1]   Or if he operates an electrically-powered milk-float or similar vehicle. Taking such a vehicle is not an offence under s. 12 if the operator is not carried in or on it.
[2]   This incongruity has always been present with regard to the petrol which is consumed.
[3]   Above, paras **2–121** to **2–124**.
[4]   This incongruity would not have arisen under the draft bill proposed by the Criminal Law Revision Committee, since the draft clause contained the words, "with intent to cause loss to another". These words were cut out by the House of Lords.

9–04   What if D obtains the benefit of the use of the electricity by fraud? Lord Airedale put the case[1] of a woodworking company allowing sea scouts to use their electrically-operated machinery and D's obtaining the use of the machinery by falsely stating that he is a sea scout. Lord Airedale thought D might escape because he had obtained authority, albeit by false pretences, and was therefore not acting "without due authority". One answer to this might be that some meaning should be given to the word "due"; and that, while D was acting with actual authority, he was not acting with "due" authority, since the authority was voidable on the ground of fraud. D is not guilty of obtaining services contrary to 1978, s. 1,[2] unless the use of the machinery had been, or was to be, paid for.

---

[1]   Parl. Debates (HL) vol 190, col 154.
[2]   Above, para **4–75**.

9–05   The corresponding provision in the Larceny Act was sometimes used to deal with persons who dishonestly used a telephone and this would seem to be perfectly possible under the Theft Act. For example, the employee who dishonestly uses his employer's telephone for his own private purposes would seem to be in no different situation from the employee who uses any other electrically-operated machine. Under the Telecommunications Act 1984, s. 42, it is a specific offence, punishable summarily with six months and on indictment with two years, dishonestly to obtain a service provided by means of of a licensed telecommunication system with intent to avoid payment of any charge. It would seem right to rely on this offence, rather than the Theft Act, whenever it is available but, for cases which do not fall within s. 42 there seems to be no reason why s. 13 should not be invoked.

CHAPTER 10
Blackmail[1]

10–01 "Blackmail" is the name which was commonly given to the group of offences contained in ss. 29–31 of the Larceny Act 1916. That term was officially adopted for the first time as the name of the offence which replaces these sections of the Larceny Act. Section 21 (1) of the 1968 Act provides:

> "A person is guilty of blackmail if, with a view to gain for himself or another or with intent to cause loss to another, he makes any unwarranted demand with menaces; and for this purpose a demand with menaces is unwarranted unless the person making it does so in the belief –
> (a) that he has reasonable grounds for making the demand; and
> (b) that the use of the menaces is a proper means of reinforcing the demand."

---

[1]   Eighth Report, Cmnd 2977, paras 108–125.

---

1   THE *ACTUS REUS*

10–02 The *actus reus* consists in a demand with menaces; and the two problems here are to determine the meaning of the expressions, "demand" and "menaces".

A. DEMAND

Under the Larceny Act, the demand had to be for "any property or valuable thing"[1] or something capable of being stolen[2] or for an appointment or office of profit or trust.[3] The Theft Act is not so limited. Section 21 (2) provides:

> "The nature of the act or omission demanded is immaterial, and it is also immaterial whether the menaces relate to action to be taken by the person making the demand."

In effect, this is limited by the requirement that the demand be made with a view to gain or intent to cause loss[4] so that the change in the law is probably slight. In the vast majority of cases, the blackmailer will be demanding money or other property, intending both a gain to himself and a loss to another. It is clearly intended that the demand for a remunerated appointment or office[5] be covered, though whether such a case satisfies the requirement of view to gain or loss requires further consideration.[6] It would seem, however, that a demand for an unremunerated office, which would formerly have been an offence, would now, prima facie, not be. To threaten one believed to have influence in these matters, if he did not procure D's appointment as a justice of the peace, or Lord Lieutenant of the County, or Chairman of the Trustees of the British Museum, would appear no longer to be an offence of blackmail. The limitation would seem to be in pursuance of a general policy of limiting the provisions of the Act to the protection of economic interests. Had there been no such limitation, the section would have extended to such cases as that where D demands with menaces that P shall have sexual intercourse with him – a case which is obviously outside the scope of an enactment dealing with "theft and similar or associated offences" and which is provided for by other legislation.[7]

176

1   Sections 29 and 31 (a).
2   Section 30.
3   Section 31 (b).
4   See below, para **10–12**.
5   *Eighth Report*, Cmnd 2977, para 117.
6   Below, para **10–18**.
7   Sexual Offences Act 1956, s. 2.

10–03   In other respects, the Act extended the scope of the law. To demand with menaces that a person abandon a claim to property or release D from some legal liability of an economic nature may now be an offence. To demand with menaces that P discontinue divorce proceedings would not, however, be within the section. Whereas under s. 29 of the Larceny Act the demand had to be in writing, it is quite immaterial whether the demand under the Theft Act be oral or written.

10–04   Whether an utterance amounts to a "demand" seems to depend on whether an ordinary literate person would so describe it.[1] A demand is made when and where a letter containing it is posted; and it probably continues to be made until it arrives and is read by the recipient.[2] To post such a letter in England addressed to P in Germany amounts to an offence in England: *Treacy v DPP*.[3] To post the letter in Germany addressed to P in England is an offence triable here, at least if the letter arrives within the jurisdiction and, according to Lord Diplock, even if it does not. The situation will be governed by Part I of the Criminal Justice Act 1993, when it is brought into force. If Lord Diplock was right, there will be no problem for the prosecutor. If he was wrong, then proof of the arrival of the letter in England is "an event . . . proof of which is required for the conviction of the offence" – a "relevant event"[4] – so, under the 1993 Act, D will be triable here for the full offence if the letter arrives and for an attempt if it does not.

An oral demand would appear to be made when uttered, though unheard by the person addressed. If an emissary, other than the Post Office, be despatched bearing a demand, whether written or oral, it would seem that it could scarcely be held to be "made" until delivered.[5] The test would seem to be whether D has done, personally or through an agent, the final act necessary in the normal course to result in a communication. The Post Office, though sometimes treated as such, is not an agent in any real sense. The posted letter is as irrevocable as the bullet expelled from a gun. Any emissary other than the Post Office, whether he carries a demand or a loaded gun, may be recalled; so the principal of the one has, as yet, no more demanded than the principal of the other has shot. As was the case under the old law, it is likely that there may be a demand although it is not expressed in words, "a demand may be implicit or explicit".[6] It is probably enough that "the demeanour of the accused and the circumstances of the case were such that an ordinary reasonable man would understand that a demand . . . was being made upon him . . . ".[7] There may also be a demand although it is couched in terms of request and obsequious in tone;[8] the addition of the menace is sufficient to show that it is truly a demand that is made.

1   *Treacy v DPP* [1971] AC 537 at 565, [1971] 1 All ER 110 at 124, HL, per Lord Diplock.
2   Ibid. Cf *Baxter* [1972] 1 QB 1, [1971] 2 All ER 359, CA.
3   See fn 1. The effect will be confirmed by the Criminal Justice Act 1993, above, para **1–18**, when it is brought into force.
4   Above, para **1–19**.
5   See Griew 12–11 to 12–15, and the discussion by Lord Reid (dissenting) in *Treacy* [1971] AC 537 at 550 and [1971] 1 All ER at 111.
6   *Clear* [1968] 1 QB 670, [1968] 1 All ER 74 at 77, CA.

7   *Collister and Warhurst* (1955) 39 Cr App Rep 100 at 102.
8   *Robinson* (1796) 2 East PC 1110; *Studer* (1915) 11 Cr App Rep 307.

B.   MENACES

10–05   The Criminal Law Revision Committee states:[1]

"We have chosen the word 'menaces' instead of 'threats' because, notwithstanding the wide meaning given to 'menaces' in *Thorne*'s case . . . we regard that word as stronger than 'threats', and the consequent slight restriction of the scope of the offence seems to us right."

It is reasonably clear, then, that it was the intention that the old law should be preserved here. In the case referred to, *Thorne v Motor Trade Association*,[2] Lord Wright said:

"I think the word 'menace' is to be liberally construed and not as limited to threats of violence but as including threats of any action detrimental to or unpleasant to the person addressed. It may also include a warning that in certain events such action is intended."

1   *Eighth Report*, Cmnd 2977, para 123.
2   [1937] AC 797 at 817, HL.

10–06   In view of the breadth of this definition, it is apparent that any restriction imposed by the use of the word "menaces" rather than "threats" must be slight. In most cases, there is no need to spell out the meaning of the word to a jury, since it is "an ordinary English word which a jury could be expected to understand".[1]

The one limitation is that the threat does not amount to a menace unless "it is of such a nature and extent that the mind of an ordinary person of normal stability and courage might be influenced or made apprehensive so as to accede unwillingly to the demand".[2] If the threat is "of such a character that it is not calculated to deprive any person of reasonably sound and ordinarily firm mind of the free and voluntary action of his mind",[3] then it does not amount to a menace; but it has been said this doctrine should receive "a liberal construction in practice",[4] that is, the court should be slow to hold that the threat would not influence an ordinary man.

1   *Lawrence* (1971) 57 Cr App Rep 64.
2   *Clear* [1968] 1 QB 670, [1968] 1 All ER 74, CA.
3   *Boyle and Merchant* [1914] 3 KB 339 at 345, CCA.
4   *Tomlinson* [1895] 1 QB 706 at 710, per Wills J; *Clear* (above) at 80.

10–07   If the threat is one of so trivial a nature that it would not influence anybody[1] to respond to the demand, it is certainly reasonable to say that it is not a menace. A letter from a student rag committee to shop-keepers offering to sell "indemnity posters" reading "these premises are immune from all rag '73 activities whatever they may be" has been held not to amount to a menace.[2] It would no doubt have been different if the '72 rag activities had been of such a nature as to cause apprehension in ordinary shop-keepers. The doctrine is satisfactory enough, then, where the person to whom the demand is addressed is a person of normal stability and courage, but it has been said that "persons who are thus practised upon are not as a rule of average firmness".[3] Suppose that P is a weak-minded person, likely to be swayed by a fanciful or trivial threat which an ordinary person would ignore; and that this is known to the threatener. It is submitted that the threat should be regarded as a menace; and that to hold the contrary would be hardly more reasonable than to say that robbery was not committed because the victim allowed himself to be overcome by a degree of force which a courageous man would have successfully resisted; or that there was no obtaining by deception because the victim was excessively gullible and was taken in by a pretence which anyone with his wits about him would have seen through. In *Garwood*,[4] it was held to be a misdirection to tell the jury, in the case of an exceptionally timid victim, that it was immaterial that an ordinary person would not have been influenced, unless they were also told that they must be satisfied that D knew of that exceptional timidity.

[1] Cf *Tomlinson* (above) per Wills J; *Boyle and Merchant* [1914] 3 KB 339 at 344.
[2] *Harry* [1974] Crim LR 32 (Judge Petre).
[3] *Tomlinson* [1895] 1 QB 706 at 710, per Wills J.
[4] [1987] 1 All ER 1032, [1987] Crim LR 476, CA.

10–08 Whether a threat amounts to a menace within this principle appears, at first sight, to be an objective question to be answered by looking at the actual facts of the case. It appears from *Clear*,[1] however, that the question is to be answered by reference to the facts known to the accused, if these are different from the actual facts – that, in effect, the question is one of intention. In that case, D had received a subpoena to appear as a witness in an action in which P was the defendant. D demanded money from P with a threat that, if the money were not paid, he would alter the statement he had made to the police and so cause P to lose the action. P was quite unmoved by this threat since the action was being defended by his insurers and, if the action succeeded, it was they and not he who would pay. D's conviction was upheld. It might be said that, in the actual circumstances of the case, the words used could not influence a person of normal stability and courage; but the court appears to have held that regard must be had, not to the actual circumstances, but to the circumstances as they appeared to the person making the demand:

> "There may be special circumstances unknown to an accused which would make the threats innocuous and unavailing for the accused's demand, but such circumstances would have no bearing on the accused's state of mind and of his intention. If an accused knew that what he threatened would have no effect on the victim it might be different."[2]

[1] Above, para **10–06**, [1968] 1 All ER 74 at 80, CA.
[2] Ibid.

10–09 It is submitted, therefore – and *Garwood*[1] appears to confirm that there is a sufficient menace if, in the circumstances known to the accused, the threat might:
   (i)   influence the mind of an ordinary person of normal stability and courage, whether or not it in fact influences the person addressed; or
   (ii) influence the mind of the person addressed, though it would not influence an ordinary person.
It is assumed, of course, that in both cases there is an intention to influence the person addressed to accede to the demand by means of the threat.

[1] Above, para **10–07**.

2   THE *MENS REA*

10–10   The *mens rea* of blackmail comprises a number of elements:
(1)   An intent to make a demand with menaces.[1]
(2)   A view to gain for himself or another, or intent to cause loss to another.
(3)   Either:
　　(a)   no belief that he has reasonable grounds for making the demand, or
　　(b)   no belief that the use of the menaces is a proper means of reinforcing the demand.

---

[1]   Above, paras **10–02** to **10–09**.

10–11   It is clear that the onus of proof of each of these elements is on the Crown; but it is enough to establish (1) and (2) and either (3) (a) or (3) (b). It may well be that, once the Crown has introduced evidence of elements (1) and (2), an evidential burden is put upon the accused as regards (3); that is, he must introduce some evidence of his belief of both (a) and (b), whereupon it will be for the Crown to prove that he did not believe one, or the other, or both. Where, on the face of it, the means used to reinforce the demand are improper, and D does not set up the case that he believed in its propriety, the jury need not be directed on the point.[1] It will be noted that whether or not a demand is "unwarranted" is primarily a question of the accused's belief, as to which no one is better informed than he; and the phraseology of the section – "a demand with menaces is unwarranted unless . . . " – suggests that it is for the accused to assert that his demand was warranted.

Where, however, D does not set up such a defence, but the evidence is such that a jury might reasonably think he had the beliefs in question, it is the duty of the judge to direct the jury not to convict unless satisfied that he did not have the beliefs or one of them.[2] The first element requires no further consideration.

---

[1]   *Lawrence* (1971) 57 Cr App Rep 64.
[2]   "It is always the duty of the judge to leave to the jury any issue (whether raised by the defence or not) which, on the evidence in the case, is an issue fit to be left to them": *Palmer* [1971] AC 814, [1971] 1 All ER 1077 at 1080, PC, per Lord Morris.

A.   A VIEW TO GAIN OR INTENT TO CAUSE LOSS

10–12   "Gain" and "loss" are defined by s. 34 (2) (a) of the Theft Act:

"'gain' and 'loss' are to be construed as extending only to gain or loss in money or other property, but as extending to any such gain or loss whether temporary or permanent; and
(i)   'gain' includes a gain by keeping what one has, as well as a gain by getting what one has not; and
(ii)   'loss' includes a loss by not getting what one might get, as well as a loss by parting with what one has."

10–13   As has already been noted,[1] this definition limits the offence to the protection of economic interests. Without it, the scope of s. 21 – demanding with menaces the performance of any act or omission – would have been very wide indeed and would certainly have extended far beyond "theft and similar or associated offences" which it is the object of the 1968 Act to revise. In most cases, the blackmailer is trying to obtain money to which he knows he has no right and there will be no doubt about his view to gain. It is clearly not necessary, however, that there should be evidence of a direct demand for money or other property. It is enough that D's purpose in demanding the act or omission, whatever it may be, is gain or loss in terms of money or other property. Suppose that D demands with menaces that P should marry him. If P is an heiress and D's object is to enrich himself, he is guilty of blackmail. A person who, to ease his pain, demands a morphine injection from his doctor at pistol-point has a view to gain. The drug is unquestionably property and it is immaterial that D's motive is relief of pain rather economic gain and that the drug is injected into his arm rather than put in his hand.[2] A similar demand for medical treatment, such as a massage, is not blackmail unless, possibly, it involves, and D knows it involves, the use of some oil or cream on his body. It is, however, arguable that there is no sufficient view to gain or intent to cause loss where the gain and loss are merely incidental to a service which is the real object of the demand. Where D demands to be driven in P's car, does he have a view to gain or intent to cause loss in respect of the petrol? To charge blackmail would have the same artificiality as to charge the "joyrider" (now guilty only of a summary offence) with theft of the petrol; but that does not necessarily rule out the charge as a matter of law. No doubt it is enough that the acquisition of money or other property is one of several objects which D has in mind in making the demand. The gain or loss must be in money or other property so it is probable that, though obtaining services by deception is now an offence,[3] obtaining them by threats is not, though D is enriched thereby.

---

[1]   Above, para **10–02**.
[2]   *Bevans* (1987) 87 Cr App Rep 64, [1988] Crim LR 236, CA.
[3]   Theft Act 1978, s. 1, above, para **4–75**.

10–14   Is it enough that D foresees that the fulfilment of his demand will result in a gain to him, even though gain is not one of the objects of the demand? D is so consumed with desire for the heiress that he would have made exactly the same demand with menaces even if she had been a pauper: but he knows that the marriage will be profitable. It is thought that this will probably not be enough. Where it is a case of causing loss rather than making a gain, "intent" is specifically required and this is likely to be construed to require a desire that loss should ensue. D demands with menaces that P should jump into a muddy pool. D's object is that P, who has offended him, should suffer discomfort and humiliation. As D foresaw, P's clothes are ruined by immersion in the pool and so he suffers a loss. It is probable that D is not guilty. If that be correct with regard to "intent to cause loss", it would seem appropriate that a similar principle should govern "view to gain".

(a)   Belief in a right to the gain

10–15   It is not necessarily a good defence that D believes he has a right to the gain. If he has such a belief, then he certainly believes that he has reasonable grounds for making the demand, but it will be recalled that this does not cause the demand to be warranted unless it is coupled with a belief that the use of the menaces is a proper means of reinforcing the demand. Section 21 does not use the word "dishonestly" which, in ss. 1, 15, 16, 17 and 20, ensures that a claim of right to the property is a defence. It is clear that the Criminal Law Revision Committee intended that the offence might be committed where D had both a claim of right and an actual right to the property which he intended to acquire.[1]

> "A may be owed £100 by B and be unable to get payment. Perhaps A needs the money badly and B is in a position to pay; or perhaps A can easily afford to wait and B is in difficulty. Should it be blackmail for A to threaten B that, if he does

not pay, A will assault him; or slash the tyres of his car; or tell people that B is a homosexual, which he is (or which he is not); or tell people about the debt and anything discreditable about the way in which it was incurred? On one view none of these threats should be enough to make the demand amount to blackmail. For it is no offence merely to utter the threats without making the demand (unless for some particular reason such as breach of the peace or defamation); nor would the threat become criminal merely because it was uttered to reinforce a demand of a kind quite different from those associated with blackmail. Why then should it be blackmail merely because it is uttered to reinforce a demand for money which is owed? On this view no demand with menaces would amount to blackmail, however harsh the action threatened, unless there was dishonesty. This is a tenable view, though an extreme one. In our opinion it goes too far and there are some threats which should make the demand amount to blackmail even if there is a valid claim to the thing demanded. For example, we believe that most people would say that it should be blackmail to threaten to denounce a person, however truly, as a homosexual unless he paid a debt. It does not seem to follow from the existence of a debt that the creditor should be entitled to resort to any method, otherwise non-criminal, to obtain payment. There are limits to the methods permissible for the purpose of enforcing payment of a debt without recourse to the courts. For example, a creditor cannot seize the debtor's goods; and in *Parker*[2] it was held that a creditor who forged a letter from the Admiralty to a sailor warning him to pay a debt was guilty of forgery notwithstanding the existence of the debt."

---

[1]   *Eighth Report*, Cmnd 2977, para 119.
[2]   (1910) 74 JP 208, above para **4–33**, fn 10.

10–16   Acts of Parliament, however, do not always carry out the intention of those who frame them, and it has been argued that the use of the words "with a view to gain" will defeat the object of the Committee in this case:[1] "There is surely no gain or loss where a person merely secures the payment of that which he is owed." The argument might be elaborated as follows:

> " . . . If I liquidate a just debt, I suffer no economic loss. In my personal balance sheet, the amount of cash in hand on the credit side is reduced, but this is offset by a corresponding reduction on the debit side in the item 'sundry creditors'."[2]

If the debtor has suffered no economic loss it follows that the creditor has acquired no economic gain for, while his cash in hand will increase, his credit balance under "sundry debtors" will diminish. If "gain in money or other property" means economic enrichment, then it is arguable that D has no view to gain when he demands that to which he is entitled.

---

[1]   Hogan [1966] Crim LR at 476.
[2]   R.N. Gooderson [1960] CLJ 199 at 205, discussing the meaning of "fraud" in relation to *Welham v DPP* [1961] AC 103, [1960] 1 All ER 805, HL.

10–17   The answer turns on the meaning of the word "gain". That word has frequently been the subject of interpretation in other statutes.[1] The meaning given to a word in one statute is by no means conclusive as to that which it should bear in another; but it may give some guidance. "Gain" certainly might mean "profit"[2] and if that is its meaning in the Theft Act, then the argument in the preceding paragraph seems a sound one. On the other hand, Jessel MR has said "'Gain' means exactly acquisition . . . Gain is something obtained or acquired."[3] Though he found that there was a profit, and therefore a gain, in that case, it would seem that he did not think that gain was necessarily to be equated with profit. If then, "gain" includes acquisition, whether at a profit or not, the difficulty disappears. A man may properly be said to have acquired that which he is entitled to have, if he secures ownership or possession of it. Apart from the intentions of the Committee which have been quoted above, the Act itself suggests that this is the right view, (a) through the omission of the word "dishonestly", which would have imported a defence of claim of right, (b) because s. 21 requires not merely a belief that D is entitled to the thing demanded but also a belief that the use of the menaces is proper, and (c) because "gain" is defined to include "getting what one has not". It is submitted, therefore, that "gain" includes the acquisition of money or other property whether it is due in law or not.[4] This view appears to be accepted by the courts. It has been held that "getting hard cash as opposed to a mere right of action is getting more than one already has".[5] It should be noted that it may also be a summary offence to harass a debtor where the debt is due.[6]

---

[1] Particularly the Companies Acts and Factories Acts. See *Stroud's Judicial Dictionary* under "gain". See also Obscene Publications Act 1964 and *Blackpool Chief Constable v Woodhall* [1965] Crim LR 660.
[2] "Any gain consequent on death" in the New Zealand Law Reform Act 1939 means "any increase in financial resources", per Ostler J in *Alley v Alfred Bucklands & Sons Ltd* [1941] NZLR 575.
[3] *Re Arthur Average Association for British, Foreign and Colonial Ships, ex p Hargrove & Co* (1875) 10 Ch App 542 at 546.
[4] Cf *Lawrence* (1971) 57 Cr App Rep 64, CA, where it appears that D believed the debt to be due.
[5] *Parkes* [1973] Crim LR 358, (Judge Dean); cf *Parkes* [1974] Crim LR 320, CA.
[6] Administration of Justice Act 1970, s. 40. Smith & Hogan 625.

(b) Intention to return an economic equivalent

10–18 If the view expressed in the preceding paragraph is wrong, similar problems arise where D intends to restore to P an economic equivalent of the alleged gain which he has in mind. As a starting point, suppose that D wishes to acquire a particular 50p piece belonging to P which has a sentimental value for both P and D. D demands of P with menaces that he exchange the desired 50p piece for another. Obviously D intends to acquire the 50p piece but he does not intend to make any profit in terms of money.[1] If there were no view to gain in this situation, many cases would be excluded from the section which it is reasonably clear that it is intended to cover. If D demands with menaces that he be given an appointment, he may have every intention of doing a good day's work and earning his wages.[2] The runner who, by menaces, gains admission to a race may have every intention of supplying a first-class performance which will be worth as much or more in terms of money to the organisers of the meeting as any prize he may win. The gambler who, by menaces, causes the bookmaker's clerk to let him bet on credit may have every intention of paying up if the horse backed loses – he is prepared to pay the full economic value of the chance he has bought. In each of these examples, D has a view to the acquisition of money or other property – his wages, the prize, the winnings – and in each case it is submitted that he is guilty of blackmail.

If this be correct, the same principle must govern "loss". D intends P to suffer a loss if he intends him to be deprived of particular money or property, though he may also intend that P be fully compensated in economic terms.

---

[1] Of course, the problem under consideration would not arise if the coin had a higher market value than its nominal value. Cf *Moss v Hancock* [1899] 2 QB 111.

[2]   Lord Denning has expressed the view that, in such a case, there is no intention to cause economic loss to the employer: *Welham v DPP* [1961] AC, 103 at 131, HL. It follows that the employee has no intention to make an economic gain.

(c)   *Temporary gain and loss*

10–19   The intent permanently to deprive – which is an essential ingredient of theft, robbery and obtaining property by deception – is not a requisite of blackmail. Suppose that D by menaces causes P to let him have a car on hire for a week. If D intends to return that car at the end of the week, he cannot be guilty of theft or of robbery.[1] He has, however, a view to a temporary gain, which is sufficient under s. 21, and he is guilty of blackmail.

This may seem strange, but it is consistent with the theory that it is the method of obtaining the property – the demand with menaces – which is the gist of the offence and not the unlawful profit made or contemplated by D or the corresponding loss to P. As we have seen, D may be demanding property which he is entitled to have.

[1]   Above, para **2–125**.

(d)   *Intent to cause loss*

10–20   In most cases "a view to gain" and an "intent to cause loss" will go hand in hand; P's loss will be D's gain. The phrase, "intent to cause loss" is not, however, superfluous. There may be circumstances in which D intends to cause a loss to P without any corresponding gain to D. If P has written his memoirs and D demands with menaces that P destroy them, D has an intent to cause loss but no view to gain.

Another instance would be the case where D demands with menaces that P dismiss Q from a remunerated office or employment or that P should not promote Q. D intends to cause Q a loss (by not getting what he might get)[1] and it is immaterial whether D has in view any gain to himself or another. Likewise where D demands with menaces that P resign his own appointment, or not apply for, or refuse promotion.

[1]   Above, para **10–12**.

(e)   *Gain by keeping and loss by not getting*

10–21   A view to gain includes an intent to keep what one has; and intent to cause a loss includes causing another not to get what he might get.[1] Thus if D owes P £10 and, by menaces, he induces him to accept £5 in full satisfaction, he has caused a gain and a loss within the meaning of s. 21.

If D, knowing that P is in financial difficulties and in urgent need of money, takes advantage of this situation in order to induce P to accept a less sum in satisfaction, he may be in danger of conviction of blackmail. D can hardly say, to any effect, that he had reasonable grounds for making the demand if he knew the larger sum was due; and in that case it is immaterial whether the use of the menaces is a proper means of reinforcing the demand. The Court of Appeal has taken the view that it is "intimidation" and holding a creditor "to ransom" to say, "We cannot pay you the £480. But we will pay you £300 if you will accept it in settlement. If you do not accept it on those terms you will get nothing. £300 is better than nothing."[2] This suggests that that court, at least, would regard such pressure on a creditor as a "menace".

¹   Section 34 (2) (a) (i) and (ii), above, para **10–12**.
²   *D & C Builders v Rees* [1966] 2 QB 617 at 625, CA, per Lord Denning MR.

(f)   Remoteness

10–22   Where a number of intermediate steps are required between the act caused by D's menace and the acquisition by him of any gain, problems of remoteness may arise.

If D gains admission to an Inn of Court by menacing the Under-Treasurer,¹ is he guilty of an offence under the section? If he intends ultimately to practise and thereby to earn fees it would seem that his action is taken with a view to gain – though this is rather far to seek. But if he has no intention to practise and merely wants the prestige of the barrister's qualification it is difficult to see that he can have committed the offence. It must appear that D at least contemplated the possibility of using his qualification to earn money, probably that this was his actual intention.

What, then, if D menaces the headmaster of the public school with a view to gaining admission for his newly-born son? If D believes that the only advantage of education at that school is that it will produce a more cultured person with a greater capacity for the enjoyment of life than education in a state school, he has no view to gain. If, however, he believes and is motivated by his belief that his son will (in about twenty years' time) have a greater earning power, is it to be said that he has a view to gain? Literally he does. Yet the gain is so distant in time and subject to so many contingencies that its connection with the demand with menaces may be thought too remote. A stronger case is that of a candidate for a university examination who menaces the examiner with a view to passing or getting a better-class degree than he would otherwise obtain. Most candidates have an eye on their earning capacity and this might be prima facie evidence of a view to gain.

¹   Cf *Bassey* (1931) 22 Cr App Rep 160.

B.   UNWARRANTED DEMANDS¹

10–23   Whether a demand is "warranted" or not appears to be exclusively a question of the accused's belief. Theoretically a demand with menaces may be unwarranted, although D is entitled to recover the property demanded and the menace is a perfectly proper means of enforcing the demand. Suppose P has stolen and disposed of D's picture. D threatens to report him to the police unless he pays D £1,000. D believes the picture is only worth £100; so he does not believe that he has reasonable grounds for making the demand. The picture is in fact worth £1,000, so he does actually have reasonable grounds. D who has looked up an out-of-date law book believes that it is the offence of compounding a felony to accept any consideration for not disclosing a theft; so he does not believe that the use of the menace is a proper means of enforcing the demand. But by the Criminal Law Act 1967, s. 5 (1) it is lawful to accept reasonable compensation for making good the injury or loss caused by an arrestable offence, in consideration for not disclosing it. The use of the menaces then – or so it seems – is a proper means of reinforcing the demand. Looking at the facts objectively, D has done nothing wrong; but he is guilty of blackmail.

It does not seem likely that this will be a serious issue in practice. Where D's conduct is objectively innocent, it is unlikely that a prosecution will ever be instituted. If it is, the onus of proof on the Crown will be very difficult to satisfy. The usual way of satisfying the jury that D did not have the beliefs referred to in s. 21 (1) (a) and (b) will be by showing that no reasonable person could have held such a belief. For example, if D says that he believed that he had reasonable grounds for demanding £1,000 from his neighbour in return for not disclosing to the neighbour's wife that her husband had committed adultery, it is safe to assume, in the absence of some extraordinary circumstances, that the jury will disbelieve him and be satisfied beyond reasonable doubt of his guilt. They will be so satisfied because they will feel that no man in his right mind could entertain such a belief for a moment.[2] If then, D's beliefs are entirely reasonable, the normal mode of proof fails; and, in the absence of some confession by D as to his belief in the unreasonableness of his demand, or the impropriety of his threat, conviction will be impossible.

---

[1]   See Williams *TBCL* 829–838.
[2]   The ultimate question is as to the state of mind of the accused person and this should always be stressed to a jury.

10–24   The problem that does arise is the converse. That is, the grounds for making the demand were not reasonable but D asserts that he believed they were; the use of the menaces is not a proper means of reinforcing the demand but D asserts that he believed it was. The question for the jury then appears to be simply whether D is speaking the truth. Juries have to determine this question often enough; but the difference about this case is that it is not a question of the accused's belief in fact, but the accused's belief in standards.

This provision of the Act has been criticised by a judicial writer:[1]

"If a defendant has acted disgracefully by making a certain demand reinforced by threats of a particular kind, I see no injustice in holding him responsible in a criminal court, even though he may have acted according to his own standard in these matters. On the other hand I see some danger to our general standards of right and wrong, if each man can claim to act according to his own, however low that standard may be. That is one objection. Another is the difficulty of the jury's ascertaining the defendant's standard, so that it may be decided whether in the case before them he acted in accordance with it. A man whose standard is below the general may fail in a particular case to observe even his own standard in which event he would, I suppose, be punishable under clause 17 [now section 21]. But are questions of this kind triable?"

---

[1]   Sir Bernard MacKenna "Blackmail: A Criticism" [1966] Crim LR 467 at 472.

10–25   If no regard whatever were paid to external standards, the crime of blackmail would virtually disappear. It is almost invariably a premeditated offence. By the accused's own standards, it is something which he might do, whatever others might think. It is his belief at the time of making the demand which is relevant. If he should later admit that his conduct was unreasonable or improper, this is probably because he knows full well that people generally regard it as unreasonable or improper. It would be unreasonable to attribute to Parliament an intention to enact an offence which would be a dead letter. It was certainly not the intention of the Committee. If we look first at the question of the propriety of the threat, some clear guidance as to their intentions can be found in the Report.[1] Some care was devoted to the choice of the word "proper":

"... we chose the word 'proper' after considering 'legitimate' or 'fair' instead. Any of the three words would, we think, be suitable. 'Fair' would provide a good test for a jury to apply. It might also be a little more favourable to the accused, because the jury might think that, even if the accused behaved improperly the prosecutor behaved so badly that it was fair that he should be treated as he was. There seems little difference between 'legitimate' and 'proper'. On the whole, 'proper' seems the best word. 'Proper' directs the mind to consideration of what is morally and socially acceptable, which seems right on a matter of this kind; 'legitimate' might suggest that it is a purely legal question whether the accused had a right to utter the menaces."

This passage clearly shows that it was intended that the jury should apply a standard and that the standard should be "what is morally and socially acceptable".

---

[1] Para 123.

10–26 We are, of course, concerned with D's beliefs in the matter, not the jury's. Once D's belief has been ascertained, it has to be decided whether it fits the words of the section. The word "proper" has to be given a meaning. According to this interpretation then, the test is: "Did the accused person believe that what he threatened to do was morally and socially acceptable?" The effect might be illustrated by considering the effect on the case, decided under the Larceny Act, of *Dymond*.[1] D wrote to P alleging that he had indecently assaulted her and adding, "I leave this to you to think what you are going to do, paid or get summons . . . If you dont send to and apologise I shall let everybody knowed in the town it." Her conviction was upheld by the Court of Criminal Appeal holding that an honest belief in "reasonable cause" for making the demand, as opposed to reasonable cause in fact, was not a defence. Probably a jury would take the view that Miss Dymond's conduct was, by their standards, morally and socially unacceptable; but the question would be whether she knew that it was morally and socially unacceptable. In the circles in which Emily Dymond moved it may well be that the advice of the neighbours was: "If he won't pay up, you ought to summons him and tell everyone." If these were the only standards known to Emily, she ought to be acquitted.

---

[1] [1920] 2 KB 260.

10–27 This is not to say that the standards of the small group to which D belongs will necessarily govern in every case. D may belong to a terrorist organisation, the members of which think it right to demand money as the price of releasing a hostage in order to further their political ends. The conduct may be morally and socially acceptable within the small group; but it is safe to assume that these are not the only standards known to D. He is well aware that, in English society generally, such conduct is morally and socially unacceptable; and it must be the known standards of English society generally which apply.

10–28 This appears to have been the interpretation adopted in the only case on the section so far to reach the Court of Appeal. In *Harvey Uylett and Plummer*,[1] P had obtained £20,000 from D by deception. He had promised to supply D with a large quantity of cannabis but had no intention of carrying out this illegal promise. D may well have thought he had reasonable grounds for demanding the return of the money; but he reinforced his demand with threats to kill or maim or rape. The judge directed that, as a matter of law, these threats could not be "proper". The Court of Appeal agreed that "no act which was not believed to be lawful could be believed to be proper within the meaning of the subsection"; but it should have been left to the jury to decide whether D knew that what he was threatening to do was a criminal act.[2] Since the threats were to do acts "which any sane man knows to be against the laws of every civilised country" the court applied the proviso.

A person might not realise that the acts he is threatening to do are crimes. It is lawful to use or threaten reasonable force to recover property which is wrongfully withheld. A person who misjudged what is reasonable might be threatening to commit a crime without realising it and so might rightly be held to believe to be "proper" what was in fact unlawful. It is difficult to imagine that anyone brought up in England could fail to know that killing, maiming or raping is an unlawful way of recovering property; but a person coming from a land where cutting off the hands of thieves is commonplace might not realise that his threat to cut off a thief's hand, if his property was not returned, was unlawful; and so might rightly be held to believe that the threat was proper.[3]

---

[1] (1981) 72 Cr App Rep 139, [1981] Crim LR 104, CA.

[2] Even if there is only one conceivable answer to the question, "Did D know that what he was threatening to do was unlawful?" it must still be left to the jury: *Stonehouse* [1978] AC 55, [1977] 2 All ER 909, HL.

[3] The view that what is known to be unlawful cannot be believed to be "proper" was advocated in the fourth edition of this book but is criticised by Williams *TBCL* 836–837, pointing out flaws in the logic of the court in *Harvey*. *Lambert* [1972] Crim LR 422 (Deputy Circuit Judge Arnold) must now be regarded as a doubtful decision, though it appears that in *Harry* [1974] Crim LR 32 the prosecution conceded that *Lambert* was correct.

10–29   Even if D does not know that it is unlawful to threaten another with a dagger in order to compel the payment of a debt,[1] a jury might well find that he knew that it was a socially and morally unacceptable way of compelling the wages clerk to pay his wages. If so, D, though not guilty of robbery or attempted robbery, would be guilty of blackmail.

In many cases of blackmail the threat is to do something not amounting to a crime. Here the exclusive test must be whether D knew that the threat in the circumstances would be condemned as improper by the community generally.

---

[1]   Cf *Skivington* [1968] 1 QB 166, [1967] 1 All ER 483, CA; above, para **3–02**.

10–30   D's plea might very well be accepted in the following cases. D, a bookmaker, being unable to obtain payment of a wagering debt due from P, another bookmaker, threatens to report P to Tattersalls if he does not pay up. D threatens P that she will tell P's wife of their immoral relationship if P does not pay her the money he promised for her immoral services. D threatens that he will warn his friends against doing business with P if P does not pay up a statute-barred debt.

10–31   A similar test might be applied to determine whether D believed he had reasonable grounds for making the demand. If he had a claim of legal right then, clearly, he believed he had reasonable grounds for making the demand. A lady who believed, wrongly but on the advice of a Hungarian lawyer, that she was entitled to money promised to her as the price of her past immoral services, would have a good defence.[1] If she knew that she had no legal right, she might nevertheless believe that the man was under a moral obligation to compensate her, and a jury could find that she believed that she had reasonable grounds for her demand. Similarly where D demands money won on a wager with P, though he knows that wagers are unenforceable in law, or demands payment of a statute-barred debt, being aware of the statute of limitations.

---

[1]   *Bernhard* [1938] 2 KB 264, [1938] 2 All ER 140.

10–32 If this view is accepted, the law is certainly lacking in precision; but this is a branch of the law in which precision is not easily obtainable. From the point of view of justice, however, the law seems unexceptionable. The defendant is not to be held liable unless it is proved that he knew he was doing something which he ought not to do, in the broad sense described, either in making the demand, or in making the threat. Moreover, it is very similar in effect to the interpretation now put upon dishonesty by *Ghosh*.[1]

---

[1] Above, para **2–122**.

CHAPTER 11

Burglary and Aggravated Burglary

1 BURGLARY

11–01 The law relating to burglary and other breaking offences contained in the Larceny Act 1916, ss. 24–27, was very complicated.[1] The Theft Act effected a considerable simplification of the law. The Act eliminated entirely the concept of "breaking", which was a requisite of burglary, and most forms of house-breaking under the Larceny Act. "Breaking" was a highly technical term on which there was a great deal of case-law and it no longer served a useful purpose in the definition of the offences. The Act also got rid of the distinction between breaking "in the night" and breaking "in the day" which was the most conspicuous difference between the old offences of burglary and house-breaking. It eliminated from the definition the concept of "dwelling house" which had its own difficulties. However, the Criminal Justice Act 1991 has now amended the law by providing for a higher penalty when burglary is committed in respect of "a dwelling". The effect of this appears to be that burglary in a dwelling becomes a separate offence.[2] If the higher penalty is to be available the indictment must allege, and the prosecution must satisfy the jury, that the premises burgled were a dwelling. It continues to be necessary to distinguish between "dwellings" and other buildings for the purposes of ascertaining the jurisdiction of magistrates' courts.[3]

---

[1] Smith & Hogan (1st edn) 397–401.
[2] *Courtie* [1984] AC 463, HL. Smith & Hogan 33. Strangely, other writers do not seem to have taken this obvious point. But the escape-from-*Courtie* route taken in *DPP v Butterworth* [1995] 1 AC 381, HL hardly seems open here.
[3] Magistrates' Courts Act 1980, Sch 1, para 28 (c).

11–02 Section 9 of the Act, as amended by the Criminal Justice Act 1991, provides:
"(1) A person is guilty of burglary if –
   (a) he enters any building or part of a building as a trespasser and with intent to commit any such offence as is mentioned in subsection (2) below; or
   (b) having entered any building or part of a building as a trespasser he steals or attempts to steal anything in the building or that part of it or inflicts or attempts to inflict on any person therein any grievous bodily harm.
(2) The offences referred to in subsection (1) (a) above are offences of stealing anything in the building or part of a building in question, of inflicting on any person therein any grievous bodily harm or raping any person therein, and of doing unlawful damage to the building or anything therein.
(3) A person guilty of burglary shall on conviction on indictment be liable to imprisonment for a term not exceeding –
   (a) where the offence was committed in respect of a building or part of a building which is a dwelling, fourteen years;
   (b) in any other case, ten years.
(4) References in subsection (1) and (2) above to a building and the reference

in subsection (3) above to a building which is also a dwelling, shall apply also to an inhabited vehicle or vessel, and shall apply to any such vehicle or vessel at times when the person having a habitation in it is not there as well as at times when he is."

Paragraphs (a) and (b) of s. 9 (1) create separate offences. Each paragraph now creates two offences (in a dwelling or not, as the case may be) so there are four offences in all. It has been decided[1] that a person charged with an offence under s. 9 (1) (b) may be convicted of an offence under s. 9 (1) (a) because (however contrary to the facts this may seem to be) the allegation of an offence under s. 9 (1) (b) is held to include an allegation of an offence under 9 (1) (a).

---

[1] *Whiting* (1987) 85 Cr App Rep 78, CA applying *Wilson and Jenkins* [1984] AC 242, [1983] 3 All ER 448, HL. *Whiting* is criticised by JCS at [1987] Crim LR 473 and by A.T.H. Smith, *Property Offences*, 28–08.

A. THE *ACTUS REUS*

(a) Enters

11–03   The common law rule was that the insertion of any part of the body, however small, was a sufficient entry. So where D pushed in a window pane and the forepart of his finger was observed to be inside the building, that was enough.[1] The Act gives no express guidance and it seems to have been assumed in Parliament that the common law rules would apply.[2] In *Collins*,[3] D, naked but for his socks, had climbed up a ladder on to a bedroom window sill, as a trespasser and with intent to rape, when the lady in the bedroom invited him in. It was not clear whether he was on the sill outside the window or on the inner sill at the moment when he ceased to be a trespasser and became an invitee. Edmund Davies LJ said that there must be "an effective and substantial entry" as a trespasser to constitute burglary. This suggests that it is no longer enough that any part of the body, however small, is intruded; but it is not clear what "effective and substantial" means. The insertion of an arm may be "effective" if it is long enough to reach property and remove it. In *Brown*,[4] there was a sufficient entry where D's feet were on the ground outside a shop and the top half of his body was inside the broken shop window, as if he was rummaging for goods displayed there. The court said that the word "substantial" did not materially assist but the entry must be "effective" and here it was. D was presumably in a position to steal. But in *Ryan*[5] D became trapped by the neck with only his head and right arm inside the window. His argument that his act was not capable of constituting an entry because he could not have stolen anything was rejected. It cannot have been the intention of the legislature that D must have got so far into the building as to be able to accomplish his unlawful purpose. The intending rapist is guilty of burglary when he enters through the ground floor window though his victim is on the fourth floor. Thus it seems that the act need be neither an "effective" nor a "substantial" entry. *Ryan* decided, not that D *had* "entered" but only that there was evidence on which a jury could find that he had. It is, however, in principle unsatisfactory that it should be left to a jury to decide whether there is an entry when all the necessary facts are established. What possible criteria can they apply?

At common law, if an instrument was inserted into the building for the purpose of committing the ulterior offence, there was an entry even though no part of the body was introduced into the building. So it was enough that hooks were inserted into the premises to drag out the carpets,[6] or that the muzzle of a gun was introduced with a view to shooting someone inside.[7] It would amount to an entry if holes were bored in the side of a granary so that wheat would run out and be stolen by D,[8] provided that the boring implement emerged on the inside. On the other hand, the insertion of an instrument for the purpose of gaining entry and not for the purpose of committing the ulterior offence, was not an entry if no part of the body entered.[9] If D bored a hole in a door with a centre bit for the purpose of gaining entry, the emergence of the point of the bit on the inside of the door was not an entry.

[1]   *Davis* (1823) Russ & Ry 499.
[2]   Parl. Debates, Official Report (HL) vol 290, cols 85–86.
[3]   [1973] QB 100 at 106, [1972] 2 All ER 1105 at 1111, CA.
[4]   [1985] Crim LR 212, CA.
[5]   (1995) 160 JP 610, [1996] Crim LR 320, CA.
[6]   (1583) 1 Anderson 114.
[7]   2 East PC 492.
[8]   *State v Crawford* (1899) 46 LRA 312 (Alabama).
[9]   *Hughes* (1785) 1 Leach 406; but cf *Tucker* (1844) 1 Cox CC 73.

11–04   Even if the courts are willing to follow the common law in holding that the intrusion of any part of the body is an entry, they may be reluctant to preserve these technical rules regarding instruments, for they seem to lead to outlandish results. Thus it seems to follow from the common law rules that there may be an entry if a stick of dynamite is thrown into the building or if a bullet is fired from outside the building into it.[1] What then if a time bomb is sent by parcel post? Has D "entered", even though he is not on the scene at all? – perhaps even abroad and outside the jurisdiction? Yet this is hardly an "entry" in the "simple language as used and understood by ordinary literate men and women" in which the Act is said to be written.[2] Perhaps D must be present at the scene, or "on the job".

[1]   Hawk PC c. 17, s. 11; 2 East PC 490; contra, 1 Hale PC 554.
[2]   Above, para **1–07**, fn 3.

11–05   There is, however, a cogent argument in favour of the common law rules which may be put as follows. If D sends a child, under the age of ten, into the building to steal, this is obviously an entry by D,[1] through an "innocent agent", under ordinary principles. Suppose that, instead of a child, D sends in a monkey. It is hard to see that this should not equally be an entry by D. But if that point be conceded, it is admitted that the insertion of an animate instrument is an entry; and are we to distinguish between animate and inanimate instruments? Unless we are, the insertion of the hooks, etc., must also be an entry.[2]

If D puts a child under ten through the window, so that the child may open a door and admit D who will himself steal, it is by no means so clear that the innocent agency argument is open; and the common law rule regarding instruments would suggest it is not an entry; since the child is being used to gain entry and not to commit the ulterior offence.

In the light of these considerations, the best course is probably to assume the continued existence of the common law rules.

[1]   1 Hale PC 555; Smith & Hogan 128–129.
[2]   Transvestites who hooked dresses worth £600 through letter boxes of shops pleaded guilty to burglary in a metropolitan magistrates' court: Daily Telegraph, 4 March 1979.

(b)   As a trespasser

11–06   Trespass is a legal concept and we must resort to the law of tort in order to ascertain its meaning.[1] It would appear that any intentional, reckless or negligent entry into a building is a trespass if the building is in fact in the possession of another who does not consent to the entry. Entry with the consent of the occupier cannot be a trespass. In *Collins*,[2] it was held that, whatever the position in the law of tort, an invitation by the occupier's daughter to enter her bedroom and have intercourse with her, without the knowledge or consent of the occupier, precluded trespass for this purpose. Suppose, however, that the occupier's daughter or servant invites her lover into the house to steal the occupier's property. This ought to be burglary if the lover realises, as he surely must, that the daughter or servant has no right to invite him in for this purpose. Where the invitation is issued by a member of the household, it is submitted that the question is whether the accused knew that, or was reckless whether, the invitation was issued without authority. In *Jones and Smith*,[3] where the occupier's son had a general permission to enter the house, entry with an accomplice, and with an intent to steal, constituted burglary. The accused had knowingly exceeded the permission. It is perhaps noteworthy that it was a case "where [DD] took elaborate precautions, going there at dead of night"; and that, even if the son's entry was covered by the general permission, this would scarcely extend to the entry of his accomplice; and, if the accomplice's entry was unlawful, the son abetted it. Williams[4] argues that *Jones and Smith* is wrongly decided, being inconsistent with *Collins*,[5] because Collins also exceeded the permission since he entered intending to use force if necessary. But as the girl saw him to be "a naked male with an erect penis" it seems clear that she invited him in for the purpose of sexual intercourse, that he knew he was so invited and that any intention to rape must have lapsed.[6]

In *Collins*, the invitation to enter was issued under a mistake as to the man's identity. It is submitted that, if he had known of the mistake, he would have intentionally entered as a trespasser. Mistake as to identity, where identity is material, generally vitiates consent. Mistake by the person entering is no defence to an action in tort; so that, if D on a very dark night were to enter the house next door in mistake for his own, this would be regarded as an intentional entry and a trespass. This would apparently be so even if D's mistake was a reasonable one, *a fortiori* if it were negligent as, for example, if he made the mistake because he was befuddled with drink. It is established, however, that it is not sufficient (though it is necessary) that D is a trespasser in the civil law. In the criminal law he must be shown to have *mens rea*. If he is charged under s. 9 (1) (a), it must appear that, when he entered, he knew the facts which caused him to be a trespasser or at least that he was reckless whether those facts existed.[7] A merely negligent entry, as where D enters another's house, honestly but unreasonably believing it to be his own, should not be enough. So too a belief in a right to enter the house of another should be a defence, for then there is no intention to enter as a trespasser. Suppose that D, being separated from his wife, wrongly supposes that he has a right to enter the matrimonial home of which she is the owner-occupier and does enter with intent to inflict grievous bodily harm upon her. Even if he is in law a trespasser it is submitted that he is not a burglar.

---

[1]   Street *Law of Torts* (8th edn) 16, 65.
[2]   [1973] QB 100 at 107, [1972] 2 All ER 1105 at 1111, CA; above, para **11–03**. Cf *Robson v Hallett* [1967] 2 QB 939, [1967] 2 All ER 407 (invitation by occupier's son effective until withdrawn by occupier).

3   [1976] 3 All ER 54, [1976] 1 WLR 672, CA.
4   *TBCL* 812–814.
5   Above, para **11–03**.
6   Cf Mason J in *Barker* (1983) 7 ALJR 426 at 429: " . . . The foundation for this conclusion (sc., that of Williams) is too frail."
7   *Collins* [1973] QB 100 at 104–105, [1972] 2 All ER 1105 at 1109–1110. "Reckless" is used in the *Cunningham* ([1957] 2 QB 396), not the *Metropolitan Police Comr v Caldwell* ([1982] AC 341, HL) sense. See Smith & Hogan 64–70.

11–07   If D's entry is involuntary, he is not a trespasser and cannot be guilty of burglary. So if he is dragged against his will into P's house and left there by his drunken companions and he steals P's vase and leaves, this is not burglary. If, however, D had intentionally entered the building, believing it to be his own house and committed theft on discovering the truth, it appears from the previous paragraph that he would have committed theft after entering as a trespasser and thus committed the *actus reus* of burglary. In this case it seems that D has *mens rea* as well, for burglary under s. 9 (1) (b) is committed, not at the time of entry, but when the ulterior crime is committed; and at that time, he knows that he has entered as a trespasser.[1]

1   The common law doctrine of trespass *ab initio* has no application to burglary under the Theft Act: *Collins* [1973] QB 100 at 107, [1972] 2 All ER 1105 at 1111, CA. See the second edition of this work at paras 377–378.

(i)   Entry for a purpose alien to a licence to enter

11–08   It seems to be entirely clear that where D gains entry by deception he enters as a trespasser. There is no need to distinguish between a licence which is void and one which is merely voidable[1] because entry under either is a trespass. For example, D gains admission to P's house by falsely pretending that he has been sent by the BBC to examine the radio set in order to trace disturbances in transmission. The old law went so far as to hold[2] that this was a constructive "breaking". That is no longer an issue and there can be no doubt that it constitutes a trespassory entry.

The authorities, however, go much farther than this, establishing that a person who has a limited authority to enter for a particular purpose enters as a trespasser though he practises no deception, if he has an unlawful purpose outside the scope of his authority. In *Taylor v Jackson*,[3] D had permission to go on P's land and hunt for rabbits. He went there to hunt for hares and the Divisional Court held that this was evidence of trespass in pursuit of game, contrary to the Game Act 1831, s. 30. In *Hillen and Pettigrew v ICI (Alkali) Ltd*,[4] members of a stevedore's gang employed to unload a barge were held to be trespassers when they placed kegs on the hatch covers, knowing that this was a wrong and dangerous thing to do. They were, therefore, not entitled to damages when the hatch covers collapsed and they were injured. Lord Atkin said:

"As Scrutton LJ has pointedly said: 'When you invite a person into your house to use the staircase you do not invite him to slide down the banisters.'[5] So far as he sets foot on so much of the premises as lie outside the invitation or uses them for purposes which are alien to the invitation he is not an invitee but a trespasser, and his rights must be determined accordingly. In the present case the stevedores knew that they ought not to use the covered hatch in order to load cargo from it; for them for such a purpose it was out of bounds: they were trespassers."

In *Farrington v Thomson and Bridgland*,[6] an Australian court held that a police officer who entered a hotel for the purpose of committing a tort was a trespasser. The tacit invitation to the public to enter the hotel did not extend to persons entering for the purpose of committing a tort or a criminal offence. In *Barker*,[7] the High Court of Australia (Murphy J dissenting) held that D committed burglary where, having been asked by his neighbour, P, to keep an eye on P's house while P was on holiday and told the whereabouts of a concealed key in case he needed to enter, D entered in order to steal. "If a person enters for a purpose outside the scope of his authority then he stands in no better position than a person who enters with no authority at all."[8]

One decision goes against this view. In *Byrne v Kinematograph Renters Society Ltd*,[9] Harman J held that it was not trespass to gain entry to a cinema by buying tickets with the purpose, not of seeing the film, but of counting the patrons. It is submitted that this decision is against the weight of authority and should not be followed.

---

[1]   See earlier editions of this book, e.g. fourth edition, paras 338–339.
[2]   *Boyle* [1954] 2 QB 292, [1954] 2 All ER 721.
[3]   (1898) 78 LT 555.
[4]   [1936] AC 65, HL.
[5]   *The Carlgarth* [1927] P 93 at 110, CA.
[6]   [1959] ALR 695, [1959] VR 286 (Smith J). See also *Gross v Wright* [1923] 2 DLR 171.
[7]   (1983) 7 ALJR 426.
[8]   Per Mason J at 429.
[9]   [1958] 2 All ER 579 at 593; distinguished in *Jones*, above, para **11–06**, fn 3 and by Mason J in *Barker* (1983) 7 ALJR 426 at 429 on the ground that "the invitation by the lessee of the cinema to the public to enter the cinema was in very general terms and could on no view be said to be limited in the way in which was contended".

11–09   It seems to follow that a person who enters a shop for the sole purpose of shop-lifting is a burglar, though two of the majority in *Barker* thought otherwise. In their view, a person with a permission to enter, not limited by reference to purpose, is not a trespasser merely because he enters with a secret unlawful intent; and the shop-keeper's invitation is not so limited: " . . . the mere presence of the prospective customer upon the premises is itself likely to be an object of the invitation and a person will be within the invitation if he enters for no particular purpose at all".[1] It is doubtful, however, if the shop-keeper's invitation can be said to extend to those who enter for the sole purpose of shop-lifting. There is no need to strain to exclude them. It is only in the exceptional case that it will be possible to prove the intent at the time of entry – as where there is evidence of a previous conspiracy, or system, or preparatory acts such as the wearing of a jacket with special pockets. Such an entry may be no more than a merely preparatory act to stealing and so not attempted theft; but it ought to be possible, where there is clear evidence, to make an arrest. Few would object to the conviction of burglary of bank robbers who enter the bank flourishing pistols, for they are clearly outside the invitation extended by the bank to the public. A person who enters a shop for the sole purpose of murdering the manager is surely a trespasser; and the case of the intending thief is no different in principle.

---

[1]   Brennan and Deane JJ (1983) 7 ALJR at 436.

(ii)   Who is the victim of the burglary?

11–10   Trespass is an interference with possession. Burglary is therefore committed against the person in possession of the building entered. Where the premises are let, the burglary is committed against the tenant and not against the landlord. The landlord could commit burglary of the premises, the tenant could not. Even if the tenant is only a tenant at will, he may maintain trespass. So may a deserted wife, though she has no proprietary interest in the matrimonial home.[1] On the other hand, "The guest at a hotel will not ordinarily have sufficient possession of his room to enable him to sue in trespass."[2] It has been held that, where a servant occupies premises belonging to his master for the more convenient performance of his duties as servant, he cannot maintain an action for trespass against the master.[3] In such a case it is, of course, necessary to look at the precise terms of the arrangement between the parties; if the servant has been given exclusive possession, he and not the master is the victim of a trespass. And it does not necessarily follow that, because the servant in a particular case may not maintain trespass against the master, he cannot do so against third parties.[4]

---

[1]   *National Provincial Bank Ltd v Ainsworth* [1965] AC 1175, [1965] 2 All ER 472, HL.
[2]   Street Law of Torts (3rd edn) 67.
[3]   *Mayhew v Suttle* (1854) 4 E & B 347; *White v Bayley* (1861) 10 CBNS 227.
[4]   Though in *White v Bayley* (above, fn 3) Byles J thought, *obiter*, that an action could not have been maintained by the servant against a stranger (10 CBNS at 235).

11–11   The position of a lodger depends on the precise terms of his contract. If he has exclusive possession so that he can refuse entry to the landlord then, no doubt, he may maintain trespass. Many lodgers, however, do not have such possession and in such cases an unauthorised entry by a third party is a trespass against the landlord.

It seems to follow that burglary is not committed where an inn-keeper enters the room of a guest, even though the entry is without the guest's consent and with intent to steal; and that, depending on the terms of the contract, the same may be true in the case of a master entering premises occupied by his servant for the purposes of his employment and a landlord entering the rooms of his lodger.

11–12   It seems that an indictment will lie although it does not allege that the building was the property of anyone. Whereas the Larceny Act 1916 required that the breaking and entering be of the dwelling house of another, there is no such expression in the Theft Act. The requirement of trespass means that evidence must be offered that someone other than the accused was in possession. If that is all that is necessary, evidence that A or B was in possession should suffice – it is equally a trespass in either event. But if a statement of ownership is required in the indictment, "A or B" will hardly do. It is submitted, therefore, that it should be sufficient that the indictment alleges that D trespassed in a building without alleging who is the owner of the building.

(c)   Any building or part of a building

11–13   The meaning of "building" in various statutes has frequently been considered by the courts. Clearly the meaning of the term varies according to the context and many things which have been held to be buildings for other purposes will not be buildings for the purpose of the Theft Act – for example, a garden wall, a railway embankment or a tunnel under the road. According to Lord Esher MR, its "ordinary and usual meaning is, a block of brick or stone work, covered in by a roof".[1] It seems clear, however, that it is not necessary that the structure be of brick or stone to be a building within this Act. Clearly all dwelling houses are intended to be protected and these may be built of wood; while "the inhabited vehicle or vessel" which is expressly included is likely to be built of steel or of wood. More helpful is the view of Byles J that a building in its ordinary sense is "a structure of considerable size and intended to be permanent or at least to endure for a considerable time".[2]

To be a building, the structure must have some degree of permanence. A substantial portable structure may be a building[3] but probably not a tent even though it is someone's home. It is again a question of the meaning of the word in the language of ordinary literate men; and this perhaps suggests that a telephone kiosk is not a building. If it is, the wreckers of these places are probably burglars.

---

[1]   *Moir v Williams* [1892] 1 QB 264, CA.
[2]   *Stevens v Gourley* (1859) 7 CBNS 99 at 112. For other descriptions, see *Stroud's Judicial Dictionary* (5th edn) 1, 311.
[3]   *B and S v Leathley* [1979] Crim LR 314 (Carlisle Crown Court). Cf *Norfolk Constabulary v Seekings and Gould* [1986] Crim LR 167.

11–14   The outbuildings of a house seem to be buildings for the purpose of the Act so that burglary may now be committed in a detached garage, a wooden toolshed or a greenhouse. Similarly, farm buildings such as a stable, cow-byre, pigsty, barn or silo, and industrial buildings such as factories, warehouses and stores, fall under the same category. Other cases are more difficult. It is not uncommon for trespassers to enter unfinished buildings and do damage. If they enter with intent to cause damage by fire or explosion are they now guilty of burglary? An unfinished building was a building within s. 6 of the Malicious Damage Act 1861.[1] Why not for the purposes of burglary? Clearly there is a difficult question as to the point in its erection at which a structure becomes a building. In *Manning*,[2] Lush J said:

" . . . it is sufficient that it should be a connected and entire structure. I do not think four walls erected a foot high would be a building."

In that case all the walls were built and finished and the roof was on. It may be that a roof will be thought necessary for a structure to be a building under the present Act, for it clearly is not intended to extend to a walled garden, yard or paddock. What if there is a roof but no walls, as in the case of a bandstand?[3] There is no obvious answer to borderline cases such as this but they are likely to be rare.

---

[1]   *Manning and Rogers* (1871) LR 1 CCR 338.
[2]   Ibid at 341.
[3]   Held to be a building for the purpose of a private act regulating the provision of public entertainments in buildings: *A-G v Eastbourne Corpn* (1934) 78 Sol Jo 633, CA.

(i)   Part of a building

11–15   It is sufficient if the trespass takes place in part of a building so that one lodger may commit burglary by entering the room of another lodger within the same house, or by entering the part of the house occupied by the landlord. A guest in a hotel may commit burglary by entering the room of another guest. A customer in a shop who goes behind the counter and takes money from the till during a short absence of the shop-keeper would be guilty of burglary even though he entered the shop with the shop-keeper's permission. The permission did not extend to his going behind the counter. It is enough that there is a defined area within the building into which D was not permitted to go and that he knew this when he entered the area or when he stole or attempted to steal, etc., within the area. It is not necessary that the building be permanently divided into parts. A temporary physical division is enough if it clearly marks out a part of the building into which D is not allowed to go. In *Walkington*,[1] there was a moveable, three-sided, rectangular counter in a shop. It was held that the rectangle bounded by the three sides of the counter was capable of being "part" of the building. A customer who entered the area with intent to steal from the till on the counter was held to have knowingly entered that part of the building as a trespasser and to be guilty of burglary.

---

¹   [1979] 2 All ER 716, [1979] Crim LR 526, CA.

11–16   Take a case put by the Criminal Law Revision Committee.¹ D enters a shop lawfully,² but conceals himself on the premises until closing time and then emerges with intent to steal. When concealing himself he may or may not have entered a part of the building to which customers are not permitted to go; but even if he did commit a trespass at this stage, he may not have done so with intent to commit an offence in that part of the building into which he has trespassed. For example, he hides in the broom cupboard of a supermarket, intending to emerge and steal tins of food. Entering the broom cupboard, though a trespass committed with intent to steal, is not burglary, for he has no intent to steal in the part of the building which he has entered as a trespasser. When he emerges from the broom cupboard after the shop has closed, he is a trespasser and it is submitted that he has entered a part of the building with intent to steal. He is just as much a trespasser as if he had been told in express terms to go, for he knows perfectly well that his licence to remain on the premises terminated when the shop closed.³

Suppose, however, having entered lawfully, he merely remained concealed behind a pile of tins of soup in the main hall of the supermarket. This was not a trespass because he had a right to be there. When he emerged and proceeded to steal, still in the main hall of the supermarket, was he entering another part of the building? It is submitted that every step he took was "as a trespasser", but it is difficult to see that he entered any part of the building as a trespasser; the whole transaction took place in a single part of the building which he had entered lawfully.

---

¹   *Eighth Report*, Cmnd 2977, para 75.
²   That is, without intent to steal; above, para **11–09**.
³   The Criminal Law Revision Committee thought, "The case is not important, because the offender is likely to go into a part of the building where he has no right to be, and this will be a trepassory entry into that part." But he has no right to be in any part of the building after closing time and the only question, it is submitted, is whether he went into another part.

11–17   It would seem that the whole reason for the words "or part of a building", is that D may enter or be in part of a building without trespass and it is desirable that he should be liable as a burglar if he trespasses in the remainder of the building with the necessary intent. It is submitted that the building need not be physically divided into "parts". It ought to be sufficient if a notice in the middle of a hall stated, "No customers beyond this point". These considerations suggest that, for present purposes, a building falls into two parts only: first, that part in which D was lawfully present and, second, the remainder of the building. This interpretation avoids anomalies which arise if physical divisions within a building are held to create "parts".¹

---

¹   See para **11–20**; Griew 4–24, n. 49, finds this interpretation "desirable but strained" and rejects it.

(ii)   The extent of a "building" and its "parts"

11–18   Under the old law, the entry had to be into a particular dwelling house, office, shop, garage, etc. A single structure might contain many dwelling houses – for example a block of flats – many offices, shops or garages. If D broke into Flat 1 with intent to pass through it, go upstairs and steal in Flat 45, the breaking and entering of Flat 1 was neither burglary nor house-breaking for D did not intend to commit a felony therein.[1] It was probably not even an attempt, not being sufficiently proximate to the intended crime. If D broke into a flat above a jeweller's shop with intent to break through the ceiling and steal in the shop, he could be convicted of burglary in the flat only if it could be said that he broke and entered the flat with intent to commit a felony therein, namely to break and enter the shop.[2] The difficulty about this argument is that while the breaking may reasonably be said to have occurred in the flat, the entering, strictly speaking, took place in the shop. On that view, there was no intent to commit a felony in the flat and it was not, therefore, burglary or house-breaking to break and enter it.

---

[1]   Cf *Wrigley* [1957] Crim LR 57.
[2]   Cf comment on *Wrigley* [1957] Crim LR 57.

11–19   The effect on this situation of the Theft Act depends on what is the extent of a "building". In its ordinary natural meaning, this term could certainly include a block of flats. If that meaning be adopted, D's entering Flat 1 as a trespasser with intent to pass through it, go upstairs and steal in Flat 45 is an entry of a building as a trespasser with intent to steal therein – that is, it is burglary. Similarly, the intending jewel thief would be guilty of burglary when he entered the flat above the jeweller's shop as a trespasser. The effect would be to make the full offence of what was previously, at the most, an attempt, and probably was only an act of preparation. There seems no good reason, however, why the law should not be extended in this way. On the contrary, there is everything to be said for enabling the police to intervene at the earliest possible moment to prevent such offences; and for forestalling defences such as "I had no intention to steal in the flat – I was only using it as a passage to another flat which I never reached." It is submitted, therefore, that the word "building" should be given its natural meaning.

11–20   Suppose, however, that D is lawfully in Flat 1, and that he can get to Flat 45 where he intends to steal only by trespassing into Flat 2. Suppose he is apprehended in Flat 2. He is guilty of burglary only if he can be shown to have intended to steal in "the part of the building in question". If Flat 2 is a separate part, he had no such intention and his act is probably too remote to constitute an attempt to enter Flat 45. But it is very odd that entering Flat 1 (from outside where D lawfully was) as a trespasser with intent to steal in Flat 45 should be burglary, and entering Flat 2 as a trespasser (from Flat 1 where D lawfully was) with intent to steal in Flat 45 should be nothing. It is therefore submitted that, as physical divisions are unnecessary to create "parts", so the existence of such divisions is insufficient to create them. If the building is divided into the part into which D may lawfully go and the part into which he may not, then Flats 2 and 45 are in the same "part" of the building and D is guilty of burglary as soon as he enters Flat 2.

11–21   Is a row of terrace houses a single building?[1] Suppose D breaks into No. 1, climbs into the rafters and makes his way above No. 2, intending to continue to No. 36, descend into the house and steal therein. Has he already committed burglary? It is difficult to discern any satisfactory principle by which this case can be distinguished from those of the block of flats and the flat above the shop considered above. In both the block of flats and the terrace a series of dwelling houses are contained within a single structure and it cannot matter that the arrangement is horizontal rather than vertical. It is true that there is internal communication between the flats; but it can hardly be said that the block of flats would cease to be "a building" because access to them was confined to an external staircase. In policy and in principle there seems to be no reason why "building" should not include the whole terrace.

---

¹ In *Hedley v Webb* [1901] 2 Ch 126, Cozens-Hardy J held that two semi-detached houses were a single building for the purpose of determining whether there was a sewer within the meaning of the Public Health Act 1875, s. 4. In *Birch v Wigan Corpn* [1953] 1 QB 136, [1952] 2 All ER 893, CA, the Court of Appeal (Denning LJ dissenting) held that one house in a terrace of six was a "house" within the meaning of s. 11 (1) and (4) of the Housing Act 1936 and not "part of a building" within s. 12 of that Act. But, since the sections were mutually exclusive, the house could not be both a "house" and "part of a building" for the purpose of the Act. Otherwise, Denning LJ would have been disposed to say that the house was both and Romer LJ also thought that "for some purposes and in other contexts two 'houses' may constitute one building".

(iii)   Inhabited vehicle or vessel

11–22   The obvious cases which are brought within the protection of burglary by this provision are a caravan or a houseboat which is someone's home. There seems to be no reason whatever why a home should lack the ordinary protection of the law because it is mobile. "Inhabited" implies, not merely that there is someone inside the vehicle, but that someone is living there. My saloon car is not an inhabited vehicle because I happen to be sitting in it when D enters against my will. The caravan or houseboat which is a man's home is, however, expressly protected, whether or not he is there at the time of the burglary. He may, for example, be away on his holidays.

11–23   The provision is not free from difficulty. Many people now own "dormobiles" or motorised caravans which they use for the ordinary purposes of a motor car during most of the year but on occasions they live in them, generally while on holiday. While the vehicle is being lived in, it is undoubtedly an inhabited vehicle. When it is being used for the ordinary purposes of a motor car, it is submitted that it is not an inhabited vehicle. The exact moment at which the dormobile becomes an inhabited vehicle may be difficult to ascertain. Is it when the family have loaded it with their belongings before departing on their holiday? When they take to the road on their journey to the sea-side? When they park the vehicle at the place where they intend to sleep? Or when they actually go to sleep in the vehicle? It can hardly be later than that. Since the vehicle is not really distinguishable from any other family car going on holiday until it reaches its destination, it probably becomes "inhabited" when it reaches the place at which it is to be used as a home. But does it then cease, for the time being, to be inhabited, if the family go for a spin in it next day? Is it burglary if a thief enters it in the car park of the swimming pool where they have gone for a swim? Similar problems arise when the holiday is concluding. If the answer tentatively suggested above regarding the beginning of the holiday is correct, then it ought to follow that when the vehicle embarks on its homeward journey, after the last night on which it is intended to sleep in it, it then ceases to be inhabited.

Very similar problems will arise in connection with boats with living accommodation. Ships where the passengers or crew sleep aboard are clearly covered. The person who trespasses into a passenger's cabin on the *Queen Elizabeth II* in order to steal is clearly guilty of burglary.[1]

---

[1]   Presumably, in such a case, the trespass is committed against the owners since, under modern conditions, they, and not the master, are in possession of the ship: *The Jupiter (No 3)* [1927] P 122 at 131; affirmed [1927] P 250, CA. The passengers would seem to be in the same situation as the guests in a hotel. See above, para **11–10**.

11–24   Difficult problems of *mens rea* may arise. According to ordinary principles, D should not be convicted unless he knew of the facts which make the thing entered "a building" in law. Suppose D enters a dormobile parked by the side of the road. If he knew that P was living in the vehicle, there is no problem. But what if he did not know? In principle it would seem that he ought to be acquitted of burglary, unless it can be shown that he was at least reckless whether anyone was living there or not; and this seems to involve showing that the possibility was present to his mind.

B.   THE *MENS REA*

(a)   Intention to enter as a trespasser; or knowledge of having trespassed

11–25   As pointed out above,[1] it must be proved on a charge under s. 9 (1) (a) that D intended to enter, knowing of the facts which, in law, made his entry trespassory; or, at least, being reckless whether such facts existed; and, on a charge under s. 9 (1) (b), that, at the time of committing the ulterior offence, D knew of or was reckless as to the facts which had made his entry a trespass. If, in a case under either paragraph, D sets up an honest belief in a right to enter, it should be for the Crown to prove the belief was not held.

---

[1]   See paras **11–06**, **11–07**.

(b)   The ulterior offence

11–26   It must be proved that D, either –
  (i)   entered with intent to commit one of the following offences:
      (a)   stealing,
      (b)   inflicting grievous bodily harm,
      (c)   rape,
      (d)   unlawful damage to the building or anything therein; or
  (ii)   entered and committed or attempted to commit one of the following:
      (a)   stealing,
      (b)   inflicting grievous bodily harm.

11–27   For some time the law of burglary was bedevilled by the ruling in *Husseyn*,[1] that "it cannot be said that one who has it in mind to steal only if what he finds is worth stealing has a present intention to steal"; but in *A-G's References (Nos 1 and 2 of 1979)*[2] these difficulties were substantially eliminated. It is now clear that, for the purposes of burglary, a person who enters intending to steal only if he finds something he thinks worth stealing has a sufficient *mens rea*. He may be interested only in money, which may or may not be on the premises, or in a particular chattel which may or may not be there. He has a sufficient intention to steal. The problem of *Husseyn* lingers on only in one rare type of case – where D intends to steal a specific thing only if he decides that the specific thing is worth stealing. He intends to take P's necklace – but only if, on examining it, he finds the pearls are real and not paste. *Husseyn* was distinguished, not overruled, and it seems that it continues to apply to this case. The result is strange. An intention to steal anything at all that comes to hand, if it is worth stealing, is an intention to steal; but an intention to steal a specific thing, if it is worth stealing, is not.[3]

---

[1]   (1978) 67 Cr App Rep 131n at 132.

[2]   [1980] QB 180, [1979] 3 All ER 143, CA; above, para **2–130**.

[3]   Cf commentaries on *Walkington* [1979] 2 All ER 716, [1979] Crim LR 526 and *A-G's References (Nos 1 and 2 of 1979)* [1980] QB 180, [1979] Crim LR 585.

(i)   Stealing

11–28   This clearly means theft, contrary to s. 1. So an entry with the intention of dishonestly using electricity contrary to s. 13 is not burglary.[1] Nor is it enough to prove that D has entered with intent to commit an offence contrary to s. 16 of the 1968 Act or an offence under the 1978 Act. Since *Gomez*,[2] however, an intention to obtain property (other than land) by deception is an intention to steal. For example, D, having entered P's "trade only" warehouse by falsely representing that he is in the trade, induces P, by a further deception, to sell him a television set at trade prices. His intention to obtain by deception is an intention to steal; and his obtaining the set is theft; so he might be convicted of burglary under either s. 9 (1) (a) or 9 (1) (b). A trespasser who receives stolen goods in the building is a burglar, either as a party to the continuing theft by others or by the theft he commits himself.[3]

---

[1]   *Low v Blease* [1975] Crim LR 513; above, para **9–01**.

[2]   Above, para **2–09**.

[3]   *Gregory* (1982) 77 Cr App Rep 41, [1981] Crim LR 229 and commentary.

(ii) Inflicting grevious bodily harm

11–29   The intention to inflict grievous bodily harm in s. 9 (1) (a) must be an intention to commit an offence. The offence in question would be causing grievous bodily harm with intent to do so, contrary to s. 18 of the Offences against the Person Act 1861. Section 9 (1) (b), however, does not use the word "offence" but simply requires that D inflicts or attempts to inflict on any person in the building any grievous bodily harm. The omission of the word "offence" is in fact a legislative accident;[1] but in *Jenkins*[2] the Court of Appeal held that the infliction need not amount to an offence of any kind. They gave this example:

> "An intruder gains access to the house without breaking in (where there is an open window for instance).[3] He is on the premises as a trespasser and his intrusion is observed by someone in the house of whom he may not even be aware, and as a result that person suffers a severe shock, with a resulting stroke . . . Should such an event fall outside the provisions of s. 9 when causing some damage to property falls fairly within it?"

This is a question (in its context) plainly expecting the answer, "no". It is submitted that the right answer is an emphatic "yes". Otherwise a person may become guilty of burglary in consequence of a wholly unforeseen and unforeseeable event. The analogy with damage to property is misplaced. Causing damage to property does not fall within the provisions of s. 9 (1) (b). There must be an actual intention to cause damage at the time of the trespassory entry. This requires a *mens rea* which is wholly absent in the example put by the court. The House of Lords allowed the appeal[4] in *Jenkins* but on a different point and no allusion was made to the interpretation by the Court of Appeal of s. 9 (1) (b). The case, therefore, stands as an authority – but, it is submitted, a bad one. When para (b) is read in the context of s. 9 (1) and (2) it is reasonably clear that the infliction of bodily harm required must be an offence – in effect, under s. 18 or s. 20 of the Offences against the Person Act 1861.

Whether or not this interpretation of para (b) is correct, it is now established that a jury may acquit D of burglary contrary to s. 9 (1) (b) and convict him on the same count of inflicting grievous bodily harm contrary to s. 20 of the 1861 Act – the latter offence is included in the former for the purposes of s. 6 (3) of the Criminal Law Act 1967.

What if D enters with intent to murder? It would be very strange if an entry with intent to inflict grievous bodily harm amounted to burglary, and an entry with intent to murder did not. It is submitted that the greater includes the less and that an intention to kill, whether by inflicting physical injuries or by poisoning, is enough.

---

1   See Smith "Burglary under the Theft Bill" [1968] Crim LR 367 and commentary on *Jenkins* [1983] 1 All ER 1000, [1983] Crim LR 386, CA.
2   [1983] 1 All ER 1000, at 1002. Cf *Watson* (1989) 139 NLJ 866, CA. (Death caused after entry is caused in the course of committing an offence under s. 9 (1) (a).)
3   The relevance of the absence of breaking is obscure.
4   [1984] AC 242, [1983] 3 All ER 448, [1984] Crim LR 36 and commentary.

(iii)   Rape

11–30   Rape is an offence under s. 1 (1) of the Sexual Offences Act 1956 punishable with life imprisonment. As re-defined by the Criminal Justice and Public Order Act 1994, s. 142, it is an offence for a man to rape a woman or another man. It consists in having unlawful sexual intercourse, whether vaginal or anal, with a person, P, who does not consent to it, knowing that P does not consent or being reckless whether P consents.[1] The recklessness referred to here can only exist at the moment of the intercourse. It is now established[2] that a man who attempts to have sexual intercourse with P, being reckless whether P consents, has an intent to commit rape for the purposes of s. 1 of the Criminal Attempts Act 1981.

The words "with intent to commit" in the Criminal Attempts Act are the same as in s. 9 (1) (a) and both relate to the ulterior intention with which a preliminary act is done. They might thus be expected to bear the same meaning. Indeed, if the entry is an act more than merely preparatory to the commission of rape, the offences of burglary and attempted rape coincide. But even if the entry is "merely preparatory" it seems that the requirement of intent must be the same and, therefore, that recklessness should be enough.

---

1   Smith & Hogan 467; *Satnam* (1983) 78 Cr App Rep 149, [1985] Crim LR 236, CA; *Breckenridge* [1984] Crim LR 174, CA.
2   *Khan* [1990] 2 All ER 783, [1990] 1 WLR 813, CA.

(iv)   Unlawful damage to the building or anything therein

11–31   The damage intended must be such that to cause it would amount to an offence. It is an offence under s. 1 of the Criminal Damage Act 1971, intentionally or recklessly to destroy or damage any property belonging to another.

Is it necessary that the object of the ulterior crime be in the building before the trespassory entry? In other words, is it burglary if D drags P into a barn with intent to rob, or inflict grievous bodily harm on, or rape her? The words of the section do not supply a clear answer, but the purpose of the offence – the protection of persons and things in a building – suggests that the crime does not extend to these cases.

2   BURGLARY IN RESPECT OF A DWELLING

11–32   As noticed above[1] burglary in respect of a dwelling, whether contrary to 9 (1) (a) or 9 (1) (b) of the Act, now appears to be a separate offence – a new aggravated form of burglary. The only constituent of the offence that requires consideration is "dwelling"; but it must be looked at in respect of both *actus reus* and *mens rea*.

Actus reus. "Dwelling" is not defined but it presumably means substantially the same as "dwelling house" in the former offence of burglary at common law and under the Larceny Acts[2] – a building or, now, a vehicle or vessel, in which someone lives as his home. Where the places are different, a person dwells in that place where he sleeps, not that where he spends his waking hours. A building, such as a block of flats, may contain many dwellings. A hotel room is probably not a dwelling unless the particular inhabitant does live there as his home. Premises which have become a dwelling will not cease to be one because of the temporary absence of the inhabitants, provided that at least one of them intends to return. A person normally dwells in the place where he sleeps; but he may have more than one dwelling as where he has a flat in London and a house in the country. The dormobile considered in para **11–23**, above, will probably be a dwelling while the family is living in it, but will cease to be a dwelling when they stop doing so.

Mens rea. As "dwelling" is an aggravating element in the offence warranting a higher maximum sentence of imprisonment, it should, in principle, import a requirement of *mens rea*. A person who commits burglary in a dwelling should be convicted only of simple burglary if he believed that no one lived there. But, in principle and by analogy to the construction of "as a trespasser" in *Collins*,[3] recklessness should be enough. If D entered knowing that someone might be living there, and someone was, he should be guilty of burglary in respect of a dwelling.

---

[1]   Above, para **11–02**.
[2]   Smith & Hogan (1st edn) 399; Russell on Crime (12th edn) 826. Cf Public Order Act 1986, s. 8.
[3]   Para **11–06**, above.

---

3   AGGRAVATED BURGLARY

11–33   By s. 10 of the Theft Act:

"(1) A person is guilty of aggravated burglary if he commits any burglary and at the time has with him any firearm or imitation firearm, any weapon of offence, or any explosive; and for this purpose –

   (a) 'firearm' includes an airgun or air pistol and 'imitation firearm' means anything which has the appearance of being a firearm, whether capable of being discharged or not; and

   (b) 'weapon of offence' means any article made or adapted for use for causing injury to or incapacitating a person, or intended by the person having it with him for such use; and

   (c) 'explosive' means any article manufactured for the purpose of producing a practical effect by explosion, or intended by the person having it with him for that purpose.

(2) A person guilty of aggravated burglary shall on conviction on indictment be liable to imprisonment for life."

The reason given by the Criminal Law Revision Committee for the creation of this offence is that "burglary when in possession of the articles mentioned . . . is so serious that it should in our opinion be punishable with imprisonment for life. The offence is comparable with robbery (which will be so punishable). It must be extremely frightening to those in the building, and it might well lead to loss of life."[1]

---

[1] *Eighth Report*, Cmnd 2977, para 80.

A. THE ARTICLES OF AGGRAVATION

11–34 "Firearm" is not defined in the Act, except to the extent that it includes an airgun or air pistol. It is possible that the courts will seek guidance as to the meaning of this term from the definition in the Firearms Act 1968, s. 57 (1). The expression is given a wide meaning in that Act, however, and it does not necessarily follow that it should bear a similarly wide meaning in the Theft Act. Thus the definition includes any component part of a firearm, but the natural meaning of the term does not include parts. If I have the body locking pin of a Bren gun in my pocket, no one would say I was carrying a firearm. As the statutory definition has not been incorporated in the Theft Act, which could easily have been done, it is submitted that the word should not be given a meaning any wider than that which it naturally bears; and that, therefore, the term "imitation firearm" be similarly limited.

11–35 The definition of "weapon of offence" is slightly wider than that of "offensive weapon" in s. 1 (4) of the Prevention of Crime Act 1953. It would seem that (i) articles made for causing injury to a person, (ii) articles adapted for causing injury to a person, and (iii) articles which D has with him for that purpose are precisely the same as under the 1953 Act.[1] Thus, (i) would include a service rifle, or bayonet, a revolver, a cosh, knuckleduster, dagger or flick-knife;[2] (ii) would include razor blades inserted in a potato, a bottle broken for the purpose, a chair leg studded with nails; and (iii) would include anything that could cause injury to the person if so desired by the person using it – a sheath-knife, a razor, a shotgun, a sandbag, a pick-axe handle, a bicycle chain or a stone.[3] To these categories, however, s. 10 (1) (b) adds (iv) any article made for incapacitating a person, (v) any article adapted for incapacitating a person, and (vi) any article which D has with him for that purpose. Articles made for incapacitating a person might include a pair of handcuffs and a gag; articles adapted for incapacitating a person might include a pair of socks made into a gag, and articles intended for incapacitating a person might include sleeping pills to put in the night-watchman's tea, a rope to tie him up, a sack to put over his head, pepper to throw in his face, and so on.

In the cases of (i), (ii), (iv) and (v) the prosecution need prove no more than that the article was made or adapted for use for causing injury or incapacitating as the case may be. In the cases of (iii) and (vi) clearly they must go further and prove that D was carrying the thing with him with the intention of using it to injure or incapacitate, not necessarily in any event, but at least if the need arose. It is not necessary to prove that D intended to use the article in the course of the burglary. It is enough that he had it with him for such use on another occasion.[4]

---

[1] Smith & Hogan 458.

2   *Gibson v Wales* [1983] 1 All ER 869, DC; *Simpson* [1984] Crim LR 39, CA.
3   *Harrison v Thornton* [1966] Crim LR 388.
4   *Stones* [1989] 1 WLR 156, CA, criticised by N.J. Reville 139 NLJ 835. Cf *Allamby* [1974] 3 All ER 126, [1974] 1 WLR 1494, CA.

11–36   The definition of "explosive" closely follows that in s. 3 (1) of the Explosives Act 1875 which, after enumerating various explosives, adds:

" . . . and every other substance, whether similar to those above mentioned or not, used or manufactured with a view to produce a practical effect by explosion or by a pyrotechnic effect . . . "

It will be observed that the definition in the Theft Act is narrower. The Explosives Act, if read literally, is wide enough to include a box of matches – these produce a "pyrotechnic effect"; but it seems clear that a box of matches would not be an "explosive" under the Theft Act.

The main difficulty about the definition – and this is unlikely to be important in practice – lies in determining the meaning of "practical effect". Perhaps it serves to exclude fireworks which, so it has been said in connection with another Act, are "things that are made for amusement",[1] but if the thing is intended to produce "a practical effect", it is immaterial that it was not manufactured for that purpose and that it is incapable of doing so.

1   *Bliss v Lilley* (1862) 32 LJMC 3, per Cockburn CJ and Blackburn J; but Wightman J thought that a fog-signal was a "firework".

B.   AT THE TIME OF COMMISSION OF BURGLARY

11–37   It must be proved that D had the article of aggravation with him at the time of committing the burglary. Where the charge is one of entry with intent this is clearly at the time of entry. Where the charge is one of committing a specified offence, having entered, it is at the time of commission of the specified offence. If D, having entered as a trespasser, is armed when he commits the specified offence, he is then guilty of aggravated burglary,[1] though he entered unarmed and whether or not he intended to commit a specified offence at the time of entry. If he did have such an intent, he is guilty of both simple and aggravated burglary. An armed person who discards his weapon before entry can be guilty of no more than simple burglary. An armed person who enters as a trespasser but without intent and discards his weapon before committing a specified offence is guilty only of simple burglary.[2]

1   *O'Leary* (1986) 82 Cr App Rep 341, CA.
2   Cf *Francis* [1982] Crim LR 363, CA.

C.   HAS WITH HIM

11–38   This phrase denotes a narrower concept than possession. A burglar who leaves a gun locked up at home when he sets out on his night's work is in possession of the gun but plainly does not have it with him. It has been held that the phrase, as used in the Firearms Act 1968, s. 18 (1), "imports an element of propinquity" but is not to be read as "to have immediately available". D need not be carrying the article: *Pawlicki*.[1] In that case there was held to be sufficient evidence – the question is one of fact – that D had guns "with him", with intent to commit a robbery, when they were in a car fifty yards from an auction room which was alleged to be the scene of a planned robbery. The court stated that it was adopting a "purposive approach". The purpose of the

Firearms Act might be held to be different from that of the Theft Act; but the decision is persuasive. If D had entered the auction room as a trespasser, it is arguable that he might have been convicted of aggravated burglary.[2] Under legislation in Northern Ireland similar to s. 10, it was held,[3] before *Pawlicki*, that it must be proved that D entered, or was on the premises, as an armed man, so that a burglar who left his pistol in a car across the road would not be guilty of the offence.

It was held in *Cugullere*,[4] where the weapon may have been inserted in D's van without his knowledge, that the words in the Prevention of Crime Act 1953 mean "knowingly has with him". It is certainly arguable that the court was concerned only with that minimum mental element which is necessary to constitute possession. But in *Russell*[5] it was held in a reserved judgment that the court in *Cugullere* was "applying the general principle of responsibility which makes it incumbent on the prosecution to prove full *mens rea*" in the sense that D must be proved to have known that he had the thing which is an offensive weapon. It was held that, where D had known of the weapon but had completely forgotten its existence, he was to be treated as if he had never known it was there at all. *Russell* was misunderstood in *Martindale*[6] which was followed by *McCalla*,[7] holding it to be no defence to having a cosh that D had picked it up a month ago, put it in the glove compartment of his car and forgotten about it. *McCalla* was followed on similar facts in *Wright*.[8] The latter two cases are inconsistent with *Russell* and it is submitted that *Russell* is to be preferred.[9] In principle (though neither *Cugullere* nor *Russell* decides this) it should be necessary to prove that D knew that the thing had those characteristics which make it an offensive weapon within the meaning of the Act. The question is not merely one of possession, as in the law relating to possession of controlled drugs,[10] but of *mens rea*. It does not seem right that no fault should be required with respect to the element which converts a ten or fourteen-year offence into one carrying life imprisonment.[11]

---

[1]   [1992] 3 All ER 902, CA explaining *Kelt* [1977] 3 All ER 1099, CA.
[2]   Professor A.T.H. Smith thinks not: *Property Offences*, 28–54. Cf Griew, 4–43.
[3]   *Murphy, Lillis and Burns* [1971] NI 193.
[4]   [1961] 2 All ER 343 at 344.
[5]   (1984) 81 Cr App Rep 315, [1985] Crim LR 231, CA.
[6]   [1986] 3 All ER 25, (1986) 84 Cr App Rep 31, CA.
[7]   (1988) 87 Cr App Rep 372, CA.
[8]   [1992] Crim LR 596, CA.
[9]   See commentary [1992] Crim LR 596.
[10]   *Warner v Metropolitan Police Comr* [1969] 2 AC 256, [1968] 2 All ER 356, HL.
[11]   It must, however, be noted that, under the Firearms Act 1968, it is unnecessary to prove that D knew the thing he used was a firearm within the meaning of the Act though it is no doubt necessary to prove that he knew he had that thing: *Pierre* [1963] Crim LR 513.

11–39   It has been decided under the Prevention of Crime Act 1953, in effect overruling earlier decisions, that a person carrying an inoffensive article for an innocent purpose does not become guilty of having an offensive weapon with him merely because he uses that article for an offensive purpose.[1] The 1953 Act is directed against the carrying abroad of articles intended to be used as weapons, not against the use of an article as a weapon. It was to be expected that the same construction would be put upon the similar words of s. 10 of the Theft Act, but in *Kelly*[2] it was held that D, who had used a screwdriver to effect an entry, became guilty of aggravated burglary when he used it to prod P in the stomach. The court purported to apply the ordinary meaning of the words of the subsection; but they seem indistinguishable in this respect from the words of the Prevention of Crime Act; and the same considerations of policy seem applicable to the two provisions. *Kelly* seems a dubious decision.

It has also been held under the 1953 Act that no offence is committed where a person arms himself with a weapon for instant attack on his victim;[3] but, if *Kelly* is right, it seems that that decision can hardly apply to s. 10. So if D is interrupted in the course of stealing after a trespassory entry and picks up an inkstand (or any object) and throws it with intent to cause injury, he will thereby become guilty of aggravated burglary. He could be adequately dealt with by a second count charging whatever offence against the person he has committed; and it is submitted that this is the proper course.

On the other hand, if D picked up a stone outside the house to use as a weapon if he should be disturbed after entry, the subsequent burglary would properly be held to be aggravated. Here D has armed himself before an occasion to use violence has arisen; and the stone is a weapon of offence.

---

[1]   *Dayle* [1973] 3 All ER 1151.
[2]   (1992) 97 Cr App Rep 245, [1993] Crim LR 763 and commentary.
[3]   *Ohlson v Hylton* [1975] 2 All ER 490; *Giles* [1976] Crim LR 253; *Bates v Bulman* [1979] 3 All ER 170, (1979) 68 Cr App Rep 21.

CHAPTER 12

Possession of House-breaking Implements, etc.[1]

12–01   By s. 25 (1) and (2) of the Theft Act:

"(1) A person shall be guilty of an offence if, when not at his place of abode, he has with him any article for use in the course of or in connection with any burglary, theft or cheat.

(2) A person guilty of an offence under this section shall on conviction on indictment be liable to imprisonment for a term not exceeding three years."

This offence replaced the more complicated provisions contained in the Larceny Act 1916, s. 28. The 1916 Act was directed chiefly against,[2] though it was not limited to, preparatory acts in contemplation of offences of breaking and entering. The new provision is expressed to be directed against acts preparatory to:

(i)   burglary contrary to s. 9,
(ii) theft contrary to s. 1,
(iii) criminal deception contrary to s. 15,[3]
(iv) taking a conveyance, contrary to s. 12.[4]

---

[1]   See J.K. Bentil (1979) 143 JP 47.
[2]   *Eighth Report*, Cmnd 2977, p 69.
[3]   By s. 25 (5), "cheat" means an offence under s. 15.
[4]   By s. 25 (5), "theft" in this section includes an offence of taking under s. 12 (1).

---

1   THE *ACTUS REUS*

A.   ANY ARTICLE

12–02   The *actus reus* consists in the accused's having with him any article. Clearly the article need not be made or adapted for use in committing one of the specified offences. It is sufficient that the *mens rea* is proved in respect of the article, that is, that the accused intended to use it in the course of, or in connection with, one of the specified offences. Thus, it might be a tin of treacle, intended for use in removing a pane of glass; a pair of gloves to be worn so as to avoid leaving fingerprints; a collecting box marked "Oxfam" when the possessor did not represent that organisation; and so on. There may occasionally be difficulty in deciding what is an "article". Does it include blacking on the face to prevent recognition, or "Bostik" on the fingers to prevent fingerprints? Having regard to the mischief at which the section is aimed, it is arguable that a substance so applied to the body, remains an "article".

12–03   The offence is thus very wide in its scope. But there must be some limits. Thus D can hardly be committing an offence because he is wearing his trousers when on his way to do a burglary. Yet he intends to wear them while he is committing the burglary and would not dream of undertaking such an enterprise without them. Similarly, he can hardly be committing an offence by wearing his shoes or any other item of everyday apparel. Yet it is stated above

209

that gloves for the avoidance of fingerprints would entail liability. This suggests that the article must be one which D would not be carrying with him but for the contemplated offence. If it is something which he would carry with him on a normal, innocent expedition, it should not fall within this section.[1] So there might be a difference between a pair of rubber gloves and a pair of fur-lined gloves which D was wearing to keep his hands warm on a freezing night, even though he did intend to keep them on so as to avoid leaving fingerprints. The latter pair of gloves is hardly distinguishable, for this purpose, from D's overcoat which seems to fall into the same category as his trousers. If D is carrying a pair of plimsolls in his car to facilitate his cat-burgling, this seems a plain enough case; but what if he has simply selected his ordinary crepe-sole shoes for wear because they are less noisy than his hob-nails?

It has been held that being in possession of a driving licence and other documents belonging to another, with intent to obtain a job that would give an opportunity to steal, is too remote from the intended theft to constitute the offence.[2]

---

[1]   See Williams *TBCL* 853–854.
[2]   *Mansfield* [1975] Crim LR 101, CA. Cf above, para **4–13**. D was guilty of an attempt to obtain a pecuniary advantage by deception contrary to s. 16 (2) (c), above, para **4–65**.

B.   HAS WITH HIM

12–04   The cross heading, "Possession of house-breaking implements, etc", and the side note, "Going equipped for stealing, etc", indicate that the offence, like s. 28 of the Larceny Act 1916 which it replaced, is aimed primarily at a person who sets out on an expedition equipped with jemmy, skeleton keys and such like. *Re McAngus*,[1] an extradition case, however, it was held that there was evidence of the offence when undercover agents said that D had agreed to sell them counterfeit clothing and shown them shirts, wrongly bearing an American brand name, in a bonded warehouse. If D intended to sell the shirts to unsuspecting buyers, he was certainly "equipped" for criminal deception and, when visiting the warehouse, he was not at his place of abode. If he had been hawking the shirts from door to door, it would have been a straightforward case; but D did not "go" anywhere with the articles. The side-note is not part of the section but it might have been taken to show that "going" is the essence of the offence.[2] Presumably it would have made no difference if the shirts had been kept in D's own warehouse which does not seem substantially different from keeping them at home. There is the further difficulty[3] that McAngus had no intention to deceive the agent buyers, so that the case cannot be rightly decided unless he intended to sell some of the shirts to other, innocent, buyers. But, even if he did, it seems extraordinary that he should commit the offence by showing his wares to – as he thought – accomplices.

The expression "has with him", is the same as in s. 10 (1) of the Act[4] and similar problems of construction arise. Questions as to D's knowledge of the nature of the thing can hardly arise here, since it must be proved that he intended to use it in the course of or in connection with a specified offence. No doubt D has an article with him if it is in his immediate possession or control; so that he will be guilty if the article is only a short distance away and he can take it up as he needs it; as where a ladder has been left in a garden by an accomplice and D enters the garden intending to use the ladder to make an entry. If the article is found in D's car some distance from the scene of the crime this will be evidence that D was in possession of the article when driving the car.

It might reasonably be expected that this phrase would be construed in the same manner as the same phrase in s. 1 of the Prevention of Crime Act 1953.[5] If the gist of that offence is the *carrying* of the weapon, so under s. 25 the gist of the offence, as indicated in the side-note, is "*Going equipped* for stealing"; so that picking up some article for use in committing a theft immediately before, or in the course of, doing so, would not constitute the offence. *Dayle* supports this opinion, but *Kelly*[6] is against it. Moreover, in *Minor v DPP*[7] it was held, in response to a question posed by magistrates, that the s. 25 offence could be committed when D was in possession of the equipment only at the time of or after preparatory acts and within a very short time of the intended theft. This suggests that D is guilty of an offence under s. 25 when he picks up a stone which he intends to use to break a window in order to steal. It is submitted that, properly construed, the section does not apply to that case.

---

[1]   [1994] Crim LR 602, DC and commentary.

[2]   As the long title showed that "carrying" was the essence of the offence under the Prevention of Crime Act 1953, above, para **11–39.**

[3]   See Griew, 16–08.

[4]   See para **11–38**, above.

[5]   Above, para **11–35.**

[6]   Cases discussed in para **11–39**, above.

[7]   (1987) 86 Cr App Rep 378, [1988] Crim LR 55 and commentary where it is pointed out that it is difficult to see how the facts of the case raised the question posed.

C.   WHEN NOT AT HIS PLACE OF ABODE

12–05   No offence is committed by being in possession of house-breaking implements in one's own home. The offence is committed as soon as D steps from his house into the street carrying the article with intent. Though the offence is primarily aimed at persons who have started out to commit crime, it extends well beyond that. It may be committed by possession of an article at a place of employment or, indeed, at any place other than D's place of abode. The burglar who keeps his house-breaking equipment in his car commits the offence every time he drives the car even though he is not starting out to commit crime but, for example, going to church. While the car is in his garage at home he is probably not committing an offence, both because the articles are at his place of abode and because he does not have them with him. Where a man had no home but his car, it was held that the car was his "place of abode" only when it was on a site where he intended to abide. While it was in transit he was committing the offence.[1]

---

[1]   *Bundy* [1977] 2 All ER 382, CA. Cf *Kelt* [1977] 3 All ER 1099, [1977] Crim LR 556 and commentary.

D.   USE IN THE COURSE OF OR IN CONNECTION WITH

12–06   It is not necessarily a defence that D did not intend to use the article while actually committing the contemplated crime. If, for example, he intended to use it only in the course of making his escape after the commission of the offence, this would be enough, being use "in connection with" the offence. Similarly if he intended to use the article while doing preparatory acts.

The offence is directed at acts preparatory to the offences specified. It is not an offence under the section merely to be in possession of articles which have been used in the course of or in connection with one of the offences.[1] A person concealing or disposing of articles which have been so used may be guilty of an offence under s. 4 of the Criminal Law Act 1967.[2]

---

1   *Ellames* [1974] 3 All ER 130, CA. Cf *Eighth Report*, Cmnd 2977, para 150. Cf *Allamby* [1974] 3 All ER 126, CA.
2   Smith & Hogan 165.

---

2   THE *MENS REA*

12–07   The *mens rea* for the offence would appear to consist in:
(i)   knowledge that one possesses the article; and
(ii)   an intention that the article be used in the course of or in connection with any of the specified crimes.

D must have it in mind that, when he uses the article, he will do so with the intention required by any one of the specified crimes. In *Rashid*,[1] a British Rail steward was charged with going equipped with his own sandwiches which he dishonestly intended to sell for personal gain to travellers instead of British Rail sandwiches. His conviction was quashed for misdirection but the court was inclined to think that D could not be guilty of the offence because it would be "a matter of complete indifference" to a passenger whether the sandwich was British Rail's or D's. In *Doukas*,[2] however, a wine waiter was held rightly convicted when he was equipped, contrary to his employer's instructions, with his own wine for sale to his employer's customers. It seemed to the court incredible that "any customer, to whom the true situation was made clear, would willingly make himself a party to what was obviously a fraud by the waiter upon his employers". *Doukas* is to be preferred to the dicta in *Rashid*. Of course D might meet dishonest customers who would not care whether the food supplied belonged to D or to his employer, but the point is that he was obviously prepared to deceive any honest customer he met.

In *Cooke*,[3] the House of Lords appeared to think that, on facts like those of *Rashid*, *Doukas* and *Cooke* itself, there is a case to leave to the jury. Since it is a question of D's intention, neither the opinion of the judge, nor even that of the jury, that the ordinary rail traveller or diner would or would not care whether the goods were D's own is not conclusive. That opinion is only evidence of D's state of mind. If D were to testify that he believed that no passenger cared whether the sandwiches were his or British Rail's, a jury which thought he might be telling the truth ought to acquit.

In *Ellames*,[4] the court expressed the opinion that it is not necessary to prove that D intended to use the article in the course of or in connection with any specific burglary, theft or cheat; it is enough that he intended to use it for some burglary, theft or cheat. Although the Committee[5] stated that they regarded the offence as a preparatory one "in contemplation of a particular crime", the dictum in *Ellames* seems to be right. It is supported by the use of the word "any". If a man sets out with a jemmy looking for a suitable house to break into, he has the article with him for use in the course of a burglary and it should not be a defence that he has not yet decided which house to break into. His conditional intention is enough. If D is equipped with car keys, having it in mind to steal anything from the cars which he thinks is worth stealing, he ought to be guilty, notwithstanding *Husseyn*.[6] Similarly, where a confidence trickster sets out with his equipment, looking for a gullible passer-by. The court in *Ellames*[7] also thought it enough that D intended the article to be used by another. There is nothing in the section to require that the contemplated use shall be by the accused.

---

1   [1977] 2 All ER 237, [1977] Crim LR 237, CA, and commentary.
2   [1978] 1 All ER 1061, [1978] Crim LR 177, CA; above, para **4–19**.
3   [1986] AC 909, [1987] Crim LR 114, HL and commentary. Lord Bridge was not convinced

that the ordinary upright citizen would not be prepared to buy from the steward whom he knew to be practising a "fiddle": *Cooke* [1986] 2 All ER 985 at 990. But there must be some passsengers of sufficient integrity to refuse and the defendant presumably intends to deceive any customer he encounters. See also *Corboz* [1984] Crim LR 629.

4 [1974] 3 All ER 130 at 136, CA.

5 Report, para 150.

6 (1978) 67 Cr App Rep 131n, CA, above, para **2–130**. But *Lyons v Owen* [1963] Crim LR 123 suggests the contrary.

7 [1974] 3 All ER 130 at 136, CA.

12–08 Section 25 (3) provides:

"Where a person is charged with an offence under this section, proof that he had with him any article made or adapted for use in committing burglary, theft or cheat shall be evidence that he had it with him for such use."

This is probably no more than enactment of the general rules regarding proof of intent.[1] The jury may take this fact into account but it is entirely for them to say what weight, if any, is to be attached to it. If D offers no explanation then the jury may be told that there is evidence upon which they may find that he had the necessary intent; but it is submitted that they should be told so to find only if satisfied beyond reasonable doubt that he in fact had that intent.[2] If D does offer an explanation then the jury should be told to acquit if they think it may reasonably be true and to convict only if satisfied beyond reasonable doubt that the explanation is untrue.[3]

Where the article in question is not made or adapted for use in any specified offence,[4] mere proof of possession without more will not amount to prima facie evidence – i.e. the case will have to be withdrawn from the jury. But, in certain circumstances, possession of articles not made or adapted for committing offences may amount to very cogent evidence of intent.[5] It is a question of law for the judge, at what point proof of other incriminating circumstances amounts to a case fit for submission to the jury.

1 Cf Criminal Justice Act 1967, s. 8.

2 Cf the case where the alleged receiver is proved to have been in possession of recently stolen property and offers no explanation: *Abramovitch* (1914) 11 Cr App Rep 45.

3 The decision in *Patterson* [1962] 2 QB 429 that the onus of proof under Larceny Act 1916, s. 28 was on the accused, was based on the express wording of that section and is entirely inapplicable to the new provision.

4 Cf *Harrison* [1970] Crim LR 415, CA.

5 Griew 16–14, 16–15

CHAPTER 13
Handling Stolen Goods

13–01 The offence created by s. 22 replaced both the indictable offences under the Larceny Act 1916, s. 33 and the summary offences under the Larceny Act 1861, s. 97. Section 22 provides:

"(1) A person handles stolen goods if (otherwise than in the course of the stealing) knowing or believing them to be stolen goods he dishonestly receives the goods, or dishonestly undertakes or assists in their retention, removal, disposal or realisation by or for the benefit of another person, or if he arranges to do so.

(2) A person guilty of handling stolen goods shall on conviction on indictment be liable to imprisonment for a term not exceeding fourteen years."

1   THE *ACTUS REUS*

A.   STOLEN GOODS

13–02 By s. 34 (2) (b):

"'goods', except in so far as the context otherwise requires, includes money and every other description of property except land, and includes things severed from the land by stealing."

This definition is narrower than the definition of "property" for the purposes of theft in s. 4 (1).[1] Since, however, land generally is excluded from theft by s. 4 (2), the effect seems to be that, with small exceptions to be discussed below, the property which can be the subject of handling is co-extensive with that which can be the subject of theft.

---

[1]   Above, para **2–89**.

(a)   Things in action

13–03 Things in action are expressly mentioned in s. 4 (1) and not in s. 34 (2) (b). They must, however, be included in the words "every other description of property except land". The remaining question is whether the context of s. 22 requires the exclusion of things in action. If s. 22 were confined, like the old law, to receiving, the context would so require. Receiving connoted taking possession or control of a physical thing and was wholly inapplicable to a thing in action. Handling, however, is not confined to receiving but may be committed by retention, removal, disposal or realisation, words which are apt to include dealing with a thing in action. A possible construction is that "property" includes things in action for all forms of handling other than receiving; but the better view probably is that things in action may also be received. "Receive" is not an inappropriate word to apply to the assignee of a thing in action. "Receive" necessarily had a limited meaning under the Larceny Acts because larceny could be committed only of tangible things. In the context of the 1968 Act, with its broader concept of stealing, a wider meaning is

214

appropriate. In *A-G's Reference (No 4 of 1979)*,[1] the Court of Appeal had no doubt that things in action were capable of being handled and did not distinguish between one form of handling and another. The only difficulty is the assumption in s. 34 (2) (b) that "goods" bears a variable meaning and it is not easy to discern any other possible variation. It may be that the draftsman used the words, "except in so far as the context otherwise requires", out of an abundance of caution. Alternatively, the phrase may apply to s. 23 which is concerned with "any goods which have been stolen or lost". It is difficult to conceive of a "lost" thing in action.

---

[1] [1981] 1 All ER 1193, (1980) 71 Cr App Rep 341, CA. A gave D a cheque drawn on an account into which she had paid stolen funds. It was held that D was guilty of handling where "part of the balance in the thief's account is transferred to the credit of the receiver's [D's] account . . .": [1981] 1 All ER 1193 at 1198. But *Preddy*, above, para **4–60,** now establishes that the balance is not "transferred". A new thing in action is created which belongs to D and has never been in the hands of a thief or handler and so is not stolen. Reliance must now be placed on s. 24A, below, para **13–51**. Cf. Law Com No 243, 36–38. The court thought there was much to be said for the view that the *cheque* given by A to D was stolen goods as representing the goods originally stolen with s. 24 (2) (a) but this view seems untenable. See para **13–19,** below and cf Griew, 15–06, para (iii).

13–04 Reported cases of handling a stolen thing in action are rare. *A-G's Reference (No 4 of 1979)* no longer provides a satisfactory precedent. Examples include A's obtaining a negotiable cheque by deception and negotiating it to D or A's selling goods on credit by deception and assigning the debt to D, who knows the relevant facts. Where E, an executor, dishonestly sells to F a copyright which belongs to a beneficiary under the will, P, F is not guilty of handling though he knows all the facts, because his participation is "in the course of the stealing" – since the stealing consists in the sale.[1] The copyright is, however, stolen goods in F's hands. If D then assists F to dispose of, or realise, the copyright for F's benefit, D is guilty of handling and F is presumably guilty of aiding and abetting him in handling. Where a thief pays stolen money into a bank account he no longer owns any money but is owed a debt by the bank.[2] The debt is a thing in action – and it is stolen. If D assists the thief to retain the "money in the bank" he will be guilty of handling the thing in action.

---

[1] But cf *Pitham and Hehl*, above, para **2–36**. If the receiving is in the course of the stealing F is, of course, guilty of aiding and abetting the theft.
[2] This point seems to have been overlooked in *Pitchley* (1972) 57 Cr App Rep 30, CA, below, para **13–32**. Cf *Forsyth* [1997] Crim LR (August).

(b) Land

13–05 "Land" which is stolen contrary to s. 4 (2) (b) can always be the subject of handling since the stealing necessarily involves severance of the thing in question. A fixture or structure which is stolen contrary to s. 4 (2) (c), on the other hand, may or may not be severed from the land. Only if it is severed can it be the subject of handling. If E, an outgoing tenant, dishonestly sells to D, the incoming tenant, a fixture belonging to P, D cannot be guilty of handling (whether or not his act is in the course of stealing) if the fixture is not severed; nor, of course, is F guilty of handling if he, knowing all the facts, takes over the premises, including the fixture, from D; yet he has knowingly taken possession of a stolen fixture.

Land which is stolen contrary to s. 4 (2) (a) will rarely be capable of being handled since the kind of conduct contemplated by s. 4 (2) (a) will not normally involve severance.

Land may be the subject of both obtaining by deception and blackmail. Again, severance may or may not take place and handling is possible only if it does so.

(c)   Meaning of "stolen"

13–06   By s. 24 (4):

"For purposes of the provisions of this Act relating to goods which have been stolen (including subsections (1) to (3) above) goods obtained in England or Wales or elsewhere either by blackmail or in circumstances described in section 15 (1) of this Act shall be regarded as stolen; and 'steal', 'theft' and 'thief' shall be construed accordingly."

By s. 24A (8):

"References to stolen goods include money which is withdrawn from an account to which a wrongful credit[1] has been made, but only to the extent that the money derives from the credit."

And by s. 24 (1):

"The provisions of this Act relating to goods which have been stolen shall apply whether the stealing occurred in England or Wales or elsewhere, and whether it occurred before or after the commencement of this Act, provided that the stealing (if not an offence under this Act) amounted to an offence where and at the time when the goods were stolen; and references to stolen goods shall be construed accordingly."

Thus goods are "stolen" for the purposes of the Act if:
(i)   they have been stolen contrary to s. 1;[2]
(ii)   they have been obtained by blackmail contrary to s. 21;
(iii) they have been obtained by deception contrary to s. 15 (1);
(iv)   they consist of money dishonestly withdrawn from a wrongful credit; or
(v)   they have been the subject of an act done in a foreign country which was (a) a crime by the law of that country and which (b), had it been done in England, would have been theft, blackmail or obtaining by deception contrary to s. 1 or s. 21 or s. 15 (1) or s. 15A (1), respectively.[3]

---

[1]   See s. 15A (obtaining a money transfer by deception), above, para **4–64** and s. 24A (dishonestly retaining a wrongful credit), below, para **13–51**.
[2]   See commentary on *Forrester* [1992] Crim LR 793, 794–795.
[3]   For a comparison with the law under the Larceny Act 1916, see editions of this book before the fifth edition – fourth edition, paras 386–388.

(d)   The "thief" must be guilty

13–07   Though s. 22 does not say so expressly, it is now established that the goods must have been stolen in fact.[1] It is not sufficient that D believed them to be "stolen" if they were not. If, because of a mistake of fact (or, possibly, of civil law[2]) D wrongly believed the goods to be stolen he might, since the Criminal Attempts Act 1981, be convicted of an attempt to handle. If D says he knew the goods were stolen because E told him so, this is excellent evidence of *mens rea* but it is not evidence that the goods were stolen in fact.[3] An admission based on hearsay is of no more value than the hearsay itself. It is a misdirection to tell the jury that they are entitled to take such an admission into account, except as evidence of *mens rea*.[4] D's admission of facts which he himself perceived is, however, evidence of those facts which might amount to evidence from which a jury could infer that the goods were stolen. Thus D's admission that he bought goods in a public house at a ridiculously low price is evidence that the goods were stolen. Similarly, where a television set is bought in a betting shop or where a publican buys cases of whisky from a lorry-driver.[5] The conduct of a person who offers a bag of jewellery to a stranger for £2,000 and then accepts £100 for it suggests strongly, as a matter of common sense, that the jewellery is stolen.[6] However, the seller's conduct in this and similar cases goes to show only that he believed the goods to be stolen, in the same way as his statement to that effect would do; and that, as the express statement is inadmissible as hearsay, so too (or *a fortiori*) should be this implied statement. The courts have been slow to recognise conduct which is not intended to be assertive as hearsay, but the House of Lords did so in *Kearley*[7] and the logical consequence of that decision is that the conduct in question would be inadmissible as evidence that the goods were stolen.

If, then, the alleged thief is not guilty, the handler cannot be convicted for there are no stolen goods for him to handle. So if the alleged thief turns out to have been under the age of ten (or under fourteen and not proved to be *doli capax*) at the time of the alleged theft, then the goods appropriated cannot be stolen goods and there can be no conviction for handling them.[8] If D believed the "thief" was fourteen, he might be convicted of an attempt to handle. Whatever his belief as to the "thief's" age, the appropriate charge would be theft of the goods.[9]

[1]   *Haughton v Smith* [1975] AC 476, [1973] 3 All ER 1109 at 1112, 1119 and 1124, HL.
[2]   Smith & Hogan 333.
[3]   *Porter* [1976] Crim LR 58; *Marshall* [1977] Crim LR 106; *Lang v Evans (Inspector of Police)* [1977] Crim LR 286; *Hack* [1978] Crim LR 359; *Overington* [1978] Crim LR 692, CA.
[4]   *Hulbert* (1979) 69 Cr App Rep 243, CA.
[5]   Example put by Lawton LJ in *McDonald* (1980) 70 Cr App Rep 288, CA.
[6]   *Korniak* (1983) 76 Cr App Rep 145, CA.
[7]   [1992] 2 All ER 345, HL.
[8]   *Walters v Lunt* [1951] 2 All ER 645, thus remains good law.
[9]   Above, paras **2–42, 2–51**.

13–08   If the appropriator of the goods is guilty of theft, it is submitted that the goods appropriated may be the subject of handling although the appropriator is immune from prosecution by reason, for example, of diplomatic immunity.[1] The thief could be prosecuted for the theft if diplomatic immunity were waived. The handler may be convicted whether that immunity is waived or not – unless, of course, he too is entitled to diplomatic immunity.

[1]   Cf *Dickinson v Del Solar* [1930] 1 KB 376; *AB* [1941] 1 KB 454; *Madan* [1961] 2 QB 1, (1961) 45 Cr App Rep 80.

13–09   It must be proved, as against an alleged handler, that another person (T) was guilty of stealing the goods. The fact that T has been acquitted of stealing the goods is no bar to the prosecution of the handler and is, indeed, inadmissible in evidence. But the fact that T has been convicted of stealing the goods is now admissible[1] and, when it is admitted, T must be taken to have committed the theft unless the contrary is proved. If D claims that T did not steal the goods – that T was wrongly convicted – it is for him to prove it on a balance of probabilities.

[1]   Police and Criminal Evidence Act 1984, s. 74 (1) and (2); *O'Connor* (1986) 85 Cr App Rep 298 at 302, CA; *Robertson* [1987] QB 920, (1987) 85 Cr App Rep 304 at 310, 311, CA; *Barnes* [1991] Crim LR 132.

B.   WHEN GOODS CEASE TO BE STOLEN

13–10   By s. 24 (3) of the Act:

"But no goods shall be regarded as having continued to be stolen goods after they have been restored to the person from whom they were stolen or to other lawful possession or custody, or after that person and any other person claiming through him have otherwise ceased as regards those goods to have any right to restitution in respect of the theft."

It is obvious that goods which have once been stolen cannot continue to be regarded as "stolen" so long as they continue to exist thereafter. A line must be drawn somewhere; and the Act draws it in the same place as did the common law. Though the word "restored" seems inappropriate to the case where the goods are taken into possession by the police, the Court of Appeal has held that the subsection applies to that case.[1] So if the stolen goods are taken from the thief by the owner or someone acting on his behalf, or by the police, and subsequently returned to the thief so that he may hand them over to a receiver, the receiver will not be guilty of handling because the goods are no longer stolen goods.[2] The owner of stolen goods does not resume possession of the goods merely by marking them and keeping them under observation.[3] More difficult is *King*,[4] where a parcel containing the stolen goods (a fur coat) was handed by E, the thief, to a policeman who was in the act of examining the contents when the telephone rang. The caller was D, the proposed receiver. The policeman discontinued his examination, D was told to come along as arranged, he did so and received the coat. It was held that D was guilty of receiving stolen goods on the ground that the coat had not been reduced into the possession of the police – though it was admitted that there was no doubt that, in a few minutes, it would have been so reduced, if the telephone had not rung. Presumably the same result would follow under the Theft Act. The case has, however, been subjected to criticism. It is easy to see that if the police are examining a parcel to see whether it contains stolen goods they do not take possession or even custody of the contents until they decide that this is what they are looking for.[5] In *King*, however, E had admitted the theft of the coat and produced the parcel. One might have expected, therefore, that the policeman had in fact made up his mind to take charge of it before the telephone rang. The decision presumably proceeds on the assumption that he had not done so.

The Court of Appeal has affirmed[6] that the question is one of the intention of the police officer. An officer correctly suspected that goods on the back seat of a car were stolen. He removed the rotor arm from the car, kept observation until D appeared and got into the car, and then questioned him. It was held that the jury ought to have been asked to consider whether the officer had decided before D's appearance to take possession of the goods or whether he was of an entirely open mind, intending to decide when he had questioned D. To immobilise a car is not the same thing as to take possession of it or its contents.

---

[1]   *Re A-G's Reference (No 1 of 1974)* [1974] QB 744, [1974] 2 All ER 899, CA. Was it the inappropriateness of the word "restored" which led some members of the House of Lords in *Haughton v Smith* to doubt whether it had properly been conceded that the goods in that case had ceased to be stolen?

[2]   Cf *Dolan* (1855) Dears CC 436; *Schmidt* (1866) LR 1 CCR 15; *Villensky* [1892] 2 QB 597.

[3]   *Greater London Metropolitan Police Comr v Streeter* (1980) 71 Cr App Rep 113, CA. Even if the owner does resume possession, the goods may be stolen again when the thief continues to deal with them: ibid, at 119.

[4]   [1938] 2 All ER 662, CCA.

[5]   Cf *Warner v Metropolitan Police Comr* [1969] 2 AC 256, [1968] 2 All ER 356, HL.

[6]   *Re A-G's Reference (No 1 of 1974)*, above, fn 1.

13–11 It is now quite clear that the goods may cease to be stolen in the case where the police are acting without the authority of the owner for they are clearly in "other lawful possession or custody" of the goods.[1]

---

[1] Cf the dictum of Cresswell J in *Dolan* (above, fn 2) that goods retained their stolen character in this situation. Presumably the police in *King* were acting with the owner's authority. The point is not discussed, but it would seem likely that the theft had been reported to the police by the owner.

13–12 Section 24 (3) also provides that the goods lose their character of stolen goods if the person from whom they were stolen has ceased to have any right of restitution in respect of the theft.

Whether a "right to restitution" exists is a question of civil law. A person whose goods have been wrongfully converted does not have a right to have those goods restored to him. He has a right to damages but it is in the discretion of the court whether to order the goods to be delivered to him.[1] It is quite clear that s. 24 (3) is not intended to be confined to those cases in which a court would exercise its discretion to order the goods to be returned to P. In the criminal proceedings, it would be impossible to identify such cases and it is submitted that the subsection is applicable to all cases in which P could succeed in a civil action based on his proprietary interest in the thing, whether in conversion or for the protection of an equitable interest.

---

[1] Torts (Interference with Goods) Act 1977, s. 3.

13–13 The provision seems to have been intended to bear a still wider meaning. The Criminal Law Revision Committee explained it as follows:[1]

"This is because, if the person who owned the goods when they were stolen no longer has any title to them, there will be no reason why the goods should continue to have the taint of being stolen goods. For example, the offence of handling stolen goods will . . . apply also to goods obtained by criminal deception under [section 15]. If the owner of the goods who has been deceived chooses on discovering the deception to ratify his disposal of the goods he will cease to have any title to them."

---

[1] *Eighth Report*, Cmnd 2977, para 139.

13–14 It is clear that "title" is here used in a broad sense to include a right to rescind. The Committee clearly has in mind a case where property passes from P to D at the moment when the goods are obtained by deception. In such a case, P, strictly, has no "title" and his right to recover the goods (or, much more likely, their value) will only arise on his rescinding the contract.[1] Such a potential right, it is submitted, is clearly a "right to restitution" within the Act.

---

[1] Cf above, para. **2-84**, where it is argued, in relation to s. 5 (4), that a person holding property under a voidable title is not "under an obligation to make restoration" until the transaction under which he obtained the property is rescinded.

13–15 Goods will cease to be stolen in the following cases:

E obtains goods by deception from P. There is a voidable contract of sale. On discovering the deception, P ratifies the contract. D, not knowing of the ratification, receives the goods believing them to be stolen. D is not guilty of handling.

E obtains goods by deception from P. There is a voidable contract of sale. E sells the goods to F, a bona-fide purchaser for value without notice of the deception. F gets a good title.[1] He delivers the goods to D who knows they have been obtained by, but was not a party to, the deception.[2] D is not guilty of handling.[3]

E steals goods from P. He sells them before 3 January 1995 in market overt to F, a bona-fide purchaser for value without notice of the theft. F gets a good title.[4] D receives the goods knowing that they were stolen by E from P. He is not guilty of handling.

P entrusts his goods to E, a mercantile agent. E dishonestly and in breach of his agreement with P, sells the goods to F who is a bona-fide purchaser for value without notice of E's dishonesty. This is theft by E but F gets a good title to the goods.[5] D receives the goods knowing that they have been dishonestly appropriated by E. D is not guilty of handling.

P delivers a motor vehicle to E under a hire-purchase or conditional sale agreement. Before the property in the vehicle has passed to E, he dishonestly sells it to F, a bona-fide purchaser for value without notice of the agreement and who is not a "trade or finance purchaser" as defined in s. 29 (2) of the Hire-Purchase Act 1964. This is theft by E but F gets a good title to[6] the vehicle. D receives the vehicle knowing that it has been dishonestly appropriated by E. He is not guilty of handling.[7]

In all the cases considered in this paragraph, D will be guilty of attempted handling if he believes the goods to be stolen because he is unaware of the facts which have caused them to cease to be stolen. If he is aware of those facts but fails to appreciate their effect in law, he is probably not guilty.[8]

---

[1] Sale of Goods Act 1979, s. 23.
[2] Cf *Peirce v London Horse and Carriage Repository* [1922] WN 170, CA.
[3] F is not guilty of theft even if he realises the goods have been obtained by deception before he sells them to D: s. 3 (2) above. Nor, of course, is D.
[4] Sale of Goods Act 1979, s. 22(1), repealed by the Sale of Goods (Amendment) Act 1994.
[5] Factors Act 1889, s. 2.
[6] Hire-Purchase Act 1964, s. 27; Consumer Credit Act 1974, Sch 4, para 22.
[7] In none of these examples is D guilty of theft from P, for P has no proprietary right or interest in the goods; but, in each case, he may be guilty of an attempt to handle.
[8] Smith & Hogan 327, 333.

C. GOODS REPRESENTING THOSE ORIGINALLY STOLEN MAY BE STOLEN GOODS

13–16   By s. 24 (2) of the Act:

"For purposes of those provisions reference to stolen goods shall include, in addition to the goods originally stolen and parts of them (whether in their original state or not) –

(a) any other goods which directly or indirectly represent or have at any time represented the stolen goods in the hands of the thief as being the proceeds of any disposal or realisation of the whole or part of the goods stolen or of goods so representing the stolen goods; and

(b) any other goods which directly or indirectly represent or have at any time represented the stolen goods in the hands of a handler of the stolen goods or any part of them as being the proceeds of any disposal or realisation of the whole or part of the stolen goods handled by him or of goods so representing them."

The effect of the interpretation put upon the corresponding provision in the Larceny Act 1916 (s. 46 (1)) was that anything into or for which the stolen goods were converted or exchanged, whether immediately or otherwise, acquired the character of stolen goods. Thus if A stole an Austin motor car from P and exchanged it with B for a Bentley; B exchanged the Austin with C for a Citroën;

and A exchanged the Bentley with D for a Daimler, all four cars would now be stolen goods even though B, C and D might be innocent. And if A, B, C and D each sold the car he had in his possession, the proceeds of each sale (as well as the cars) would be stolen, as would any property purchased with the proceeds. Thus the stolen goods might be multiplied to an alarming extent. The provision did not seem to give rise to any difficulty in practice and it seems that it was very rarely invoked; but it was clearly undesirable to re-enact a provision with such far-reaching theoretical possibilities. Section 24 (2) imposes a limitation upon the possible multiplication of stolen goods.

13–17   The Criminal Law Revision Committee stated[1] of this provision:

> "It may seem technical; but the effect will be that the goods which the accused is charged with handling must, at the time of the handling or at some previous time, (i) have been in the hands of the thief or of a handler, and (ii) have represented the original stolen goods in the sense of being the proceeds, direct or indirect, of a sale or other realisation of the original goods."

---

[1]   Cmnd 2977, para 138.

13–18   Thus, in the example above, if B, C and D were innocent (i) the Austin would continue to be stolen throughout unless P ceased to have any right to restitution of it in respect of the theft;[1] (ii) the Bentley would be stolen goods since it directly represented the goods originally stolen in the hands of the thief as the proceeds of a disposition of them;[2] (iii) the Citroën would not be stolen since B was neither a thief nor a handler; (iv) the Daimler would be stolen since it indirectly represented the stolen goods in the hands of the thief; and the proceeds of sale of the Daimler would also be stolen goods; but the proceeds of sale of the Austin, the Bentley and the Citroën would not, since they came into the hands of C, D and B respectively, none of whom was a thief or a handler.

The difference between the old law and the new is, of course, that a disposition or realisation of the stolen goods by a person who is neither a thief nor a handler (i.e. by one who is in fact appropriating or handling the goods but who has no *mens rea*) no longer causes the proceeds to be stolen. So if D innocently receives stolen goods and converts them into another form – for example, he buys a car with stolen money, or pays stolen money into a bank – the property in the changed form is not stolen; and the dishonest retention of it by D is not handling,[3] nor is it theft if value was given for the goods.[4] In the case where he pays the money into his bank, however, he may now commit the offence of dishonestly retaining a wrongful credit; and money which he dishonestly withdraws from the account will be stolen goods.[5]

Where goods are stolen in such circumstances that the property does not pass, s. 24 (2) probably makes no difference: any goods notionally stolen by virtue of that subsection are probably also "stolen" by virtue of other provisions in the Act, read in the light of the rules of common law and equity under which an owner can trace his property when it is converted into another form. But where the goods are "stolen" in such circumstances that the property passes to the "thief", the subsection has a potentially wider effect. The reasons for this are examined in the fourth and earlier editions of this work.[6]

---

[1]   Section 24 (3), above, para **13–10**. Cf *Forsyth* [1997] Crim LR (August).
[2]   Because a car representing stolen money is stolen goods, an action by one who conspired to steal the money will fail: *ex turpi causa non oritur actio*: *Solomon v Metropolitan Police Comr* [1982] Crim LR 606 (Milmo J).

3   The point seems to have been overlooked in *Pitchley* (1972) 57 Cr App Rep 30, [1972] Crim LR 705, CA. Cf Griew 15–23. See also *Forsyth* [1997] Crim LR (August)
4   Above, para **2–43**.
5   Theft Act 1968, s 24A, below, para **13–51**.
6   See the fourth edition, paras 401–404.

13–19 Difficult questions may arise where a thief or handler pays stolen money or a stolen cheque into his bank account. If it is a new account or one with a zero balance then the stolen money or cheque has been converted into an identifiable thing in action, i.e. the right to recover an equivalent sum from the bank, which is therefore also "stolen".

If, however, the account already has a credit balance, representing money lawfully acquired by the holder, the question is whether the owner of the stolen money retains any proprietary interest in the mixed fund.[1] If he does not, it seems impossible to say that he has any "right to restitution" in respect of the theft: the stolen money or cheque has ceased to exist and nothing remains which can be the subject of handling. If, however, the theft was a breach of trust, the fiduciary relationship between trustee and beneficiary would enable the latter to trace his money into the mixed fund so that he would have a proprietary interest in it, sufficient, it is submitted, to amount to a right to restitution within the meaning of s. 24 (3). The portion of the mixed fund representing the stolen property would then be stolen goods. Where the theft does not amount to a breach of a fiduciary relationship, the position is more doubtful;[2] but a recent case suggests readiness in the criminal courts to recognise the existence of the interests of victims of thefts in mixed funds.[3] If a person is under an obligation to P to "retain and deal" with property under s. 5 (3) it seems logical that P has "a right to restitution".

If the victim of the theft can trace into the mixed fund, "The correct rule appears to be that the beneficiary [i.e. the victim of the theft] may claim a charge upon any part of the fund which he can identify as being part of the mixed fund."[4] The effect is, where D steals £100 from P and pays it into his bank account which has a credit balance of £100 –

(a)   if he draws out £100 and dissipates it, the remaining £100 belongs in equity to P and is stolen goods; but

(b)   if he draws out £100 and invests it in premium bonds and then dissipates the remaining £100, the premium bonds belong in equity to P and are stolen goods.

If the goods have ceased to be stolen no one can thereafter be convicted of handling them as stolen goods, whatever his intention or belief. If the parties intend and believe the payment to represent the stolen property, even though it does not do so in law, it is possible that they might, since the Criminal Attempts Act 1981, be convicted of an attempt to handle.[5]

Assuming that the credit balance in the account of the thief or handler does represent stolen property, is a cheque, drawn on it and intended to enable D to obtain a transfer of part of the credit balance, or of cash, stolen goods?[6] If the delivery of the cheque operated as an assignment of part of the debt represented by the bank balance then the answer would be in the affirmative; but it is clear that it does not so operate.[7]

1   See Hanbury and Maudsley *Modern Equity* (12th edn) 637–640.
2   See Hanbury and Maudsley, *loc cit* and [1981] Crim LR at 52–53.
3   *Governor of Brixton Prison, ex p Levin* [1997] QB 65, [1996] 4 All ER 350, 364–365, HL.
4   Hanbury and Maudsley (10th edn) 569. *Clowes (No 2)* [1994] 2 All ER 316, 335–336, CA.
5   The case is quite analagous to *Haughton v Smith* [1975] AC 476, HL which is reversed by the Act.
6   The question was raised in *A-G's Reference (No 4 of 1979)* (1981) 71 Cr App Rep 341 at 349.

The court was inclined to think it did but it was unnecessary to decide the point.

[7] *Schroeder v Central Bank of London Ltd* (1876) 34 LT 735, above, para **4–57**.

When proceeds of stolen goods cease to be stolen

13–20   It has already been seen that stolen goods cease to be stolen when the conditions laid down by s. 24 (3) are fulfilled. What then, is the position of goods which have been stolen notionally under s. 24 (2)? Do they cease to be notionally stolen when the goods which they represent cease to be stolen? They must do so when the original goods are restored to the possession of the owner, for then the right to restitution of the proceeds lapses. Do the proceeds also cease to be stolen when the owner loses his right to restitution of the original goods? It seems clear that the answer must be in the negative. If it were otherwise, s. 24 (2) would be almost completely ineffective. Suppose that A obtains a car by deception from P. The contract of sale is voidable, so that A gets ownership of the car. He sells it to B who knows all the facts and who re-sells it to C who is bona-fide and without notice of A's dishonesty. C gets an unimpeachable title to the car, i.e. P's right to restitution of it is lost and it ceases to be stolen goods. A then gives the proceeds of the sale to D who knows all the facts. This is just the situation in which it might be desirable to rely on s. 24 (2) but it would not be possible to do so if the money (notionally stolen, as the proceeds of the car) ceased to be stolen on the car's so ceasing. It is submitted, therefore, that the money does not cease to be stolen. It continues to be stolen until the conditions specified in s. 24 (3) are satisfied in respect of it.

13–21   Section 24 (3) may be applicable to "stolen" proceeds since the person from whom the original goods were stolen may assert a right to restitution as against the proceeds. Suppose that a thief used stolen money to purchase a necklace from a bona-fide seller so that the right to restitution of the money was lost and it ceased to be stolen. Suppose further that the necklace had been given to D who knew all the facts. The necklace would be stolen by virtue of s. 24 (2).[1] P would have a right to restitution in respect of it and there would be room for the application of s. 24 (3) in that this right might be lost in the various ways[2] in which the right to restitution of the original goods might be lost. Additionally, it would be lost if the original property were restored to the possession of the owner, since he could not recover the value of his property twice.

[1] It would also be stolen independently of s. 24 (2).
[2] Above, paras **13–14** and **13–15**.

13–22   To sum up, it is submitted that:
1. Goods notionally stolen as being the proceeds of other stolen goods do not necessarily cease to be notionally stolen when the original stolen goods cease, by virtue of s. 24 (3), to be stolen.
2. Goods notionally stolen cease to be notionally stolen when the conditions of s. 24 (3) are satisfied in respect of those goods.
3. Goods notionally stolen are usually also actually stolen.

D.   FORMS OF HANDLING

13–23   The term "handling" was adopted because "receiving" – the only way of committing the offence under s. 33 (1) of the 1916 Act – is now one of several ways in which the new offence can be committed. As the section has been interpreted by the House of Lords in *Bloxham*,[1] these are:

(i) Receiving the goods.

(ii) Undertaking the retention, removal, disposal or realisation of the goods for the benefit of another person.

(iii) Assisting in the retention, removal, disposal or realisation of the goods by another person.

(iv) Arranging to do (i), (ii) or (iii).

Although in *Bloxham* Lord Bridge stated that, "It is, I think, well settled that this subsection creates two distinct offences but no more than two", it is submitted that the subsection creates only one offence[2] which may be committed in a variety of ways. What was well settled before *Bloxham* was that, where the evidence justified it, the proper practice was to have one count for receiving (or perhaps arranging to receive) and a second count for all the other forms of handling.[3] In law, however, the subsection created only one offence. Thus in *Nicklin*[4] it was held that an indictment alleging unparticularised handling is not defective. If, as Lord Bridge suggested, the subsection creates two offences, the indictment would have been bad for duplicity. The dictum is incorrect.

If D is charged only with receiving, he may not be convicted on that indictment of some other form of handling;[5] and vice versa. Since receiving is "a single finite act" each receipt of stolen goods is a separate offence and, therefore, a single count for receiving a quantity of goods found in D's possession will be bad for duplicity if the receipt took place on more than one occasion.[6] The other forms of handling include "an activity which may be continuing"; so that a single count may encompass goods which have been received on a number of different occasions. The word, "retention", in particular, would be apt to include a large quantity of goods found in D's possession and perhaps received by him over a long period of time. In order to obtain a conviction under the single count it would of course be necessary to prove, not merely that D received the goods, but that he was retaining them for the benefit of another person, or that he was assisting another person in retaining them.

Particulars should be given so as to enable the accused to understand the ingredients of the charge he has to meet.[7] The maximum number of counts for a single instance of handling in the ordinary case is two.[8]

---

[1] [1983] 1 AC 109, [1982] 1 All ER 582, HL.
[2] *Griffiths v Freeman* [1970] 1 All ER 1117, [1970] 1 WLR 659.
[3] *Willis and Syme* [1972] 3 All ER 797, CA; *Deakin* [1972] 3 All ER 803, CA.
[4] [1977] 2 All ER 444, CA.
[5] *Nicklin* [1977] 2 All ER 444, [1977] Crim LR 221, CA.
[6] *Smythe* (1980) 72 Cr App Rep 8, CA. Cf *Skipp*, above, para **2–13**, (overruled, but still relevant on this issue).
[7] *Sloggett* [1972] 1 QB 430, [1971] 3 All ER 264, CA.
[8] *Ikpong* [1972] Crim LR 432, CA.

(a) Receiving

13–24 All forms of handling other than receiving or arranging to receive are subject to the qualification that it must be proved that D was assisting another person or acting "for the benefit of another person".[1] If there is no evidence of this – as will frequently be the case – then it must be proved that D received or arranged to receive the goods and evidence of no other form of handling will suffice. The Act does not define receiving in any way and it must be assumed that all the old authorities remain valid.

It must be proved, then, that D took possession or control of the stolen property or joined with others to share possession or control of it. "Receiving" the thief who has the goods in his possession does not necessarily amount to receiving the goods. If the thief retains exclusive control, there is no receiving.[2] There may, however, be a joint possession in thief and receiver, so it is unnecessary to prove that the thief ever parted with possession – it is sufficient that he shared it with the alleged receiver. In *Smith*,[3] it was held that a recorder had correctly directed a jury when he told them that if they believed "that the watch was then in the custody of a person with the cognizance of the prisoner, that person being one over whom the prisoner had absolute control, so that the watch would be forthcoming if the prisoner ordered it, there was ample evidence to justify them in convicting . . . ". Lord Campbell CJ said that if the thief had been employed by D to commit larceny, so that the watch was in D's control, D was guilty of receiving. In such a case D was an accessory before the fact to larceny and today he would be guilty of theft. If the facts were as put by Lord Campbell, when did D become a receiver? As soon as the theft was committed? If so, we have the extraordinary result that D became guilty of both theft and receiving at the same moment. But, if this moment is not selected, it is difficult to see what other is appropriate. This may, however, appear less anomalous under the new law than under the old. Virtually all handling is now theft, so it is the general rule that the two offences are committed simultaneously. In the ordinary case, however, the offence is handling because there has been a previous theft. The peculiarity of the present problem is that there has been no previous theft; and it may be, therefore, that the requirement that the handling be "otherwise than in the course of the stealing", would prevent D from being guilty of handling until he did some act amounting to that offence, after the theft was complete.

---

[1] Below, para **13–35**.
[2] *Wiley* (1850) 2 Den 37.
[3] (1855) Dears CC 494.

13–25 As is clear from *Smith*, actual manual possession by D need not be proved. It is enough if the goods are received by his servant or agent with his authority.[1] The receipt may be for a merely temporary purpose such as concealment from the police.[2] It is unnecessary that the receiver should receive any profit or advantage from the possession of the goods. If D took possession of the goods from the thief without his consent, this was formerly only larceny (from the thief) and not receiving.[3] There seems to be no reason why it should not be both theft and handling under the Act, since it is clear that the two offences can be committed by one and the same act.

---

[1] *Miller* (1854) 6 Cox CC 353.
[2] *Richardson* (1834) 6 C & P 335.
[3] *Wade* (1844) 1 Car & Kir 739.

13–26 It continues to be essential for the judge to give a careful direction as to possession or control.[1] If the only evidence against D is that he ran away on being found by the police in a house where stolen property had been left, there would appear to be no case to leave to a jury. Likewise where the evidence is consistent with the view that D went to premises where stolen goods were stored with the intention of assuming possession, but had not actually done so;[2] or where the only evidence of receiving a stolen car is that D's fingerprint was found on the driving mirror.[3] The mere fact that the stolen goods were found on D's premises is not sufficient evidence. It must be shown that the goods had come either by invitation or arrangement with him or that he had exercised some control over them.[4] D is not necessarily in possession of a stolen safe simply because he assists others in trying to open it.[5]

---

[1]   *Frost and Hale* (1964) 48 Cr App Rep 284.
[2]   *Freedman* (1930) 22 Cr App Rep 133.
[3]   *Court* (1960) 44 Cr App Rep 242.
[4]   *Cavendish* [1961] 2 All ER 856. Cf *Lloyd* [1992] Crim LR 361, CA.
[5]   *Tomblin* [1964] Crim LR 780.

(b)   Arranging to receive

13–27   D's preparations to receive, not yet amounting to an attempt to do so, may constitute a sufficient "arrangement". The goods must be stolen at the time the arrangement is made. D must know or believe the goods to be stolen. If his belief is mistaken, the full offence is not committed but he may be guilty of an attempt to commit it. An agreement to handle goods to be stolen in the future may be a conspiracy to handle but it is not handling even when the goods are actually stolen.[1] The crime is complete as soon as the arrangement is made. It is not undone if D repents or does nothing to carry out the arrangement, or it becomes impossible of performance. So in a case like *King*[2] it might now be possible to get a conviction for handling by showing that the arrangement was made while the goods were still stolen. It is odd that the offence is committed both by arranging to receive and by actually doing so. Is it two offences or one continuing offence? The latter view is preferable, for *Griffiths v Freeman*[3] by no means solves all the problems of duplicity. Most arrangements will involve agreement with another. An arrangement with an innocent person will be enough. If the other knows the goods are stolen, there will usually be a conspiracy.

---

[1]   *Park* (1987) 87 Cr App Rep 164, [1988] Crim LR 238, CA, disapproving a tentative suggestion in the fifth edition of this book, para 403.
[2]   Above, para **13–10**.
[3]   Above, para **13–23**, fn 2.

(c)   Undertaking and assisting

13–28   Handling can be committed by retention, removal, disposal or realisation in one or other of two ways.

> "First, the offender may himself undertake the activity for the benefit of another person. Secondly, the activity may be undertaken by another person and the offender may assist him. Of course, if the thief or an original receiver and his friend act together in, say, removing the stolen goods, the friend may be committing the offence in both ways."[1]

Some examples drawn from the old law will illustrate the kind of case to which the law extends.

D negotiates the sale to F of goods which he knows to have been stolen by E. D is never in possession or control of the goods.[2] He has undertaken the disposal and realisation of stolen goods.

D assists E to lift from a van a barrel of gin which he knows to have been stolen by E or another. Even if he never has possession or control[3] he has assisted the removal of the stolen goods.

D's fifteen-year-old son, E, brings home a bicycle which he has stolen. D assists in its retention if (i) he agrees that E may keep the bicycle in the house, or (ii) he tells the police there is no bicycle in the house, or (iii) he gives E a tin of paint so that he may disguise it.

D lights the way for E to carry stolen goods from a house to a barn so that E may negotiate the sale of the goods. D has assisted in the removal of the goods.[4]

It has been held that where a seller employs a sub-contractor to make goods which are delivered to the buyer, the seller may be guilty of handling by assisting in the realisation of stolen goods if, knowing or believing the materials to have been stolen, he pays the sub-contractor for the goods.[5] The buyer of stolen goods may be assisting in the realisation of them but is not "undertaking" the realisation.[6]

1   *Bloxham* [1983] 1 AC 109, [1982] 1 All ER 582 at 585, HL, per Lord Bridge.
2   Cf *Watson* [1916] 2 KB 385.
3   *Gleed* (1916) 12 Cr App Rep 32; *Hobson v Impett* (1957) 41 Cr App Rep 138.
4   *Wiley* (1850) 2 Den 37.
5   *Tamm* [1973] Crim LR 115 (Judge R. David).
6   *Bloxham* at 585, disapproving a statement by Phillimore LJ in *Deakin* [1972] 3 All ER 803 at 808, CA.

13–29   Merely to use goods knowing them to be stolen does not in itself amount to assisting in their retention. D did not commit the offence by using a stolen heater and battery charger in his father's garage,[1] nor by erecting stolen scaffolding in the course of a building operation.[2] Nothing was done with the purpose, or with the effect, of assisting in retention. According to *Kanwar*,[3] "something must be done by the offender, and done intentionally and dishonestly, for the purpose of enabling the goods to be retained". However, it was held to be sufficient in that case that D told lies to protect her husband who had dishonestly brought the stolen goods into the house. She knew that, if the deception succeeded, the effect would be that her husband would be enabled to retain the goods.

A person does not "assist" in the disposition of stolen property merely by accepting the benefit of the disposition. There must be proof that D gave help or encouragement. In *Coleman*,[4] D knew that his wife was using money which she had stolen to pay solicitors' fees relating to the purchase of a flat in the couple's joint names. That did not in itself amount to assisting though it was evidence from which a jury might infer that he had assisted by telling his wife to use the stolen money or agreeing that she should do so.

It was said in *Kanwar* that, "The requisite assistance need not be successful in its object." But does one who attempts to assist and fails "assist"? This seems to involve reading the section as if it read, "does an act with the purpose of assisting". The would-be assister who fails to assist in any way would surely be more properly convicted of an attempt.

1   *Sanders* (1982) 75 Cr App Rep 84, CA.
2   *Thornhill* unreported; discussed in *Sanders*, above.
3   [1982] 2 All ER 528, (1982) 75 Cr App Rep 87.
4   [1986] Crim LR 56, CA.

(d)   *Arranging or undertaking to assist*

13–30   Far-reaching though the extension of the law to undertaking and assisting is, the Act goes further. A mere arrangement to do any of the acts amounting to undertaking or assisting is enough. D simply agrees or prepares to negotiate the sale of stolen goods, to lift down the barrel of stolen gin or to do any act for the purpose of enabling E to retain, remove or dispose of the goods. Nothing more is required.

E. HANDLING BY OMISSION

13–31 "Receiving", "undertaking" and "arranging" all suggest that an act of some kind is required. It is difficult to envisage any of these forms of handling being committed by omission. It is, however, possible to assist another by inactivity; but this will not constitute an offence except in the rather rare case where the law imposes a duty to act.

In *Brown*,[1] it was held that D's mere failure to reveal to the police the presence of stolen goods on his premises did not amount to assisting in their retention. (Nor did his advice to the police to "Get lost".) Clearly the thief was in fact assisted by D's silence in the sense that D's omission to disclose the truth delayed the finding of the stolen goods. There is, however, no duty to give information to the police.[2] No doubt the answer would have been different if D had not merely refused information but had told lies.[3]

The court thought that D's conduct was evidence that D was permitting the goods to remain and thereby assisting in their retention. It would obviously be an act of assistance for D, expressly or tacitly, to give a thief permission to keep stolen goods on D's premises. The court's remarks (and, indeed, decision for they applied the proviso) seem to go farther and suggest that it would be enough if D did not communicate with the thief at all but simply allowed stolen goods which had been placed on his premises to remain there. This comes very close to making the mere omission to remove goods or report their presence an offence. But the result is perhaps reasonable. If a lorry-driver were to observe that his mate had secretly inserted some stolen goods in the lorry and were then to drive the lorry to its destination without comment, there would be no difficulty in saying that he had assisted in the removal of the goods. Where the goods are planted on static premises, the assistance consists in the maintenance of the premises where the goods lie and the exclusion of strangers, just as in the lorry case it consists in driving the lorry.

---

1 [1970] 1 QB 105, [1969] 3 All ER 198, CA.
2 Refusal to answer a constable is not an obstruction in the course of his duty: *Rice v Connolly* [1966] 2 QB 414, [1966] 2 All ER 649; Smith & Hogan 432–436.
3 This probably is obstruction of the police: *Rice v Connolly* (fn 2, above); *Mathews v Dwan* [1949] NZLR 1037.

13–32 The dicta in *Brown* were followed in *Pitchley*.[1] D's son stole £150 and on 5 November gave it to D to look after for him. D may not have known the money was stolen when he received it and, on 6 November, he paid it into a savings bank account. On 7 November D learnt that the money was stolen. He did nothing about it. He was indicted for handling the sum of £150 between 5 and 11 November. The prosecution case was that he either received the money dishonestly or assisted dishonestly in its retention. The court thought that the word "retain" in the section bears its dictionary meaning – "keep possession of, not lose, continue to have".[2] D, by permitting the "money"[3] to remain under his control, was retaining it,[4] and was guilty. He was, it appears, under a duty to withdraw "the money" and return it to its owner.

---

1 (1973) 57 Cr App Rep 30, [1972] Crim LR 705, CA, and commentary thereon.
2 "The meaning of the word 'retention' in the section is a matter of law in so far as the construction of the word is necessary", per Cairns LJ at 57 Cr App Rep 37. Cf *Feely*, above, para **2–121**.
3 The stolen money in fact had ceased to exist and it appears that the thing in action which replaced it was not "stolen" because D was neither a thief nor a handler at the time of the "realisation". See Griew 15–23, fn 62; Williams *TBCL* 873: above, para **13–18**. It is thus very doubtful whether Pitchley was rightly convicted. A better charge would have been theft. The

thing in action, being the proceeds of the stolen money, probably continued to belong to P; and D, by keeping it as owner, appropriated it: s. 3 (2).

⁴   But is "retaining" (as distinct from undertaking the retention) an offence? If D alone retains, it is odd to describe him as assisting in retention. D's conduct might have been better described as undertaking the retention, but he was not dishonest when he "undertook".

F.   OTHERWISE THAN IN THE COURSE OF THE STEALING

13–33   Almost every handling is also stealing but the stealing here referred to is the stealing which caused the goods to be stolen goods before the alleged handling. If D was a party to that theft, his participation in it cannot be the offence of handling stolen goods. The provision was necessary to keep handling within proper bounds. Without it, virtually every instance of theft by two or more persons would also have been handling by one or other or, more likely, both of them.

In the fifth edition of this book it was stated that "whatever the form of handling alleged, it must be proved that it was done 'otherwise than in the course of the stealing'". In *Cash*,[1] the court said this statement "might be unhappily worded". It is a general principle that the judge must direct the jury as to all the elements of an offence[2] but in *Cash* it was held that "where in reality [D] had to be acquitted if he could not be shown to be a handler", the words, "otherwise than in the course of the stealing", have little importance and the jury should not even be told about them. Perhaps these words, being in parentheses, are regarded as an exception to, or exemption from, rather than an element of, the offence; so that it is for D to introduce sufficient evidence to raise a doubt whether he received the goods in the course of the stealing, or even (though this seems unlikely) to prove on the balance of probabilities that he did so receive them.[3] The case envisaged is one where, in the opinion of the judge, no reasonable jury could be satisfied beyond reasonable doubt that D, the alleged handler, was the thief – it is, in his judgment, handling or nothing. But, even if no reasonable jury could be satisfied beyond reasonable doubt that D was the thief, they might think it quite possible, or even probable, that he was. If the matter were left to them, they would not be satisfied beyond reasonable doubt that D received the goods otherwise than in the course of the stealing and they would acquit; but because they are not told about this provision they will convict. This seems wrong. It is certainly exceptional for the prosecution to have to prove that D is not guilty of an offence,[4] but this seems to be what Parliament has provided.

In *Cash*, stolen goods were found in D's possession on 25 February. The property was stolen (by a burglar) not later than 16 February. It was held that it was not open to the jury to infer that D was the burglar rather than a receiver. Perhaps the evidence was insufficient to satisfy the jury beyond reasonable doubt that D was the burglar but may they not, given the opportunity, have thought that it was reasonably possible, if not probable, that he was the burglar? Is it unheard of for burglars to retain possession of the stolen property for nine days? In *Greaves*,[5] it was held that the judge had properly left it open to the jury to convict of burglary where the time lapse was 17 days.

---

¹   [1985] QB 801, [1985] Crim LR 311, CA and commentary.
²   *McVey* [1988] Crim LR 127.
³   Section 101 of the Magistrates' Courts Act 1980 provides that the onus of proof is on a defendant to an information or complaint who relies on an exception, exemption, etc. and the House of Lords in *Hunt* [1987] AC 352, [1987] 1 All ER 1 held that the section is a statement of the common law which applies in trials on indictment; but, in fact, the application of the

supposed principle is haphazard, inconsistent and, in serious offences, rare. See "The Presumption of Innocence" (1987) 38 NILQ 223.
4   But see *McMonagle v Westminster City Council* [1989] Crim LR 455, DC.
5   (1987) Times, 11 July, discussed Archbold 21–127, 128. *Cash* was also distinguished in *Bruce* [1988] VR 579.

13–34   The duration of "the course of the stealing" depends on the extent to which appropriation is a continuing act.[1] As has been observed, one case involving handling, *Pitham and Hehl*,[2] suggested that appropriation is an instantaneous act, concluded at the moment the goods are stolen. If this were right, the words "in the course of the stealing" would be rendered nugatory. It is submitted that, in the light of *Hale*[3] and *Atakpu*,[4] cases concerned with robbery and theft respectively, *Pitham* must be wrongly decided in this respect. *Atakpu* adopts the transaction test – was E still "on the job"? This does not, of course, solve all the problems. A thief is likely to be held to be on the job while he is in a building which he has entered for the purpose of stealing and from which he intends to remove the stolen goods. But is he still in the course of theft as he walks down the garden path with the swag? as he drives home? and as he shows it to his wife in the kitchen? It does not necessarily follow that the theft is still in the course of commission because the stolen property has not yet been removed from the premises on which it was stolen. E may have completed his part of "the job", leaving it to others to take possession of the goods. Arguably, in such a case, E is no longer in the course of stealing. If so, some of the old cases on larceny are no longer in point. Thus in *Atwell and O'Donnell*,[5] goods were left in the warehouse in which they had been stolen for some time thereafter and the court held that it was a continuing transaction as to those who joined in the plot before the goods were finally carried away from the premises. Presumably until this occurred, the larceny was incomplete. It does not necessarily follow that the course of stealing under the Theft Act continues so long. If E appropriates goods in his employer's warehouse and conceals them so that they may be taken by D who comes to the warehouse a week later, is it to be said that D's taking is in the course of the stealing? Surely not.

---

1   Above, para **2–49**.
2   (1977) 65 Cr App Rep 45, CA above, paras **2–36, 2–49**.
3   (1978) 68 Cr App Rep 415, CA above, paras **2–49, 3–09**.
4   [1994] QB 69, [1993] 4 All ER 215, above, paras **2–46, 2–49**.
5   (1801) 2 East PC 768.

G.   BY OR FOR THE BENEFIT OF ANOTHER PERSON

13–35   Each of the nouns, "retention", "removal", "disposal" and "realisation" is governed by the words "by or for the benefit of another person".[1] It must therefore be proved that:
(a)   D undertook or arranged the retention, removal, disposal or realisation *for the benefit of another person*; or
(b)   D assisted or arranged the retention, removal, disposal or realisation *by another person*.[2]

There can hardly ever have been a thief who did not retain, remove, dispose of or realise the stolen goods, and the qualification created by the italicised words prevents all thieves from being handlers as well. The italicised words are an essential part of the offence and the indictment must allege that the handling was "by or for the benefit of another person".[3] The thief may himself be guilty of handling (by undertaking) if he himself retains, removes, etc., the goods for the benefit of another person. It would seem to be immaterial that the other person is guilty of no offence and even unaware of what is going on.

In *Bloxham*,[4] it was held that a purchaser, as such, of stolen goods is not "another person" within the meaning of the section. Sellers usually sell for their own benefit, not the benefit of the purchaser but, even if the sale could be described as for the purchaser's benefit, it would not, in the opinion of Lord Bridge, be within the ambit of the section. This is to give a special meaning to "another person", the limits of which are not clear. An attractive solution is proposed by Professor Spencer:[5]

> " . . . the requirement that the act be 'for the benefit of another' serves no intelligible purpose unless it limits the offence to those who act on another's behalf."

---

[1] *Sloggett* [1972] 1 QB 430, [1971] 3 All ER 264 at 267, CA.
[2] Cf *Blake* "The Innocent Purchaser and Section 22 of the Theft Act" [1972] Crim LR 494.
[3] *Sloggett* [1972] 1 QB 430, [1971] 3 All ER 264, CA.
[4] Above, para **13–23**.
[5] "The Mishandling of Handling" [1981] Crim LR 682 at 685.

13-36 In *Bloxham*, D in good faith purchased a stolen car for £1,300. Eleven months later, suspecting the truth, he sold it for £200 to a person unknown who was prepared to buy it without documents. D was charged with handling by undertaking or assisting in the realisation of the car for the benefit of the buyer. A submission of no case to answer was rejected, whereupon he pleaded guilty. His conviction was upheld by the Court of Appeal who thought that the buyer's use of the car, for which he had paid less than its true value, was a benefit to him. Maybe it was; but it seems a travesty to say that the sale was for his benefit. The House of Lords quashed the conviction. The buyer was not "another person". In fact, of course, he was "another person"; but the sale was certainly not effected "on his behalf".

13-37 In *Roberts*[1] it was held that, if A and B are jointly charged in one count with an act of handlng "by or for the benefit of another", the other must be some person other than A or B. This seems logical if, indeed, only one act, jointly done by A and B, is alleged. A might, however, arrange the disposition of the goods *by* B; and B might undertake the disposition *for the benefit of* A. In that case both have committed an offence under s. 22 and there is no need to show that any third person was involved.

---

[1] (9 July 1993, unreported); see *Slater and Suddens* [1996] Crim LR 494, CA.

13–38 *Conspiracy to handle.* As s. 22 creates only one offence (*pace* Lord Bridge in *Bloxham*) an indictment for conspiracy to handle contrary to s. 22, not particularising the form of handling, is good. It is not an allegation of conspiracy to commit crime X or crime Y. An agreement by A and B that B would, for example, dispose of the goods for the benefit of A is, notwithstanding *Roberts*, a conspiracy. A and B have agreed that B will commit the offence of handling, and that is enough. If B does dispose of the goods as agreed, he commits the offence under s. 22; and, obviously A has counselled or procured him to do so. They are both guilty of the same offence. There seems to be every reason, *pace* the court in *Roberts*, why A and B should be jointly charged with committing it.

H.   INNOCENT RECEIPT AND SUBSEQUENT RETENTION WITH *MENS REA*

13–39   If D receives the stolen goods either believing them not to be stolen or knowing them to be stolen but intending to return them to the true owner he commits no offence. Suppose he subsequently discovers the goods to be stolen or decides not to return them to the true owner or disposes of them. He has, presumably dishonestly, undertaken the retention of or has disposed of stolen goods knowing them to be stolen. Whether he is guilty of an offence depends on a number of factors.

1. Where D does not get ownership of the goods (the normal situation where goods are stolen):

  (i)   D gives value for the goods.

   (a)   D retains or disposes of the goods for his own benefit. This is not theft because of s. 3 (2);[1] nor is it handling by undertaking, assisting or arranging since it is not for the benefit of another. D might be guilty of handling by aiding and abetting the receiving by the person to whom he disposes of the goods, if that person has *mens rea*.

   (b)   D retains or disposes of the goods "for the benefit of another person" – whatever that means. This is not theft (s. 3 (2)) but is handling.

  (ii)   D does not give value.

   (a)   D retains or disposes of the goods for his own benefit. This is theft but not handling unless it amounts to aiding and abetting receipt by another.

   (b)   D retains or disposes of the goods "for the benefit of another person". This is theft and handling.

2. Where D gets ownership of the goods. (Because the rogue obtained them by deception and acquired a voidable title or because of some exception to the *nemo dat* rule.)

  (i)   D gives value for the goods.

Retention or disposal of the goods cannot be theft, since P has no property in the goods, nor handling since P has lost his right to restitution,[2] his right to rescind being destroyed on the goods coming into the hands of D who was a bona-fide purchaser for value.

  (ii)   D does not give value.

Again this cannot be theft, since P has no property in the goods, but it may be handling since P's right to rescind and secure restitution of his property is not extinguished by the goods coming into the hands of one who does not give value. It will be handling if this is so and D either aids and abets a guilty receipt by another or disposes of the goods "for the benefit of another person".

---

[1]   Above, para **2–43**.
[2]   Above, para **13–10**.

I.   HANDLING BY THE THIEF

13–40   The common law rules regulating the liability of a thief to a charge of receiving goods feloniously stolen by him were complicated by the distinction between principals and accessories.

That distinction[1] was abolished in 1967 and all participants in a crime are now classed as prinicipals.[2] The effect is that any thief may be convicted of handling the goods stolen by him by receiving them – if the evidence warrants this conclusion[3] and proves that he handled, or aided and abetted the handling of, goods, otherwise than in the course of the theft which caused the goods to be stolen. In the majority of cases the thief can only be guilty of handling by receiving where he aids and abets the receipt by another. Since he is already in possession or control, he cannot receive as the principal offender. In some circumstances, however, a thief might be convicted of handling the stolen goods by receiving them as the principal offender. For example, D steals goods and, in the course of the theft, delivers them to E. Two days later E returns the goods to D.

---

1   See the third edition of this book, para 405.
2   Criminal Law Act 1967, s. 1.
3   *Dolan* (1976) 62 Cr App Rep 36 at 39, CA, where this passage was followed. Cf *Stapylton v O'Callaghan* [1973] 2 All ER 782.

---

2   THE *MENS REA*

A. KNOWLEDGE OR BELIEF

13–41   It must be proved that D handled the goods, "knowing or believing them to be stolen goods", i.e. that he knew or believed the goods to be stolen at the time when he received them or did such other act as is alleged to amount to handling.[1] The test is subjective. The fact that any reasonable man would have known that the goods were stolen is evidence, but no more, that D knew or believed that this was so.[2] There is some difficulty about the function of the words, "or believing". The law of receiving stolen goods under the Larceny Acts used the word "knowing" alone. To say that a person "knows" a thing to be so implies that it is so. To say that he "believes" it to be so means that he thinks it is (or, perhaps, probably is) so, whether it is in fact so or not. It might have been supposed that "believing" was introduced to extend the law to cover one who received the goods believing them to be stolen when they were not. It has already been noticed that this interpretation was considered and rejected by the House of Lords in *Haughton v Smith*.[3] The CLRC intended the words "or believing" to extend the *mens rea* of the offence. They said:[4]

> "It is a serious defect of the present law that actual knowledge that the property was stolen must be proved. Often the prosecution cannot prove this. In many cases indeed guilty knowledge does not exist, although the circumstances of the transaction are such that the receiver ought to be guilty of an offence. The man who buys goods at a ridiculously low price from an unknown seller whom he meets in a public house may not know that the goods were stolen, and he may take the precaution of asking no questions. Yet it may be clear on the evidence that he believes that the goods were stolen. In such cases the prosecution may fail (rightly, as the law now stands) for want of proof of guilty knowledge."

It seems clear that they intended to include the concept of "wilful blindness" which is often held by the courts to be included in the word "knowing" standing alone.[5] But, if this was their intention, it has not been achieved. Wilful blindness postulates that D has a strong suspicion that something is so and consciously decides not to take steps which he could take to confirm or deny that fact. But the courts have constantly said that, for the purposes of s. 22, suspicion is not to be equated with belief.[6] It is a misdirection to tell the jury that it is enough that D, "suspecting that the goods were stolen deliberately shut his eyes to the consequences".[7] What, if anything, then, does "believing" add? According to *Hall*:[8]

> "A man may be said to know that goods are stolen when he is told by someone with first-hand knowledge (someone such as the thief or the burglar) that such is the case. Belief, of course, is something short of knowledge. It may be said to

233

be the state of mind of a person who says to himself: 'I cannot say I know for certain that these goods are stolen but there can be no other reasonable conclusion in the light of all the circumstances, in the light of all that I have heard and seen.'"

But this seems to be merely a distinction between two sources of D's knowledge or belief: if D had direct evidence, he knows, if he has circumstantial evidence, he believes. This section requires a distinction between two states of mind, not two modes of arriving at the same state of mind. D may be left in varying degrees of certainty whether he has been told by the thief or deduced the fact from his own observation. If both processes cause D to be certain that the goods are stolen, there is no difference in his state of mind. What seems to be implied in *Hall* is that the person with direct information is certain and the person with circumstantial evidence is nearly certain. But it would be dangerous so to direct a jury because "near certainty" is strong suspicion and that is not enough.

In general, however, it seems that a judge cannot be wrong if he simply directs the jury in accordance with the words of the section and offers no elaboration or explanation of "believing".[9] Of course, it may be that the jury will then apply the word as if it included wilful blindness, but no one will ever know.

---

[1]   *Brook* [1993] Crim LR 455, CA.
[2]   *Stagg* [1978] Crim LR 227, CA; *Brook*, above, fn 1.
[3]   [1975] AC 476 at 485; above, para **13–07**.
[4]   *Eighth Report*, Cmnd 2977, at p 64.
[5]   Smith & Hogan 107.
[6]   *Grainge* [1974] 1 All ER 928, CA. Cf *Woods* [1969] 1 QB 447, [1968] 3 All ER 709, CA; *Ismail* [1977] Crim LR 557, CA and commentary. Cf Griew 15.29–15.33, Williams *TBCL* 39–36, *Spencer* [1985] Crim LR 101.
[7]   *Griffiths* (1974) 60 Cr App Rep 14, CA. *Atwal v Massey* [1971] 3 All ER 881, DC, is definitely misleading on this point and seems to have misled the judge in *Pethick* [1980] Crim LR 242, CA where it was said that suspicion, "however strong", does not amount to knowledge.
[8]   (1985) 81 Cr App Rep 260 at 264, [1985] Crim LR 377; criticised in *Forsyth* [1997] Crim LR (August).
[9]   *Reader* (1977) 66 Cr App Rep 33, CA *Harris* (1987) 84 Cr App Rep 75, CA *Toor* (1986) 85 Cr App Rep 116, [1987] Crim LR 122, CA.

13–42   It is sufficient that D knows or believes that the goods, whatever they are, are stolen. His knowledge or belief need not extend to the identity of the thief, or the owner,[1] or the nature of the stolen goods.[2] If D knows he is in possession of a box containing stolen goods, it is no defence that he does not know what the contents are and is shocked to discover that the box contains guns; nor would it be a defence that he believed the box contained stolen watches.[3]

---

[1]   *Fuschillo* [1940] 2 All ER 489; but it may be necessary to name the owner where the property is of a common and indistinctive type: *Gregory* [1972] 2 All ER 861, CA.
[2]   *McCullum* (1973) 57 Cr App Rep 645, CA.
[3]   Ibid at 649–650. An argument that D was not in possession of the contents because he was mistaken as to their nature would probably fail because he knew there was "something wrong" with the goods: *Warner v Metropolitan Police Comr* [1969] 2 AC 256 at 308, [1968] 2 All ER 356 at 390, HL.

B.   DISHONESTY

13–43   D may receive goods knowing or believing them to be stolen and yet not be guilty if, for example, he intends to return them to the true owner or the police.[1] A claim of right will amount to a defence, but it will be difficult to establish such a claim where D knows or believes the goods to be stolen except in the case put above, where he intends to return the goods to the owner. Whether there is dishonesty is presumably now a question of fact for the jury in each case, as in theft.[2]

---

[1] Cf *Matthews* [1950] 1 All ER 137.
[2] *Feely* [1973] QB 530, [1973] 1 All ER 341, CA.

C. PROVING THEFT AND HANDLING

13–44 The general principles of evidence in criminal cases apply to the proof of offences under the Theft Act as they apply to other crimes. This is not the place to examine those rules but their application to some Theft Act offences has created special problems and an exposition of the substantive law which did not examine these matters would be incomplete.

The "doctrine of recent possession". Where D is found in possession of, or dealing with, property which has recently been stolen, a jury may be directed that they may infer that he is guilty of an offence if he offers no explanation or if they are satisfied beyond reasonable doubt that any explanation he has offered is untrue. They are not bound so to infer and should be directed to do so only if satisfied beyond reasonable doubt that D was in fact guilty of the particular offence. The onus of proof remains on the Crown throughout. Whether D offers an explanation or not, the jury must not convict unless they are sure that he committed the offence in question.[1]

These principles are sometimes misleadingly referred to as "the doctrine of recent possession". The "doctrine" is nothing more than the application to this constantly recurring situation of the ordinary principles of circumstantial evidence. Sometimes the correct inference will be that D was the thief (or robber or burglar if the goods were stolen in the course of a robbery or burglary), sometimes that he was a handler. If the lead is stolen off the church roof at midnight and D is found dragging it across a field at 1 a.m., this is very cogent evidence that he stole the lead from the roof. If it is found in his backyard next day and he offers no explanation, or an explanation which is shown to be untrue, as to how he came by it, this is slightly less cogent evidence that he was the thief but very persuasive that he either stole it or received it knowing it to be stolen. As the time lengthens between the theft and discovery of D's connection with the stolen property, the weight of the evidence diminishes but it will vary according to the nature of the property stolen and other circumstances. One relevant circumstance will be the nature of D's conduct in relation to the goods, but the same principles apply whether D is charged with receiving or with one of the other forms of handling. So in *Ball*,[2] it was held that there was evidence of handling otherwise than by receiving where D assisted the thief in physically handling stolen goods and accompanying him on an expedition to sell the stolen property.

---

[1] *Abramovitch* (1914) 11 Cr App Rep 45; *Aves* (1950) 34 Cr App Rep 159; *Hepworth and Fearnley* [1955] 2 QB 600.
[2] (1983) 77 Cr App Rep 131, [1983] Crim LR 546, CA.

13–45 Because of the impossibility of predicting which inference the jury will decide to be the right one, the prosecution may find it convenient to include two counts, count 1, say, for robbery and count 2 for receiving the goods which were stolen in the course of that robbery. These two counts are mutually contradictory. If D is guilty of robbery he came by the goods in the course of the stealing and therefore cannot be guilty of the alleged handling;[1] but, if he is guilty of handling, he received the goods otherwise than in the course of the stealing and is not guilty of robbery. On count 1 the prosecution are alleging that D received the goods in the course of the theft. On count 2 they are alleging that he did not receive the goods in the course of the theft. It is established[2] that it is lawful to include two such "mutually destructive" counts in an indictment where there is a prima facie case on each count.

---

[1]   Section 22 (1), above.
[2]   *Bellman* [1989] 1 All ER 22, [1989] 2 WLR 37, HL.

13–46 The difficulty which then arises is that a jury may be quite certain that the defendant was either the thief or a receiver but not satisfied beyond reasonable doubt that he was the one rather than the other. Indeed, it may be that there is no evidence on which they could possibly be satisfied that he was the one rather than the other. In that case, it appears that neither offence is proved beyond reasonable doubt and the only proper course is a complete acquittal – a conclusion satisfactory to no one but the accused. A solution which has been adopted in some jurisdictions, following *Langmead* (1864),[1] is to direct the jury that, if they are satisfied beyond reasonable doubt that D was either the thief or a receiver, they may convict of the offence which they think more probable – i.e. it is enough that they are satisfied on a balance of probabilities that D was the thief, or that he was the receiver. As the jury is unlikely to find that the evidence is exactly evenly balanced, this is a practical solution. It was, however, rejected by the Privy Council in *A-G of Hong Kong v Yip Kai-foon*.[2] It was inconsistent with the principle that the jury must be satisfied beyond reasonable doubt of the accused's guilt of a particular offence. *Langmead* had not been cited in any English judgment and was not found a persuasive authority for the proposition relied on.

In *Yip Kai-foon*, D was indicted for robbery. In Hong Kong a jury may convict of handling on a robbery charge and D was so convicted. The Hong Kong Court of Appeal quashed his conviction, holding that it was incumbent on the prosecution to prove beyond reasonable doubt that the receiving took place otherwise than in the course of the robbery. The Privy Council, following *Cash*,[3] disagreed. The jury had been rightly directed to consider the robbery charge first. Once they had decided that they were not satisfied beyond reasonable doubt that D was guilty of robbery, he was to be presumed to be innocent of the theft of the goods and it followed that any handling that occurred took place "otherwise then in the course of the stealing" so there was no need for more than a passing reference to those words. This is a novel use of the presumption of innocence against a defendant. Because the jury are not satisfied beyond reasonable doubt that D was guilty of theft it is apparently to be conclusively presumed that he was not guilty of that offence. If the jury are satisfied that he was guilty of one offence or the other, it follows inevitably that he was guilty of handling. But this is arbitrary. The outcome depends on which offence the jury consider first. Since, *ex hypothesi*, they are not satisfied that D committed that offence, they will convict of the second offence.

---

[1]   (1864) Le & Ca 427.
[2]   [1988] AC 642, [1988] 1 All ER 153, followed in *Foreman* [1991] Crim LR 702 and *Ryan and French v DPP* [1994] Crim LR 457, DC; but see commentaries thereon.
[3]   Above, para **13–33**.

13–47 A person guilty of handling stolen goods almost inevitably dishonestly appropriates, or aids and abets the appropriation, of property belonging to another and so is guilty of theft as well. In *Devall*,[1] where D was charged in two counts with stealing a generator and handling the stolen generator, the Court of Appeal approved, *obiter*, of the judge's direction to the jury that they could convict on an alternative basis of such "a second appropriation". D had equally stolen the goods and committed the theft charged whether he was the original thief or a thief-by-handling. But the court suggested that there should be a separate count giving particulars of the second appropriation. There is a difficulty about this. If the jury cannot decide whether D was the thief or a handler, they cannot be satisfied that he was guilty on the first count; and they cannot be satisfied that he was guilty on the second count. We are no farther forward. An alternative is a single count of theft drawn in sufficiently wide terms to cover both the first and second appropriations. This solution was found attractive by the Court of Appeal in *More*[2] and seems in effect to have been the solution adopted in *Shelton*.[3] There seems to be no particular difficulty about alleging that D committed theft between two specified dates – the dates of the theft and of D's being found in possession. But it is not a case where it is merely uncertain on which day a particular act was done. Two distinct acts are envisaged and the prosecution are saying that D committed the one or the other. It has been held that it is not sufficient to prove that D attempted to pervert the course of justice either (a) by making false allegations, or (b) by resiling from those allegations at an ensuing trial.[4] This is very close to the case envisaged and the decision may be a fatal objection. Perhaps legislation is the only satisfactory solution to the problem.

[1] [1984] Crim LR 428. Cf. *Falconer-Atlee* (1973) 58 Cr App R 348, CA and *Japes* [1994] Crim LR 605, CA.
[2] (1987) 86 Cr App Rep 234 at 238.
[3] [1986] Crim LR 637.
[4] *Tsang Ping-Nam* [1981] 1 WLR 1462.

13–48 Because of the difficulty of proving guilty knowledge, the Larceny Act provided for the admission of certain evidence on a receiving charge which would not be admissible in criminal cases generally. The Theft Act has corresponding but somewhat different provisions. By s. 27 (3):

"Where a person is being proceeded against for handling stolen goods (but not for any offence other than handling stolen goods), then at any stage of the proceedings, if evidence has been given of his having or arranging to have in his possession the goods the subject of the charge, or of his undertaking or assisting in, or arranging to undertake or assist in, their retention, removal, disposal or realisation, the following evidence shall be admissible for the purpose of proving that he knew or believed the goods to be stolen goods—
(a) evidence that he has had in his possession, or has undertaken or assisted in the retention, removal, disposal or realisation of, stolen goods from any theft taking place not earlier than twelve months before the offence charged; and
(b) (provided that seven days' notice in writing has been given to him of the intention to prove the conviction) evidence that he has within the five years preceding the date of the offence charged been convicted of theft or of handling stolen goods."

Whereas under (b) the previous conviction must have occurred within five years preceding the offence charged, the possession, etc. under (a) must have occurred "not earlier" than twelve months before the offence charged. The possession, etc. which is admissible under (a) may have taken place later than the offence charged.[1] The section has been strictly construed. Paragraph (a) allows proof of the fact of possession of stolen goods and probably of their description but not of the circumstances in which D came into possession of them.[2] Under paragraph (b) it was formerly held that not even the description of the goods is allowed: "the prosecution is not permitted to go further than to relate the fact of conviction for handling stolen goods and where and when". However in *Hacker*[3] the House of Lords has held that paragraph (b) must now be read with s. 73 (2) of the Police and Criminal Evidence Act 1984 (PACE) which provides that a certificate of conviction on indictment which is admitted to prove the conviction must give the substance and effect of the indictment. As was stated in the Court of Appeal and repeated by Lord Slynn, "[The jury] might, quite sensibly, take the point that if it was handling of a stolen motorcar it might be quite different from handling of half a pound of sugar." It appears to be assumed that the conviction is evidence that the convicted person committed the offence. By s. 74 (3) of PACE the person proved to have been convicted is taken to have committed the offence until the contrary is proved but only where the evidence is relevant for a reason other than to show that the accused has a disposition to commit the kind of offence with which he is charged. It is not clear whether the reason for the admissibility of a conviction under s. 27 is to show the disposition of the accused to handle stolen goods.

---

[1] *Davis* [1972] Crim LR 431, CA.
[2] *Bradley* (1980) 70 Cr App Rep 200, CA; criticised in [1980] Crim LR 173.
[3] [1994] 1 All ER 45, [1994] 1 WLR 1659, HL.

13–49 It appears that these provisions supplement and do not replace the common law.[1] Thus a handling of goods stolen earlier than twelve months before the handling now charged might be admissible at common law if it fell within the "similar facts" rule of admissibility.[2] So too might a conviction of theft or handling after the date of the offence charged or more than five years before it – though this is rather unlikely. Section 27 (3) imposes limitations upon admissibility which do not exist at common law. The evidence in question may not be given until after some evidence of the *actus reus* has been given; and evidence admissible under (b) may not be given without seven days' notice in writing of intention to tender it. Commonly, evidence admissible under the Act will not be admissible at common law because there is an insufficient degree of similarity or other nexus. Where the evidence is admissible at common law as well as under the Act, it is submitted that the statutory restrictions must be observed. If the evidence is inadmissible under the Act – for example it is a handling of goods stolen more than twelve months before the offence charged – but is admissible at common law because of the striking similarity of the facts, the statutory restrictions cannot apply. It is submitted, however, that the rule requiring evidence of the *actus reus* of the offence charged to be given before the evidence of the other handling or theft ought to be observed as a rule of practice. If it is a desirable precaution in the case of evidence sanctioned by statute, it is equally desirable in the case of that admitted by the common law.

---

[1] *Davis*, para **13–48**, fn 1, above.
[2] Cross *Evidence* (7th edition) Ch 9.

13–50 Although evidence has been given of the *actus reus* – for example that D was in possession – D may dispute that fact. Evidence admitted under s. 27 (3) may not be considered on the question whether D was in possession. It is admissible for one purpose only – to prove the knowledge or belief that the goods were stolen. Since proof of possession also requires proof of a mental element, these questions may become virtually indistinguishable. In *Wilkins*,[1] evidence was given that stolen goods were found in D's garden and behind a drawer in her bedroom. This was evidence that she was in possession, permitting the admission of evidence under s. 27 (3). Her defence was that the articles had been put there without her knowledge, that she did not know they were there, and, accordingly, that she was never in possession. Since the judge's direction failed to make clear that the evidence could be taken into account only on the issue of guilty knowledge or belief that the goods were stolen, the convictions were quashed. Where there is a danger that the jury may think the evidence relevant to some other issue, the judge might be wise to exercise his discretion to exclude the evidence.

---

[1]   [1975] 2 All ER 734, CA.

---

3   DISHONESTLY RETAINING A WRONGFUL CREDIT

13–51 Section 24A of the Theft Act 1968 (inserted by s. 2 of the Theft (Amendment) Act 1996) provides:

"(1) A person is guilty of an offence if–
  (a) a wrongful credit has been made to an account kept by him or in respect of which he has any right or interest,
  (b) he knows or believes that the credit is wrongful; and
  (c) he dishonestly fails to take such steps as are reasonable in the circumstances to secure that the credit is cancelled.
(2) References to a credit are to a credit of an amount of money
(3) A credit to an account is wrongful if it is the credit side of a money transfer obtained contrary to section 15A of this Act."

The offence is punishable under s. 24A on indictment with imprisonment for ten years.

13–52 The effect is that D1, a person who has committed an offence under the new s.15A,[1] commits a second offence if he does not take steps within a reasonable time to divest himself of his ill-gotten gains. The provision is not, of course, aimed at him but at D2, where D1 has procured the crediting, not of his own, but of D2's account. If this was done with D2's connivance, D2 would be guilty as a secondary party to D1's offence under s. 15A. There would be no need to invoke s. 24A. Suppose, however, that the credit was made without D2's connivance. One day D2 finds that an unexpected credit has been made to his account. As soon as he knows or believes that the credit has been made in such circumstances as amount to an offence under s. 15A he comes under a duty to divest himself of this unforeseen windfall. If he fails to do so within a reasonable time he commits the offence. It is an offence of omission,[2] rather like theft where s. 5 (4) applies. Whereas, however, s. 5 (4) requires D to intend to "make restoration" of the property, s. 24A (1) (c) merely requires him to cancel the credit. Does he do this merely by withdrawing the money to spend on riotous living?

---

[1]   Above, para **4–64**.
[2]   The argument of the Law Commission that this is necessary is in Law Com No 243 at p 39.

13–53 The Act does not stop there. It extends to other conduct which was not an offence even before the decision of the House of Lords in *Preddy*. Section 24A (4) provides:

> "(4) A credit to an account is also wrongful to the extent that it derives from–
>   (a) theft;
>   (b) an offence under section 15A of this Act;
>   (c) blackmail; or
>   (d) stolen goods."

So D2 may be guilty of the offence if:
(i)   D1 steals money and pays it into D2's account;
(ii) D1 procures a wrongful credit to his own account and then transfers funds from it to D2's account;
(iii) D1 obtains money by blackmail and pays that money into D2's account;
(iv) D1 receives stolen money and pays it into D2's account.

In each of these cases the credit in D2's account is a new item of property – a thing in action belonging to D2 – which has never been "in the hands" of a thief or handler and so is not "stolen goods" within s. 24 (2). D2 is not guilty of handling by retaining it. Now, however, he commits an offence under s. 24A (1) if he dishonestly fails to cancel "the wrongful credit" within a reasonable time. Presumably he can cancel the wrongful credit and escape liability under s. 24A by immediately withdrawing the money. But s. 24A (8) provides that any money which is withdrawn from a wrongful credit will be stolen goods and subject to the general law of handling so D2 may commit an offence under s. 22.

13–54   An incidental effect is that the thief, blackmailer or handler who pays the proceeds of his offence into his own account commits another offence when he fails to take reasonable steps to cancel the credit. This is so because the Law Commission thought "It would be difficult, if not impossible, to devise a simple way of excluding the case where A dishonestly secures a credit to his own account, while including the case where A dishonestly secures a credit to B's."[1] The Commission comforted themselves with the consideration that there was already an enormous degree of overlap in the existing offences under the Theft Acts.

---

[1]   Law Com No 243, paras 6.16–6.17.

13–55   Section 24A (5) provides that it is immaterial whether an account is overdrawn before or after a credit is made. So if D2's account is overdrawn to the tune of £100 when a wrongful credit of £50 arrives, he is under a duty, somehow, to get his overdraft restored to its former level.

There is no provision corresponding to s. 24 (3)[1] (stolen goods cease to be "stolen" when they are restored to lawful custody or when the owner and any others claiming through him have ceased to have any right to restitution of the goods). Nor is there any exemption for the bona-fide purchaser such as is to be found in s. 3 (2).[2] Suppose that D sells his car in good faith to A who pays him with stolen money. After learning that the money was stolen D spends it. He did not commit any offence before the enactment of s. 24A. He still commits no offence if A paid him in cash and he spends the cash. But if D paid the cash into his own bank account, or if he was paid by a cheque which he has paid into that account, he has received a wrongful credit and it appears that he will (subject to proof of dishonesty) commit an offence under s. 24A when he spends the money, because he has failed to take reasonable steps to disgorge. That would create not only an unsatisfactory anomaly but also a conflict with the civil law. A transferee of stolen currency for value and without notice gets a good title: *Miller v Race*.[3] The money, whether in cash or in the bank, is surely his to dispose of as he chooses. How then can he be guilty of a crime by doing so? It may be that a court will think it necessary to read into s. 24A (1) (c) some such qualification as "except where no person has any right to restitution of the credit," on the ground that Parliament could not have intended to change, or create a conflict with, such a fundamental rule of the civil law. This would introduce a limitation to the same effect as that relating to stolen goods generally in s. 24 (4).

---

[1]   Above, para **13–10**
[2]   Above, para **2–43**
[3]   (1758) 1 Burr 452.

---

4   ADVERTISING REWARDS FOR RETURN OF GOODS STOLEN OR LOST

13–56   It is a summary offence to advertise publicly for the return of stolen or lost goods, using any words to the effect that no questions will be asked, or no inquiries made, or that any money paid for the goods will be repaid.[1] The history of this provision goes back to 1828. Until the Common Informers Act 1951 it was not punishable in criminal proceedings but was enforceable by any person who sued in debt for the sum of £50 which the defendant forfeited for every offence – "a penal action". The 1951 Act abolished penal actions and provided that conduct formerly subject to this procedure should be an offence punishable on summary conviction by a fine (now a fine not exceeding level 3 of the standard scale). After some hesitation, the CLRC decided to keep the offence as "advertisements of this kind may encourage dishonesty".[2] In *Denham v Scott*,[3] it was held that the offence is one of strict liability so that the advertising manager of a free weekly newspaper in which such an advertisement appeared was guilty, as the controlling mind of the company for the purpose of publication, although he had not inspected the advertisement before it was published and did not know it had appeared.

---

[1]   1968 Act, s. 23, below, p 267.
[2]   *Eighth Report*, Cmnd 2977, para 144.
[3]   (1983) 77 Cr App Rep 210, [1983] Crim LR 558, DC.

PROCEDURE

13–57   By s. 27 (1):

"Any number of persons may be charged in one indictment with reference to the same theft, with having at different times or at the same time handled all or any of the stolen goods, and the persons so charged may be tried together."

If £500 is stolen from a bank and the thief, on separate occasions, hands £100 to each of five persons, all five may be tried together for handling the stolen money, though they have no connection with one another except through the thief.

By s. 27 (2):

"On the trial of two or more persons indicted for jointly handling any stolen goods the jury may find any of the accused guilty if the jury are satisfied that he handled all or any of the stolen goods, whether or not he did so jointly with the other accused or any of them."

Under the rule in *DPP v Merriman*[1] where two persons are jointly charged with committing the same act and it emerges that they were not acting in concert, each may be convicted of committing the act independently. The subsection goes further in that it allows conviction not only where there is separate participation in a single act but where there are different acts in relation to the same stolen goods. In *French*,[2] D received stolen goods and took them to E's shop where E received them. It was held that they were properly jointly indicted, although the handlings were quite separate and the case against each must be considered separately.

---

[1] [1973] AC 584, [1972] 3 All ER 42, [1972] 3 WLR 545, HL.
[2] [1973] Crim LR 632, CA.

CHAPTER 14

Enforcement and Procedure

1 SEARCH FOR STOLEN GOODS

14–01 Power to issue a warrant or authority to search premises for stolen goods is given by s. 26 of the 1968 Act.[1] Only a policeman may be authorised to search, though the information may be sworn by any person. Other enactments authorising the issue of search warrants to persons other than police officers are expressly preserved. In any such Act a reference to stolen goods shall be construed in accordance with s. 24 of the Theft Act.[2] The power of search includes goods which have been obtained by blackmail and by deception.

It is submitted that the constable's authority to seize goods under s. 26 (3) extends to any goods on the premises in question which he believes to be stolen goods, whether they are named in the warrant or not.[3] Even if the section did not justify such a seizure, it would be lawful under the Police and Criminal Evidence Act 1984, s. 19, or by the common law.[4]

---

[1] Below, p 269.
[2] See s. 32 (2) (b), below, p 272.
[3] Contrast the wording of s. 42 (1) of the Larceny Act 1916.
[4] *Chic Fashions (West Wales) Ltd v Jones* [1968] 2 QB 299, [1968] 1 All ER 229, CA.

---

2 JURISDICTION

A. TERRITORIAL

14–02 It is a general rule of construction that unless there is something which points to a contrary intention, a statute will be taken to apply to the United Kingdom and only to the United Kingdom. The Theft Acts expressly provide that, with small exceptions, they do not extend to Scotland or Northern Ireland.[1] The majority of the House of Lords in *Treacy v DPP*[2] assumed that the general principle of construction applied to offences under the 1968 Act, with the result that they are triable only if committed in England and Wales – but this will have to be read in the light of the provisions of the Criminal Justice Act 1993 when they are brought into force.[3]

An exception is created by the 1968 Act, ss. 14 and 33. Where a person is charged with theft, attempted theft, robbery, attempted robbery or assault with intent to rob, with respect to the theft of a mail-bag or postal packet, or the contents of either when in course of transmission in the British postal area,[4] then he may be tried in England and Wales without proof that the offence was committed there.

---

[1] Section 36 (3) of the 1968 Act and s. 7 (3) of the 1978 Act.
[2] [1971] AC 537, [1971] 1 All ER 110, HL.
[3] Above, paras **1–18** to **1–24**.
[4] Section 14 (2).

14–03 By Part I of Schedule 3, the provisions of the Post Office Act 1953 which relate to stealing and receiving were repealed for England and Wales (but not for Scotland). Anyone prosecuted in England and Wales for stealing or handling mail-bags, etc. must therefore be prosecuted under the appropriate section of the Theft Act. If the charge is one of handling mail-bags, etc., then it seems that it must be proved that the offence was committed in England and Wales. The other offences under the Post Office Act, including those akin to but not amounting to theft, such as unlawfully taking away or opening a mail-bag, continue in force.

B. COURTS

(a) The Crown Court

14–04 The Courts Act 1971 abolished courts of assize and quarter sessions and all proceedings on indictment are now brought in the Crown Court. Of the indictable offences under the Theft Acts, aggravated burglary, burglary in the circumstances described in Sch 1, para 28 of the Magistrates' Courts Act 1980 are "Class 3" offences and the remainder are "Class 4" offences.[1] The effect is that all the offences may be listed for trial by a High Court judge or by a circuit judge or recorder but the Class 4 offences may be tried by an assistant recorder and will not be listed for trial by a High Court judge except with his consent or that of a presiding judge.

---

[1]   *Practice Direction (Crown Court: Allocation of Business)* [1995] 2 Cr App Rep 295.

(b) Magistrates' courts

14–05 All indictable offences under the Theft Acts 1968 and 1978 are triable either way except –
  (a) robbery, aggravated burglary, blackmail and assault with intent to rob;
  (b) burglary comprising the commission of, or an intention to commit, an offence which is triable only on indictment;
  (c) burglary in a dwelling if any person in the dwelling was subjected to violence or the threat of violence.[1]
The offences triable only on indictment which are likely to be relevant under (b) are causing grievous bodily harm with intent, contrary to s. 18 of the Offences against the Person Act 1861, rape and damaging property with intent to endanger life, contrary to the Criminal Damage Act 1971, s. 1 (2). "Dwelling" under (c) will include inhabited vehicles or vessels.

---

[1]   Magistrates' Courts Act 1980, Sch 1, para 28.

3   RESTITUTION[1]

14–06 The Theft Act 1968, s. 28, provides a summary procedure whereby the court before which a person is convicted of certain offences may order that the property concerned be restored to the owner.[2] Under the old law, conviction might affect the title to goods. This is no longer so.[3] Who is the owner of property is a question for the civil law and the fact that there has been a conviction of any criminal offence with respect to the property is irrelevant, so far as title is concerned. Section 28 (1) provides:

"Where goods have been stolen, and either a person is convicted of any offence with reference to the theft (whether or not the stealing is the gist of his offence) or a person is convicted of any other offence but such an offence as aforesaid is taken into consideration in determining his sentence, the court by or before which the offender is convicted may on the conviction exercise any of the following powers–

(a) the court may order anyone having possession or control of the goods to restore them to any person entitled to recover them from him; or

(b) on the application of a person entitled to recover from the person convicted any other goods directly or indirectly representing the first-mentioned goods (as being the proceeds of any disposal or realisation of the whole or part of them or of goods so representing them), the court may order those other goods to be delivered or transferred to the applicant; or

(c) the court may order that a sum not exceeding the value of the first-mentioned goods shall be paid out of any money of the person convicted which was taken out of his possession on his apprehension to any person who, if those goods were in the possession of the person convicted, would be entitled to recover them from him."

---

[1] Macleod, "Restitution under the Theft Act" [1968] Crim LR 577.

[2] Police have no power to retain property seized from the accused solely in anticipation of a compensation, forfeiture or restitution order being made: *Malone v Metropolitan Police Comr* [1980] QB 49, [1979] 1 All ER 256, CA.

[3] Section 31 (2), below, p 272.

A. STOLEN GOODS

14–07 "Goods" are defined in s. 34 (2) (b) which is considered above.[1] "Stolen" bears the same meaning as in s. 24 (4)[2] and thus extends to goods obtained by blackmail or by deception and money dishonestly withdrawn from an account to which a wrongful credit has been made, to the extent that the money derives from the credit.[3]

---

[1] See para **13–02**.

[2] Above, para **13–06**.

[3] Sections 24 (4), 24A (8) and 28 (6).

B. CONVICTION

14–08 The court's power arises on a conviction, or a taking into consideration, "of any offence with reference to the theft[1] (whether or not the stealing is the gist of his offence)". The convictions would include handling the stolen goods, robbery, burglary and aggravated burglary. The two latter offences do not necessarily involve theft and it would, of course, be necessary for the court to be satisfied on the evidence admissible under s. 28 (1),[2] that a theft of the goods which were the object of the burglary had in fact been committed. It is not necessary that the conviction should be an offence against the Act. It might be, for example, a conviction of assisting an arrestable offender under s. 4 (1) of the Criminal Law Act 1967 or of concealing an arrestable offence under s. 5 (1) of that Act; of conspiracy or an attempt to commit theft where there is proof that the theft was actually committed; or of a forgery done for the purpose of committing the theft in question.

---

[1] That is, the theft, blackmail, deception or wrongful credit.

[2] Below, para **14–14**.

C.   AGAINST WHOM THE ORDER MAY BE MADE

14–09   An order under s. 28 (1) (a) may be made against anyone having possession or control of the goods. A bona-fide purchaser may thus be ordered to surrender the goods to someone with a better title. The order may be made against a person holding the goods on behalf of another as, for example, a servant who has custody of goods, possession being in the employer.

An order under s. 28 (1) (b)[1] may be made only against the person convicted.

---

[1]   Cf *Eighth Report*, Cmnd 2977, para 165.

D.   IN WHOSE FAVOUR THE ORDER MAY BE MADE

14–10   An order may be made in favour of any person who is entitled to recover the goods from the person in possession or control (para (a)) or who would be entitled to recover the goods if they were in the possession of the person convicted (para (c)); and any applicant[1] entitled to recover the proceeds of the stolen goods from the person convicted (para (b)).

As has been pointed out above,[2] it is only in exceptional cases that the owner of goods has a literal right to recover them, even from a thief, in civil law. Generally his remedy is an action in conversion in which he will be awarded damages. It is submitted that, as with "right to restitution", so also "entitled to recover" must be given a broad interpretation to extend to cases in which the claimant would be able to succeed in an action based upon his proprietary rights in the thing in question. This would therefore extend to a case in which the ownership has passed to the rogue under a voidable transaction which the owner has rescinded.

The person entitled will generally be the victim of the theft or someone standing in his shoes, as his executor, administrator or trustee in bankruptcy. If the victim has received compensation for the loss of the stolen goods under an insurance policy, then the insurance company may be subrogated to his rights.[3] If the victim had not the best right to possession of the goods (as, for example, if he himself had stolen them from another) the person with that right is the person entitled.

---

[1]   *Thibeault* (1983) Cr App Rep 201, CA.
[2]   In discussing the meaning of "a right to restitution" in s. 24 (3); para **13–12**.
[3]   *Church* (1970) 55 Cr App Rep 65 at 71.

E.   THE PROPERTY IN RESPECT OF WHICH THE ORDER MAY BE MADE

14–11   The property in respect of which the order may be made is as follows:

Section 28 (1) (a): such of the goods[1] which have been stolen as are in the possession or control of the person against whom the order is made.

Section 28 (1) (b): such of the proceeds of the goods which have been stolen as are in the possession or control of the person against whom the order is made.

Section 28 (1) (c): any money of the person convicted which was taken out of his possession on his apprehension, not exceeding the value of the stolen goods.

Two questions arise here. The first relates to the meaning of "taken out of his possession on his apprehension". This is not confined, as might have been supposed, to money which is taken from D's person when he is arrested. In *Ferguson*,[2] it was held to include money in a safe deposit box at Harrods, of which D had the key, which was properly appropriated by the police as the suspected proceeds of the theft, ten days after D's arrest. This decision seems to attribute to "possession" its legal rather than its popular meaning but the court said that it was "difficult to think of a clearer case of money being in the possession" of the accused and that, giving "'on his apprehension' a commonsense meaning", the money was so taken. If the money had been deposited in a bank account, the result would have been different since D would have been only a creditor of the bank and not in possession. It seems then that money at D's home or in his car is in his possession for this purpose.

Presumably the taking must be lawful. The police have no right to seize money which they do not reasonably believe to be the proceeds of a crime or evidence of its commission. It is submitted that money unlawfully seized, though literally taken from the accused on his apprehension, could not be used to compensate the victim. The provision may thus work somewhat capriciously. Money wrongly but reasonably suspected to be the proceeds of the theft may be taken and used to compensate, but other money in the possession of the accused may not. It is odd that a wrong, though reasonable, suspicion should make the difference.

Any provision containing the word "possession" is likely to present problems. In *Parker*,[3] D apparently threw away a wallet containing money shortly before his arrest, and this was found in a garden by the police the following day; the court refused to answer the question whether the money was taken from his possession on his apprehension. On one view, he had abandoned possession by throwing the wallet away; but so to hold would seem to depart from the broad "commonsense" view taken in *Ferguson*.[4]

Finally, the money must be "money of the person convicted" so that if, as in *Ferguson*, any doubt is raised as to D's ownership of the money, no order may be made.

---

[1]   Cf s. 34 (2) (b), above, paras **13–02** to **13–04**.
[2]   [1970] 2 All ER 820, CA.
[3]   [1970] 2 All ER 458, CA.
[4]   See fn 2 above.

14–12   The second problem concerns the extent to which D may be required to make compensation. Section 28 (1) (c) says to the extent of "a sum not exceeding the value of the first mentioned goods" – i.e. the goods which have been stolen. This presents no difficulty where D is convicted of the theft. He may, however, be convicted of an offence "with reference to the theft" and his participation may relate only to a small part of the stolen property. For example, it may be proved that £1,000 was stolen from a bank and that D dishonestly received £10 of that money which was taken from him when he was arrested. On a literal reading, it would seem that D might be ordered to pay £990 out of other money taken from him on his arrest which was not the proceeds of the theft. However, in *Parker*,[1] the court held that, whatever the proper construction of the section:

> "If a man is charged with handling stolen goods and the whole of the goods in respect of which he has been convicted are recovered, then it must, we hold, be an incorrect exercise of any discretion which exists under the section to make him pay compensation in addition in respect of other goods which are not the subject of a charge against him."

---

[1]   [1970] 2 All ER 458 at 462 to 463.

F.   COMPENSATION TO A THIRD PARTY

14–13   By s. 28 (3):

"Where under subsection (1) above[1] the court on a person's conviction makes an order under paragraph (a) for the restoration of any goods, and it appears to the court that the person convicted has sold the goods to a person acting in good faith, or has borrowed money on the security of them from a person so acting, the court may order that there shall be paid to the purchaser or lender, out of any money of the person convicted which was taken out of his possession on his apprehension, a sum not exceeding the amount paid for the purchase by the purchaser or, as the case may be, the amount owed to the lender in respect of the loan."

Thus if D has stolen a necklace from P and pawned it with Q for a loan of £100, on D's conviction, Q may be ordered to restore the necklace to P and be compensated out of the money taken from D on his apprehension. The provision is confined to money taken from D on his apprehension so Q will have no remedy under s. 28 if D, when apprehended, is wearing a gold watch but carrying no money, though he has large sums in his bank. Q, may, however, be compensated by an order made under s. 35 of the Powers of Criminal Courts Act 1973.[2]

---

[1]   See above, para **14–06**.
[2]   Below, para **14–21**.

G.   WHEN AN ORDER SHOULD BE MADE

14–14   It is provided by s. 28 (4)[1] that: "The court shall not exercise the powers conferred by this section unless in the opinion of the court the relevant facts sufficiently appear from the evidence given at the trial or the available documents, together with admissions made by or on behalf of any person in connection with any proposed exercise of the powers . . . "

The court must be satisfied on the evidence given at the trial that an order should be made; and the trial concludes when sentence is passed.[2] The court may not embark on a new inquiry at the end of the trial. The words, "on the conviction" in s. 28 (1), mean the same as "immediately after the conviction" in the Forfeiture Act 1870, s. 4 (repealed).

The court is never bound to make an order under s. 28; when the condition in s. 28 (4) is satisfied it is a matter for the discretion of the court. Clearly, however, when the relevant facts do sufficiently appear, an order should generally be made unless there is a real dispute as to the title to the goods. Even when the facts are absolutely clear the question of entitlement to the goods may involve difficult questions of law. Where they have been transferred to a third party, many of the subtleties of the old law of larceny by a trick and false pretences may arise. If there is any real dispute or any doubt as to title, then an order should not be made; the parties should be left to their civil remedies. Only in the plainest cases, where there is no doubt of fact or law, should an order be made.[3]

"In practice the power will be exercisable only where there is no real dispute as to ownership. It would seriously hamper the work of the criminal courts if at the end of a trial they had to investigate disputed titles."[4]

No right to be heard is given to a third party against whom an order might be made – and it has been said that he has no *locus standi*,[5] but it is submitted that it would be improper to make an order against a party without allowing him to be heard on the subject,[6] particularly since, where the order is made by the Crown Court, the third party has no right of appeal.[7] An order made against a person not afforded a hearing would seem to offend against the rules of natural justice and, where made by a magistrates' court, liable to be quashed by *certiorari*; but *certiorari* will not lie to the Crown Court, which is part of the Supreme Court.

[1]   Below, p 270.
[2]   *Church* (1970) 55 Cr App Rep 65, CA.
[3]   *Ferguson* [1970] 2 All ER 820, CA.
[4]   *Eighth Report*, Cmnd 2977, para 164: "it would probably be impracticable (as well as being undesirable) that an order should be made in any but straightforward cases".
[5]   *Ferguson* [1970] 2 All ER 820 at 822.
[6]   ". . . certainly it is intended that he should be heard, either in person or through counsel" – Parl. Debate Official Report (HL) 290, col 865, per Lord Stonham. Cf *Macklin* (1850) 5 Cox CC 216.
[7]   Below, para **14–18**.

H.   EXERCISE OF MORE THAN ONE POWER

14–15   The question may arise as to whether the court may exercise more than one of its powers in respect of the same theft.[1] Though paras (a), (b) and (c) of s. 28 (1) are expressed in the alternative, s. 28 (2) contemplates that an order may be made against the thief under both (b) and (c). The situation contemplated is that where the thief has disposed of the goods for less than their true value. If power is exercised under (b) to award these proceeds to the applicant, the balance may be made up from money taken from D on his apprehension. Normally, where the power under (a) is exercised to restore the goods to the owner, no further compensation will be required. If, however, only a part of the goods can be restored by exercising power (a), there seems to be no reason why power (b) or (c) should not be exercised in relation to the remainder.

Where P gets the whole of his goods back under (a) but they are damaged, he might succeed in an application for compensation under (c). The court might also exercise its power under s. 35 of the Powers of Criminal Courts Act 1973.[2] There seems to be nothing to prevent the court exercising these various statutory powers on the same occasion and in combination if it thinks it just to do so.

Where D has succeeded in passing a good title to a bona-fide purchaser (B), and the court, in the exercise of power (a), consequently orders possession to be given to B, may it then exercise power (c) in favour of the original owner, A? This is the converse of a more usual situation expressly provided for in s. 28 (3)[3] where the bona-fide purchaser gets no title and consequently is ordered to surrender the goods to A. It is submitted that the above question should be answered in the affirmative. If the goods were in the possession of D, A "would be entitled to recover them from him". The superior right of B would not defeat an action by A against D. A therefore satisfies the condition in para (c), and it seems entirely right that he should be compensated out of money taken from D where D has succeeded in depriving him of his title to the goods. The situation will probably rarely arise, since it will not often be absolutely clear that D has passed a good title to B; and where there is a doubt, the court must refrain from making orders.[4]

[1]   Cf Macleod [1968] Crim LR at 586–587.
[2]   Below, para **14–21**.

3   Above, para **14–13**.
4   Above, para **14–14**.

I. ENFORCEMENT OF AN ORDER

14–16   The Act makes no provision for the enforcement of orders made under s. 28.

"Disobedience to an order made by a court of assize or quarter sessions for the handing over of goods could, we think, be dealt with as contempt. Disobedience to a similar order made by a magistrates' court could be dealt with under s. 54 (3) of the Magistrates' Courts Act 1952."[1]

1   *Eighth Report*, Cmnd 2977, para 163. See now Magistrates' Courts Act 1980, s. 63 (3).

J. THE EFFECT OF AN ORDER

14–17   The Act contains no provision similar to that in the Police (Property) Act 1897, protecting the person in whose favour an order is made against claims to the property on the expiration of six months from the order.[1] It is submitted that an order should have no effect whatever on the rights under the civil law of any claimant to the property, except possibly where those rights consist in a merely possessory title.[2]

It may frequently happen that a magistrates' court is in a position to order the return of the property either under the Police (Property) Act or under the Theft Act, and, when this is so, the court should make it clear under which provision it is acting since there is the difference in effect referred to.[3] In general it is thought that it would be better to utilise the power under the Theft Act, since the 1897 Act may interfere in a rather arbitrary fashion with the rights at civil law, even of persons who are unaware that the proceedings are taking place.[4]

1   Below, para **14–24**.
2   Cf *Irving v National Provincial Bank Ltd* [1962] 2 QB 73, [1962] 1 All ER 157, CA.
3   Moreover the order under the Theft Act does not take effect if the conviction is quashed (below, para **14–20**) whereas that under the Police (Property) Act is quite unaffected by the quashing of any conviction since the power does not depend upon the existence of a conviction, but only of a charge.
4   Below, para **14–24**.

K. APPEAL

(a)   From an order in the Crown Court

14–18   It has now been decided[1] that where an order is made against a person convicted on indictment, he may appeal against it to the Court of Appeal. Though the point has not been made clear by the courts, it seems that the appeal is an appeal against sentence under s. 9 of the Criminal Appeal Act 1968; for, by s. 50 (1) of that Act:

" . . . 'sentence', in relation to an offence, includes any order made by a court when dealing with an offender . . . "

It was held that this was wide enough to include an order made under s. 4 of the Forfeiture Act 1870 for payment of money by way of satisfaction or compensation,[2] and it would seem to follow that an order made under s. 28 is also part of the sentence.[3] Leave to appeal against sentence must be obtained from the Court of Appeal.

Where an order is made against a person other than the person convicted no appeal by him will lie;[4] though if the convicted person appeals, the court may then annul or vary[5] a restitution order made against a third party. This is anomalous – particularly since it is possible for an order to be made against a third party who has not been heard; but it will be of no practical importance if orders are made only in undisputed and straightforward cases.

---

[1]   *Parker* [1970] 2 All ER 458, CA; *Ferguson* [1970] 2 All ER 820.
[2]   *Jones* [1929] 1 KB 211.
[3]   In *Thebith* (1969) 54 Cr App Rep 35 at 37, CA, it was stated that there was (unspecified) authority that a restitution order was not part of the sentence, and consequently there was no appeal. The author has been unable to trace the authority, and it would appear to be overruled by the cases cited above.
[4]   Cf *Elliott* [1908] 2 KB 452; Central Criminal Court Justices (1886) 18 QBD 314.
[5]   Criminal Appeal Act 1968, s. 30 (4).

(b)   From an order in the magistrates' court

14–19   Section 108 of the Magistrates' Courts Act 1980 gives a right of appeal against sentence to the Crown Court and sentence includes (with inapplicable exceptions) "any order made on conviction". This clearly gives a right of appeal to the convicted person against an order made under s. 28. Both the convicted person and a third party against whom an order has been made might appeal by way of case stated to the High Court on a question of law or jurisdiction, under s. 111 (1) of the Magistrates' Courts Act which applies to any person aggrieved by an order.

L.   SUSPENSION OF ORDERS MADE ON INDICTMENT

14–20   The operation of an order for restitution is suspended for 28 days after the date of conviction on indictment unless, "in any case in which, in their opinion, the title to the property is not in dispute",[1] the court directs otherwise. Where notice of appeal or leave to appeal is given within those 28 days, then the operation of the order is suspended until the conviction is quashed or, if it is not quashed, until time for applying for leave to the House of Lords has run out or so long as any appeal to that House is pending.[2] If the conviction is quashed by the Court of Appeal or the House of Lords then the order does not take effect. When a conviction is quashed by the Court of Appeal and restored by the House of Lords, the House may make any order for restitution which could have been made by the court which convicted the respondent.[3]

---

[1]   Criminal Appeal Act 1968, s. 30; and Theft Act 1968, s. 28 (4).
[2]   Criminal Appeal Act 1968, s. 42 (1).
[3]   Ibid, s. 42 (3).

M.   OTHER POWERS TO AWARD COMPENSATION

(a)   Under the Powers of Criminal Courts Act 1973

14–21   Section 35 of the Powers of Criminal Courts Act 1973, as amended by the Criminal Justice Act 1982, s. 67, provides that a court by or before which a person is convicted of any offence may, instead of, or in addition to, dealing with him in any other way and whether on application or otherwise, make an order requiring the offender to pay compensation for any personal injury, loss or damage resulting from that offence or any other offence which is taken into consideration in determining the sentence.[1] The court is required to have regard to the offender's means so far as they appear or are known to the court. In the Crown Court there is no other limit but in a magistrates' court the maximum for one offence is £5,000.[2] In the case of an offence under the Theft Act, where the property in question is recovered, any damage to the property occurring while it was out of the owner's possession is to be treated as having resulted from the offence, however and by whomsoever the damage was caused.[3] If D takes P's car, contrary to 1968, s. 12, and crashes into Q's car, the damage to P's car is covered but not the damage to Q's car.[4]

Unlike s. 28 of the Theft Act, these provisions do not relate to any particular property. They may thus be relied on where neither the stolen property nor its proceeds has been recovered and nothing has been taken from D on his apprehension.

---

[1] For the principles to be applied, see *Kneeshaw* [1975] QB 57, [1974] 1 All ER 896, CA; *Oddy* [1974] 2 All ER 666, CA.
[2] Magistrates' Courts Act 1980, s. 32 (9), as amended by the Criminal Justice Act 1991.
[3] Section 35 (2).
[4] *Quigley v Stokes* [1977] 2 All ER 317, applying s. 35 (3).

(b)   Under the Police (Property) Act 1897

14–22   Where any property has come into the possession of the police in their investigation of a suspected offence, a magistrates' court may, under s. 1 (1) of the Police (Property) Act 1897, make an order for the delivery of the property to the person appearing to be the owner, or, if the owner cannot be ascertained, make "such order with respect to the property as to the magistrate or court may seem meet". The procedure should be used only in straightforward cases, where there is no difficulty of law.[1] The word "owner" is to be given its ordinary, popular meaning; so that a jeweller to whom a ring has been handed for valuation and who, suspecting it to be stolen, has given it to the police, is not "the owner". Though no one with a better title has appeared, somewhere (presumably) there is a person who "owns" the ring in the ordinary popular sense. No order may be made in favour of the jeweller.[2]

---

[1] *Raymond Lyons & Co Ltd v Metropolitan Police Comr* [1975] QB 321, [1975] 1 All ER 335.
[2] Ibid.

14–23   The property must not be restored to the person who is the owner in the popular sense, if it appears that there is some person with a better right to immediate possession, such as a person with a valid lien on the property. It was so held in *Marsh v Police Comr*,[1] though the court declined to decide whether the lienor was the "owner" for this purpose. According to *Raymond Lyons* case,[2] he is not. The curious result is that where another person has a better right to possession than the owner, no order can be made in favour of either claimant. Moreover, the magistrates cannot exercise the discretion given to them by the section where "the owner cannot be ascertained", because the owner is ascertained. It is submitted that, notwithstanding *Raymond Lyons* case, if it is wrong to deliver to the owner in the strict sense where there is another with a better right to possession, this can only be because the owner in the strict sense is not "the owner" for the purpose of the Act; and that it should follow that "the owner" is the person with the best right to possession.[3]

1 [1945] KB 43, [1944] 2 All ER 392, CA.
2 Above, para **14–22**.
3 Howard argues that the property must in all cases be awarded to the owner in the strict sense; [1958] Crim LR 744. A forfeiture order made by the Crown Court under s. 43 of the Powers of Criminal Courts Act 1973 does not determine the issue of the ownership of the property: *Chester Justices, ex p Smith* [1978] RTR 373, [1978] Crim LR 226, DC.

14–24 It is provided by s. 1 (2) of the Police (Property) Act 1897 that an order made under s. 1 (1) does not affect any person's right to bring legal proceedings within six months of the order to recover the property from the person to whom it has been delivered under the order of the court; but on the expiration of those six months, the right shall cease. An order may, however, affect the onus of proof: *Irving v National Provincial Bank Ltd*[1] where it was held that, in the absence of any evidence as to the ownership of the money, the defendant bank's title arising from an order made under the Act was superior to that of the plaintiff from whose possession the money had been taken by the police; the onus was on the plaintiff and not on the defendant to establish actual ownership in the money.

It is submitted that this provision should defeat the title only of one who might have asserted a better right to possess before the magistrates' court. If, for example, D steals a car from P and, on D's conviction, the magistrates order that it be returned to P, the rights of Q, from whom P had the car on hire or hire-purchase, should not be affected. If, after the expiration of six months, Q seeks to recover the car in accordance with the terms of the contract he should not be debarred from doing so by the order made under the Act.

Even thus limited, the provision could lead to arbitrary and unjust interference with civil rights. Suppose that the court makes an order in favour of P from whom goods have been stolen. The goods had been the subject of an earlier theft from Q. More than six months after the order, Q discovers that the goods are in the possession of P. His right to recover them would appear to be barred. It is not obvious why P should have this windfall arising out of the dishonest intervention of a third party.

1 [1962] 2 QB 73, [1962] 1 All ER 157, CA.

14–25 It has been held by a metropolitan magistrate that "property" includes anything into or for which the property has been converted or exchanged by analogy to s. 46 (1) of the Larceny Act 1916.[1] It is submitted that this was the correct decision, though it would be better to rely on the common law concerning ownership[2] than on the analogy of a criminal statute. Difficult questions might arise where the property has been converted into a more valuable thing by the expenditure of skill and labour.[3]

1 (1959) 123 JPJ 640.
2 *Taylor v Plumer* (1815) 3 M & S 562.
3 See 104 LJ 296 and Torts (Interference with Goods) Act 1977, s. 6.

14–26 The Theft Act no longer provides that the 1897 Act shall apply to any property seized by the police under the authority of s. 26 of the Theft Act.[1] Such property appears to be covered by the amended words of s. 1 (1) of the 1897 Act.

1 Section 26 (4) is repealed by the Criminal Justice Act 1972, s. 64 (2), Sch 6, Part II.

4   HUSBAND AND WIFE[1]

14–27   Under the Larceny Act 1916, a husband could steal from a wife and vice versa only if, at the time of the theft, either, they were not living together or the property was taken with a view to their ceasing to live together. So where a wife took her husband's property and gave it to her lover, the lover was not guilty of receiving stolen goods.[2] This rule was abolished by s. 30 (1) of the 1968 Act which also applies to the 1978 Act[3] and provides:

"This Act shall apply in relation to the parties to a marriage, and to property belonging to the wife or husband whether or not by reason of an interest derived from the marriage, as it would apply if they were not married and any such interest subsisted independently of the marriage."

The effect is that wives and husbands can steal, or commit any other offence under the Acts in relation to, the property of each other.

[1]   *Eighth Report*, Cmnd 2977, paras 189–199.
[2]   *Creamer* [1919] 1 KB 564.
[3]   1978, s. 5 (2).

A.   PROCEEDINGS INSTITUTED BY INJURED SPOUSE

14–28   The proceedings may be instituted by the injured spouse. The 1968 Act, s. 30 (2) provides:

"Subject to subsection (4) below, a person shall have the same right to bring proceedings against that person's wife or husband for any offence (whether under the Act or otherwise) as if they were not married, and a person bringing any such proceedings shall be competent to give evidence for the prosecution at every stage of the proceedings."

This subsection is not confined to offences under the Acts but applies to "any offence". Thus, for example, a wife may prosecute her husband for stealing or damaging the property of a third party, for an offence against the person of a third party, or for perjury; and in any such prosecution the wife would now be a competent witness for the prosecution.

B.   RESTRICTIONS ON PROSECUTION

14–29   The 1968 Act, s. 30 (4) provides:

"Proceedings shall not be instituted against a person for any offence of stealing or doing unlawful damage to property which at the time of the offence belongs to that person's wife or husband, or for any attempt, incitement or conspiracy to commit such an offence, unless the proceedings are instituted by or with the consent of the Director of Public Prosecutions:

Provided that –
(a)   this subsection shall not apply to proceedings against a person for an offence–
   (i)   if that person is charged with committing the offence jointly with the wife or husband; or
   (ii)   if by virtue of any judicial decree or order (wherever made) that person and the wife or husband are at the time of the offence under no obligation to cohabit; and
(b)   (Repealed.)"[1]

¹   For s. 30 (5), see below, p 271.

14–30   Where it is a case of stealing or the doing of unlawful damage by one spouse to the property of the other, consent is required whether the proceedings are to be instituted by the aggrieved spouse or by a third party.¹ Outside these cases, however, no consent is required whether the proceedings be instituted by the aggrieved spouse or by a third party. If a wife alleges, or a third party alleges, that her husband has obtained her property by deception, blackmailed her, wounded her or raped her, no consent is required. Presumably consent will be required on a robbery charge since this is within "any offence of stealing". It is not obvious why this clause (which was not in the draft bill produced by the Criminal Law Revision Committee) should be thus limited.

¹   *Withers* [1975] Crim LR 647.

14–31   Proviso (a) (i) is not very clear. It is a proviso to a subsection dealing with a case of a person who steals or damages his spouse's property; and so one would expect a proviso to qualify the rule that such a person cannot be prosecuted except with the consent of the Director. That is, the natural meaning of "that person" in the proviso is the person who has stolen or damaged the property of his wife or husband.

If that be correct, proviso (a) (i) deals with the case where the husband and wife are jointly charged with theft of or criminal damage to property which belongs to one of them. This looks a little curious; but it will be recalled¹ that it is perfectly possible for a person to be convicted of stealing his own property where some third person has a proprietary interest in it. Suppose that a husband has pawned his watch. While his wife engages the pawnbroker's attention, he secretly takes the watch back again. Proceedings may be brought against the couple without the consent of the Director. It is very reasonable that consent should not be necessary in this case; and perhaps the proviso is required because the proceeding, literally, is for an offence of stealing property belonging to the husband.

¹   Above, para **2–57**.

14–32   The position would seem to be much the same in the case of criminal damage. Generally a man may damage property which is his own with impunity, no matter how barbarous his action may be. But if another has a proprietary interest in the property, this would surely be an offence. For example, D has mortgaged a valuable painting to P by bill of sale. If he deliberately destroys the painting, he is surely guilty of an offence of criminal damage. If then, his wife destroys the painting with his connivance, they may both be prosecuted without consent.

If this interpretation is correct, it follows that if, in the above examples, the wife had taken the watch and destroyed the painting, without the husband's connivance, the Director's consent would have been required, for proceedings instituted by P. This looks strange because, though it is the husband's property which is destroyed, the offence is committed against a third party.

Moreover, property may "belong" to one of the spouses, at least for the purposes of theft,¹ although the ownership in the strict sense is in a third party. Suppose that H has a television set on hire or hire-purchase from P. If his wife, W, sells the television set without H's consent, it is clearly right that he should have to get consent to prosecute her for stealing from him. The same should apply if she smashes the set and he alleges that she has criminally damaged his property. On the other hand, it looks distinctly odd that P has to get the consent of the Director to prosecute W; but that appears to be the effect.

---

[1]   See s. 5, above, para **2–55**.

14–33   It may well be that the proviso was not actually intended to deal with this situation at all, but to apply to the case where D, a third party, assists H to steal or destroy W's property and D and H are prosecuted jointly. It may be intended to say that, in those circumstances, no consent shall be required so far as the proceedings against D are concerned. If that is the intention, the proviso is not strictly necessary because D is not within the main part of the subsection. It would mean, moreover, that consent would still be necessary for the proceedings against H; so that joint proceedings would still have to wait on consent. That would not be very sensible; so probably the better course (if not the only proper course) is to assume that the proviso means what it says. In that event, the situation envisaged in this paragraph is the same as if the proviso did apply to it. No consent is required so far as D is concerned (because he is not a person charged with an offence against his wife's property) but consent is required so far as H is concerned. There must either be separate trials or the Director's consent obtained.

Proviso (a) (ii) means that if H and W have been judicially separated or if a non-molestation order has been made[1] and one of them steals or damages the other's property, proceedings may be brought without the consent of the Director, whether they were in fact living together at the time of the offence or not. If the parties have merely separated in pursuance of an agreement, the Director's consent is required even if they are in fact living apart at the time of the alleged offence.

---

[1]   *Woodley v Woodley* [1978] Crim LR 629, DC.

APPENDIX
Theft Act 1968

(1968 C. 60)

ARRANGEMENT OF SECTIONS

257

Enforcement and procedure

General and consequential provisions

Supplementary

SCHEDULES
Schedules 2 (Miscellaneous and Consequential Amendments) and 3 (Repeals) are omitted from this edition.

An Act to revise the law of England and Wales as to theft and similar or associated offences, and in connection therewith to make provision as to criminal proceedings by one party to a marriage against the other, and to make certain amendments extending beyond England and Wales in the Post Office Act 1953 and other enactments; and for other purposes connected therewith

[26th July 1968]

Definition of "theft"

1. Basic definition of theft

(1) A person is guilty of theft if he dishonestly appropriates property belonging to another with the intention of permanently depriving the other of it; and "thief" and "steal" shall be construed accordingly.

(2) It is immaterial whether the appropriation is made with a view to gain, or is made for the thief's own benefit.

(3) The five following sections of this Act shall have effect as regards the interpretation and operation of this section (and, except as otherwise provided by this Act, shall apply only for purposes of this section).

2. "Dishonestly"

(1) A person's appropriation of property belonging to another is not to be regarded as dishonest—

    (a) if he appropriates the property in the belief that he has in law the right to deprive the other of it, on behalf of himself or of a third person; or

    (b) if he appropriates the property in the belief that he would have the other's consent if the other knew of the appropriation and the circumstances of it; or

    (c) (except where the property came to him as trustee or personal representative) if he appropriates the property in the belief that the person to whom the property belongs cannot be discovered by taking reasonable steps.

(2) A person's appropriation of property belonging to another may be dishonest notwithstanding that he is willing to pay for the property.

3. "Appropriates"

(1) Any assumption by a person of the rights of an owner amounts to an appropriation, and this includes, where he has come by the property (innocently or not) without stealing it, any later assumption of a right to it by keeping or dealing with it as owner.

(2) Where property or a right or interest in property is or purports to be transferred for value to a person acting in good faith, no later assumption by him of rights which he believed himself to be acquiring shall, by reason of any defect in the transferor's title, amount to theft of the property.

4. "Property"

(1) "Property" includes money and all other property, real or personal, including things in action and other intangible property.

(2) A person cannot steal land, or things forming part of land and severed from it by him or by his directions, except in the following cases, that is to say—

   (a) when he is a trustee or personal representative, or is authorised by power of attorney, or as liquidator of a company, or otherwise, to sell or dispose of land belonging to another, and he appropriates the land or anything forming part of it by dealing with it in breach of the confidence reposed in him; or

   (b) when he is not in possession of the land and appropriates anything forming part of the land by severing it or causing it to be severed, or after it has been severed; or

   (c) when, being in possession of the land under a tenancy, he appropriates the whole or part of any fixture or structure let to be used with the land.

For purposes of this subsection "land" does not include incorporeal hereditaments; "tenancy" means a tenancy for years or any less period and includes an agreement for such a tenancy, but a person who after the end of a tenancy remains in possession as statutory tenant or otherwise is to be treated as having possession under the tenancy, and "let" shall be construed accordingly.

(3) A person who picks mushrooms growing wild on any land, or who picks flowers, fruit or foliage from a plant wild on any land, does not (although not in possession of the land) steal what he picks, unless he does it for reward or for sale or other commercial purpose.

For purposes of this subsection "mushroom" includes any fungus, and "plant" includes any shrub or tree.

(4) Wild creatures, tamed or untamed, shall be regarded as property; but a person cannot steal a wild creature not tamed nor ordinarily kept in captivity, or the carcase of any such creature, unless either it has been reduced into possession by or on behalf of another person and possession of it has not since been lost or abandoned, or another person is in course of reducing it into possession.

5. "Belonging to another"

(1) Property shall be regarded as belonging to any person having possession

or control of it, or having in it any proprietary right or interest (not being an equitable interest arising only from an agreement to transfer or grant an interest).

(2) Where property is subject to a trust, the persons to whom it belongs shall be regarded as including any person having a right to enforce the trust, and an intention to defeat the trust shall be regarded accordingly as an intention to deprive of the property any person having that right.

(3) Where a person receives property from or on account of another, and is under an obligation to the other to retain and deal with that property or its proceeds in a particular way, the property or proceeds shall be regarded (as against him) as belonging to the other.

(4) Where a person gets property by another's mistake, and is under an obligation to make restoration (in whole or in part) of the property or its proceeds or of the value thereof, then to the extent of that obligation the property or proceeds shall be regarded (as against him) as belonging to the person entitled to restoration, and an intention not to make restoration shall be regarded accordingly as an intention to deprive that person of the property or proceeds.

(5) Property of a corporation sole shall be regarded as belonging to the corporation notwithstanding a vacancy in the corporation.

6. "With the intention of permanently depriving the other of it"

(1) A person appropriating property belonging to another without meaning the other permanently to lose the thing itself is nevertheless to be regarded as having the intention of permanently depriving the other of it if his intention is to treat the thing as his own to dispose of regardless of the other's rights; and a borrowing or lending of it may amount to so treating it if, but only if, the borrowing or lending is for a period and in circumstances making it equivalent to an outright taking or disposal.

(2) Without prejudice to the generality of subsection (1) above, where a person, having possession or control (lawfully or not) of property belonging to another, parts with the property under a condition as to its return which he may not be able to perform, this (if done for purposes of his own and without the other's authority) amounts to treating the property as his own to dispose of regardless of the other's rights.

Theft, robbery, burglary, etc

7. Theft

A person guilty of theft shall on conviction on indictment be liable to imprisonment for a term not exceeding seven years.

8. Robbery

(1) A person is guilty of robbery if he steals, and immediately before or at the time of doing so, and in order to do so, he uses force on any person or puts or seeks to put any person in fear of being then and there subjected to force.

(2) A person guilty of robbery, or of an assault with intent to rob, shall on conviction on indictment be liable to imprisonment for life.

9. Burglary

(1)   A person is guilty of burglary if—

    (a) he enters any building or part of a building as a trespasser and with intent to commit any such offence as is mentioned in subsection (2) below; or

    (b) having entered any building or part of a building as a trespasser he steals or attempts to steal anything in the building or that part of it or inflicts or attempts to inflict on any person therein any grievous bodily harm.

(2)   The offences referred to in subsection (1)(a) above are offences of stealing anything in the building or part of a building in question, of inflicting on any person therein any grievous bodily harm or raping any person therein, and of doing unlawful damage to the building or anything therein.

(3)   A person guilty of burglary shall on conviction on indictment be liable to imprisonment for a term not exceeding—

    (a)   where the offence was committed in respect of a building or part of a building which is a dwelling, fourteen years;

    (b)   in any other case, ten years.

(4)   References in subsections (1) and (2) above to a building, and the reference in subsection (3) above to a building which is a dwelling, shall apply also to an inhabited vehicle or vessel, and shall apply to any such vehicle or vessel at times when the person having a habitation in it is not there as well as at times when he is.

10. Aggravated burglary

(1)   A person is guilty of aggravated burglary if he commits any burglary and at the time has with him any firearm or imitation firearm, any weapon of offence, or any explosive; and for this purpose—

    (a)   "firearm" includes an airgun or air pistol, and "imitation firearm" means anything which has the appearance of being a firearm, whether capable of being discharged or not; and

    (b)   "weapon of offence" means any article made or adapted for use for causing injury to or incapacitating a person, or intended by the person having it with him for such use; and

    (c)   "explosive" means any article manufactured for the purpose of producing a practical effect by explosion, or intended by the person having it with him for that purpose.

(2)   A person guilty of aggravated burglary shall on conviction on indictment be liable to imprisonment for life.

11. Removal of articles from places open to the public

(1)   Subject to subsections (2) and (3) below, where the public have access to a building in order to view the building or part of it, or a collection or part of a collection housed in it, any person who without lawful authority removes from the building or its grounds the whole or part of any article displayed or kept for display to the public in the building or that part of it or in its grounds shall be guilty of an offence.

For this purpose "collection" includes a collection got together for a temporary purpose, but references in this section to a collection do not apply to a collection made or exhibited for the purpose of effecting sales or other commercial dealings.

(2)   It is immaterial for purposes of subsection (1) above, that the public's access to a building is limited to a particular period or particular occasion; but where anything removed from a building or its grounds is there otherwise than as forming part of, or being on loan for exhibition with, a collection intended for permanent exhibition to the public, the person removing it does not thereby commit an offence under this section unless he removes it on a day when the public have access to the building as mentioned in subsection (1) above.

(3) A person does not commit an offence under this section if he believes that he has lawful authority for the removal of the thing in question or that he would have it if the person entitled to give it knew of the removal and the circumstances of it.

(4) A person guilty of an offence under this section shall, on conviction on indictment, be liable to imprisonment for a term not exceeding five years.

12. Taking motor vehicle or other conveyance without authority

(1) Subject to subsections (5) and (6) below, a person shall be guilty of an offence if, without having the consent of the owner or other lawful authority, he takes any conveyance for his own or another's use or, knowing that any conveyance has been taken without such authority, drives it or allows himself to be carried in or on it.

(2) A person guilty of an offence under subsection (1) above shall be liable on summary conviction to a fine not exceeding level 5 on the standard scale, to imprisonment for a term not exceeding six months, or to both.

(3) [Repealed.]

(4) If on the trial of an indictment for theft the jury are not satisfied that the accused committed theft, but it is proved that the accused committed an offence under subsection (1) above, the jury may find him guilty of the offence under subsection (1) and if he is found guilty of it, he shall be liable as he would have been liable under subsection (2) above on summary conviction.

(5) Subsection (1) above shall not apply in relation to pedal cycles; but, subject to subsection (6) below, a person who, without having the consent of the owner or other lawful authority, takes a pedal cycle for his own or another's use, or rides a pedal cycle knowing it to have been taken without such authority, shall on summary conviction be liable to a fine not exceeding level 3 on the standard scale.

(6) A person does not commit an offence under this section by anything done in the belief that he has lawful authority to do it or that he would have the owner's consent if the owner knew of his doing it and the circumstances of it.

(7) For purposes of this section—

 (a) "conveyance" means any conveyance constructed or adapted for the carriage of a person or persons whether by land, water or air, except that it does not include a conveyance constructed or adapted for use only under the control of a person not carried in or on it, and "drive" shall be construed accordingly; and

 (b) "owner", in relation to a conveyance which is the subject of a hiring agreement or hire-purchase agreement, means the person in possession of the conveyance under that agreement.

12A. Aggravated vehicle-taking

(1) Subject to subsection (3) below, a person is guilty of aggravated taking of a vehicle if—

 (a) he commits an offence under section 12(1) above (in this section referred to as a "basic offence") in relation to a mechanically propelled vehicle; and

 (b) it is proved that, at any time after the vehicle was unlawfully taken (whether by him or another) and before it was recovered, the vehicle was driven, or injury or damage was caused, in one or more of the circumstances set out in paragraphs (a) to (d) of subsection (2) below.

(2) The circumstances referred to in subsection (1)(b) above are—

(a) that the vehicle was driven dangerously on a road or other public place;
(b) that, owing to the driving of the vehicle, an accident occurred by which injury was caused to any person;
(c) that, owing to the driving of the vehicle, an accident occurred by which damage was caused to any property, other than the vehicle;
(d) that damage was caused to the vehicle.

(3) A person is not guilty of an offence under this section if he proves that, as regards any such proven driving, injury or damage as is referred to in subsection (1)(b) above, either—

(a) the driving, accident or damage referred to in subsection (2) above occurred before he committed the basic offence; or
(b) he was neither in nor on nor in the immediate vicinity of the vehicle when that driving, accident or damage occurred.

(4) A person guilty of an offence under this section shall be liable on conviction on indictment to imprisonment for a term not exceeding two years or, if it is proved that, in circumstances falling within subsection (2)(b) above, the accident caused the death of the person concerned, five years.

(5) If a person who is charged with an offence under this section is found not guilty of that offence but it is proved that he committed a basic offence, he may be convicted of the basic offence.

(6) If by virtue of subsection (5) above a person is convicted of a basic offence before the Crown Court, that court shall have the same powers and duties as a magistrates' court would have had on convicting him of such an offence.

(7) For the purposes of this section a vehicle is driven dangerously if—

(a) it is driven in a way which falls far below what would be expected of a competent and careful driver; and
(b) it would be obvious to a competent and careful driver that driving the vehicle in that way would be dangerous.

(8) For the purposes of this section a vehicle is recovered when it is restored to its owner or to other lawful possession or custody; and in this subsection "owner" has the same meaning as in section 12 above.

13. Abstracting of electricity

A person who dishonestly uses without due authority, or dishonestly causes to be wasted or diverted, any electricity shall on conviction on indictment be liable to imprisonment for a term not exceeding five years.

14. Extension to thefts from mails outside England and Wales, and robbery etc on such a theft

(1) Where a person—

(a) steals or attempts to steal any mail bag or postal packet in the course of transmission as such between places in different jurisdictions in the British postal area, or any of the contents of such a mail bag or postal packet; or
(b) in stealing or with intent to steal any such mail bag or postal packet or any of its contents, commits any robbery, attempted robbery or assault with intent to rob;

then, notwithstanding that he does so outside England and Wales, he shall be guilty of committing or attempting to commit the offence against this Act as if he had done so in England or Wales, and he shall accordingly be liable to be prosecuted, tried and punished in England and Wales without proof that the offence was committed there.

(2) In subsection (1) above the reference to different jurisdictions in the British postal area is to be construed as referring to the several jurisdictions of England and Wales, of Scotland, of Northern Ireland, of the Isle of Man and of the Channel Islands.

(3) For purposes of this section "mail bag" includes any article serving the purpose of a mail bag.

Fraud and blackmail

15. Obtaining property by deception

(1) A person who by any deception dishonestly obtains property belonging to another, with the intention of permanently depriving the other of it, shall on conviction on indictment be liable to imprisonment for a term not exceeding ten years.

(2) For purposes of this section a person is to be treated as obtaining property if he obtains ownership, possession or control of it, and "obtain" includes obtaining for another or enabling another to obtain or to retain.

(3) Section 6 above shall apply for purposes of this section, with the necessary adaptation of the reference to appropriating, as it applies for purposes of section 1.

(4) For purposes of this section "deception" means any deception (whether deliberate or reckless) by words or conduct as to fact or as to law, including a deception as to the present intentions of the person using the deception or any other person.

15A. Obtaining a money transfer by deception

(1) A person is guilty of an offence if by any deception he dishonestly obtains a money transfer for himself or another.

(2) A money transfer occurs when—

(a) a debit is made to one account,

(b) a credit is made to another, and

(c) the credit results from the debit or the debit results from the credit.

(3) References to a credit and to a debit are to a credit of an amount of money and to a debit of an amount of money.

(4) It is immaterial (in particular)—

(a) whether the amount credited is the same as the amount debited;

(b) whether the money transfer is effected on presentment of a cheque or by another method;

(c) whether any delay occurs in the process by which the money transfer is effected;

(d) whether any intermediate credits or debits are made in the course of the money transfer;

(e) whether either of the accounts is overdrawn before or after the money transfer is effected.

(5) A person guilty of an offence under this section shall be liable on conviction on indictment to imprisonment for a term not exceeding ten years.

15B. Section 15A: supplementary

(1) The following provisions have effect for the interpretation of section 15A of this Act.

(2) "Deception" has the same meaning as in section 15 of this Act.

(3) "Account" means an account kept with—

(a) a bank; or
(b) a person carrying on a business which falls within subsection (4) below.

(4) A business falls within this subsection if—

(a) in the course of the business money received by way of deposit is lent to others; or
(b) any other activity of the business is financed, wholly or to any material extent, out of the capital of or the interest on money received by way of deposit;

and "deposit" here has the same meaning as in section 35 of the Banking Act 1987 (fraudulent inducement to make a deposit).

(5) For the purposes of subsection (4) above—

(a) all the activities which a person carries on by way of business shall be regarded as a single business carried on by him; and
(b) "money" includes money expressed in a currency other than sterling or in the European currency unit (as defined in Council Regulation No 3320/94/EC or any Community instrument replacing it).

16. Obtaining pecuniary advantage by deception

(1) A person who by any deception dishonestly obtains for himself or another any pecuniary advantage shall on conviction on indictment be liable to imprisonment for a term not exceeding five years.

(2) The cases in which a pecuniary advantage within the meaning of this section is to be regarded as obtained for a person are cases where—

(a) [Repealed.]
(b) he is allowed to borrow by way of overdraft, or to take out any policy of insurance or annuity contract, or obtains an improvement of the terms on which he is allowed to do so; or
(c) he is given the opportunity to earn remuneration or greater remuneration in an office or employment, or to win money by betting.

(3) For purposes of this section "deception" has the same meaning as in section 15 of this Act.

17. False accounting

(1) Where a person dishonestly, with a view to gain for himself or another or with intent to cause loss to another,—

(a) destroys, defaces, conceals or falsifies any account or any record or document made or required for any accounting purpose; or
(b) in furnishing information for any purpose produces or makes use of any account, or any such record or document as aforesaid, which to his knowledge is or may be misleading, false or deceptive in a material particular;

he shall, on conviction on indictment, be liable to imprisonment for a term not exceeding seven years.

(2) For purposes of this section a person who makes or concurs in making in an account or other document an entry which is or may be misleading, false or deceptive in a material particular, or who omits or concurs in omitting a material particular from an account or other document, is to be treated as falsifying the account or document.

18. Liability of company officers for certain offences by company

(1) Where an offence committed by a body corporate under section 15, 16 or 17 of this Act is proved to have been committed with the consent or connivance of any director, manager, secretary or other similar officer of the body corporate, or any person who was purporting to act in any such capacity, he as well as the body corporate shall be guilty of that offence, and shall be liable to be proceeded against and punished accordingly.

(2) Where the affairs of a body corporate are managed by its members, this section shall apply in relation to the acts and defaults of a member in connection with his functions of management as if he were a director of the body corporate.

19. False statements by company directors, etc

(1) Where an officer of a body corporate or unincorporated association (or person purporting to act as such), with intent to deceive members or creditors of the body corporate or association about its affairs, publishes or concurs in publishing a written statement or account which to his knowledge is or may be misleading, false or deceptive in a material particular, he shall on conviction on indictment be liable to imprisonment for a term not exceeding seven years.

(2) For purposes of this section a person who has entered into a security for the benefit of a body corporate or association is to be treated as a creditor of it.

(3) Where the affairs of a body corporate or association are managed by its members, this section shall apply to any statement which a member publishes or concurs in publishing in connection with his functions of management as if he were an officer of the body corporate or association.

20. Suppression, etc of documents

(1) A person who dishonestly, with a view to gain for himself or another or with intent to cause loss to another, destroys, defaces or conceals any valuable security, any will or other testamentary document or any original document of or belonging to, or filed or deposited in, any court of justice or any government department shall on conviction on indictment be liable to imprisonment for a term not exceeding seven years.

(2) A person who dishonestly, with a view to gain for himself or another or with intent to cause loss to another, by any deception procures the execution of a valuable security shall on conviction on indictment be liable to imprisonment for a term not exceeding seven years; and this subsection shall apply in relation to the making, acceptance, indorsement, alteration, cancellation or destruction in whole or in part of a valuable security, and in relation to the signing or sealing of any paper or other material in order that it may be made or converted into, or used or dealt with as, a valuable security, as if that were the execution of a valuable security.

(3) For purposes of this section "deception" has the same meaning as in section 15 of this Act, and "valuable security" means any document creating, transferring, surrendering or releasing any right to, in or over property, or authorising the payment of money or delivery of any property, or evidencing the creation, transfer, surrender or release of any such right, or the payment of money or delivery of any property, or the satisfaction of any obligation.

21. Blackmail

(1) A person is guilty of blackmail if, with a view to gain for himself or another or with intent to cause loss to another, he makes any unwarranted demand with menaces; and for this purpose a demand with menaces is unwarranted unless the person making it does so in the belief—

  (a) that he has reasonable grounds for making the demand; and

  (b) that the use of the menaces is a proper means of reinforcing the demand.

(2) The nature of the act or omission demanded is immaterial, and it is also immaterial whether the menaces relate to action to be taken by the person making the demand.

(3) A person guilty of blackmail shall on conviction on indictment be liable to imprisonment for a term not exceeding fourteen years.

Offences relating to goods stolen etc

22. Handling stolen goods

(1) A person handles stolen goods if (otherwise than in the course of the stealing) knowing or believing them to be stolen goods he dishonestly receives the goods, or dishonestly undertakes or assists in their retention, removal, disposal or realisation by or for the benefit of another person, or if he arranges to do so.

(2) A person guilty of handling stolen goods shall on conviction on indictment be liable to imprisonment for a term not exceeding fourteen years.

23. Advertising rewards for return of goods stolen or lost

Where any public advertisement of a reward for the return of any goods which have been stolen or lost uses any words to the effect that no questions will be asked, or that the person producing the goods will be safe from apprehension or inquiry, or that money paid for the purchase of the goods or advanced by way of loan on them will be repaid, the person advertising the reward and any person who prints or publishes the advertisement shall on summary conviction be liable to a fine not exceeding level 3 on the standard scale.

24. Scope of offences relating to stolen goods

(1) The provisions of this Act relating to goods which have been stolen shall apply whether the stealing occurred in England or Wales or elsewhere, and whether it occurred before or after the commencement of this Act, provided that the stealing (if not an offence under this Act) amounted to an offence where and at the time when the goods were stolen; and references to stolen goods shall be construed accordingly.

(2) For purposes of those provisions references to stolen goods shall include, in addition to the goods originally stolen and parts of them (whether in their original state or not),—

  (a) any other goods which directly or indirectly represent or have at any time represented the stolen goods in the hands of the thief as being the proceeds of any disposal or realisation of the whole or part of the goods stolen or of goods so representing the stolen goods; and

  (b) any other goods which directly or indirectly represent or have at any time represented the stolen goods in the hands of a handler of the stolen goods or any part of them as being the proceeds of any disposal or realisation of the whole or part of the stolen goods handled by him or of goods so representing them.

(3) But no goods shall be regarded as having continued to be stolen goods after they have been restored to the person from whom they were stolen or to other lawful possession or custody, or after that person and any other person claiming through him have otherwise ceased as regards those goods to have any right to restitution in respect of the theft.

(4)   For purposes of the provisions of this Act relating to goods which have been stolen (including subsections (1) to (3) above) goods obtained in England or Wales or elsewhere either by blackmail or in the circumstances described in section 15(1) of this Act shall be regarded as stolen; and "steal", "theft" and "thief" shall be construed accordingly.

24A. Dishonestly retaining a wrongful credit

(1)   A person is guilty of an offence if—

  (a)   a wrongful credit has been made to an account kept by him or in respect of which he has any right or interest;
  (b)   he knows or believes that the credit is wrongful; and
  (c)   he dishonestly fails to take such steps as are reasonable in the circumstances to secure that the credit is cancelled.

(2)   References to a credit are to a credit of an amount of money.

(3)   A credit to an account is wrongful if it is the credit side of a money transfer obtained contrary to section 15A of this Act.

(4)   A credit to an account is also wrongful to the extent that it derives from—

  (a)   theft;
  (b)   an offence under section 15A of this Act;
  (c)   blackmail; or
  (d)   stolen goods.

(5)   In determining whether a credit to an account is wrongful, it is immaterial (in particular) whether the account is overdrawn before or after the credit is made.

(6)   A person guilty of an offence under this section shall be liable on conviction on indictment to imprisonment for a term not exceeding ten years.

(7)   Subsection (8) below applies for purposes of provisions of this Act relating to stolen goods (including subsection (4) above).

(8)   References to stolen goods include money which is dishonestly withdrawn from an account to which a wrongful credit has been made, but only to the extent that the money derives from the credit.

(9)   In this section "account" and "money" shall be construed in accordance with section 15B of this Act.

Possession of house breaking implements, etc

25. Going equipped for stealing, etc

(1)   A person shall be guilty of an offence if, when not at his place of abode, he has with him any article for use in the course of or in connection with any burglary, theft or cheat.

(2)   A person guilty of an offence under this section shall on conviction on indictment be liable to imprisonment for a term not exceeding three years.

(3)   Where a person is charged with an offence under this section, proof that he had with him any article made or adapted for use in committing a burglary, theft or cheat shall be evidence that he had it with him for such use.

(4)   Any person may arrest without warrant anyone who is, or whom he, with reasonable cause, suspects to be, committing an offence under this section.

(5)   For purposes of this section an offence under section 12(1) of this Act of taking a conveyance shall be treated as theft, and "cheat" means an offence under section 15 of this Act.

Enforcement and procedure

26. Search for stolen goods

(1)   If it is made to appear by information on oath before a justice of the peace that there is reasonable cause to believe that any person has in his custody or possession or on his premises any stolen goods, the justice may grant a warrant to search for and seize the same; but no warrant to search for stolen goods shall be addressed to a person other than a constable except under the authority of an enactment expressly so providing.

(2)   [Repealed.]

(3)   Where under this section a person is authorised to search premises for stolen goods, he may enter and search the premises accordingly, and may seize any goods he believes to be stolen goods.

(4)   [Repealed.]

(5)   This section is to be construed in accordance with section 24 of this Act; and in subsection (2) above the references to handling stolen goods shall include any corresponding offence committed before the commencement of this Act.

27. Evidence and procedure on charge of theft or handling stolen goods

(1)   Any number of persons may be charged in one indictment, with reference to the same theft, with having at different times or at the same time handled all or any of the stolen goods, and the persons so charged may be tried together.

(2)   On the trial of two or more persons indicted for jointly handling any stolen goods the jury may find any of the accused guilty if the jury are satisfied that he handled all or any of the stolen goods, whether or not he did so jointly with the other accused or any of them.

(3)   Where a person is being proceeded against for handling stolen goods (but not for any offence other than handling stolen goods), then at any stage of the proceedings, if evidence has been given of his having or arranging to have in his possession the goods the subject of the charge, or of his undertaking or assisting in, or arranging to undertake or assist in, their retention, removal, disposal or realisation, the following evidence shall be admissible for the purpose of proving that he knew or believed the goods to be stolen goods:—

(a)   evidence that he has had in his possession, or has undertaken or assisted in the retention, removal, disposal or realisation of, stolen goods from any theft taking place not earlier than twelve months before the offence charged; and

(b)   (provided that seven days' notice in writing has been given to him of the intention to prove the conviction) evidence that he has within the five years preceding the date of the offence charged been convicted of theft or of handling stolen goods.

(4)   In any proceedings for the theft of anything in the course of transmission (whether by post or otherwise), or for handling stolen goods from such a theft, a statutory declaration made by any person that he despatched or received or failed to receive any goods or postal packet, or that any goods or postal packet when despatched or received by him were in a particular state or condition, shall be admissible as evidence of the facts stated in the declaration, subject to the following conditions—

(a)   a statutory declaration shall only be admissible where and to the extent to which oral evidence to the like effect would have been admissible in the proceedings; and

(b) a statutory declaration shall only be admissible if at least seven days before the hearing or trial a copy of it has been given to the person charged, and he has not, at least three days before the hearing or trial or within such further time as the court may in special circumstances allow, given the prosecutor written notice requiring the attendance at the hearing or trial of the person making the declaration.

(4A) Where the proceedings mentioned in subsection (4) above are proceedings before a magistrates' court inquiring into an offence as examining justices that subsection shall have effect with the omission of the words from "subject to the following conditions" to the end of the subsection.

(5) This section is to be construed in accordance with section 24 of this Act; and in subsection 3(*b*) above the reference to handling stolen goods shall include any corresponding offence committed before the commencement of this Act.

28. Orders for restitution

(1) Where goods have been stolen, and either a person is convicted of any offence with reference to the theft (whether or not the stealing is the gist of his offence) or a person is convicted of any other offence but such an offence as aforesaid is taken into consideration in determining his sentence, the court by or before which the offender is convicted may on the conviction (whether or not the passing of sentence is in other respects deferred) exercise any of the following powers—

(a) the court may order anyone having possession or control of the goods to restore them to any person entitled to recover them from him; or

(b) on the application of a person entitled to recover from the person convicted any other goods directly or indirectly representing the first-mentioned goods (as being the proceeds of any disposal or realisation of the whole or part of them or of goods so representing them), the court may order those other goods to be delivered or transferred to the applicant; or

(c) the court may order that a sum not exceeding the value of the first-mentioned goods shall be paid, out of any money of the person convicted which was taken out of his possession on his apprehension, to any person who, if those goods were in the possession of the person convicted, would be entitled to recover them from him.

(2) Where under subsection (1) above the court has power on a person's conviction to make an order against him both under paragraph (b) and under paragraph (c) with reference to the stealing of the same goods, the court may make orders under both paragraphs provided that the person in whose favour the orders are made does not thereby recover more than the value of those goods.

(3) Where under subsection (1) above the court on a person's conviction makes an order under paragraph (a) for the restoration of any goods, and it appears to the court that the person convicted has sold the goods to a person acting in good faith, or has borrowed money on the security of them from a person so acting, the court may order that there shall be paid to the purchaser or lender, out of any money of the person convicted which was taken out of his possession on his apprehension, a sum not exceeding the amount paid for the purchase by the purchaser or, as the case may be, the amount owed to the lender in respect of the loan.

(4) The court shall not exercise the powers conferred by this section unless in the opinion of the court the relevant facts sufficiently appear from evidence given at the trial or the available documents, together with admissions made by

or on behalf of any person in connection with any proposed exercise of the powers; and for this purpose "the available documents" means any written statements or admissions which were made for use, and would have been admissible, as evidence at the trial, the depositions taken at any committal proceedings and any written statements or admissions used as evidence in those proceedings and such written statements, depositions and other documents as were tendered by or on behalf of the prosecutor at any committal proceedings.

(5) Any order under this section shall be treated as an order for the restitution of property within the meaning of section 30 of the Criminal Appeal Act 1968 (which relates to the effect on such orders of appeals).

(6) References in this section to stealing are to be construed in accordance with section 24(1) and (4) of this Act.

(7) An order may be made under this section in respect of money owed by the Crown.

29. [Repealed]

General and consequential provisions

30. Husband and wife

(1) This Act shall apply in relation to the parties to a marriage, and to property belonging to the wife or husband whether or not by reason of an interest derived from the marriage, as it would apply if they were not married and any such interest subsisted independently of the marriage.

(2) Subject to subsection (4) below, a person shall have the same right to bring proceedings against that person's wife or husband for any offence (whether under this Act or otherwise) as if they were not married, and a person bringing any such proceedings shall be competent to give evidence for the prosecution at every stage of the proceedings.

(3) [Repealed.]

(4) Proceedings shall not be instituted against a person for any offence of stealing or doing unlawful damage to property which at the time of the offence belongs to that person's wife or husband, or for any attempt, incitement or conspiracy to commit such an offence, unless the proceedings are instituted by or with the consent of the Director of Public Prosecutions:

Provided that—

(a) this subsection shall not apply to proceedings against a person for an offence—
   (i) if that person is charged with committing the offence jointly with the wife or husband; or
   (ii) if by virtue of any judicial decree or order (wherever made) that person and the wife or husband are at the time of the offence under no obligation to cohabit;

(5) Notwithstanding section 6 of the Prosecution of Offences Act 1979 subsection (4) of this section shall apply—

(a) to an arrest (if without warrant) made by the wife or husband, and
(b) to a warrant of arrest issued on an information laid by the wife or husband.

31. Effect on civil proceedings and rights

(1) A person shall not be excused, by reason that to do so may incriminate that person or the wife or husband of that person of an offence under this Act—

    (a) from answering any question put to that person in proceedings for the recovery or administration of any property, for the execution of any trust or for an account of any property or dealings with property; or

    (b) from complying with any order made in any such proceedings;

but no statement or admission made by a person in answering a question put or complying with an order made as aforesaid shall, in proceedings for an offence under this Act, be admissible in evidence against that person or (unless they married after the making of the statement or admission) against the wife or husband of that person.

(2) Notwithstanding any enactment to the contrary, where property has been stolen or obtained by fraud or other wrongful means, the title to that or any other property shall not be affected by reason only of the conviction of the offender.

32. Effect on existing law and construction of references to offences

(1) The following offences are hereby abolished for all purposes not relating to offences committed before the commencement of this Act, that is to say—

    (a) any offence at common law of larceny, robbery, burglary, receiving stolen property, obtaining property by threats, extortion by colour of office or franchise, false accounting by public officers, concealment of treasure trove and, except as regards offences relating to the public revenue, cheating; and

    (b) any offence under an enactment mentioned in Part I of Schedule 3 to this Act, to the extent to which the offence depends on any section or part of a section included in column 3 of that Schedule;

but so that the provisions in Schedule 1 to this Act (which preserve with modifications certain offences under the Larceny Act 1861 of taking or killing deer and taking or destroying fish) shall have effect as there set out.

(2) Except as regards offences committed before the commencement of this Act, and except in so far as the context otherwise requires,—

    (a) references in any enactment passed before this Act to an offence abolished by this Act shall, subject to any express amendment or repeal made by this Act, have effect as references to the corresponding offence under this Act, and in any such enactment the expression "receive" (when it relates to an offence of receiving) shall mean handle, and "receiver" shall be construed accordingly; and

    (b) without prejudice to paragraph (*a*) above, references in any enactment, whenever passed, to theft or stealing (including references to stolen goods), and references to robbery, blackmail, burglary, aggravated burglary or handling stolen goods, shall be construed in accordance with the provisions of this Act, including those of section 24.

33. Miscellaneous and consequential amendments, and repeal

(1) The Post Office Act 1953 shall have effect subject to the amendments provided for by Part I of Schedule 2 to this Act and (except in so far as the contrary intention appears) those amendments shall have effect throughout the British postal area.

(2) The enactments mentioned in Parts II and III of Schedule 2 to this Act shall have effect subject to the amendments there provided for, and (subject to subsection (4) below) the amendments made by Part II to enactments extending beyond England and Wales shall have the like extent as the enactment amended.

(3) The enactments mentioned in Schedule 3 to this Act (which include in Part II certain enactments related to the subject matter of this Act but already obsolete or redundant apart from this Act) are hereby repealed to the extent specified in column 3 of that Schedule; and, notwithstanding that the foregoing sections of this Act do not extend to Scotland, where any enactment expressed to be repealed by Schedule 3 does so extend, the Schedule shall have effect to repeal it in its application to Scotland except in so far as the repeal is expressed not to extend to Scotland.

(4) No amendment or repeal made by this Act in Schedule 1 to the Extradition Act 1870 or in the Schedule to the Extradition Act 1873 shall affect the operation of that Schedule by reference to the law of a British possession; but the repeal made in Schedule 1 to the Extradition Act 1870 shall extend throughout the United Kingdom.

Supplementary

34. Interpretation

(1) Sections 4(1) and 5(1) of this Act shall apply generally for purposes of this Act as they apply for purposes of section 1.

(2) For purposes of this Act—

    (a) "gain" and "loss" are to be construed as extending only to gain or loss in money or other property, but as extending to any such gain or loss whether temporary or permanent; and—

        (i) "gain" includes a gain by keeping what one has, as well as a gain by getting what one has not; and

        (ii) "loss" includes a loss by not getting what one might get, as well as a loss by parting with what one has;

    (b) "goods", except in so far as the context otherwise requires, includes money and every other description of property except land, and includes things severed from the land by stealing.

35. Commencement and transitional provisions

(1) This Act shall come into force on the 1st January 1969 and, save as otherwise provided by this Act, shall have effect only in relation to offences wholly or partly committed on or after that date.

(2) Sections 27 and 28 of this Act shall apply in relation to proceedings for an offence committed before the commencement of this Act as they would apply in relation to proceedings for a corresponding offence under this Act, and shall so apply in place of any corresponding enactment repealed by this Act.

(3) Subject to subsection (2) above, no repeal or amendment by this Act of any enactment relating to procedure or evidence, or to the jurisdiction or powers of any court, or to the effect of a conviction, shall affect the operation of the enactment in relation to offences committed before the commencement of this Act or to proceedings for any such offence.

36. Short title, and general provisions as to Scotland and Northern Ireland

(1) This Act may be cited as the Theft Act 1968.

(2) [Repealed.]

(3) This Act does not extend to Scotland or, . . . to Northern Ireland, except as regards any amendment or repeal which in accordance with section 33 above is to extend to Scotland or Northern Ireland.

273

SCHEDULES

SCHEDULE 1

OFFENCES OF TAKING, ETC, DEER OR FISH

Taking or killing deer

[Paragraph 1 is repealed and superseded by the Deer Act 1991, ss. 1–9.]

Taking or destroying fish

2.—(1)   Subject to subparagraph (2) below, a person who unlawfully takes or destroys, or attempts to take or destroy, any fish in water which is private property or in which there is any private right of fishery shall on summary conviction be liable to imprisonment for a term not exceeding three months or to a fine not exceeding level 3 on the standard scale or to both.

(2)   Subparagraph (1) above shall not apply to taking or destroying fish by angling in the daytime (that is to say, in the period beginning one hour before sunrise and ending one hour after sunset); but a person who by angling in the daytime unlawfully takes or destroys, or attempts to take or destroy, any fish in water which is private property or in which there is any private right of fishery shall on summary conviction be liable to a fine not exceeding level 1 on the standard scale.

(3)   The court by which a person is convicted of an offence under this paragraph may order the forfeiture of anything which, at the time of the offence, he had with him for use for taking or destroying fish.

(4)   Any person may arrest without warrant anyone who is, or whom he, with reasonable cause, suspects to be, committing an offence under subparagraph (1) above, and may seize from any person who is, or whom he, with reasonable cause, suspects to be, committing any offence under this paragraph anything which on that person's conviction of the offence would be liable to be forfeited under subparagraph (3) above.

Schedules 2 (Miscellaneous and Consequential Amendments) and 3 (Repeals) are omitted from this edition.

Theft Act 1978

(1978 C. 31)

ARRANGEMENT OF SECTIONS

An Act to replace section 16(2)(a) of the Theft Act 1968 with other provision against fraudulent conduct; and for connected purposes

[20th July 1978]

1. Obtaining services by deception

(1) A person who by any deception dishonestly obtains services from another shall be guilty of an offence.

(2) It is an obtaining of services where the other is induced to confer a benefit by doing some act, or causing or permitting some act to be done, on the understanding that the benefit has been or will be paid for.

(3) Without prejudice to the generality of subsection (2) above, it is an obtaining of services where the other is induced to make a loan, or to cause or permit a loan to be made, on the understanding that any payment (whether by way of interest or otherwise) will be or has been made in respect of the loan.

2. Evasion of liability by deception

(1)   Subject to subsection (2) below, where a person by any deception—

    (a) dishonestly secures the remission of the whole or part of any existing liability to make a payment, whether his own liability or another's; or

    (b) with intent to make permanent default in whole or in part on any existing liability to make a payment, or with intent to let another do so, dishonestly induces the creditor or any person claiming payment on behalf of the creditor to wait for payment (whether or not the due date for payment is deferred) or to forgo payment; or

    (c) dishonestly obtains any exemption from or abatement of liability to make a payment;

he shall be guilty of an offence.

(2) For purposes of this section "liability" means legally enforceable liability; and subsection (1) shall not apply in relation to a liability that has not been accepted or established to pay compensation for a wrongful act or omission.

(3) For purposes of subsection (1)(b) a person induced to take in payment a cheque or other security for money by way of conditional satisfaction of a pre-

existing liability is to be treated not as being paid but as being induced to wait for payment.

(4) For purposes of subsection (1)(*c*) "obtains" includes obtaining for another or enabling another to obtain.

3. Making off without payment

(1) Subject to subsection (3) below, a person who, knowing that payment on the spot for any goods supplied or service done is required or expected from him, dishonestly makes off without having paid as required or expected and with intent to avoid payment of the amount due shall be guilty of an offence.

(2) For purposes of this section "payment on the spot" includes payment at the time of collecting goods on which work has been done or in respect of which service has been provided.

(3) Subsection (1) above shall not apply where the supply of the goods or the doing of the service is contrary to law, or where the service done is such that payment is not legally enforceable.

(4) Any person may arrest without warrant anyone who is, or whom he, with reasonable cause, suspects to be, committing or attempting to commit an offence under this section.

4. Punishments

(1) Offences under this Act shall be punishable either on conviction on indictment or on summary conviction.

(2) A person convicted on indictment shall be liable—

    (a) for an offence under section 1 or section 2 of this Act, to imprisonment for a term not exceeding five years; and

    (b) for an offence under section 3 of this Act, to imprisonment for a term not exceeding two years.

(3) A person convicted summarily of any offence under this Act shall be liable—

    (a) to imprisonment for a term not exceeding six months; or

    (b) to a fine not exceeding the prescribed sum for the purposes of section 32 of the Magistrates' Courts Act 1980 (punishment on summary conviction of offences triable either way: £1,000 or other sum substituted by order under that Act),

or to both.

5. Supplementary

(1) For purposes of sections 1 and 2 above "deception" has the same meaning as in section 15 of the Theft Act 1968, that is to say, it means any deception (whether deliberate or reckless) by words or conduct as to fact or as to law, including a deception as to the present intentions of the person using the deception or any other person; and section 18 of that Act (liability of company officers for offences by the company) shall apply in relation to sections 1 and 2 above as it applies in relation to section 15 of that Act.

(2) Sections 30(1) (husband and wife), 31(1) (effect on civil proceedings) and 34 (interpretation) of the Theft Act 1968, so far as they are applicable in relation to this Act, shall apply as they apply in relation to that Act.

(3) [Repealed]

(4) In the Visiting Forces Act 1952, in paragraph 3 of the Schedule (which defines for England and Wales "offence against property" for purposes of the exclusion in certain cases of the jurisdiction of United Kingdom courts) there shall be added at the end—

"(j) the Theft Act 1978"

(5) In the Theft Act 1968 section 16(2)(a) is hereby repealed.

6. Enactment of same provisions for Northern Ireland

An Order in Council under paragraph 1(1)(*b*) of Schedule 1 to the Northern Ireland Act 1974 (legislation for Northern Ireland in the interim period) which contains a statement that it operates only so as to make for Northern Ireland provision corresponding to this Act—

(a) shall not be subject to paragraph 1(4) and (5) of that Schedule (affirmative resolution of both Houses of Parliament); but

(b) shall be subject to annulment by resolution of either House.

7. Short title, commencement and extent

(1) This Act may be cited as the Theft Act 1978.

(2) This Act shall come into force at the expiration of three months beginning with the date on which it is passed.

(3) This Act except section 5(3), shall not extend to Scotland; and except for that subsection, and subject also to section 6, it shall not extend to Northern Ireland.

Index

Note: references to paragraph numbers relate to body of text; references to page numbers relate to Appendix